John Adams

The Works of Alexander Pope, Esq

In four volumes. Vol. 4

John Adams

The Works of Alexander Pope, Esq
In four volumes. Vol. 4

ISBN/EAN: 9783337245320

Printed in Europe, USA, Canada, Australia, Japan

Cover: Foto ©Thomas Meinert / pixelio.de

More available books at **www.hansebooks.com**

THE

WORKS

O F

ALEXANDER POPE, Efq;

In Four Volumes, Complete.

V O L U M E IV.

CONTAINING

The reft of his LETTERS, and WILL.

EDINBURGH:
Printed in the year MDCCLXIV.

CONTENTS.

† a 2 .   II. Excuf

CONTENTS.

LETTERS to and from Mr GAY, &c.

From 1712 to 1732.

a 3 XVII. From

vi CONTENTS.

XLVII. From

LETTERS to and from Dr SWIFT.

XVII. Anſwer

CONTENTS.

Ireland: Character. of Mrs Pope: Reflections on Mr
Pope's and Mr Gay's circumstances, 272
XL. Mr Pope's anfwer : His fituation and contentment : An
account of his other friends, 273
XLI. Lord Bolingbroke to Dr Swift : A review of his life,
his thoughts of œconomy, and concerning fame, 275
XLII. Dr Swift's anfwer. The misfortunes attending great
talents : Concerning fame, and the defire of it, 278
XLIII. Dr Swift to Mr Pope. Concerning the Dunciad,
and of his fituation of life, 280
XLIV. From Lord B. That the fenfe of friendfhip increa-
fes with increafe of years. Concerning a hiftory of his
own times, and Mr P.'s moral poem, 282
XLV. Of the ftyle of his letters, of his condition of life,
his paft friendfhips, diflike of party-fpirit, and thoughts of
penfions and preferment, 283
XLVI. Of Mr Weftley's differtations on Job.—Poftfcript by
Lord Bol. on the pleafure we take in reading letters, 287
XLVII. From Lord B. to Dr Swift. Inviting him to England, and concerning reformation of manners by writing, 289
XLVIII. From the fame. The temper proper to men in
years: An account of his own. The character of his lady.—Poftfcript by Mr P. on his mother, and the effects of
the tender paffions, 290
XLIX. From the fame. Of his ftudies, particularly a me-
taphyfical work. Of retirement and exercife.—Poftfcript
by Mr P. His wifh that their ftudies were united in fome
work ufeful to manners, and his diftafte of all party-wri-
tings, 292
L. Concerning the Duchefs of Q—y. Perfuafions to œco-
nomy, 295
LI. On the fame fubjects, 296
LII. A letter of raillery, 298
LIII. In the fame ftyle, to Mr Gay and the Duchefs, 301
LIV. A ftrange end of a law-fuit. His way of life, &c.
Poftfcript to the Duchefs, 304
LV. Two new pieces of the Dean's: Anfwer to his invita-
tion into England. Advice to write, &c. 306
LVI. More on the fame fubjects. A happy union againft
corruption. Poftfcript to the Duke of Q. and to the
Duchefs, 308
LVII. Mr Gay to Dr Swift. His account of himfelf : His
laft fables : His œconomy.—Poftfcript by Mr Pope, of
their common ailments, and œconomy ; and againft party-
fpirit in writing, 311
LVIII. From Dr Swift to Mr Gay. Congratulation on Mr
Gay's leaving the court : Lord Cornbury's refufal of a pen-
fion : Character of Mr Gay, 315
LIX. From the fame. Concerning the writing of fables : -
Advice about œconomy, and provifion for old age ; of in-
attention, &c. Poftfcript to the Duchefs, 317
LX. From-

of

CONTENTS. xi

XCII. Of

CONTENTS.

LETTERS to Mr WARBURTON.

L E T T E R S.

LETTERS to and from EDWARD BLOUNT, Efq;

From 1714 to 1725.

LETTER I.

Mr POPE *to* EDWARD BLOUNT, *Efq;*

Auguſt 27. 1714.

Whatever ſtudies on the one hand, or a-muſements on the other, it ſhall be my fortune to fall into, I ſhall be equally in-capable of forgetting you in any of them. The taſk I undertook *, though of weight enough in it-ſelf, has had a voluntary increaſe by the enlarging my deſign of the *notes* †; and the neceſſity of con-ſulting a number of books has carried me to Oxford. But I fear, through my Lord Harcourt's and Dr Clarke's means, I ſhall be more converſant with the pictures and company of the place, than with the books and manuſcripts of it.

I find ſtill more reaſon to complain of the negli-gence of the geographers in their maps of old Greece, ſince I looked upon two or three more no-ted names in the public libraries here. But, with all the care I am capable of, I have ſome cauſe to fear the engraver will prejudice me in a few ſitua-

* The tranſlation of Homer's Iliad.
† The notes on the Iliad were his own; thoſe on the Odyſſey were Dr Broome's.——But they ſpeak their reſpective authors.

tions. I have been forced to write to him in fo high
a ftyle, that, were my epiftle intercepted, it would
raife no fmall admiration in an ordinary man. There
is fcarce an order in it of lefs importance, than to
remove fuch and fuch mountains, alter the courfe of
fuch and fuch rivers, place a large city on fuch a
coaft, and rafe another in another country. I have
fet bounds to the fea, and faid to the land, Thus
far fhalt thou advance, and no further *. In the
mean time, I, who talk and command at this rate,
am in danger of lofing my horfe, and ftand in fome
fear of a country-juftice †. To difarm me indeed,
may be but prudential, confidering what armies I
have at prefent on foot, and in my fervice. A hundred thoufand Grecians are no contemptible body :
for all that I can tell, they may be as formidable as
four thoufand priefls; and they feem proper forces
to fend againft thofe in Barcelona. That fiege deferves as fine a poem as the Iliad; and the machi-
ning part of poetry would be the jufter in it, as, they
fay, the inhabitants expect angels from heaven to
their affiftance. May I venture to fay who am a
Papift, and fay to you who are a Papift, that nothing is more aftonifhing to me, than that people
fo greatly warmed with a fenfe of liberty, fhould be
capable of harbouring fuch weak fuperftition, and
that fo much bravery and fo much folly can inhabit
the fame breafts ?

I could not but take a trip to London on the death
of the Queeen, moved by the common curiofity of
mankind, who leave their own bufinefs to be looking upon other mens. I thank God, that, as for
myfelf, I am below all the accidents of ftate-chan-
ges by my circumftances, and above them by my
philofophy. Common charity of man to man, and

---

* This relates to the map of ancient Greece, laid down by
our author in his obfervations on the fecond Iliad.

† Some of the laws were, at this time, put in force againft
the Papifts,

univerfal

univerfal good-will to all, are the points I have moſt
at heart ; and I am fure thofe are not to be broken
for the fake of any governours or government. I am
willing to hope the beſt ; and what I more wifh than
my own or any particular man's advancement, is,
that this turn may put an end entirely to the divifions of Whig and Tory ; that the parties may love
each other as well as I love them both, or at leaſt
hurt each other as little as I would either ; and that
our own people may live as quietly as we fhall certainly let theirs ; that is to fay, that want of power
itfelf in us may not be a furer prevention of harm,
than want of will in them. I am fure, if all Whigs
and all Tories had the fpirit of one Roman Catholic
that I know, it would be well for all Roman Catholics ; and if all Roman Catholics had always had
that fpirit, it had been well for all others ; and we
had never been charged with fo wicked a fpirit as
that of perfecution.

I agree with you in my fentiments of the ſtate of
our nation fince this change. I find myfelf juſt in
the fame fituation of mind you defcribe as your own ;
heartily wifhing the good, that is, the quiet of my
country, and hoping a total end of all the unhappy
divifions of mankind by party-fpirit, which at beſt
is but the madnefs of many for the gain of a few.

I am, &c.

LETTER II.

From Mr BLOUNT.

IT is with a great deal of pleafure I fee your letter, dear Sir, written in a ſtyle that fhews you
full of health, and in the midſt of diverfions. I
think thofe two things neceffary to a man who has
fuch undertakings in hand as yours. All lovers of
Homer are indebted to you for taking fo much pains
about the fituation of his hero's kingdoms. It will
not only be of great ufe with regard to his works,

A 2 but

but to all that read any of the Greek hiftorians; who generally are ill underſtood through the difference of the maps as to the places they treat of, which makes one think one author contradicts another. You are going to fet us right; and it is an advantage every body will gladly fee you ingrofs the glory of.

You can draw rules to be free and eafy, from formal pedants; and teach men to be ſhort and pertinent, from tedious commentators. However, I congratulate your happy deliverance from fuch authors, as you (with all your humanity) cannot wiſh alive again to converfe with. Critics will quarrel with you, if you dare to pleafe without their leave; and zealots will ſhrug up their ſhoulders at a man that pretends to get to heaven out of their form, drefs, and diet. I would no more make a judgment of an author's genius from a damning critic, than I would of a man's religion from an unfaving zealot.

I could take great delight in affording you the new glory of making a Barceloniad, (if I may venture to coin fuch a word). I fancy you would find a jufter parallel than it feems at firſt fight; for the Trojans too had a great mixture of folly with their bravery; and I am out of countenance for them, when I read the wife refult of their council, where, after a warm debate between Antenor and Paris, about reſtoring Helen, Priam fagely determines that they ſhall go to fupper. And as for the Greeks, what can equal their fuperftition in facrificing an innocent lady?

Tantum relligio potuit, &c.

I have a good opinion of my politics, fince they agree with a man who always thinks fo juftly as you. I wiſh it were in our power to perfuade all the nation into as calm and fteady a difpofition of mind.

We have received the late melancholy news, with the ufual ceremony, of condoling in one breath for the lofs of a gracious Queen, and in another rejoicing for an illuftrious King. My views carry me no
farther,

farther, than to wifh the peace and welfare of my country; and my morals and politics teach me to leave all that to be adjufted by our reprefentatives a-bove, and to divine Providence. It is much at one to you and me, who fit at the helm, provided they will permit us to fail quietly in the great fhip. Ambi-tion is a vice that is timely mortified in us poor Pa-pifts; we ought in recompenfe to cultivate as many virtues in ourfelves as we can, that we may be truly great. Among my ambitions, that of being a fin-cere friend is one of the chief: yet I will confefs that I have a fecret pleafure to have fome of my de-fcendents know, that their anceftor was great with Mr Pope.

I am, &c.

LETTER III.

From Mr BLOUNT.

Nov. 11. 1715.

IT is an agreement of long date between you and me, that you fhould do with my letters juft as you pleafed, and anfwer them at your leifure; and that is as foon as I fhall think you ought. I have fo true a tafte of the fubftantial part of your friendfhip, that I wave all ceremonials; and am fure to make you as many vifits as I can, and leave you to return them whenever you pleafe, afluring you they fhall at all times be heartily welcome to me.

The many alarms we have from your parts, have no effect upon the genius that reigns in our country, which is happily turned to preferve peace and quiet among us. What a difmal fcene has there been o-pened in the North? what ruin have thofe unfortu-nate rafh gentlemen drawn upon themfelves and their miferable followers, and perchance upon many o-thers too, who upon no account would be their fol-lowers? however it may look ungenerous to reproach people in diftrefs. I do not remember you and I e-ver ufed to trouble ourfelves about politics; but when any matter happened to fall into our difcourſe, we uſed to condemn all undertakings that tended towards the diſturbing the peace and quiet of our country, as contrary to the notions we had of morality and religion, which oblige us on no pretence whatſoever to violate the laws of charity. How many lives have there been loſt in hot blood, and how many more are there like to be taken off in cold? If the broils of the nation affect you, come down to me; and though we are farmers, you know Eumeus made his friends welcome. You ſhall here worſhip the Echo at your eaſe. Indeed we are forced to do ſo, becauſe we cannot hear the firſt report, and therefore are obliged to liſten to the ſecond; which, for ſecurity's fake, I do not always believe neither.

It is a great many years ſince I fell in love with the character of Pomponius Atticus. I longed to imitate him a little; and have contrived hitherto to be, like him, engaged in no party, but to be a faithful friend to ſome in both. I find myſelf very well in this way hitherto; and live in a certain peace of mind by it, which, I am perſuaded, brings a man more content than all the perquiſites of wild ambition. I with pleaſure join with you in wiſhing, nay I am not aſhamed to ſay, in praying for the welfare temporal and eternal of all mankind. How much more affectionately then ſhall I do ſo for you, ſince I am in a moſt particular manner, and with all ſincerity,   Your, &c.

L E T T E R   IV.

Jan. 21. 1715-16.

I Know of nothing that will be ſo intereſting to you at preſent, as ſome circumſtances of the laſt act of that eminent comic poet, and our friend, Wycherley. He had often told me, as I doubt not he did all his acquaintance, that he would marry as ſoon as his life was deſpaired of. Accordingly, a few days before his death, he underwent the ceremony; and joined together thoſe two ſacraments, which,

which, wife men fay, fhould be the laft we receive; for, if you obferve, matrimony is placed after extreme unction in our catechifm, as a kind of hint of the order of time in which they are to be taken. The old man then lay down, fatisfied in the confcience of having by this one act paid his juft debts, obliged a woman, who (he was told) had merit, and fhewn an heroic refentment of the ill ufage of his next heir. Some hundred pounds which he had with the lady, difcharged thofe debts; a jointure of four hundred a-year made her a recompenfe; and the nephew he left to comfort himfelf as well as he could, with the miferable remains of a mortgaged eftate. I faw our friend twice after this was done, lefs peevifh in his ficknefs than he ufed to be in his health; neither much afraid of dying, nor (which in him had been more likely) much afhamed of marrying. The evening before he expired, he called his young wife to the bedfide, and earneftly entreated her not to deny him one requeft, the laft he fhould make. Upon her affurances of confenting to it, he told her, " My dear, it is only this, that " you will never marry an old man again." I cannot help remarking, that ficknefs, which often deftroys both wit and wifdom, yet feldom has power to remove that talent which we call humour. Mr Wycherley fhewed his, even in this laft compliment; though I think his requeft a little hard, for why fhould he bar her from doubling her jointure on the fame eafy terms?

So trivial as thefe circumftances are, I fhould not be difpleafed myfelf to know fuch trifles, when they concern or characterife any eminent perfon. The wifeft and wittieft of men are feldom wifer or wittier than others in thefe fober moments. At leaft, our friend ended much in the character he had lived in: and Horace's rule for a play, may as well be applied to him as a play-wright,

——————— *Servetur ad imum*
Qualis ab incepto proceffserit, et fibi conftet.

I am, &c.

L E T-

LETTER V.

Feb. 10. 1715-16.

I Am juft returned from the country, whither Mr
Rowe accompanied me, and paffed a week in
the foreft. I need not tell you how much a man of
his turn entertained me; but I muft acquaint you,
there is a vivacity and gaiety of difpofition almoft
peculiar to him, which make it impoffible to part
from him without that uneafinefs which generally
fucceeds all our pleafures. I have been juft taking
a folitary walk by moonfhine, full of reflections on
the tranfitory nature of all human delights; and giving my thoughts a loofe in the contemplation of
thofe fatisfactions which probably we may hereafter
tafte in the company of feparate fpirits, when we
fhall range the walks above, and perhaps gaze on
this world at as vaft a diftance as we now do on
thofe worlds. The pleafures we are to enjoy in that
converfation muft undoubtedly be of a nobler kind,
and (not unlikely) may proceed from the difcoveries
each fhall communicate to another, of God and of
Nature; for the happinefs of minds can furely be
nothing but knowledge.

The higheft gratification we receive here from
company, is mirth; which at the beft is but a flut-
tering unquiet motion, that beats about the breaft
for a few moments, and after leaves it void and
empty. Keeping good company, even the beft, is
but a lefs fhameful art of lofing time. What we
here call fcience and ftudy, are little better: the
greater number of arts to which we apply ourfelves,
are mere groping in the dark; and even the fearch
of our moft important concerns in a future being, is
but a needlefs, anxious, and uncertain hafte to be
knowing, fooner than we can, what without all this
folicitude we fhall know a little later. We are but
curious impertinents in the cafe of futurity. It is
not our bufinefs to be gueffing what the ftate of fouls
fhall

shall be, but to be doing what may make our own state happy. We cannot be knowing, but we can be virtuous.

If this be my notion of a great part of that high science, Divinity, you will be so civil as to imagine I lay no mighty stress upon the rest. Even of my darling poetry I really make no other use, than horses of the bells that gingle about their ears, (though now and then they toss their heads as if they were proud of them), only to jog on a little more merrily.

Your observations on the narrow conceptions of mankind in the point of friendship, confirm me in what I was so fortunate as at my first knowledge of you to hope, and since so amply to experience. Let me take so much decent pride and dignity upon me, as to tell you, that, but for opinions like these which I discovered in your mind, I had never made the trial I have done; which has succeeded so much to mine, and, I believe, not less to your satisfaction: for, if I know you right, your pleasure is greater in obliging me; than I can feel on my part, till it falls in my power to oblige you.

Your remark, That the variety of opinions in politics or religion is often rather a gratification, than an objection, to people who have sense enough to consider the beautiful order of nature in her variations, makes me think you have not construed Joannes Secundus wrong, in the verse which precedes that which you quote. *Bene nota fides*, as I take it, does no way signify the Roman-Catholic religion, though Secundus was of it. I think it was a generous thought, and one that flowed from an exalted mind, That it was not improbable but God might be delighted with the various methods of worshipping him, which divided the whole world. I am pretty sure you and I should no more make good inquisitors to the modern tyrants in faith, than we could have been qualified for lictors to Procrustes, when he converted refractory members with the rack.

In

In a word, I can only repeat to you what I think I have formerly faid, That I as little fear God will damn a man who has charity, as I hope that any prieſt can ſave him without it.

I am, &c.

LETTER VI.

March 20. 1715-16.

I Find that a real concern is not only a hinderance to ſpeaking, but to writing too. The more time we give ourſelves to think over one's own or a friend's unhappineſs, the more unable we grow to expreſs the grief that proceeds from it. It is as natural to delay a letter at ſuch a ſeaſon as this, as to retard a melancholy viſit to a perſon one cannot relieve. One is aſhamed in that circumſtance, to pretend to entertain people with trifling, inſignificant affectations of ſorrow on the one hand, or unſeaſonable and forced gaieties on the other. It is a kind of profanation of things ſacred, to treat ſo ſolemn a matter as a generous voluntary ſuffering, with compliments, or heroic gallantries. Such a mind as yours has no need of being ſpirited up into honour, or, like a weak woman, praiſed into an opinion of its own virtue. It is enough to do and ſuffer what we ought; and men ſhould know, that the noble power of ſuffering bravely is as far above that of enterpriſing greatly, as an unblemiſhed-conſcience and inflexible reſolution are above an accidental flow of ſpirits, or a ſudden tide of blood. If the whole religious buſineſs of mankind be included in reſignation to our Maker, and charity to our fellow-creatures, there are now ſome people who give us as good an opportunity of practiſing the one, as themſelves have given an inſtance of the violation of the other. Whoever is really brave, has always this comfort when he is oppreſſed, that he knows himſelf to be ſuperiour to thoſe who injure him : for the greateſt power on earth can no ſooner do him that injury,

jury, but the brave man can make himself greater by forgiving it.

If it were generous to feek for alleviating confolations in a calamity of fo much glory, one might fay, that to be ruined thus in the grofs, with a whole people, is but like perilhing in the general conflagration, where nothing we can value is left behind us.

Methinks, the moft heroic thing we are left capable of doing, is to endeavour to lighten each other's load, and (oppreffed as we are) to fuccour fuch as are yet more oppreffed. If there are too many who cannot be affifted, but by what we cannot give, our money; there are yet others who may be relieved by our counfel, by our countenance, and even by our cheerfulnefs. The misfortunes of private families, the mifunderftandings of people whom diftreffes make fufpicious, the coldneffes of relations whom change of religion may difunite, or the neceffities of half-ruined eftates render unkind to each other; thefe at leaft may be foftened in fome degree, by a general well-managed humanity among ourfelves; if all thofe who have your principles of belief, had alfo your fenfe and conduct. But indeed moft of them have given lamentable proofs of the contrary; and it is to be apprehended, that they who want fenfe, are only religious through weaknefs, and good-natured through fhame. Thefe are narrow-minded creatures that never deal in effentials; their faith never looks beyond ceremonials, nor their charity beyond relations. As poor as I am, I would gladly relieve any diftreffed confcientious French refugee at this inftant. What muft my concern then be, when 1 perceive fo many anxieties now tearing thofe hearts, which I have defired a place in, and clouds of melancholy rifing on thofe faces which I have long looked upon with affection? I begin already to feel both what fome apprehend, and what others are yet too ftupid to apprehend. I grieve with the old, for fo many additional inconveniencies and

chagrins,

chagrins, more than their fmall remain of life feemed deftined to undergo; and with the young, for fo
many of thofe gaieties and pleafures (the portion of
youth) which they will by this means be deprived of.
This brings into my mind one or other of thofe I
love beft, and among them the widow and fatherlefs,
late of— As I am certain no people living had an
earlier and truer fenfe of others misfortunes, or
a more generous refignation as to what might be
their own ; fo I earneftly wifh, that whatever part
they muft bear, may be rendered as fupportable to
them, as it is in the power of any friend to make it.
    But I know you have prevented me in this thought,
as you always will in any thing that is good or generous.   I find by a letter of your lady's, (which I
have feen), that their eafe and tranquillity is part of
your care.   I believe there is fome fatality in it,
that you fhould always, from time to time, be doing
thofe particular things that make me enamoured of
you.
    I write this from Windfor foreft, of which I am
come to take my laft look.   We here bid our neighbours adieu, much as thofe who go to be hanged do
their fellow-prifoners, who are condemned to follow
them a few weeks after.   I parted from honeft Mr
D * * with tendernefs ; and from old Sir William
Trumbull as from a venerable prophet, foretelling
with lifted hands the miferies to come, from which
he is juft going to be removed himfelf.
    Perhaps now I have learned fo far as

    No: dulcia linquimus arva ;

my next leffon may be,

    Nos patriam fugimus. ·

Let that, and all elfe be as Heaven pleafes ! I have
provided juft enough to keep me a man of honour.
I believe you and I fhall never be afhamed of each
other.   I know I wifh my country well ; and if it
undoes me, it fhall not make me wifh it otherwife.
                                    L E T·

LETTER VII.

From Mr BLOUNT.

March 24. 1715-16.

YOur letters give me a gleam of fatisfaction, in
the midft of a very dark and cloudy fituation
of thoughts, which it would be more than human to
be exempt from at this time, when our homes muft
either be left, or be made too narrow for us to turn in.
Poetically fpeaking, I fhould lament the lofs Windfor foreft and you fuftain of each other ; but that,
methinks, one cannot fay you are parted, becaufe
you will live by and in one another, while verfe is
verfe. This confideration hardens me in my opinion
rather to congratulate you ; fince you have the pleafure of the profpect whenever you take it from your
fhelf, and at the fame time the folid cafh you fold it
for, of which Virgil in his exile knew nothing in
thofe days, and which will make every place eafy to
you. I for my part am not fo happy. My *parva
rura* are faftened to me, fo that I cannot exchange
them, as you have, for more portable means of fub-
fiftence ; and yet I hope to gather enough to make
the *Patriam fugimus* fupportable to me : it is what
I am refolved on, with my *Penate*. If therefore you
afk me, to whom you fhall complain ? I will exhort
you to leave lazinefs and the elms of St James's
park, and chufe to join the other two propofals in
one, fafety and friendfhip, (the leaft of which is a
good motive for moft things, as the other is for almoft every thing), and go with me where war will
not reach us, nor paltry conftables fummon us to
veftries.

The future epiftle you flatter me with, will find
me ftill here ; and I think I may be here a month
longer. Whenever I go from hence, one of the
few reafons to make me regret my home will be,
that I fhall not have the pleafure of faying to you,

Hic tamen hanc mecum poteris requiescere noctem;
which would have rendered this place more agreeable, than ever else it could be to me : for I protest,
it is with the utmost sincerity that I assure you, I am
entirely,

Dear Sir,

Your, &c.

LETTER VIII.

June 22. 1717.

IF a regard both to public and private affairs may
plead a lawful excuse in behalf of a negligent
correspondent, I have really a very good title to it.
I cannot say whether it is a felicity or unhappiness,
that I am obliged at this time to give my whole application to Homer ; when, without that employment, my thoughts must turn upon what is less a-
greeable, the violence, madness, and resentment of
modern war-makers *, which are likely to prove
(to some people at least) more fatal, than the same
qualities in Achilles did to his unfortunate country-
men.

Though the change of my scene of life, from
Windsor forest to the side of the Thames, be one of
the grand æra's of my days, and may be called a
notable period in so inconsiderable a history ; yet you
can scarce imagine any hero passing from one stage
of life to another, with so much tranquillity, so easy a transition, and so laudable a behaviour. I am
become so truly a citizen of the world, (according
to Plato's expression), that I look with equal indifference on what I have left, and on what I have
gained. The times and amusements past are not more
like a dream to me, than those which are present. I
lie in a refreshing kind of inaction ; and have one
comfort at least from obscurity, that the darkness
helps me to sleep the better. I now and then reflect

* This was written in the year of the affair of Preston.

upon

upon the enjoyment of my friends, whom, I fancy,
I remember much as feparate fpirits do us, at tender
intervals; neither interrupting their own employments, nor altogether carelefs of ours : but in general conftantly wifhing us well, and hoping to have
us one day in their company.

To grow indifferent to the world, is to grow philofophical, or religious, (which foever of thofe turns
we chance to take) : and indeed the world is fuch a
thing, as one that thinks pretty much, muft either
laugh at, or be angry with : but if we laugh at it,
they fay we are proud ; and if we are angry with it,
they fay we are ill-natured. So the moft politic way
is to feem always better pleafed than one can be,
greater admirers, greater lovers, and in fhort greater
fools, than we really are : fo fhall we live comfortably with our families, quietly with our neighbours,
favoured by our mafters, and happy with our mi-
ftreffes. I have filled my paper, and fo adieu.

LETTER IX.

Sept. 8. 1717.

I Think your leaving England was like a good
man's leaving the world, with the bleffed confcience of having acted well in it ; and I hope you
have received your reward, in being happy where
you are. I believe, in the religious country you inhabit, you will be better pleafed to find I confider
you in this light, than if I compared you to thofe
Greeks and Romans, whofe conftancy in fuffering
pain, and whofe refolution in purfuit of a generous
end, you would rather imitate than boaft of.

But I had a melancholy hint the other day, as if
you were yet a martyr to the fatigue your virtue
made you undergo on this fide the water. I beg, if
your health be reftored to you, not to deny me the
joy of knowing it. Your endeavours of fervice and
good advice to the poor Papifts, put me in mind of
Noah's preaching forty years to thofe folks that were

to

to be drowned at laſt. At the worſt, I heartily wiſh your ark may find an Ararat, and the wife and family (the hopes of the good patriarch) land ſafely after the deluge upon the ſhore of Totneſs.

If I durſt mix profane with ſacred hiſtory, I would cheer you with the old tale of Brutus the wandering Trojan, who found on that very coaſt the happy end of his peregrinations and adventures.

I have very lately read Jeffery of Monmouth, (to whom your Cornwall is not a little beholden), in the tranſlation of a clergyman in my neighbourhood. The poor man is highly concerned to vindicate Jeffery's veracity as an hiſtorian; and told me, he was perfectly aſtoniſhed, we of the Roman communion could doubt of the legends of his giants, while we believe thoſe of our ſaints. I am forced to make a fair compoſition with him; and, by crediting ſome of the wonders of Corinæus and Gogmagog, have brought him ſo far already, that he ſpeaks reſpectfully of St Chriſtopher's carrying Chriſt, and the reſuſcitation of St Nicholas Tolentine's chicken. Thus we proceed apace in converting each other from all manner of infidelity.

Ajax and Hector are no more to be compared to Corinæus and Arthur, than the Guelphs and Ghibellines are to the Mohocks of ever dreadful memory. This amazing writer has made me lay aſide Homer for a week! and when I take him up again, I ſhall be very well prepared to tranſlate, with belief and reverence, the ſpeech of Achilles's horſe.

You will excuſe all this trifling, or any thing elſe which prevents a ſheet full of compliment: and believe, there is nothing more true, (even more true than any thing in Jeffery is falſe), than that I have a conſtant affection for you, and am, &c.

P. S. I know you will take part in rejoicing for the victory of Prince Eugene over the Turks, in the zeal you bear to the Chriſtian intereſt; though your couſin of Oxford (with whom I dined yeſterday) *ſays,* fays, there is no other difference in the Chriſtians beating the Turks, or the Turks beating the Chriſtians, than whether the Emperor ſhall firſt declare war againſt Spain, or Spain declare it againſt the Emperor.

LETTER X.

Nov. 27. 1717.

THE queſtion you propoſed to me is what at preſent I am the moſt unfit man in the world to anſwer, by my loſs of one of the beſt of fathers *.

He had lived in ſuch a courſe of temperance as was enough to make the longeſt life agreeable to him, and in ſuch a courſe of piety as ſufficed to make the moſt ſudden death ſo alſo. Sudden indeed it was. However, I heartily beg of God to give me ſuch a one, provided I can lead ſuch a life. I leave him to the mercy of God, and to the piety of a religion that extends beyond the grave : *Si qua eſt ea cura,* &c.

He has left me to the ticklish management of ſo narrow a fortune, that any one falſe ſtep would be fatal. My mother is in that diſpirited ſtate of reſignation, which is the effect of long life, and the loſs of what is dear to us. We are really each of us in want of a friend, of ſuch an humane turn as yourſelf, to make almoſt any thing deſirable to us. . I feel your abſence more than ever ; at the ſame time I can leſs expreſs my regards to you than ever ; and ſhall make this, which is the moſt ſincere letter I ever writ to you, the ſhorteſt and fainteſt perhaps of any you have received. It is enough if you reflect, that barely to remember any perſon when one's mind is taken up with a ſenſible ſorrow, is a great degree of friendſhip. I can ſay no more, but that I love you, and all that are yours; and that I wiſh it may be very long before any of yours ſhall feel for you what I now feel for my father. Adieu.

. * See Mr Pope's epitaph on his father and mother, vol. 1. p. 308.

LET-

Rentcomb in Gloucefterfhire, Oct. 3. 1721.

YOur kind letter has overtaken me here; for I have been in and about this country ever .fince your departure. I am well pleafed to date this from a place fo well known to Mrs Blount, where I write as if I were dictated to by her anceftors, whofe faces are all upon me. I fear none fo much as Sir Chriftopher Guife, who, being in his fhirt, feems as ready to combat me, as her own Sir John was to demolifh Duke Lancaftere. I dare fay your lady will recollect his figure. I looked upon the manfion, walls, and terraces; the plantations, and flopes, which nature has made to command a variety of valleys and rifing woods, with a veneration mixed with a pleafure, that reprefented her to me in thofe puerile amufements which engaged her fo many years ago in this place. I fancied I faw her fober over a fampler, or gay over a jointed baby. I dare fay fhe did one thing more, even in thofe early times; " remembered her Creator in the days of " her youth."

You defcribe fo well your hermitical ftate of life, that none of the ancient anchorites could go beyond you, for a cave in a rock, with a fine fpring, or any of the accommodations that befit a folitary. Only I do not remember to have read, that any of thofe venerable and holy perfonages took with them a lady, and begat fons and daughters. You muft modeftly be content to be accounted a patriarch. But were you a little younger, I fhould rather rank you with Sir Amadis, and his fellows. If piety be fo romantic, I fhall turn hermit in good earneft; for I fee one may go fo far as to be poetical, and hope to fave one's foul at the fame time. I really wifh myfelf fomething more, that is, a prophet; for I wifh I were, as Habakkuk, to be taken by the hair of his head, and vifit Daniel in his den. You are very obliging

liging in faying, I have now a whole family upon
my hands to whom to difcharge the part of a friend :
I affure you, I like them all fo well, that I will never quit my hereditary right to them ; you have made
me yours, and confequently them mine. I ftill fee
them walking on my green at Twickenham ; and
gratefully remember, not only their green gowns,
but the inftructions they gave me how to flide down
and trip up the fteepeft flopes of my mount.

Pray think of me fometimes, as I fhall often of
you ; and know me for what I am, that is,

Your, &c.

LETTER XII.

Oct. 21. 1721.

YOur very kind and obliging manner of inquiring after me, among the firft concerns of life,
at your refufcitation, fhould have been fooner anfwered and acknowledg-d. I fincerely rejoice at
your recovery from an illnefs which gave me lefs pain
than it did you, only from my ignorance of it. I
fhould have elfe been ferioufly and deeply afflicted,
in the thought of your danger by a fever. I think it
a fine and a natural thought, which I lately read in
a letter of Montaigne's publifhed by P. Cofte, giving
an account of the laft words of an intimate friend of
his : " Adieu, my friend ! the pain I feel will foon
" be over; but I grieve for that you are to feel,
" which is to laft you for life."

I join with your family in giving God thanks for
lending us a worthy man fomewhat longer. The
comforts you receive from their attendance, put me
in mind of what old Fletcher of Salton faid one day
to me. " Alas, I have nothing to do but to die ; I
" am a poor individual ; no creature to wifh, or to
" fear, for my life or death. It is the only reafon
" I have to repent being a fingle man ; now I grow
" old, I am like a tree without a prop, and with-

" out

" out young trees to grow round me, for company
" and defence."

I hope the gout will foon go after the fever, and
all evil things remove far from you.   But pray tell
me, when will you move towards us ? If you had an
interval to get hither, I care not what fixes you afterwards except the gout.   Pray come, and never
ftir from us again.   Do away your dirty acres, caft
them to dirty people, fuch as in the fcripture-phrafe
poffefs the land.   Shake off your earth like the noble
animal in Milton,

The tawny lion, pawing to get free
His hinder parts, he fprings as broke from bonds,
And rampant fhakes his brinded mane : the ounce,
The lizard, and the tyger, as the mole
Rifing, the crumbled earth above them threw
In hillocks ! ———

But, I believe, Milton never thought thefe fine very
fes of his fhould be applied to a man felling a parcel
of dirty acres ; though in the main I think it may
have fome refemblance.   For, God knows ! this little fpace of ground nourifhes, buries, and confines
us, as that of Eden did thofe creatures, till we can
fhake it loofe, at leaft in our affections and defires.

Believe, dear Sir, I truly love and value you. Let
Mrs Blount know that fhe is in the lift of my *Memen-*
to, Domine, famulorum famularumque's, &c. My poor
mother is far from well, declining ; and I am watch-
ing over her, as we watch an expiring taper, that e-
ven when it looks brighteft, waftes faiteft.   I am (as
you will fee from the whole air of this letter) not in
the gayeft nor eafieft humour, but always with fincerity,

Your, &c.

L E T T E R   XIII.

June 27. 1723.

YOU may truly do me the juftice to think no man
is more your fincere wellwifher than myfelf,

or

or more the fincere wellwifher of your whole family ; with all which, I cannot deny but I have a mixture of envy to you all, for loving one another fo
well ; and for enjoying the fweets of that life, which
can only be tafted by people of good-will.

They from all fhades the darknefs can exclude,
And from a defert banifh folitude.

Torbay is a paradife, and a ftorm is but an amufement to fuch people. If you drink tea upon a pro-
montory that over-hangs the fea, it is preferable to
an affembly ; and the whiftling of the wind better
mufic to contented and loving minds, than the opera
to the fpleenful, ambitious, difeafed, diftafted, and
diftracted fouls which this world affords ; nay, this
world affords no other. Happy they who are banifhed from us ! but happier they who can banifh
themfelves, or more properly banifh the world from
them !

Alas ! I live at Twickenham !

I take that period to be very fublime, and to include more than a hundred. fentences that might be
writ to exprefs diftraction, hurry, multiplica ion of
nothings, and all the fatiguing perpetual bufinefs of
having no bufinefs to do. You will wonder I reckon tranflating the Odyffey as nothing. But whenever I think ferioufly, (and of late I have met with
fo many occafions of thinking ferioufly, that I begin
never to think otherwif), I cannot but think thefe
things very idle ; as idle as if a beaft of burden
fhould go on gingling his bells, without bearing any
thing valuable about him, or ever ferving his mafter.

Life's vain amufements, amidft which we dwell ;
Not weigh'd, or underftood, by the grim god of hell !

faid a Heathen poet ; as he is tranflated by a Chriftian Bifhop, who has, firft by his exhortations, and
fince by his example, taught me to think as becomes
a reafonable creature—but he is gone !

I

I remember I promifed to write to you, as foon as
I fhou'd hear you were got home. You mult look on
tuis as the firft day I have been myfelf, and pafs over
the mad interval unimputed to me. How punctual
a correfponent I fhall henceforward be able or not
able to be, God knows : but he knows, I fhall ever
be a punctual and gratefui friend, and all the good
wifhes of fuch an one will ever attend you.

L E T T E R   XIV.

Twick'nam, June 2. 1725.

YOU fhew yourfelf a juft man and a friend in
thofe guefles and fuppofitions you make at the
poflible reafons of my filence ;· every one ʳf which is
a true one. As to forgetfulnefs of you or yours, I
affure you, the promifcuous converfations of the
town ferve only to put me in mind of better, and
more quiet, to be had in a corner of the world (un-
difturbed, innocent, ferene, and fenfible) with fuch
as you. Let no accefs of any diftruft make you
think of me differently in a cloudy day from what
you do in the moft funfhiny weather. Let the young.
ladies be affured I make nothing new in my gardens
without wifhing to fee the print of their fairy fteps in
every part of them. I have put the laft hand to my
works of this kind, in happily finifhing the fubterra-
neous way and grotto. I there found a fpring of
the cleareft water, which falls in a perpetual rill,
that echoes through the cavern day and night. From
the river Thames, you fee through my arch up a
walk of the wildernefs, to a kind of open temple,
wholly compofed of fhells in the ruftic manner; and
from that diftance under the temple you lo k down
through a floping arcade of trees, and· fee the fails
on the river pafling fuddenly and vanifhing, as
through a perfpective glafs. When you fhut the
doors of this grotto, it becomes on the inftant, from
a luminous room, a *camera obfcura* ; on the walls of
which all the objects of the river, hills, woods, and
boats,

boats, are forming a moving picture in their visible
radiations : and when you have a mind to light it
up, it affords you a very different scene. It is finished with shells intersperfed with pieces of looking-
glass in angular forms; and in the ceiling is a star of
the fame material, at which when a lamp (of an or-
bicular figure of thin alabaster) is hung in the middle, a thousand pointed rays glitter, and are reflected over the place. There are connected to this grotto by a narrower passage two porches, one towards
the river of fmooth stones full of light, and open ;
the other toward the garden shadowed with trees,
rough with shells, flints, and iron-ore. The bottom
is paved with simple pebble, as is also the adjoining
walk up the wildernefs to the temple, in the natural
tafte, agreeing not ill with the little dripping murmur, and the aquatic idea of the whole place. It
wants nothing to complete it but a good flatue with
an inscription, like that beautiful antique one which
you know I am fo fond of,

Hujus Nympha loci, facri cuftodia fontis,
Dormio, dum blandæ fentio murmur aquæ.
Parce meum, quifquis tangis cava marmora, fomnum
Rumpere; fi bibas, five lavere, tace.

Nymph of the grot, thefe facred fprings I keep,
And to the murmur of thefe waters fleep ;
Ah fpare my flumbers, gently tread the cave!
And drink in filence, or in filence lave !

You will think I have been very poetical in this
defcription, but it is pretty near the truth *. I
wifh you were here to bear teftimony how little it

* He had greatly enlarged and improved this grotto not long
before his death : and, by incrufting it about with a vaft number of ores and minerals of the richeft and rareft kinds, had made
it one of the moft elegant and romantic retirements that was a-
ny where to be feen. He has made it the fubject of a very
pretty pcem of a fingular caft and compofition, — See this pcem
vol. 2. *p.* 154.

owes

owes to art, either the place itfelf, or the image I give of it.

am, &c.

LETTER XV.

Sept. 13. 1725.

I Should be afhamed to own the receipt of a very kind letter from you, two whole months from the date of this; if I were not more afhamed to tell a lie, or to make an excufe, which is worfe than a lie; (for being built upon fome probable circum-ftance, it makes ufe of a degree of truth to falfify with, and is a lie guarded). Your letter has been in my pocket in conflant wearing, till that, and the pocket, and the fuit, are worn out; by which means I have read it forty times, and I find, by fo doing, that I have not enough confidered and reflected upon many others you have obliged me with; for true friendfhip, as they fay of good writing, will bear reviewing a thoufand times, and ftill difcover new beauties.

I have had a fever, a fhort one, but a violent. I am now well; fo it fhall take up no more of this paper.

I begin now to expect you in town to make the winter to come more tolerable to us both. The fummer is a kind of heaven, when we wander in a para-difiacal fcene among groves and gardens : but at this feafon, we are, like our poor firft parents, turned out of that agreeable though folitary life, and forced to look about for more people to help to bear our la-bours, to get into warmer houfes, and live together in cities.

I hope you are long fince perfectly reftored, and rifen from your gout, happy in the delights of a con-tented family, fmiling at ftorms, laughing at great-nefs, merry over a Chriftmas fire, and exercifing all the functions of an old patriarch in charity and ho-fpitality. I will not tell Mrs B * * what I think fhe

is

is doing : for I conclude it is her opinion, that he only ought to know it for whom it is done ; and she will allow herself to be far enough advanced above a fine lady, not to defire to fhine before men.

Your daughters perhaps may have fome other thoughts, which even their mother muft excufe them for, becaufe fhe is a mother. I will not however fuppofe thofe thoughts get the better of their devotions, but rather excite them, and affift the warmth of them ; while their prayer may be, that they may raife up and breed as irreproachable a young family as their parents have done. In a word, I fancy you all well, eafy, and happy, juft as I wifh you ; and next to that, I wifh you all with me.

Next to God, is a good man ; next in dignity, and next in value. *Minuifti eum paullo minus ab an-gelis.* If therefore I wifh well to the good and the deferving, and defire they only fhould be my companions and correfpondents, I muft very foon and very much think of you. I want your company, and your example. Pray make hafte to town, fo as not again to leave us. Difcharge the load of earth that lies on you, like one of the mountains under which the poets fay the giants (the men of the earth) are whelmed : leave earth to the fons of the earth ; your converfation is in heaven. Which that it may be accomplifhed in us all, is the prayer of him who maketh this fhort fermon ; value (to you) three pence. Adieu.

Mr Blount died in London the following year, 1726.

L_E T T E R S to and from the Hon,
R o b e r t D i g b y.

From 1714 to 1727.

L E T T E R I.

To the Hon. R o b e r t D i g b y *.

I Had pleafed myfelf fooner in writing to you, but that I have been your fucceffor in a fit of ficknefs, and am not yet fo much recovered, but that I have thoughts of ufing your phyficians †. They are as grave perfons as any of the faculty, and (like the an-cients) carry their own medicaments about with them. But indeed the moderns are fuch lovers of raillery, that nothing is grave enough to efcape them. Let them laugh, but people will ftill have their opinions. As they think our doctors affes to them, we will think them affes to our doctors.

I am glad you are fo much in a better ftate of health, as to allow me to jeft about it. My con-cern, when I heard of your danger, was fo very ferious, that I almoft take it ill Dr Evans fhould tell you of it, or you mention it. I tell you fairly, if you and a few more fuch people were to leave the world, I would not give fixpence to ftay in it.

I am not fo much concerned as to the point whe-ther you are to live fat or lean : moft men of wit or honefty are ufually decreed to live very lean : fo I am inclined to the opinion that it is decreed you fhall ; however, be comforted, and reflect, that you will make the better bufto for it.

* See Mr Pope's epitaph on him and his fifter, vol. 2,
† Affes.

It

It is fomething particular in you, not to be fatif-
fied with fending me your own books, but to make
your acquaintance continue the frolic. Mr Wharton
forced me to take Gorboduc, which has fince done
me great credit with feveral people, as it has done
Dryden and Oldham fome difkindnefs, in fhewing
there is as much difference between their Gorboduc
and this, as between Queen Anne and King George.
It is truly a fcandal, that men fhould write with contempt of a piece which they never once faw, as thofe
two poets did, who were ignorant even of the fex,
as well as fenfe of Gorboduc *.

Adieu ! 1 am going to forget you. This minute
you took up all my mind ; the next I fhall think of
nothing but the reconciliation with Agamemnon, and
the recovery of Brifeis. I fhall be Achilles's humble
fervant thofe two months, (with the good leave of
all my friends). I have no ambition fo ftrong at prefent, as that noble one of Sir Salathiel Lovel, record-
er of London, to furnifh out a decent and plentiful
execution of Greeks and Trojans. It is not to be
expreffed how heartily I wifh the death of all Homer's heroes, one after another. The Lord preferve
me in the day of battle, which is juft approaching !
Join in your prayers for me, and know me to be always

Your, &c.

LETTER II.

London, March 31. 1718.

TO convince you how little pain I give myfelf
in correfponding with men of good nature
and good underftanding, you fee I omit to anfwer
your letters till a time, when another man would be
afhamed to own he had received them. If therefore
you are ever moved on my account by that fpirit,
which I take to be as familiar to you as a quotidian

---

* There is a correct edition of it in that valuable collection of
old Plays publifhed by Dodfley.

ague, I mean the spirit of goodness, pray never stint it in any fear of obliging me to a civility beyond my natural inclination. I dare trust you, Sir, not only with my folly when I write, but with my negligence when I do not : and expect equally your pardon for either.

If I knew how to entertain you through the rest of this paper, it should be spotted and diversified with conceits all over; you should be put out of breath with laughter at each sentence, and pause at each period, to look back over how much wit you have passed. But I have found by experience, that people now-a-days regard writing as little as they do preaching. The most we can hope, is to be heard just with decency and patience, once a-week, by folks in the country. Here in town we hum over a piece of fine writing, and we whistle at a sermon. The stage is the only place we seem alive at ! There indeed we stare, and roar, and clap hands for K. George and the government. As for all other virtues but this loyalty, they are an obsolete train, so ill-dressed, that men, women, and children hiss them out of all good company. Humility knocks so sneakingly at the door, that every footman outraps it, and makes it give way to the free entrance of Pride, Prodigality, and Vain-glory.

My Lady Scudamore, from having rusticated in your company too long, really behaves herself scandalously among us. She pretends to open her eyes for the sake of seeing the sun, and to sleep because it is night; drinks tea at nine in the morning, and is thought to have said her prayers before ; talks, without any manner of shame, of good books, and has not seen Cibber's play of the Nonjuror. I rejoiced the other day to see a libel on her toilette; which gives me some hope, that you have, at least, a taste of scandal left you, in defect of all other vices.

Upon the whole matter, I heartily wish you well ; but as I cannot entirely desire the ruin of all the joys

of

of this city, so all that remains is to wish you would
keep your happiness to yourselves, that the happiest
here may not die with envy at a bliss which they cannot attain to.

I am, &c.

LETTER III.

From Mr D I G B Y.

Celeshill, April 17. 1718.

I Have read your letter over and over with delight.
By your description of the town, I imagine it
to lie under some great inchantment, and am very
much concerned for you and all my friends in it. I
am the more afraid, imagining, since you do not
fly those horrible monsters, rapine, dissimulation, and
luxury, that a magic circle is drawn about you, and
you cannot escape. We are here in the country in
quite another world, surrounded with blessings and
pleasures, without any occasion of exercising our
irascible faculties. Indeed we cannot boast of good-
breeding and the art of life, but yet we do not live
unpleasantly in primitive simplicity and good-humour. The fashions of the town affect us but just
like a raree-show; we have a curiosity to peep at
them, and nothing more. What you call pride,
prodigality, and vain-glory, we cannot find in
pomp and splendour at this distance: it appears to
us a fine glittering scene; which if we do not envy
you, we think you happier than we are, in your enjoying it. Whatever you may think to persuade us
of the humility of Virtue, and her appearing in rags,
amongst you, we can never believe. Our uninformed
minds represent her so noble to us, that we necessari-
ly annex splendour to her, and we could as soon
imagine the order of things inverted, and that there is
no man in the moon, as believe the contrary. I cannot forbear telling you, we indeed read the spoils of
rapine as boys do the English rogue, and hug our-

C 3   selves

felves full as much over it; yet our rofes are not
without thorns. Pray give me the pleafure of the r-
ing (when you are at leifure) how foon I may expect
to fee the next volume of Homer.

I am, &c.

L E T T E R   IV.

May 1. 1720.

YOU will think me very full of myfelf, when
after long filence (which however, to fay
truth, has rather been employed to contemplate of
you, than to forget you) I begin to talk of my own
works. I find it is in the finifhing a book, as in
concluding a feffion of parliament; one always
thinks it will be very foon, and finds it very late.
There are many unlooked-for incidents to retard the
clearing any public account; and fo I fee it is in
mine. I have plagued myfelf, like great minifters,
with undertaking too much for one man; and with
a defire of doing more than was expected from me,
have done lefs than I ought.

For having defigned four very laborious and uncommon fort of indexes to Homer, I am forced,
for want of time, to publifh two only; the defign
of which you will own to be pretty, though far
from being fully executed. I have alfo been obliged
to leave unfinifhed in my defk the heads of two
effays, one on the theology and morality of Homer, and another on the oratory of Homer and Virgil. So they muft wait for future editions, or pe-
rifh: and (one way or other, no great matter which)
dabit Deus his quoque finem. I think of you every
day, I affure you, even without fuch good memorials
of you as your fifters, with whom I fometimes talk
of you, and find it one of the moft agreeable of all
fubjects to them. My Lord Digby muft be perpetually remembered by all who ever knew him, or
knew his children. There needs no more than an

acquaintance

acquaintance with your family, to make all elder
fons wifh they had fathers to their lives end.

I cannot touch upon the fubject of filial love,
without putting you in mind of an old woman, who
has a fincere, hearty old-fafhioned refpect for you,.
and conftantly blames her fon for not having writ to
you oftener to tell you fo.

I very much wifh (but what fignifies my wifhing?
my Lady Scudamore wifhes, your fifters wifh) that
you were with us, to compare the beautiful contraft
this feafon affords us, of the town and the country.
No ideas you could form in the winter can make you
imagine what Twickenham is (and what your friend
Mr Johnfon of Twickenham is) in this warmer
feafon. Our river glitters beneath an unclouded fun,
at the fame time that its banks retain the verdure of
fhowers : our gardens are offering their firft nofe-
gays ; our trees, like new acquaintance brought
happily together, are ftretching their arms to mcct
each other, and growing nearer and nearer every
hour ; the birds are paying their thankfgiving-fongs
for the new habitations I have made them ; my
building iifes high enough to attract the eye and curiofity of the paffenger from the river, where, upon
beholding a mixtuie of beauty and ruin, he inquires
what houfe is falling, or what church is iifing ? So
little tafte have our common Tritons of Vitruvius.;
whatever delight the poetical gods of the river may
take, in reflecting on their ftreams, by Tufcan por-
ticoes, or Ionic pilafters.

But (to defcend fiom all this pomp of ftyle) the
beft account of what I am building, is, that it will
afford me a few pleafant rooms for fuch a friend as
yourfelf, or a cool fituation for an hour or two for
Lady Scudamore,. when fhe will do me the honour
(at this public houfe on the road) to drink her own
cyder.

The moment I am writing this, I am furprifed
with the account of the death of a friend of mine ;
which makes all I have here been talking of, a
mere

mere jeſt ! Building, gardens, writings, pleaſures, works of whatever ſtuff man can raiſe ! none of them (God knows) capable of advantaging a crea- ture that is mortal, or of ſatisfying a ſoul that is immortal ! Dear Sir,

I am, &c.

LETTER V.

From Mr DIGBY.

May 21. 1720.

YOur letter, which I had two poſts ago, was very medicinal to me; and I heartily thank you for the relief it gave me. I was ſick of the thoughts of my not having in all this time given you any teſtimony of the affection I owe you, and which I as conſtantly indeed feel as I think of you. This indeed was a troubleſome ill to me, till, after reading your letter, I found it was a moſt idle weak imagination to think I could ſo offend you. Of all the impreſſions you have made upon me, I never re- ceived any with greater joy than this of your abun- dant good-nature, which bids me be aſſured of ſome ſhare of your affections.

I had many other pleaſures from your letter. That your mother remembers me, is a very ſincere joy to me. I cannot but reflect how alike you are ; from the time you do any one a favour, you think yourſelves obliged as thoſe that have received one. This is indeed an old-faſhioned reſpect, hardly to be found out of your houſe. I have great hopes how- ever, to ſee many old-faſhioned virtues revive, ſince you have made our age in love with Homer. I heartily wiſh you, who are as good a citizen as a poet, the joy of ſeeing a reformation. from your works. I am in doubt whether I ſhould congratulate your having finiſhed Homer, while the two eſſays you mention are not completed ; but if you expect

no

no great trouble from finishing these, I heartily rejoice with you.

I have some faint notion of the beauties of Twickenham from what I here see round me. The verdure of showers is poured upon every tree and field about us; the gardens unfold variety of colours to the eye every morning, the hedges breath is beyond all perfume, and the song of birds we hear as well as you. But though I hear and see all this, yet I think they would delight me more if you was here. I found the want of these at Twickenham while I was there with you, by which I guess what an increase of charms it must now have. How kind is it in you to wish me there, and how unfortunate are my circumstances that allow me not to visit you? If I see you, I must leave my father alone; and this uneasy thought would disappoint all my proposed pleasures. The same circumstance will prevent my prospect of many happy hours with you in Lord Bathurst's wood, and I fear of seeing you till winter; unless Lady Scudamore comes to Sherburne, in which case I shall press you to see Dorsetshire, as you proposed. May you have a long enjoyment of your new favourite portico.

Your, &c.

L E T T E R VI.

From Mr D I G B Y.

Sherburne, July 9. 1720.

THE London language and conversation is, I find, quite changed since I left it, though it is not above three or four months ago. No violent change in the natural world ever astonished a philosopher so much as this does me. I hope this will calm all party-rage, and introduce more humanity than has of late obtained in conversation. All scandal will sure be laid aside; for there can be no such disease any more as spleen in this new golden age.

I

I am pleafed with the thoughts of feeing nothing but a general good-humour when I come up to town; I rejoice in the univerfal riches I hear of, in the thought of their having this effect. They tell me you was foon content; and that you cared not for fuch an increafe as others wifhed you. By this account I judge you the richeft man in the South-fea, and congratulate you accordingly. I can wifh you only an increafe of health; for of riches and fame you have enough.

Your, &c.

LETTER VII.

July 20. 1720.

YOur kind defire to know the ftate of my health had not been unfatisfied fo long, had not that ill ftate been the impediment. Nor fhould I have feemed an unconcerned party in the joys of your family, which I heard of from Lady Scudamore, whofe fhort efchantillon of a letter (of a quarter of a page) I value as the fhort glimpfe of a vifion afforded to fome devout hermit; for it includes (as thofe revelations do) a promife of a better life in the Elyfian groves of Cirencefter, whither, I could fay almoft in the ftyle of a fermon, the Lord bring us all, &c. Thither may we tend, by various ways, to one blifsful bower; thither may health, peace, and good-humour wait upon us as affociates; thither may whole cargoes of nectar (liquor of life and longævity!) by mortals called fpaw-water, be conveyed; and there (as Milton has it) may we, like the deities,

On flow'rs repos'd, and with frefh garlands crown'd,
Quaff immortality and joy.

When I fpeak of garlands, I fhould not forget the green veftments and fcarfs which your fifters promifed to make for this purpofe. I expect you too in green, with a hunting-horn by your fide, and a green hat,

hat, the model of which you may take from Of-
borne's defcription of King James I.

What words, what numbers, what oratory, or
what poetry, can fuffice, to exprefs how infinitely I
efteem, value, love, and defire you all, above all the
great ones of this part of the world ; above all the
Jews, jobbers, bubblers, fubfcribers, projectors,
directors, governours, treafurers, &c. &c. &c. in
fæcula fæculorum !

Turn your eyes and attention from this miferable
mercenary period ; and turn yourfelf, in a juft contempt of thefe fons of Mammon, to the contemplation of books, gardens, and marriage : in which I
now leave you, and return (wretch that I am) to wa-
ter-gruel and Palladio.

I am, &c.

LETTER VIII.

From Mr DIGBY.

Sherburne, July 30.

I Congratulate you, dear Sir, on the return of the
golden age ; for fure this muft be fuch, in which
money is fnowered down in fuch abundance upon us.
I hope this overflowing will produce great and good
fruits, and bring back the figurative moral golden
age to us. I have fome omens to induce me to believe it may ; for when the Mufes delight to be near
a court, when I find you frequently with a firft minifter, I cannot but expect from fuch an intimacy an
encouragement and revival of the polite arts. I know,
you defire to bring them into honour, above the gold-
en image which is fet up and worfhipped ; and if
you cannot effect it, adieu to all fuch hopes. You
feem to intimate in yours another face of things
from this inundation of wealth, as if beauty, wit,
and valour would no more engage our paffions in the
pleafurable purfuit of them, though affifted by this
increafe : if fo, and if monfters only as various as
thofe

thofe of Nile arife from this abundance, who that has
any fpleen about him will not hafte to town to laugh?
What will become of the playhoufe? who will go
thither, while there is fuch entertainment in the
ftreets? I hope we fhall neither want good fatire nor
comedy; if we do, the age may well be thought
barren of geniufes, for none has ever produced better fubjects.

Your, &c.

L E T T E R IX.

From Mr D I G B Y.

Colefhill, Nov. 12. 1720.

I Find in my heart that I have a taint of the corrupt age we live in. I want the public fpirit fo
much admired.in old Rome, of facrificing every thing
that is dear to us to the commonwealth. I even
feel a more intimate concern for my friends who have
fuffered in the S. fea, than for the public, which is
faid to be undone by it. But I hope the reafon is,
that I do not fee fo evidently the ruin of the public
to be a confequence of it, as I do the lofs of my
friends. I fear there are few befides yourfelf that
will be perfuaded by old Hefiod, that *half is more
than the whole.* I know not whether I do not rejoice in your fufferings *; fince they have fhewn me
your mind is principled with fuch a fentiment, I affure you I expect from it a performance greater ftill
than Homer. I have an extreme joy from your com-
municating to me this affection of your mind;

Quid voveat dulci nutricula majus alumno?

Believe me, dear Sir, no equipage could fhew you
to my eye in fo much fplendour. I would not indulge this fit of philofophy fo far as to be tedious to
you, elfe I could profecute it with pleafure.

* See note on ver. 133. fat. 2. book 2. of Horace, in vol. 1.
p. 329.

I

I long to fee you, your mother, and your villa;
till then I will fay nothing of Lord Bathurft's wood,
which I faw in my return hither. Soon after Chriftmas I defign for London, where I fhall mifs Lady
Scudamore very much, who intends to ftay in the
country all winter. I am angry with her, as I am
like to fuffer by this refolution; and would fain
blame her, but cannot find a caufe. The man is
curfed that has a longer letter than this to write
with as bad a pen; yet I can ufe it with pleafure to
fend my fervices to your good mother, and to write
myfelf

Your, &c.

LETTER X.

DOctor Arbuthnot is going to Bath, and will ftay
there a fortnight or more. Perhaps you
would be comforted to have a fight of him, whether
you need him or not. I think him as good a doctor
as any man for one that is ill, and a better doctor for
one that is well. He would do admirably for Mrs
Mary Digby. She needed only to follow his hints,
to be in eternal bufinefs and amufement of mind, and
even as active as fhe could defire. But indeed I fear
fhe would out-walk him; for (as Dean Swift obferved to me the very firft time I faw the Doctor) " he
" is a man that can do every thing but walk." His
brother, who is lately come into England, goes alfo
to the Bath; and is a more extraordinary man than
he, worth your going thither on purpofe to know
him. The fpirit of philanthropy, fo long dead to
our world, is revived in him : he is a philofopher
all of fire; fo warmly, nay fo wildly in the right,
that he forces all others about him to be fo too, and
draws them into his own vortex. He is a ftar that
looks as if it were all fire, but is all benignity, all
gentle and beneficial influence. If there be other
men in the world that would ferve a friend, yet he

VOL. IV.   † D   is

is the only one, I believe, that could make even an enemy ſerve a friend.

As all human life is chequered and mixed with ac-quiſitions and loſſes, (though the latter are more cer-tain and irremediable, than the former laſting or ſa-tisfactory); ſo at the time I have gained the acquain-tance of one worthy man, I have loſt another, a very eaſy, humane, and gentlemanly neighbour, Mr Stonor. It is certain the loſs of one of this character puts us naturally upon ſetting a greater value on the few that are left, though the degree of our eſteem may be different. Nothing, ſays Seneca, is ſo me-lancholy a circumſtance in human life, or ſo ſoon re-conciles us to the thought of our own death, as the reflection and proſpect of one friend after another dropping round us! Who would ſtand alone, the ſole remaining ruin, the laſt tottering column of all the fabric of friendſhip once ſo large, ſeemingly ſo ſtrong, and yet ſo ſuddenly ſunk and buried?

I am, &c.

LETTER XI.

I Have belief enough in the goodneſs of your whole family, to think you will all be pleaſed that I am arrived in ſafety at Twickenham; though it is a ſort of earneſt that you will be troubled again with me, at Sherburne, or Coleſhill: for however I may like one of your places, it may be in that as in liking one of your family; when one ſees the reſt, one likes them all. Pray make my ſervices acceptable to them. I wiſh them all the happineſs they may want, and the continuance of all the happineſs they have; and I take the latter to compriſe a great deal more, than the former. I muſt ſeparate Lady Scudamore from you, as, I fear, ſhe will do herſelf before this letter reaches you: ſo I wiſh her a good journey, and I hope one day to try if ſhe lives as well as you do: though I much queſtion if ſhe can live as quiet-ly. I ſuſpect the bells will be ringing at her arrival,

and

and on her own and Miss Scudamore's birth-days'
and that all the clergy in the country come to pay
respects; both the clergy and their bells expecting
from her, and from the young lady, further business
and further employment. Besides all this, there
dwells on the one side of her the Lady Conningsby,
and on the other Mr W * *. Yet I shall, when the
days and the years come about, adventure upon all
this for her sake.

I beg my Lord Digby to think me a better man
than to content myself with thanking him in the
common way. I am in as sincere a sense of the
word, his servant, as you are his son, or he your father.

I must in my turn insist upon hearing how my last
fellow-travellers got home from Clarendon, and defire Mr Philips to remember me in his cyder, and to
tell Mr W * * that I am dead and buried.

I wish the young ladies, whom I almost robbed of
their good name, a better name in return (even that
very name to each of them, which they shall like
best, for the sake of the man that bears it).

Your, &c.

LETTER XII.

1722.

YOur making a sort of apology for your not
writing, is a very genteel reproof to me. I
know I was to blame; but I know I did not intend
to be so, and (what is the happiest knowledge in the
world) I know you will forgive me; for, sure, nothing is more satisfactory, than to be certain of such
a friend as will overlook one's failings, since every
such instance is a conviction of his kindness.

If I am all my life to dwell in intentions, and never to rise to actions, I have but too much need of
that gentle disposition which I experience in you.
But I hope better things of myself, and fully purpose to make you a visit this summer at Sherburne.

D 2

I am told you are all upon removal very fpeedily,
and that Mrs Mary Digby talks in a letter to Lady
Scudamore, of feeing my Lord Bathurft's wood in
her way. How much I wifh to be her guide through
that inchanted foreit, is not to be expreffed. I look
upon myfelf as the magician appropriated to the
place, without whom no mortal can penetrate into
the receffes of thofe facred fhades. I could pafs whole
days, in only defcribing to her the future, and as
yet vifionary beauties, that are to rife in thofe fcenes;
the palace that is to be built, the pavilions that are
to glitter, the colonades that are to adorn them; nay
more, the meeting of the Thames and the Severn,
which (when the noble owner has finer dreams than
ordinary) are to be led into each other's embraces
through fecret caverns of not above twelve or fifteen
miles, till they rife and celebrate their marriage in
the midft of an immenfe amphitheatre, which is to be
the admiration of pofterity, a hundred years hence.
But till the deftined time fhall arrive that is to manifeft thefe wonders, Mrs Digby muft content herfelf
with feeing what is at prefent no more than the fineft
wood in England.

The objects that attract this part of the world, are
of a quite different nature. Women of quality are
all turned followers of the camp in Hyde-park this
year, whither all the town refort to magnificent entertainments given by the officers, &c. The Scy-
thian ladies that dwelt in the waggons of war, were
not more clofely attached to the luggage. The ma-
trons, like thofe of Sparta, attend their fons to the
field, to be the witneffes of their glorious deeds; and
the maidens, with all their charms difplayed, provoke the fpirit of the foldiers. Tea and coffee fupply the place of Lacedæmonian black broth. This
camp feems crowned with perpetual victory, for e-
very fun that rifes in the thunder of cannon, fets in
the mufic of violins. Nothing is yet wanting but
the conftant prefence of the Princefs, to reprefent the
mater exercitus.

At

At Twickenham the world goes otherwife. There are certain old people who take up all my time, and will hardly allow me to keep any other company. They were introduced here by a man of their own fort, who has made me perfectly rude to all contemporaries, and will not fo much as fuffer me to look upon them. The perfon I complain of, is the Bifhop of Rochefter. Yet he allows me (from fomething he has heard of your character and that of your family, as if you were of the old fect of moralifts) to write three or four fides of paper to you, and to tell you (what thefe fort of people never tell but with truth and religious fincerity) that I am, and ever will be,

Your, &c.

LETTER XIII.

THE fame reafon that hindered your writing, hindered mine, the pleafing expectation to fee you in town. Indeed, fince the willing confinement I have lain under here with my mother, (whom it is natural and reafonable I fhould rejoice with, as well as grieve), I could the better bear your abfence from London, for I could hardly have feen you there; and it would not have been quite reafonable to have drawn you to a fick room hither from the firft embraces of your friends. My mother is now (I thank God) wonderfully recovered, though not fo much as yet to venture out of her chamber, but enough to enjoy a few particular friends, when they have the good-nature to look upon her. I may recommend to you the room we fit in, upon one (and that a favourite) account, that it is the very warmeft in the houfe. We and our fires will equally fmile upon your face. There is a Perfian proverb that fays (I think very prettily), " The converfation of a friend brightens " the eyes." This I take to be a fplendour ftill more agreeable than the fires you fo delightfully defcribe.

D 3

That

That you may long enjoy your own fire-fide in the
metaphorical fenfe, that is, all thofe of your family
who make it pleafing to fit and fpend whole wintry
months together, (a far more rational delight, and
better felt by an honeft heart, than all the glaring entertainments, numerous lights, and falfe fplendours,
of an affembly of empty heads, aking hearts, and
falfe faces); this is my fincere wifh to you and
yours.

You fay you propofe much pleafure in feeing fome
new faces about town of my acquaintance. I guefs
you mean Mrs Howard's and Mrs Blount's. And I
affure you, you ought to take as much pleafure in
their hearts, if they are what they fometimes exprefs
with regard to you.

Believe me, dear Sir, to you all, a very faithful
fervant.

L E T T E R   XIV.

From Mr D I G B Y.

Sherburne, Aug. 14. 1723.

I Cannot return from fo agreeable an entertainment
as yours in the country, without acknowledging
it. I thank you heartily for the new agreeable idea
of life you there gave me; it will remain long with
me, for it is very ftrongly impreffed upon my imagination. I repeat the memory of it often; and
fhall value that faculty of the mind now more than
ever, for the power it gives me of being entertained
in your villa, when abfent from it. As you are poffeffed of all the pleafures of the country, and, as I
think, of a right mind, what can I wifh you but
health to enjoy them ? This I fo heartily do, that I
fhould be even glad to hear your good old mother
might lofe all her prefent pleafures in her unwearied
care of you, by your better health convincing them
it is unneceffary.

I am troubled, and fhall be fo, till I hear you
have

have received this letter : for you gave me the greateft pleafure imaginable in yours, and I am impatient
to acknowledge it. If I any wife deferve that
friendly warmth and affection with which you write,
it is, that I have a heart full of love and efteem for
you ; fo truly, that I fhould lofe the greateft pleafure of my life if I loft your good opinion. It rejoices me very much to be reckoned by you in the clafs
of honeft men : for though I am not troubled over
much about the opinion moft may have of me, yet
I own it would grieve me not to be thought well of
by you and fome few others. I will not doubt my
own ftrength ; yet I have this further fecurity to
maintain my integrity, that I cannot part with that,
without forfeiting your efteem with it.

Perpetual diforder and ill health have for fome
years fo difguifed me, that I fometimes fear I do not
to my beft friends enough appear what I really am.
Sicknefs is a great oppreffor ; it does great injury to
a zealous heart, ftifling its warmth, and not fuffering it to break out in action. But I hope I fhall not
make this complaint much longer. I have other
hopes that pleafe me too, though not fo well grounded. Thefe are, that you may yet make a journey
weftward with Lord Bathurft ; but of the probability of this I do not venture to reafon, becaufe I would
not part with the pleafure of that belief. It grieves
me to think how far I am removed from you, and
from that excellent Lord, whom I love ! Indeed I remember him, as one that has made ficknefs eafy to
me, by bearing with my infirmities in the fame manner that you have always done. I often too confider
him in other lights that make him valuable to me.
With him, I know not by what connection, you never fail to come into my mind, as if you were infeparable. I have, as you guefs, many philofophical
reveries in the fhades of Sir Walter Raleigh, of which
you are a great part. You generally enter there with
me, and, like a good genius, applaud and ftrengthen
all my fentiments that have honour in them. This
good

good office which you have often done me unknow-
ingly, I muſt acknowledge now, that my own breaſt
may not reproach me with ingratitude, and diſquiet
me when I would muſe again in that ſolemn ſcene.
I have not room now left to aſk you many queſtions I
intended about the Odyſſey. I beg I may know how
far you have carried Ulyſſes on his journey, and how
you have been entertained with him on the way ? I
deſire I may hear of your health, of Mrs Pope's,
and of every thing elſe that belongs to you.

How thrive your garden-plants ? how look the
trees ? how ſpring the brocoli and the fenochio ? hard
names to ſpell ! how did the poppies bloom ? and how
is the great room approved ? what parties have you
had of pleaſure ? what in the grotto ? what upon the
Thames ? I would know how all your hours paſs,
all you ſay, and all you do; of which I ſhould queſtion you yet farther, but my paper is full, and ſpares
you. My brother Ned is wholly yours; ſo my father deſires to be, and every ſoul here whoſe name is
Digby. My ſiſter will be yours in particular. What
can I add more ? ·

                              I am, &c.

L E T T E R XV.

Oꞔ. 10.

I Was upon the point of taking a much greater
journey than to Bermudas, even to that *undiſ-
covered country, from whoſe bourn no traveller returns !*
A fever carried me on the high gallop towards it
for ſix or ſeven days.—But here you have me now,
and that is all I ſhall ſay of it : ſince which time an
impertinent lameneſs kept me at home twice as long;
as if Fate ſhould ſay, (after the other dangerous illnefs), " You ſhall neither go into the other world,
" nor any where you like in this." Elſe who knows
but I had been at Hom-lacy ?
I conſpire in your ſentiments, emulate your plea-
                                                          ſures,

fures, wifh for your company. You are all of one
heart and one foul, as was faid of the primitive Chriftians : it is like the kingdom of the juft upon earth ;
not a wicked wretch to interrupt you, but a fet of
tried, experienced friends, and fellow-comforters,
who have feen evil men and evil days, and have, by
a fuperior rectitude of heart, fet yourfelves above
them, and reap your reward. Why will you ever,
of your own accord, end fuch a millenary year in
London ? tranfmigrate (if I may fo call it) into other
creatures, in that fcene of folly militant, when you
may reign for ever at Hom-lacy in fenfe and reafon
triumphant ? I appeal to a third lady in your family,
whom I take to be the moft innocent, and the leaft
warped by idle fafhion and cuftom of you all ; I appeal to her, if you are not every foul of you better
people, better companions, and happier, where you
are ? I defire her opinion under her hand in your next
letter, I mean Mifs Scudamore's *. I am confident,
if fhe would or durft fpeak her fenfe, and employ
that reafoning which God has given her, to infufe
more thoughtfulnefs into you all ; thofe arguments
could not fail to put you to the blufh, and keep you
out of town, like people fenfible of your own felici-
ties. I am not without hopes, if fhe can detain a
parliament-man and a lady of quality from the world
one winter, that I may come upon you with fuch ir-
refiftible arguments another year, as may carry you
all with me to Bermudas †, the feat of all earthly
happinefs, and the new Jerufalem of the righteous.

Do not talk of the decay of the year, the feafon
is good where the people are fo. It is the beft time
in the year for a painter.; there is more variety of
colours in the leaves, the profpects begin to open,

---

* Afterwards Duchefs of Beaufort, at this time very
young.

† About this time the Rev. Dean Berkley conceived his project of erecting a fettlement in Bermudas for the propagation
of the Chriftian faith, and introduction of fciences into Ame-
rica.

through

through the thinner woods, over the valleys ; and
through the high canopies of trees to the higher arch
of heaven : the dews of the morning impearl every
thorn, and fcatter diamonds on the verdant mantle
of the earth ; the frofts are frefh and wholefome :
what would you have ? the moon fhines too, though
not for lovers thefe cold nights, but for aftrono-
mers.

Have ye not reflecting telefcopes *, whereby ye
may innocently magnify her fpots and blemifhes ?
Content yourfelves with them, and do not come to
a place where your own eyes become reflecting telefcopes, and where thofe of all others are equally
fuch upon their neighbours. Stay you at leaft, (for
what I have faid before relates only to the ladies :
do not imagine I will write about any eyes but theirs),
ftay, I fay, from that idle, bufy-looking fanhedrim,
where wifdom or no wifdom is the eternal debate, not
(as it lately was in Ireland) an accidental one.

If, after all, you will defpife good advice, and
refolve to come to London, here you will find me,
doing juft the things I fhould not, living where I
fhould not, and as worldly, as idle, in a word, as
much an Anti-Bermudanift as any body. Dear
Sir, make the ladies know I am their fervant ; you
know I am

Yours, &c.

LETTER XVI.

Aug. 12.

I Have been above a month ftrolling about in
Buckinghamfhire and Oxfordfhire, from garden
to garden, but ftill returning to Lord Cobham's
with frefh fatisfaction. I fhould be forry to fee my
Lady Scudamore's, till it has had the full advantage
of Lord B * *'s improvements ; and then I will expect fomething like the waters of Rifkins, and the
woods of Oakley together, which (without flattery)

* Thefe inftruments were juft then brought to perfection.

would

would be at leaft as good as any thing in our world: For as to the hanging gardens of Babylon, the paradife of Cyrus, and the Sharawaggi's of China, I have little or no ideas of them, but, I dare fay, Lord B * * has, becaufe they were certainly both very great, and very wild. I hope Mrs Mary Digby is quite tired of his Lordfhip's *extravagante bergerie*; and that fhe is juft now fitting, or rather reclining on a bank, fatigued with over much dancing and finging at his unwearied requeft and inftigation. I know your love of eafe fo well, that you might be in danger of being too quiet to enjoy quiet, and too philofophical to be a philofopher; were it not for the ferment Lord B. will put you into. One of his Lordfhip's maxims is, That a total abftinence from intemperance or bufinefs, is no more philofophy, than a total confopition of the fenfes is repofe; one muft feel enough of its contrary to have a relifh of either. But, after all, let your temper work, and be as fedate and contemplative as you will, I will engage you fhall be fit for any of us, when you come to town in the winter. Folly will laugh you into all the cuftoms of the company here; nothing will be able to prevent your converfion to her, but indifpofition, which I hope will be far from you. I am telling the worft that can come of you: for as to vice, you are fafe; but folly is many an honeft man's, nay every good-humoured man's lot: nay, it is the feafoning of life; and fools (in one fenfe) are the falt of the earth: a little is excellent, though indeed a whole mouthful is juftly called the devil.

So much for your diverfions next winter, and for mine. I envy you much more at prefent, than I fhall then; for if there be on earth an image of paradife, it is fuch perfect union and fociety as you all poffefs. I would have my innocent envies and wifhes of your ftate known to you all; which is far better than making you compliments, for it is inward approbation and efteem. My Lord Digby has in me a

fincere

fincere fervant, or would have, were there any occafion for me to manifeft it.

·L·E·T·T·E·R XVII.

Dec. 28. 1724.

IT is now the feafon to wifh you a good end of
one year, and a happy beginning of another :
but both thefe you know how to make yourfelf, by
only continuing fuch a life as you have been long ac-
cuftomed to lead. As for good works, they are
things I dare not name, either to thofe that do them,
or to thofe that do them not : the firft are too modeft,
and the latter too felfifh, to bear the mention of
what are become either too old-fafhioned, or too
private, to conftitute any part of the vanity or reputation of the prefent age. However, it were to be
wifhed, people would now and then look upon good
works as they do upon old wardrobes, merely in
cafe any of them fhould by chance come into fafhion
again ; as ancient fardingales revive in modern
hooped petticoats, (which may be properly compared to charities, as they cover a multitude of fins.)
    They tell me, that at Colefhill certain antiquated
charities and obfolete devotions are yet fubfifting ;
that a thing called Chriftian cheerfulnefs, (not in-
compatible with Chryftmas-pes and plum-broth),
whereof frequent is the mention in old fermons and
almanacks, is really kept alive and in practice ; that
feeding the hungry, and giving alms to the poor,
do yet make a part of good houfekeeping, in a latitude not more remote from London than fourfcore
miles ; and, laftly, that prayers and roaft-beef ac-
tually make fome people as happy, as a whore and a
bottle. But here in town, I affure you, men, women, and children have done with thefe things.
Charity not only begins, but ends, at home. Inftead
of the four cardinal virtues, now reign four courtly
ones : we have cunning for prudence, rapine for juftice, time-ferving for fortitude, and luxury for tem-
                                                perance.

perance. Whatever you may fancy, where you live
in a ftate of ignorance, and fee nothing but quiet,
religion, and good-humour, the cafe is juft as I tell
you where people underftand the world, and know
how to live with credit and glory.

I wifh that Heaven would open the eyes of men,
and make them fenfible which of thefe is right;
whether, upon a due conviction, we are to quit faction, and gaming, and high-feeding, and all manner of luxury, and to take to your country-way? or
you to leave prayers, and almfgiving, and reading,
and exercife, and come into our meafures? I wifh (I
fay) that this matter were as clear to all men, as it
is to

Your affectionate, &c.

LETTER XVIII.

DEAR SIR, *April* 21. 1726.

I Have a great inclination to write to you, though
I cannot by writing, any more than I could by
words, exprefs what part I bear in your fufferings.
Nature and efteem in you are joined to aggravate your
affliction. The latter I have in a degree equal even
to yours, and a tie of friendfhip approaches near to
the tendernefs of nature : yet, God knows, no man
living is lefs fit to comfort you, as no man is more
deeply fenfible than myfelf of the greatnefs of the
lofs. That very virtue which fecures his prefent
ftate from all the forrows incident to ours, does but
aggrandife our fenfation of its being removed from
our fight, from our affection, and from our imitation.
For the friendfhip and fociety of good men does not
only make us happier, but it makes us better.
Their death does but complete their felicity before
our own, who probably are not yet arrived to that
degree of perfection which merits an immediate reward. That your dear brother and my dear friend
was fo, I take his very removal to be a proof. Providence would certainly lend virtuous men to a world

that fo much wants them, as long as in its juſtice,
to them it could ſpare them to us. May my ſoul be
with thoſe who have meant well, and have acted well
to that meaning! and I doubt not, if this prayer be
granted, I ſhall be with him. Let us preſerve his memory in the way he would beſt like, by recollecting
what his behaviour would have been, in every incident of our lives to come, and doing in each juſt as
we think he would have done; ſo we ſhall have him
always before our eyes, and in our minds, and
(what is more) in our lives and manners. I hope,
when we ſhall meet him next, we ſhall be more of a
piece with him, and conſequently not to be ever-
more ſeparated from him. I will add but one word
that relates to what remains of yourſelf and me,
ſince ſo valued a part of us is gone; it is to beg you
to accept, as yours by inheritance, of the vacancy he
has left in a heart, which (while he could fill it with
ſuch hopes, wiſhes, and affections for him as ſuited
a mortal creature) was truly and warmly his; and
ſhall (I aſſure you in the ſincerity of ſorrow for my
own loſs) be faithfully at your ſervice while I continue to love his memory, that is, while I continue to
be myſelf.

N. B. *Mr Digby died in the year* 1726, *and is buried in the church of Sherburne in Dorſetſhire, with
an epitaph written by the author,* vol. 2. p. 159.

LETTERS to and from Dr ATTER-
BURY *, Bishop of ROCHESTER.

From the year 1716 to 1723.

LETTER I.

The Bishop of ROCHESTER *to Mr* POPE.

Dec. 1716.

I Return your preface †, which I have read twice with pleasure. The modesty and good sense there is in it, must please every one that reads it : and since there is nothing that can offend, I see not why you should balance a moment about printing it—always provided, that there is nothing said there which you may have occasion to unsay hereafter : of which you yourself are the best, and the only judge. This is my sincere opinion, which I give, because you ask it : and which I would not give, though asked, but to a man I value as much as I do you ; being sensible how improper it is, on many accounts, for me to interpose in things of this nature ; which I never understood well, and now understand some-what less than ever. I did. But I can deny you no-thing ; especially since you have had the goodness often, and patiently, to hear what I have said against rhyme, and in behalf of blank verse ; with little discretion perhaps, but, I am sure, without the least prejudice : being myself equally incapable of writing well in either of those ways, and leaning therefore to neither side of the question, but as the appearance of reason inclines me. Forgive me this

* See Mr Pope's epitaph on him, vol. 2. p. 163.
† The general preface to Mr Pope's poems, first printed 1717, the year after the date of this letter.

E 2   errour,

errour, if it be one; an errour. of above thirty years ſtanding, and which therefore I ſhall be very loath to part with. In other matters which relate to polite writing, I ſhail ſeldom differ from you; or, if I do, ſhall, I hope, have the prudence to conceal my opinion. I am as much as I ought to be, that is, as much as any man can be,

Your, &c.

L E T T E R   II.

The Biſhop of R O C H E S T E R *to Mr* P O P E.

Feb. 13, 1717.

I Hoped to find you laſt night at Lord Bathurſt's, and came but a few minutes after you had left him. I brought *Gorboduc* * with me; and Dr Arbuthnot telling me he ſhould ſee you, I depoſited the book in his hands: out of which, I think, my Lord Bathurſt got it before we parted, and from him therefore you are to claim it. If Gorboduc ſhould ſtill miſs his way to you, others are to anſwer for it; I have delivered up my truſt. I am not ſorry your *Alcander* † is burnt. Had I known your intentions, I would have interceded for the firſt page, and put it, with your leave, among my curioſities. In truth, it is the only inſtance of that kind I ever met with, from a perſon good for any thing elſe, nay for every thing elſe to which he is pleaſed to turn himſelf.

Depend upon it, I ſhall ſee you with great pleaſure at Bromley; and there is no requeſt you can make to me, that I ſhall not moſt readily comply with. I wiſh you health and happineſs of all ſorts, and would be glad to be inſtrumental in any degree

---

* A tragedy written in the reign of Edward VI. (and much the beſt performance of that age), by Sackville, afterwards Earl of Dorſet, and Lord Treaſurer to Queen Eliſabeth. It was then very ſcarce, but lately reprinted by R. Dodſley in Pallmall.

† An heroic poem writ at 15 years old.

towards

towards helping you to the leaft fhare of either. I
am always, every where, moft affectionat:ly and
faithfully

Your, &c.

LETTER III.

The Bifhop of ROCHESTER *to* Mr POPE,.

Bromley, Nov. 8. 1717.

I Have nothing to fay to you on that melancholy
fubject, with an account of which the printed
papers have furnifhed me, but what you have already
faid to yourfelf.

When you have paid the debt of tendernefs you
owe to the memory of a father, I doubt not but
you will turn your thoughts towards improving that
accident to your own eafe and happinefs. You have
it now in your power, to purfue that method of
thinking and living which you like beft. Give me
leave, if I am not a little too early in my applications of this kind, to congratulate you upon it;
and to affure you, that there is no man living, who
wifhes you better, or would be more pleafed to contribute any wife to your fatisfaction or fervice.

I return you your Milton, which, upon collation,
I find to be revifed, and augmented, in feveral places,
as the title-page of my third edition pretends it to be.
When I fee you next, I will fhew you the feveral
paffages altered, and added by the author, befide
what you mentioned to me.

I proteft to you, this laft perufal of him has given
me fuch new degrees, I will not fay of pleafure, but
of admiration and aftonifhment, that I look upon the
fublimity of Homer, and the majefty of Virgil, with
fomewhat lefs reverence than I ufed to do. I challenge you, with all your partiality, to fhew me in
the firft of thefe any thing equal to the allegory of
fin and death, either as to the greatnefs and juftnefs
of the invention, or the height and beauty of the

E 3   colouring.

colouring. What I looked upon as a rant of Barrow's, I now begin to think a ferious truth, and could almoft venture to fet my hand to it:

*Hæc quicunque legit, tantum ceciniffe putabit
Mæonidem ranas, Virgilium culices.*

But more of this when we meet. When I left the town, the D. of Buckingham continued fo ill that he received no meffages ; oblige me fo far as to let me know how he does : at the fame time I fhall know how you do, and that will be a double fatisfaction to

Your, &c.

LETTER IV.

The Anfwer.

My LORD,   *Nov.* 20. 1717.

I Am truly obliged by your kind condolence on my father's death, and the defire you exprefs that I fhould improve this incident to my advantage. I know your Lordfhip's friendfhip to me is fo extenfive, that you include in that wifh both my fpiritual and my temporal advantage ; and it is what I owe to that friendfhip, to open my mind unrefervedly to you on this head. It is true, I have loft a parent for whom no gains I could make would be any equivalent. But that was not my only tie : I thank God, another ftill remains (and long may it remain) of the fame tender nature : *Genitrix eft mihi*—and excufe me if I fay with Euryalus,

——*nequeam lacrymas perferre parentis.*

A rigid divine may call it a carnal tie, but fure it is a virtuous one : at leaft I am more certain that it is a duty of nature to preferve a good parent's life and happinefs, than I am of any fpeculative point whatever.

—— *Ignaram*

———— Ignaram hujus quodcunque pericli
————Hanc ego, nunc, linquam ?

For she, my Lord, would think this separation more grievous than any other ; and I, for my part, know as little as poor Euryalus did, of the success of such an adventure, (for an adventure it is, and no small one, in spite of the most positive divinity). Whether the change would be to my spiritual advantage, God only knows. This I know, that I mean as well in the religion I now profess, as I can possibly ever do in another. Can a man who thinks so, justify a change, even if he thought both equally good? To such an one, the part of *joining* with any one body of Christians might perhaps be easy : but I think it would not be so to *renounce* the other.

Your Lordship has formerly advised me to read the best controversies between the churches. Shall I tell you a secret? I did so at fourteen years old, (for I loved reading, and my father had no other books) : there was a collection of all that had been written on both sides in the reign of King James II. I warmed my head with them ; and the consequence was, that I found myself a Papist and a Protestant by turns, according to the last book I read. I am afraid most seekers are in the same case ; and when they stop, they are not so properly converted, as outwitted. You see how little glory you would gain by my conversion. And after all, I verily believe your Lordship and I are both of the same religion, if we were thoroughly understood by one another, and that all honest and reasonable Christians would be so, if they did but talk enough together every day ; and had nothing to do together, but to serve God, and live in peace with their neighbour.

As to the *temporal* side of the question, I can have no dispute with you. It is certain, all the beneficial circumstances of life, and all the shining ones, lie on the part you would invite me to. But if I could bring myself to fancy, what I think you do but

fancy,

fancy, that I have any talents for active life, I want health for it; and besides, it is a real truth, I have less inclination (if possible) than ability. Contemplative life is not only my scene, but it is my habit too. I begun my life where most people end theirs, with a disrelish of all that the world calls ambition. I do not know why it is called so; for to me it always seemed to be rather *stooping* than *climbing*. I will tell you my politic and religious sentiments in a few words. In my politics, I think no further than how to prefer the peace of my life, in any government under which I live; nor in my religion, than to preserve the peace of my conscience in any church with which I communicate. I hope all churches and all governments are so far of God, as they are rightly understood, and rightly administered: and where they are, or may be wrong, I leave it to God alone to mend or reform them; which whenever he does, it must be by greater instruments than I am. I am not a Papist; for I renounce the temporal invasions of the Papal power, and detest their arrogated authority over princes and states. I am a Catholic in the strictest sense of the word. If I was born under an absolute prince, I would be a quiet subject; but I thank God I was not. I have a due sense of the excellence of the British constitution. In a word, the things I have always wished to see, are, not a Roman Catholic, or a French Catholic, or a Spanish Catholic, but a true Catholic; and not a King of Whigs, or a King of Tories, but a King of England. Which God of his mercy grant his present Majesty may be, and all future Majesties. You see, my Lord, I end like a preacher. This is *sermo ad clerum*, not *ad populum*. Believe me, with infinite obligation and sincere thanks, ever

Your, &c.

LET.

LETTER V.

Sept. 23. 1720.

I Hope you have fome time ago received the ful-
phur, and the two volumes of Mr Gay, as inftances how (fmall ones foever) that I wifh you both
health and diverfion. What I now fend for your
perufal, I fhall fay nothing of; not to foreftall by a
fingle word what you promifed to fay upon that fubject. Your Lordfhip may criticife from Virgil to
thefe tales; as Solomon wrote of every thing from
the cedar to the hyffop. I have fome caufe, fince I
laft waited on you at Bromley, to look upon you as
a prophet in that retreat, from whom oracles are to
be had, were mankind wife enough to go thither to
confult you. The fate of the South-fea fcheme has,
much fooner than I expected, verified what you told
me. Moft people thought the time would come,
but no man prepared for it; no man confidered it
would come *like a thief in the night*; exactly as it
happens in the cafe of our death. Methinks God
has punifhed the avaricious, as he often punifhes finners, in their own way, in the very fin itfelf. The
thirft of gain was their crime, that thirft continued
became their punifhment and ruin. As for the few
who have the good fortune to remain with half of
what they imagined they had, (among whom is your
humble fervant), I would have them fenfible of their
felicity, and convinced of the truth of old Hefiod's
maxim, who, after half his eftate was fwallowed by
the *directors* of thofe days, refolved that *half* to be
more than the whole.

Does not the fate of thefe people put you in mind
of two paffages, one in Job, the other from the
Pfalmift?

Men fhall groan out of the CITY, *and hifs them out
of their* PLACE.

*They have dreamed out their dream, and awaking
have found nothing in their hands.*

Indeed

Indeed the univerfal poverty, which is the confe-- quence of univerfal avarice, and which will fall hardeft upon the guiltlefs and induftrious part of mankind, is truly lamentable. The univerfal de- luge of the S. fea, contrary to the old deluge, has drowned all except a few *unrighteous* men. But it is fome comfort to me that I am not one of them, even though I were to furvive, and rule the world by it. I am much pleafed with a thought of Dr· Arbuthnot's. He fays, the government and South- fea company have only locked up the money of the· people, upon conviction of their lunacy, (as is ufual in the cafe of lunatics), and intend to reftore them as much as may be fit for fuch people, as faft as they fhall fee them return to their fenfes.

The latter part of your letter does me fo much ho- nour, and fhews me fo much kindnefs, that I muft both be proud and pleafed, in a great degree: but I affure you, my Lord, much more the laft than the firft. For I certainly know, and feel, from my own heart which truly refpects you, that there may be a ground for your partiality, one way; but I find not the leaft fymptoms in my head, of any foundation for the other. In a word, the beft reafon I know for my being pleafed, is, that you continue your favour toward me; the beft I know for being proud, would be that you might cure me of it; for I have found you to be fuch a phyfician as does not only *repair*, but *improve*. I am, with the fincereft efteem, and moft grateful acknowledgment,

Your, &c.

LETTER VI.

From the Bifhop of ROCHESTER.

THE Arabian tales, and Mr Gay's books, I re- ceived not till Monday night, together with your letter; for which I thank you. I have had a fit of the gout upon me ever fince I returned hither from

from Weftminfter on Saturday night laft. It has
found its way into my hands as well as legs, fo that
I have been utterly incapable of writing. This is
the firft letter that I have ventured upon ; which will
be written, I fear, *vacillantibus literis*, as, Tully fays,
Tyro's letters were, after his recovery from an illnefs.
What I faid to you in mine about the monument, was
intended only to quicken, not to alarm you. It is
not worth your while to know what I meant by it:
but when I fee you, you fhall. I hope you may be
at the deanery towards the end of October ; by which
time I think of fettling there for the winter. What
do you think of fome fuch fhort infcription as this in
Latin, which may, in a few words, fay all that is to
be faid of Dryden, and yet nothing more than he deferves ?

IOHANNI DRYDENO.

CVI POESIS ANGLICANA
VIM SVAM AC VENERES DEBET ;
ET SIQVA IN POSTERVM AVGEBITVR LAVDE,
EST ADHVC DEBITVRA :
HONORIS ERGO P. &c.

To fhew you that I am as much in earneft in the
affair as you yourfelf, fomething I will fend you too
of this kind in Englifh. If your defign holds of
fixing Dryden's name only below, and his bufto a-
bove—may not lines like thefe be graved juft under
the name ?

This SHEFFIELD *rais'd, to* DRYDEN's *afhes juft ;*
Here fix'd his name, and there his laurel'd buft.
What elfe the Mufe in marble might exprefs,
Is known already ; praife would make him lefs.

Or thus——

More needs not ; where acknowledg'd merits reign,
Praife is impertinent, and cenfure vain.

This

This you will take as a proof of my zeal at leaft, though it be none of my talent in poetry. When you have read it over, I will forgive you if you fhould not once in your lifetime again think of it.

And now, Sir, for your *Arabian Tales :* Ill as I have been, almoft ever fince they came to hand, I have read as much of them, as ever I fhall read while I live. Indeed they do not pleafe my tafte : they are writ with fo romantic an air, and, allowing for the difference of eaftern manners, are yet, upon any fuppofition that can be made, of fo wild and abfurd a contrivance, (at leaft to my northern understanding), that I have not only no pleafure, but no patience, in perufing them. They are to me like the odd paintings on Indian fcreens, which at firft glance may furprife and pleafe a little; but when you fix your eye intently upon them, they appear fo extravagant, difproportioned, and monftrous, that they give a judicious eye pain, and make him feek for relief from fome other object.

They may furnifh the mind with fome new images : but I think the purchafe is made at too great an expenfe : for to read thofe two volumes through, liking them as little as I do, would be a terrible penance ; and to read them with pleafure, would be dangerous on the other fide, becaufe of the infection. I will never believe, that you have any keen relifh of them, till I find you write worfe than you do, which I dare fay I never fhall. Who that *Petit de la Croife* is, the pretended author of them, I cannot tell : but obferving how full they are in the defcriptions of drefs, furniture, &c. I cannot help thinking them the product of fome woman's imagination : and, believe me, I would do any thing but break with you, rather than be bound to read them over with attention.

I am forry that I was fo true a prophet in refpect of the S. fea ; forry, I mean, as far as your lofs is concerned : for in the general I ever was, and ftill am of opinion, that had that project taken root and flourifhed,

flourifhed, it would by degrees have overturned our conftitution. Three or four hundred millions was fuch a weight, that whichfoever way it had leaned, muft have borne down all before it. — But of the dead we muft fpeak gently; and therefore, as Mr Dryden fays fomewhere, *Peace be to its manes!*

Let me add one reflection, to make you eafy in your ill luck. Had you got all that you have loft beyond what you ventured, confider that your fuperfluous gains would have fprung from the ruin of feveral families that now want neceffaries! a thought, under which a good and good-natured man that grew rich by fuch means, could not, I perfuade myfelf, be perfectly eafy. Adieu, and believe me, ever

Your, &c.

LETTER VII.

From the Bifhop of ROCHESTER.

March 26. 1721.

YOU are not yourfelf gladder you are well than I am; efpecially fince I can pleafe myfelf with the thought, that when you had loft your health elfewhere, you recovered it here. May thefe lodgings never treat you worfe, nor you at any time have lefs reafon to be fond of them !

I thank you for the fight of your verfes * ; and with the freedom of an honeft, though perhaps injudicious friend, muft tell you, that though I could like fome of them, if they were any body's elfe but yours, yet as they are yours, and to be owned as fuch, I can fcarce like any of them. Not but that the four firft lines are good, efpecially the fecond couplet; and might, if followed by four others as good, give reputation to a writer of a lefs eftablifhed fame : but from you I expect fomething of a more perfect kind, and which the oftener it is read, the

* Epitaph on Mr Harcourt, vol. 2, p. 156.

more it will be admired. When you barely exceed
other writers, you fall much beneath yourfelf: it is
your misfortune now to write without a rival, and
to be tempted by that means to be more carelefs,
than you would otherwife be in your compofures.

Thus much I could not forbear faying, though I
have a motion of confequence in the houfe of Lords
to-day, and muft prepare for it. I am even with you
for your ill paper; for I write upon worfe, having
no other at hand. I wifh you the continuance of
your health moft heartily; and am ever

Yours, &c.

I have fent Dr Arbuthnot the Latin MS. which I
could not find when you left me; and I am fo angry
at the writer for his defign, and his manner of exe-
cuting it, that I could hardly forbear fending him
a line of Virgil along with it. The chief reafoner
of that philofophic farce is a *Gallo-Ligur*, as he is
called — what that means in Englifh or French, I
cannot fay — but all he fays, is in fo loofe, and flip-
pery, and trickifh a way of reafoning, that I could
not forbear applying the paffage of Virgil to him,

Vane Ligur, fruftraque animis elate fuperbis!
Nequicquam patrias tentafti lubricus artes —

To be ferious, I hate to fee a book gravely written,
and in all the forms of argumentation, which proves
nothing, and which fays nothing; and endeavours
only to put us into a way of diftrufting our own faculties, and doubting whether the marks of truth and
falfehood can in any cafe be diftinguifhed from each
other. Could that bleffed point be made out, (as
it is a contradiction in terms to fay it can), we fhould
then be in the moft uncomfortable and wretched ftate
in the world; and I would in that cafe be glad to exchange my reafon, with a dog for his inftinct, to-
morrow.

L E T-

LETTER VIII.

Lord Chancellor HARCOURT *to Mr* POPE.

Dec. 6. 1722.

I Cannot but fufpect myfelf of being very unreafon-
able in begging you once more to review the inclofed. Your friendfhip draws this trouble on you.
I may freely own to you, that my tendernefs makes
me exceeding hard to be fatisfied with any thing
which can be faid on fuch an unhappy fubject. I
caufed the Latin epitaph to be as often altered before
I could approve it.

When once your epitaph is fet up, there can be no
alteration of it; it will remain a perpetual monument
of your friendfhip, and, I affure myfelf, you will fo
fettle it, that it fhall be worthy of you. I doubt
whether the word, *denied*, in the third line, will
juftly admit of that conftruction which it ought to
bear, *(viz.)* renounced, deferted, &c. *Denied* is capable, in my opinion, of having an ill fenfe put upon it, as too great uneafinefs, or more good-nature,
than a wife man ought to have. I very well remember you told me, you could fcarce mend thofe two
lines, and therefore I can fcarce expect your forgivenefs for my defiring you to reconfider them.

HARCOURT *ftands dumb, and* POPE *is forc'd to fpeak.*

I cannot perfectly, at leaft without further difcourfing
you, reconcile myfelf to the firft part of that line;
and the word *forced* (which was my own, and, I perfuade myfelf, for that reafon only fubmitted to by
you) feems to carry too doubtful a conftruction for an
epitaph, which, as I apprehend, ought as eafily to
be underftood as read. I fhall acknowledge it as a
very particular favour, if at your beft leifure you will
perufe the inclofed, and vary it, if you think it capable of being amended; and let me fee you any
morning next week.

I am, &c.

LET.

LETTER IX.

The Bishop of ROCHESTER *to Mr* POPE.

Sept. 21. 1721.

I AM now confined to my bedchamber, and to the matted room, wherein I am writing, feldom venturing to be carried down even into the parlour to dinner, unlefs when company to whom I cannot excufe myfelf, comes, which I am not ill pleafed to find is now very feldom.˙ This is my cafe in the funny part of the year : what muft I expect, when

inverfum contriftat Aquarius annum ?

If thefe things be done in the green tree, what fhall be done in the dry ? Excufe me for employing a fentence of fcripture on this occafion ; I apply it very feriouf-ly. One thing relieves me a little under the ill pro-fpect I have of fpending my time at the deanery this winter ; that I fhall have the opportunity of feeing you oftener ; though, I am afraid, you will have little pleafure in feeing me there. So much for my ill ftate of health ; which I had not touched on, had not your friendly letter been fo full of it. One civil thing that you fay in it, made me think you had been reading Mr Waller ; and poffeffed of that image at the end of his copy, *à la malade*, had you not be-ftowed it on one who has no right to the leaft part of the character. If you have not read the verfes lately, I am fure you remember them becaufe you forget nothing.

With fuch a grace you entertain,
And look with fuch contempt on pain, &c.

I mention them not on the account of that couplet, but one that follows ; which ends with the very fame rhymes and words *(appear and clear)* that the cou-plet but one after that does ; — and therefore in my

Waller

Waller there is a various reading of the firſt of theſe couplets ; for there it runs thus,

So lightnings in a ſtormy air
Scorch more, than when the ſky is fair.

You will ſay that I am not very much in pain, nor very buſy, when I can reliſh theſe amuſements; and you will ſay true : for at preſent I am in both theſe reſpects very eaſy.

I had not ſtrength enough to attend Mr Prior to his grave; elſe I would have done it, to have ſhewed his friends that I had forgot and forgiven what he wrote on me. He is buried, as he deſired, at the feet of Spenſer, and I will take care to make good in every reſpect what I ſaid to him when living ; particularly as to the triplet he wrote for his own epitaph ; which, while we were in good terms, I promiſed him ſhould never appear on his tomb, while I was Dean of Weſtminſter.

I am pleaſed to find you have ſo much pleaſure, and (which is the foundation of it) ſo much health at Lord Bathurſt's. May both continue till I ſee you! may my Lord have as much ſatisfaction in building the houſe in the wood, and uſing it when built, as you have in deſigning it! I cannot ſend a wiſh after him that means him more happineſs, and yet I am ſure I wiſh him as much as he wiſhes himſelf.

I am, &c.

LETTER X.

From the ſame.

Bromley, Oct. 15. 1721.

NOtwithſtanding I write this on Sunday even, to acknowledge the receipt of yours this morning ; yet I foreſee it will not reach you till Wedneſday morning. And before ſet of ſun that day I hope to reach my winter-quarters at the deanery. I hope,

F 3. did

did I fay ? I recall that word, for it implies defire ;
and, God knows, that is far from being the cafe.
For I never part with this place but with regret,
though I generally keep here what Mr Cowley calls
the worft of company in the world, my own ; and
fee either none befide, or what is worfe than none,
fcme of the *Arrii* or *Sebofi* of my neighbourhood :
charaƈers, which Tully paints fo well in one of his
epiftles, and complains of the too civil, but impertinent interruption they gave him in his retirement.
Since I have named thofe gentlemen, and the book
is not far from me, I will turn to the place, and by
pointing it out to you, give you the pleafure of perufing the epiftle ; which is a very agreeable one, if
my memory does not fail me.

I am furprifed to find that my Lord Bathurft and
you are parted fo foon.   He has been fick, I know,
of fome late tranfaƈtions; but fhould that ficknefs
continue ftill in fome meafure, I prophefy it will be
quite off by the beginning of November.   A letter or
two from his London friends, and a furfeit of folitude,
will foon make him change his refolution and his
quarters.   I vow to you, I could live here with pleafure all the winter, and be contented with hearing no
more news than the London Journal, or fome fuch
trifling paper, affords me, did not the duty of my
place require, abfolutely require my attendance at
Weftminfter; where, I hope, the prophet will now
and then remember he has a bed and a candleftick.
In fhort, I long to fee you, and hope you will come,
if not a day, at leaft an hour fooner to town than you
intended, in order to afford me that fatisfaƈtion.   I
am now, I thank God ! as well as ever I was in my
life, except that I can walk fcarce at all without
crutches : and I would willingly compound the matter with the gout, to be no better, could I hope to be
no worfe. But that is a vain thought; I expeƈt a new
attack long before Chriftmas.   Let me fee you therefore while I am in a condition to relifh you, before
the

the days (and the nights) come, when I fhall (and muſt) fay, I have no pleafure in them.

I will bring your fmall volume of paſtorals along with me, that you may not be difcouraged from lending me books, when you find me fo punctual in returning them. Shakefpear fhall bear it company, and be put into your hands as clear and as fair as it came out of them, though you, I think, have been dabbling here and there with the text. I have had more reverence for the writer and the printer, and left every thing ſtanding juſt as I found it. However, I thank you for the pleafure you have given me in putting me upon reading him once more before I die.

I believe I fhall fcarce repeat that pleafure any more, having other work to do, and other things to think of; but none that will interfere with the offices of friendfhip, in the exchange of which with you, Sir, I hope to live and die

Your, &c.

P. S. Addifon's works came to my hands yeſter-day. I cannot but think it a very odd fet of incidents, that the book fhould be dedicated by a * dead man to † a dead man ; and even that the new ‡ patron to whom Tickel chofe to infcribe his verfes, fhould be dead alfo before they were publifhed. Had I been in the editor's place, I fhould have been a little apprehenſive for myfelf, under a thought that every one who had any hand in that work was to die before the publication of it. You fee, when I am converfing with you, I know not how to give over, till the very bottom of the paper admenifhes me once more to bid you adieu!

* Mr Addifon.   † Mr Craggs.   ‡ Lord Warwick.

L E T-

L E T T E R XI.

My LORD,   *Feb.* 8. 1721-2.

IT is fo long fince I had the pleafure of an hour
with your Lordfhip, that I fhould begin to think
myfelf no longer *amicus omnium horarum,* but for finding myfelf fo in my conftant thoughts of you. In
thofe I was with you many hours this very day, and
had you (where I wifh and hope cne day to fee you
really) in my garden at Twit'nam. When I went
laft to town, and was on wing for the deanery, I
heard your Lordfhip was gone the day before to
Bromley, and there you continued till after my return hither. I fincerely wifh you whatever you wifh
yourfelf, and all you wifh your friends or family. All
I mean by this word or two, is juft to tell you fo,
till in perfon I find you as I defire, that is, find you
well. Eafy, refigned, and happy you will make
yourfelf, and (I believe) every body that converfes
with you ; if I may judge of your power over other
mens minds and affections, by that which ycu will e-
ver have over thofe of   Your, &c.

L E T T E R XII.

From the Bifhop of ROCHESTER.

Feb. 26. 1721.

PErmit me, dear Sir, to break into your retirement, and to defire of you a complete copy of
thofe verfes on Mr Addifon * ; fend me alfo your laft
refolution, which fhall punctually be obferved in relation to my giving out any copy of it ; for I am a-
gain folicited by another Lord, to whom I have given the fame anfwer as formerly. No fmall piece of
your writing has been ever fought after fo much : it

* An imperfect copy was got out, very much to the author's
furprife, who never would give any.

                                    has

has pleafed every man without exception, to whom it
has been read. Since you now therefore know
where your real ftrength lies, I hope you will not
fuffer that talent to lie unemployed. For my part, I
fhould be fo glad to fee you finifh fomething of that
kind, that I could be content to be a little fneered at in
a line or fo, for the fake of the pleafure I fhould have
in reading the reft. I have talked my fenfe of this
matter to you once or twice ; and now I put it under
my hand, that you may fee it is my deliberate opinion. What weight that may have with you, I cannot fay : but it pleafes me to have an opportunity of
fhewing you how well I wifh you, and how true a
friend I am to your fame; which I defire may grow
every day, and in every kind of writing, to which
you fhall pleafe to turn your pen. Not but that I
have fome little intereft in the propofal, as I fhall be
known to have been acquainted with a man that was
capable of excelling in fuch different manners, and
did fuch honour to his country and language ; and
yet was not difpleafed fometimes to read what was
written by his humble fervant.

LETTER XIII.

March 14. 1721-2.

I Was difappointed (much more than thofe who
commonly ufe that phrafe on fuch occafions) in
miffing you at the deanery, where I lay folitary two
nights. Indeed I truly partake in any degree of
concern that affects you ; and I wifh every thing may
fucceed as you defire in your own family, and in that
which, I think, you no lefs account your own, and
is no lefs your family, the whole world : for I take
you to be one of the true friends of it, and to your
power its protector. Though the noife and daily
buftle for the public be now over, I dare fay, a
good man is ftill tendering its welfare ; as the fun in
the winter when feeming to retire from the world,
is preparing benedictions and warmth for a better
feafon.

feafon. No man wifhes your Lordfhip more quiet; more tranquillity, than I, who know you fhould underftand the value of it : but I do not wifh you a jot lefs concerned or lefs active than you are in all fincere, and therefore warm defires of public good.

I beg the kindnefs (and it is for that chiefly I trouble you with this letter) to favour me with notice as foon as you return to London, that I may come and make you a proper vifit of a day or two : for hitherto I have not been your vifitor, but your lodger, and I accufe myfelf of it. I have now no earthly thing to oblige my being in town, (a point of no fmall fatisfaction to me), but the beft reafon, the feeing a friend. As long, my Lord, as you will let me call you fo, (and I dare fay you will, till I forfeit what, I think, I never fhall, my veracity and integrity), I fhall efteem myfelf fortunate, in fpite of the Southfea, poetry, Popery, and poverty.

I cannot tell you how forry I am, you fhould be troubled anew by any fort of people. I heartily wifh, *Quod fupereft, ut tibi vivas*; — that you may teach me how to do the fame ; who, without any real impediment to acting and living rightly, do act and live as foolifhly as if I were a great man.

I am, &c.

LETTER XIV.

From the Bifhop of ROCHESTER.

March 16. 1721-2.

AS a vifitant, a lodger, a friend, (or under what other denomination foever), you are always welcome to me ; and will be more fo, I hope, every day that we live : for, to tell you the truth, I like you as I like myfelf, beft when we have both of us leaft bufinefs. It has been my fate to be engaged in it much and often, by the ftations in which I was placed ; but God, that knows my heart, knows I never loved it ; and am ftill lefs in love with it than ever,

ever, as I find lefs temptation to act with any hope
of fuccefs. If I am good for any thing, it is *in an-
gulo cum libello* ; and yet a good part of my time has
been fpent, and perhaps muft be fpent, far otherwife. For I will never, while I have health, be
wanting to my duty in my poft, or in any refpect,
how little foever I may like my employment, and
how hopelefs foever I may be in the difcharge of it.

In the mean time, the judicious world is pleafed
to think that I delight in work which I am obliged
to undergo, and aim at things which I from my
heart defpife : let them think as they will, fo I
might be at liberty to act as I will, and fpend my
time in fuch a manner as is moft agreeable to me.
I cannot fay I do fo now ; for I am here without any
books, and if I had them, could not ufe them to my
fatisfaction, while my mind is taken up in a more
melancholy manner* : and how long or how little a
while it may be fo taken up, God only knows ;
and to his will I implicitly refign myfelf in every
thing.

I am, &c.

LETTER XV.

My LORD,   *March* 19. 1721-2.

I AM extremely fenfible of the repeated favour of
your kind letters, and your thoughts of me in
abfence, even among thoughts of much nearer concern to yourfelf on the one hand, and of much more
importance to the world on the other, which cannot
but engage you at this juncture. I am very certain
of your good-will, and of the warmth which is in
you infeparable from it.

Your remembrance of Twitenham is a frefh inftance of that partiality. I hope the advance of the
fine feafon will fet you upon your legs, enough
to enable you to get into my garden, where I will
carry you up a mount, in a point of view to fhew

* In his lady's laft ficknefs.

you

you the glory of my little kingdom. If you approve
it, I shall be in danger to boast, like Nebuchadnez-
zar, of the things I have made, and to be turned to
converse, not with the beasts of the field, but with
the birds of the grove, which I shall take to be no
great punishment. For indeed I heartily despise the
ways of the world, and most of the great ones of it.

Oh keep me innocent, make others great !

And you may judge how comfortably I am strength-
ened in this opinion, when such as your Lordship
bear testimony to its vanity and emptiness. *Tinnit,
inane est*, with the picture of one ringing on the
globe with his finger, is the best thing I have the
luck to remember in that great poet Quarles, (not
that I forget the devil at bowls ; which I know to
be your Lordship's favourite cut, as well as favourite
diversion.)

The situation here is pleasant, and the view rural
enough, to humour the most retired, and agree with
the most contemplative. Good air, solitary groves,
and sparing diet, sufficient to make you fancy yourself (what you are in temperance, though elevated
into a greater figure by your station) one of the fathers of the desert. Here you may think, (to use
an author's words, whom you so justly prefer to all
his followers, that you will receive them kindly,
though taken from his worst work *),

That in Eliah's banquet you partake,
Or sit a guest with Daniel, at his pulse.

I am sincerely free with you, as you desire I
should, and approve of your not having your coach
here ; for if you would see Lord C * * or any body
else, I have another chariot, besides that little one
you laughed at when you compared me to Homer in
a nut-shell ; but if you would be entirely private,
nobody shall know any thing of the matter. Be-

* The *Paradise regain'd*. Supposed to be in compliment to
the Bishop, it could never be his own opinion.

lieve

lieve me, (my Lord), no man is with more perfect acquiefcence, nay with more willing acquiefcence, (not
even any of your own fons of the church),

Your obedient, &c.

LETTER XVI.

From the Bifhop of ROCHESTER.

April 6. 1722.

UNder all the leifure in the world, I have no
leifure, no ftomach to write to you. The
gradual approaches of death are before my eyes. I
am convinced that it muft be fo; and yet make a
fhift to flatter myfelf fometimes with the thought,
that it may poffibly be otherwife. And that very
thought, though it is directly contrary to my reafon,
does for a few moments make me eafy — however
not eafy enough in good earneft to think of any
thing, but the melancholy object that employs them.
Therefore wonder not that I do not anfwer your kind
letter. I fhall anfwer it too foon, I fear, by accepting your friendly invitation. When I do fo, no conveniencies will be wanting : for I will fee no body
but you and your mother, and the fervants. Vifits
to ftatefmen always were to me (and are now more
than ever) infipid things. Let the men that expect,
that wifh to thrive by them, pay them that homage;
I am free. When I want them, they fhall hear of
me at their doors ; when they want me, I fhall be
fure to hear of them at mine. But probably they
will defpife me fo much, and I fhall court them fo
little, that we fhall both of us keep our diftance.

When I come to you, it is in order to be with you
only. A prefident of the council, or a ftar and
garter, will make no more impreffion upon my mind,
at fuch a time, than the hearing of a bag-pipe, or
the fight of a puppet-fhew. I have faid to Greatnefs fome time ago, — *Tuas tibi res habeto, egomet
curabo meas.* The time is not far off when we

ſhall all be upon the level : and I am refolved, for my part, to anticipate that time, and be upon the level with them now ; for he is fo, that neither feeks nor wants them. Let them have more virtue, and lefs pride; and then I will court them as much as any body : but till they refolve to diſtinguiſh them- felves fome way elfe than by their outward trappings, I am determined (and I think I have a right) to be as proud as they are: though I truſt in God, my pride is neither of fo odious a nature as theirs, nor of fo mifchievous a confequence.

I know not how I have fallen into this train of thinking ; — when I fat down to write, I intended on- ly to excufe myfelf for not writing, and to tell you that the time drew nearer and nearer, when I muſt diſlodge ; I am preparing for it : for I am at this moment building a vault in the Abbey, for me and mine. It was to be in the Abbey, becaufe of my relation to the place ; but it is at the weſt door of it ; as far from Kings and Cæfars as the fpace will admit of.

I know not but I may ſtep to town to-morrow, to fee how the work goes forward ; but if I do, I ſhall return hither in the evening. I would not have given you the trouble of this letter, but that they tell me it will coſt you nothing, and that our privilege of franking (one of the moſt valuable we have left) is again allowed us.

Your, &c.

LETTER XVII.

From the Biſhop of ROCHESTER.

Bromley, May 25. 1722.

I Had much ado to get hither laſt night, the water being fo rough, that the ferrymen were unwill- ing to venture. The firſt thing I faw this morning after my eyes were open, was your letter, for the freedom and kindnefs of which I thank you. Let all
compliments

compliments be laid afide between us for the future; and depend upon me as your faithful friend in all things within my power, as one that truly values you, and wifhes you all manner of happinefs. I thank you and Mrs Pope for my kind reception, which has left a pleafing impreffion upon me that will not foon be effaced.

Lord * * has preffed me terribly to fee him at * *, and told me in a manner betwixt kindnefs and refentment, that it is but a few miles beyond Twitenham.

I have but a little time left, and a great deal to do in it; and muft expeét that ill health will render a good fhare of it ufelefs; and therefore what is likely to be left at the foot of the account, ought by me to be cherifhed, and not thrown away in compliments. You know the motto of my fun-dial, *Vivite, ait, fugio*. I will, as far, as I am able, follow its advice, and cut off all unneceflary avocations and amufements. There are thofe that intend to employ me this winter in a way I do not like. If they perfift in their intentions, I muft apply myfelf to the work they cut out for me, as well as I can. But withal, that fhall not hinder me from employing myfelf alfo in a way which they do not like. The givers of trouble one day fhall have their fhare of it another; that at laft they may be induced to let me be quiet, and live to myfelf, with the few (the very few) friends I like: for that is the point, the fingle point, I now aim at; though I know, the generality of the world who are unacquainted with my intentions and views, think the very reverfe of this charaéter belongs to me. I do not know how I have rambled into this account of myfelf; when I fat down to write, I had no thought of making that any part of my letter.

You might have been fure without my telling you, that my right hand is at eafe; elfe I fhould not have overflowed at this rate. And yet I have not done; for there is a kind intimation in the end of yours, which I underftood, becaufe it feems to tend towards

G 2

employing

employing me in fomething that is agreeable to you, Pray explain yourfelf; and believe, that you have not an acquaintance in the world that would be more in earneft on fuch an occafion than I; for I love you, as well as efteem you.

All the while I have been writing, pain, and a fine thrufh have been feverally endeavouring to call off my attention ; but both in vain: nor fhould I yet part with you, but that the turning over a new leaf, frights me a little, and makes me refolve to break through a new temptation, before it has taken too faft hold on me.

I am, &c.

L E T T E R   XVIII.

From the fame.

June 15. 1722.

YOU have generally written firft, after our part- ing; I will now be beforehand with you in my inquiries how you got home, and how you do, and whether you met with Lord **; and delivered my civil reproach to him in the manner I defired ? I fuppofe you did not, becaufe I have heard nothing either from you, or from him on that head ; as, I fuppofe, I might have done, if you had found him.

I am fick of thefe men of quality ; and the more fo, the oftener I have any bufinefs to tranfact with them. They look upon it as one of their diftin- guifhing privileges, not to be punctual in any bufi- nefs, of how great importance foever ; nor to fet other people at eafe with the lofs of the leaft part of their own. This conduct of his vexes me ; but to what purpofe ? or how can I alter it ?

I long to fee the original MS. of Milton : but do not know how to come at it without your repeat- ed affiftance.

I hope you will not utterly forget what paffed in the coach about Samfon Agoniftes. I fhall not prefs you as to time ; but fome time or other, I wifh you
would

would review and polifh that piece. If upon a new perufal of it (which I defire you to make) you think as I do, that it is written in the very fpirit of the ancients ; it deferves your care, and is capable of being improved, with little trouble, into a perfect model and ftandard of tragic poetry—always allowing for its being a ftory taken out of the Bible ; which is an objection that at this time of day, I know, is not to be got over.

I am, &c.

L E T T E R XIX.

July 27.

I Have been .as conftantly at Twitenham as your Lordfhip has at Bromley, ever fince you faw Lord Bathurft. At the time of the Duke of Marlborough's funeral, I intend to lie at the deanery, and moralife one evening with you on the vanity of human glory. —

The Duchefs's * letter concerns me nearly, and you know it, who know all my thoughts without difguife. I muft keep clear of flattery ; I will : and as this is an honeft refolution, I dare hope, your Lordfhip will not be fo unconcerned for my keeping it, as not to affift me in fo doing. I beg therefore you would reprefent thus much at leaft to her Grace, that as to the fear fhe feems touched with, [That the Duke's memory fhould have no advantage but what he muft give himfelf, without being beholden to any one friend], your Lordfhip may certainly, and agreeably to your character, both of rigid honour and Chriftian plainnefs, tell her, that no man can have any other advantage ; and that all offerings of friends in fuch a cafe pafs for nothing. Be but fo good as to confirm what I have reprefented to her, that an infcription in the ancient way, plain, pompous, yet modeft, will be the moft uncommon, and therefore the moft diftinguifhing manner of doing it.

* The Duchefs of Buckingham.

G 3 And

And fo I hope fhe will be fatisfied, the Duke's honour be preferved, and my integrity alfo : which is
too facred a thing to be forfeited, in confideration of
any little (or what people of quality may call great)
honour or diflinction whatever, which thofe of their
rank can beftow on one of mine; and which indeed they are apt to over-rate, but never fo much, as
when they imagine us under any obligation to fay
one untrue word in their favour.

I can only thank you, my Lord, for the kind
tranfition you make from common bufinefs, to that
which is the only real bufinefs of every reafonable
creature. Indeed I think more of it than you ima--
gine, though not fo much as I ought. I am pleafed
with thofe Latin verfes extremely, which are fo very
good that I thought them yours, till you called them
an Horatian cento, and then I recollected the *dif-
jecta membra poetæ*. I will not pretend I am fo totally in thofe fentiments which you compliment me
with, as I yet hope to be. You tell me I have them,
as the civilleft method to put me in mind how much
it fits me to have them. I ought, firft, to prepare
my mind by a better knowledge even of good profane writers, efpecially the moralifts, &c. before I
can be worthy of tafting that fupreme of books,
and fublime of all writings. In which, as in all
the intermediate ones, you may (if your friendfhip
and charity toward me continue fo far) be the beft
guide to

Your, &c.

L E T T E R   XX.

From the Bifhop of R O C H E S T E R.

July 30. 1722.

I Have written to the Duchefs * juft as you defired, and referred her to our meeting in town
for a further account of it. I have done it the ra.

* Duchefs of Buckingham,

ther,

ther, becaufe your opinion in the cafe is fincerely
mine : and if it had not been fo, you yourfelf
fhould not have induced me to give it. Whether,
and how far fhe will acquiefce in it, I cannot fay ;
efpecially in a cafe where fhe thinks the Duke's honour concerned : but fhould fhe feem to perfift a little at prefent, her good fenfe (which I depend upon)
will afterwards fatisfy her that we are in the right.

I go to-morrow to the deanery, and I believe I fhall
ftay there, till I have faid duft to duft, and fhut up
that laft fcene of pompous vanity *.

It is a great while for me to ftay there at this
time of year, and I know I fhall often fay to myfelf,
while I am expecting the funeral,

O Rus, quando ego te afpiciam ! quandoque licebit
Ducere folicitæ jucunda oblivia vitæ !

In that cafe I fhall fancy I hear the ghoft of the
dead, thus entreating me,

At tu facratæ ne parce malignus arenæ
    Offibus et capiti inhumato
Particulam dare—

Quanquam feftinas, non eft mora longa ; licebit,
    Injecto ter pulvere, curras.

There is an anfwer for me fomewhere in Hamlet to
this requeft, which you remember, though I do not.
Poor Ghoft ! thou fhalt be fatisfied !— or fomething
like it. However that be, take care you do not fail
in your appointment, that the company of the living
may make me fome amends for my attendance on
the dead.

I know you will be glad to hear that I am well :
I fhould always, could I always be here —

————————————*Sed me*
Imperiofa trahit Proferpina : vive, valeque.

* This was the funeral of the Duke of Marlborough, at which
the Bifhop officiated as Dean of Wefminfter, in Auguft 1722.

You are the firſt man I ſent to this morning, and the
laſt man I deſire to converſe with this evening,
though at twenty miles diſtance from you.

Te, veniente die, te, decedente, requiro.

L E T T E R   XXI.

From the Biſhop of R o c h e s t e r.

Dear Sir,   *The Tower, April* 10. 1723.

I Thank you for all the inſtances of your friendſhip, both before and ſince my misfortunes. A
little time will complete them, and ſeparate you and
me for ever. But in what part of the world ſoever I
am, I will live mindful of your ſincere kindneſs to
me ; and will pleaſe myſelf with the thought, that
I ſtill live in your eſteem and affeation, as much as
ever I did ; and that no accidents of life, no diſtance
of time or place will alter you in that reſpect. It
never can me ; who have loved and valued you, ever
ſince I knew you, and ſhall not fail to do it when I
am not allowed to tell you ſo ; as the caſe will ſoon
be. Give my faithful ſervices to Dr Arbuthnot, and
thanks for what he ſent me ; which was much to the
purpoſe, if any thing can be ſaid to be to the purpoſe, in a caſe that is already determined. Let him
know my defence will be ſuch, that neither my
friends need bluſh for me, nor will my enemies have
great occaſion of triumph, though ſure of the victory. I ſhall want his advice before I go abroad, in
many things. But I queſtion whether I ſhall be permitted to ſee him, or any body, but ſuch as are abſolutely neceſſary towards the diſpatch of my private
affairs. If ſo, God bleſs you both ! and may no part
of the ill fortune that attends me, ever purſue either
of you ! I know not but I may call upon you at my
hearing, to ſay ſomewhat about my way of ſpending
my time at the deanery, which did not ſeem calcula-
ted towards managing plots and conſpiracies. But
of

of that I fhall confider——You and I have fpent many
hours together upon much pleafanter fubjects; and,
that I may preferve the old cuftom, I fhall not part
with you now till I have clofed this letter, with three
lines of Milton, which you will, I know, readily,
and not without fome degree of concern, apply to
your ever affectionate, &c.

> *Some nat'ral tears he dropt, but wip'd them foon :*
> *The world was all before him, where to chufe*
> *His place of reft,* and Providence *his guide.*

LETTER XXII.

The Anfwer.

April. 20. 1723.

IT is not poffible to exprefs what I think, and what
I feel ; only this, that I have thought and felt for
nothing but you, for fome time paft ; and fhall think
of nothing fo long for the time to come. The greateft comfort I had, was an intention (which I would
have made practicable) to have attended you in your
journey ; to which I had brought that perfon to confent, who only could have hindered me, by a tie
which, though it may be more tender, I do not think
more ftrong, than that of friendfhip. But I fear
there will be no way left me to tell you this great
truth, that I remember you, that I love you, that I
am grateful to you, that I entirely efteem and value
you : no way but that one, which needs no open
warrant to authorife it, or fecret conveyance to fecure
it ; which no bills can preclude, and no kings prevent ; a way that can reach to any part of the world
where you may be, where the very whifper or even
the wifh of a friend muft not be heard, or even fufpected : by this way, I dare tell my efteem and affection of you, to your enemies in the gates, and
you, and they, and their fons, may hear of it.

You prove yourfelf, my Lord, to know me for
the

the friend I am ; in judging that the manner of your
defence, and your reputation by it, is a point of the
higheſt concern to me ; and aſſuring me, it ſhall be
ſuch, that none of your friends ſhall bluſh for you.
Let me further prompt you to do yourſelf the beſt
and moſt laſting juſtice : the inſtruments of your
fame to poſterity will be in your own hands.   May
it not be, that Providence has appointed you to ſome
great and uſeful work, and calls you to it this ſevere
way ? You may more eminently and more effectually
ſerve the public even now, than in the ſtations you
have ſo honourably filled.   Think of Tully, Bacon,
and Clarendon *.   Is it not the latter, the diſgraced
part of their lives, which you moſt envy, and which
you would chuſe to have lived ?

   I am tenderly ſenſible of the wiſh you expreſs,
that no part of your misfortune may purſue me. But,
God knows, I am every day leſs and leſs fond of
my native country, (ſo torn as it is by party-rage),
and begin to conſider a friend in exile as a friend in
death ; one gone before, where I am not unwilling
nor unprepared to follow after ; and where (however
various or uncertain the roads and voyages of another
world may be) I cannot but entertain a pleaſing hope
that we may meet again.

   I faithfully aſſure you, that in the mean time there
is no one, living or dead, of whom I ſhall think
oftener, or better than of you. I ſhall look upon
you as in a ſtate between both, in which you will
have from me all the paſſions and warm wiſhes that
can attend the living, and all the reſpect and tender
ſenſe of loſs that we feel for the dead.   And I ſhall
ever depend upon your conſtant friendſhip, kind memory, and good offices, though I were never to ſee
or hear the effects of them : like the truſt we have in
benevolent ſpirits, who, though we never ſee or hear

_____

* Clarendon indeed wrote his beſt works in his baniſhment:
but the beſt of Bacon's were written before his diſgrace, and the
beſt of Tully's after his return from exile.

them,

them, we think, are conſtantly ſerving us, and praying for us.

Whenever I am wiſhing to write to you, I ſhall
conclude you are intentionally doing ſo to me. And
every time that I think of you, I will believe you
are thinking of me. I never ſhall ſuffer to be forgotten (nay to be but faintly remembered) the honour, the pleaſure, the pride I muſt ever have, in
reflecting how frequently you have delighted me, how
kindly you have diſtinguiſhed me, how cordially you
have adviſed me ! In converſation, in ſtudy, I ſhall
always want you, and wiſh for you: in my moſt
lively, and in my moſt thoughtful hours, I ſhall e-
qually bear about me the impreſſions of you: and
perhaps it will not be in this life only, that I ſhall
have cauſe to remember and acknowledge the friendſhip of the Biſhop of Rocheſter.

I am, &c.

LETTER XXIII.

To the ſame.

May 17. 1723.

ONce more I write to you, as I promiſed, and
this once, I fear, will be the laſt ! the curtain
will ſoon be drawn between my friend and me, and
nothing left but to wiſh you a long good-night. May
you enjoy a ſtate of repoſe in this life, not unlike that
ſleep of the ſoul which ſome have believed is to ſucceed it, where we lie utterly forgetful of that world
from which we are gone, and ripening for that to
which we are to go. If you retain any memory of
the paſt, let it only image to you what has pleaſed
you beſt; ſometimes preſent a dream of an abſent
friend, or bring you back an agreeable converſation.
But, upon the whole, I hope you will think leſs of
the time paſt than of the future ; as the former has
been leſs kind to you than the latter infallibly will
be. Do not envy the world your ſtudies ; they will

tend.

tend to the benefit of men againſt whom you can have
no complaint, I mean of all poſterity ; and perhaps,
at your time of life, nothing elſe is worth your care.
What is every year of a wife man's life, but a cenſure or critic on the paſt ? Thoſe whoſe date is the
ſhorteſt, live long enough to laugh at one half of it :
the boy deſpiſes the infant, the man the boy, the
philoſopher both, and the Chriſtian all. You may
now begin to think your manhood was too much a
puerility ; and you will never ſuffer your age to be
but a ſecond infancy. The toys and baubles of your
childhood are hardly now more below you, than
thoſe toys of our riper and of our declining years, the
drums and rattles of Ambition, and the dirt and bub-
bles of Avarice. At this time, when you are cut off
from a little ſociety and made a citizen of the world
at large, you ſhould bend your talents not to ſerve a
party, or a few, but all mankind. Your genius
ſhould mount above that miſt in which its participa-
tion and neighbourhood with earth long involved it.
To ſhine abroad and to heaven, ought to be the buſineſs, and the glory of your preſent ſituation. Remember it was at ſuch a time, that the greateſt lights
of antiquity dazzled and blazed the moſt, in their
retreat, in their exile, or in their death : but why
do I talk of dazzling or blazing ? it was then that
they did good, that they gave light, and that they
became guides to mankind.

Thoſe aims alone are worthy of ſpirits truly great,
and ſuch I therefore hope will be yours. Reſentment
indeed may remain, perhaps cannot be quite extin-
guiſhed, in the nobleſt minds ; but Revenge never
will harbour there : higher principles than thoſe of
the firſt, and better principles than thoſe of the latter, will infallibly influence men, whoſe thoughts and
whoſe hearts are enlarged, and cauſe them to prefer
the whole to any part of mankind, eſpecially to ſo
ſmall a part as one's ſingle ſelf.

Believe me, my Lord, I look upon you as a ſpirit

rit entered into another life *, as one juft upon the edge of immortality; where the paffions and affections muft be much more exalted, and where you ought to defpife all little views, and all mean retrofpects †. Nothing is worth your looking back; and therefore look forward, and make (as you can) the world look after you. But take care that it be not with pity, but with efteem and admiration.

I am with the greateft fincerity, and paffion for your fame as well as happinefs,

Your, &c.

LETTER XXIV.

From the Bifhop of ROCHESTER.

Paris, Nov. 23. 1731.

YOU will wonder to fee me in print; but how could I avoid it? The dead and the living, my friends and my foes, at home and abroad, called upon me to fay fomething; and the reputation of an hiftory ‡ which I and all the world value, muft have fuffered, had I continued filent. I have printed it here, in hopes that fomebody may venture to reprint it in England, notwithftanding thofe two frightening words at the clofe of it ||. Whether that happens

---

* The Bifhop of Rochefter went into exile the month following, and continued in it till his death, which happened at Paris, on the 15th day of February in the year 1732.

† Notwithftanding this, Mr Pope was convinced, before the Bifhop's death, that, during his banifhment, he was in the intrigues of the pretender: though, when he took his laft leave of Mr Pope, he told him, he would allow him to fay his fentence was juft, if he ever found he had any concerns with that family in his exile.

‡ Earl of Clarendon's.

|| The Bifhop's name, fet to his vindication of Bifhop Smolridge, Dr Aldrich, and himfelf, from the fcandalous reflections of Oldmixon, relating to the publication of Lord Clarendon's hiftory. Paris, 1731, 4to, fince reprinted in England.

or not, it is fit you fhould have a fight of it, who, I
know, will read it with fome degree of fatisfaction,
as it is mine, though it fhould have (as it really has)
nothing elfe to recommend it. Such as it is, *Extre-
mum hoc munus morientis habeto :* for that may well
be the cafe, confidering that within a few months I
am entering into my feventieth year; after which, e-
ven the healthy and the happy cannot much depend
upon life, and will not, if they are wife, much defire it. Whenever I go, you will lofe a friend who
loves and values you extremely, if in my circumftances I can be faid to be loft to any one, when dead,
more than I am already whilft living. I expected to
have heard from you by Mr Morice, and wondered
a little that I did not ; but he owns himfelf in a fault,
for not giving you due notice of his motions. It
was not amifs that you forbore writing, on a head
wherein I promifed more than I was able to perform.
Difgraced men fancy fometimes, that they preferve
an influence, where when they endeavour to exert it,
they foon fee their miftake. I did fo, my good
friend, and acknowledge it under my hand. You
founded the coaft, and found out my errour, it feems,
before I was aware of it. But enough on this fubject.

What are they doing in England to the honour of
letters ? and particularly what are you doing ? *Ipfe
quid audes ? quæ circumvolitas agilis thyma ?* Do you
purfue the moral plan you marked out, and feemed
fixteen months ago fo intent upon ? Am I to fee it
perfected ere I die, and are you to enjoy the reputation of it while you live ? or do you rather chufe to
leave the marks of your friendfhip, like the legacies
of a will, to be read and enjoyed only by thofe who
furvive you ? Were I as near you as I have been, I
fhould hope to peep into the manufcript before it
was finifhed. But alas! there is, and will ever probably be a great deal of land and fea between us.
How many books have come out of late in your parts,
which you think I fhould be glad to perufe ? Name
them.

them. The catalogue; I believe, will not coft you much trouble. They muft be good ones indeed to challenge any part of my time, now I have fo little of it left. I, who fquandered whole days heretofore, now hufband hours when the glafs begins to run low, and care not to mifpend them on trifles. At the end of the lottery of life, our laft minutes, like tickets left in the wheel, rife in their valuation. They are not of fo much worth perhaps in themfelves as thofe which preceded, but we are apt to prize them more, and with reafon. I do fo, my dear friend; and yet think the moft precious minutes of my life are well employed, in reading what you write. But this is a fatisfaction I cannot much hope for, and therefore muft betake myfelf to others lefs entertaining. Adieu! dear Sir, and forgive me engaging with one, whom you, I think, have reckoned among the heroes of the Dunciad. It was neceffary for me either to accept of his dirty challenge, or to have fuffered in the efteem of the world by declining it.

My refpects to your mother. I fend one of thefe papers for Dean Swift, if you have an opportunity, and think it worth while to convey it. My country at this diftance feems to me a ftrange fight; I know not how it appears to you, who are in the midft of the fcene, and yourfelf a part of it; I wifh you would tell me. You may write fafely to Mr Morice, by the honeft hand that conveys this, and will return into thefe parts before Chriftmas; fketch out a rough draught of it, that I may be able to judge whether a return to it be really eligible, or whether I fhould not, like the chemift in the bottle, upon hearing Don Quevedo's account of Spain, defire to be corked up again.

After all, I do and muft love my country, with all its faults and blemifhes; even that part of the conftitution which wounded me unjuftly, and itfelf through my fide, fhall ever be dear to me. My laft wifh fhall be like that of father Paul, *Efto perpetua !*

and when I die at a diftance from it, it will be in the fame manner as Virgil defcribes the expiring Pelo-ponnefian,

Sternitur, ————————
———————— *et dulces moriens reminifcitur Argos.*

Do I ftill live in the memory of my friends, as they certainly do in mine ? I have read a good many of your paper-fquabbles about me, and am glad to fee fuch free conceffions on that head, though made with no view of doing me a pleafure, but merely of load-ing another.

I am, &c.

LETTER XXV.

From the Bifhop of ROCHESTER.

On the death of his daughter.

Montpelier, Nov. 20. 1729.

I AM not yet mafter enough of myfelf, after the late wound I have received, to open my very heart to you, and am not content with iefs than that, whenever I converfe with you. My thoughts are at prefent vainly, but pleafingly employed, on what I have loft, and can never recover. I know well I ought, for that reafon, to call them off to other fub-jects; but hitherto I have not been able to do it. By giving them the rein a little, and fuffering them to fpend their force, I hope in fome time to check and fubdue them. *Multis fortunæ vulneribus perculfus, huic uni me imparem fenfi, et pene fuccubui.* This is weaknefs, not wifdom, I own; and on that account fitter to be trufted to the bofom of a friend, where I may fafely lodge all my infirmities. As foon as my mind is in fome meafure corrected and calmed, I will endeavour to follow your advice, and turn to fome-thing of ufe and moment; if I have ftill life enough left to do any thing that is worth reading and preferving.

ferving. In the mean time I fhall be pleafed to hear,
that you proceed in what you intend, without any
fuch melancholy interruption as I have met with.
Your mind is as yet unbroken by age and ill accidents; your knowledge and judgment are at the
height: ufe them in writing fomewhat that may
teach the prefent and future times, and if not gain
equally the applaufe of both, may yet raife the envy
of the one, and fecure the admiration of the other.
Employ not your precious moments, and great talents, on little men and little things; but chufe a
fubject every way worthy of you, and handle it as
you can, in a manner which nobody elfe can equal
or imitate. As for me, my abilities, if I ever had
any, are not what they were: and yet I will endeavour to recollect and employ them.

———*Gelidus tardante feneta*
Sanguis hebet, frigentque effæto in corpore vires.

However, I fhould be ungrateful to this place, if I
did not own that I have gained upon the gout in the
fouth of France, much more than I did at Paris;
though even there I fenfibly improved. I believe my
cure had been perfected, but the earneft defire of
meeting one I dearly loved, called me abruptly to
Montpelier; where after continuing two months,
under the cruel torture of a fad and fruitlefs expectation, I was forced at laft to take a long journey to
Touloufe; and even there I had miffed the perfon I
fought, had fhe not, with great fpirit and courage,
ventured all night up the Garonne to fee me, which
fhe above all things defired to do before fhe died.
By that means fhe was brought where I was, between
feven and eight in the morning, and lived twenty
hours afterwards; which time was not loft on either
fide, but paffed in fuch a manner as gave great fatif-
faction to both, and fuch as, on her part, every way
became her circumftances and character. For fhe
had her fenfes to the very laft gafp, and exerted them
to give me, in thofe few hours, greater marks of du-

H 3   ty

ty and love than fhe had done in all her lifetime,
though fhe had never been wanting in either. The
laft words fhe faid to me were the kindeft of all ; a
reflection on the goodnefs of God, which had allowed us in this manner to meet once more, before we
parted for ever. Not many minutes after that, fhe
laid herfelf on her pillow, in a fleeping pofture,

placidaque ibi demum morte quievit.

Judge you, Sir, what I felt, and ftill feel on this
occafion, and fpare me the trouble of defcribing it.
At my age, under my infirmities, among utter ftrangers, how fhall I find out proper reliefs and fupports?
I can have none, but thofe with which Reafon and Religion furnifh me ; and thofe I lay hold on, and grafp
as faft as I can. I hope, that he who laid the burthen upon me, (for wife and good purpofes no doubt),
will enable me to bear it, in like manner as I have
borne others, with fome degree of fortitude and firmnefs.

You fee how ready I am to relapfe into an argument which I had quitted once before in this letter.
I fhall probably again commit the fame fault, if I
continue to write ; and therefore I ftop fhort here,
and with all fincerity, affection, and efteem, bid you
adieu ! till we meet either in this world, if God pleafes, or elfe in another.

I am, &c.

LETTERS to and from Mr GAY, &c.

From 1712 to 1732.

LETTER I.

Binfield, Nov. 13. 1712.

YOU writ me a very kind letter some months ago, and told me you were then upon the point of taking a journey into Devonshire. That hindered my answering you; and I have since several times inquired of you, without any satisfaction; for so I call the knowledge of your welfare, or of any thing that concerns you. I passed two months in Suffex, and since my return have been again very ill. I writ to Lintot in hopes of hearing of you, but had no answer to that point. Our friend Mr Cromwell too has been silent all this year; I believe he has been displeased at some or other of my freedoms *, which I very innocently take, and most with those I think most my friends. But this I know nothing of: perhaps he may have opened to you; and if I know you right, you are of a temper to cement friendships, and not to divide them. I really much love Mr Cromwell, and have a true affection for yourself; which, if I had any interest in the world, or power with those who have, I should not be long without manifesting to you. I desire you will not, either out of modesty, or a vicious distrust of another's value for you, (those two eternal foes to merit), imagine that your letters and conversation are

---

* We see by the letters to Mr Cromwell, that Mr Pope was used to rally him on his turn for trifling and pedantic criticism. So he lost his two early friends, Cromwell and Wycherley, by his zeal to correct the bad poetry of the one, and the bad taste of the other.

not

not always welcome to me. There is no man more
entirely fond of good-nature or ingenuity than myfelf, and I have feen too much of thofe qualities in
you to be any thing lefs than

Your, &c.

L E T T E R II.

Dec. 24. 1721.

IT has been my good fortune within this month
paft, to hear more things that have pleafed me
than (I think) almoft in all my time befide. But nothing, upon my word, has been fo home-felt a fatif-
faction as the news you tell me of yourfelf: and you
are not in the leaft miftaken, when you congratulate
me upon your own good fuccefs: for I have more
people out of whom to be happy, than any ill-natu-
red man can boaft of. I may with honefty affirm to
you, that, notwithftanding the many inconveniencies and difadvantages they commonly talk of in the
Res angufti demi, I have never found any other, than
the inability of giving people of merit the only certain proof of our value for them, in doing them
fome real fervice. For after all, if we could but
think a little, felf-love might make us philofophers,
and convince us *quantuli indiget natura!* Ourfelves
are eafily provided for; it is nothing but the cir-
cumftantials, and the apparatus or equipage of human life, that cofts fo much the furnifhing. Only
what a luxurious man wants for horfes and footmen,
a good-natured man wants for his friends or the in-
digent.

I fhall fee you this winter with much greater pleafure than I could the laft; and, I hope, as much of
your time, as your attendance on the Duchefs * will
allow you to fpare to any friend, will not be thought
loft upon one who is as much fo as any man. I muft
alfo put you in mind, though you are now fecretary

* Duchefs of Monmouth, to whom he was juft then made
fecretary.

to

to this lady, that you are likewife fecretary to nine other ladies, and are to write fometimes for them too. He who is forced to live wholly upon thofe ladies favours, is indeed in as precarious a condition as any he who does what Chaucer fays for fuftenance; but they are very agreeable companions, like other ladies, when a man only paffes a night or fo with them at his leifure, and away. I am

Your, &c.

LETTER III.

Aug. 23. 1713.

JUft as I received yours, I was fet down to write to you, with fome fhame that I had fo long deferred it. But I can hardly repent my neglect, when it gives me the knowledge how little you infift upon ceremony, and how much a greater fhare in your memory I have than I deferve. I have been near a week in London, where I am like to remain, till I become, by Mr Jervas's help, *elegans formarum fpectator.* I begin to difcover beauties that were till now imperceptible to me. Every corner of an eye, or turn of a nofe or ear, the fmalleft degree of light or fhade on a cheek, or in a dimple, have charms to diftract me. I no longer look upon Lord Plaufible as ridiculous, for admiring a lady's fine tip of an ear, and pretty elbow, (as the *Plain Dealer* has it), but am in fome danger even from the ugly and difagreeable, fince they may have their retired beauties, in one trait or other about them. You may guefs in how uneafy a ftate I am, when every day the performances of others appear more beautiful and excellent, and my own more defpicable. I have thrown away three Dr Swifts, each of which was once my vanity, two Lady Bridgwaters, a Duchefs of Montague, befides half a dozen earls, and one knight of the garter. I have crucified Chrift over again in effigie, and made a Madona as old as her mother St Anne. Nay, what is yet more miraculous, I have

rivalled

rivalled St Luke himself in painting ; and as, it is said, an angel came and finished his piece, so, you would swear, a devil put the last hand to mine, it is so begrimed and smutted. However I comfort my-self with a Christian reflection, that I have not bro-ken the commandment ; for my pictures are not the likeness of any thing in heaven above, or in earth below, or in the water under the earth. Neither will any body adore or worship them, except the Indians should have a sight of them, who, they tell us, worship certain idols purely for their ugliness.

I am very much recreated and refreshed with the news of the advancement of the *Fan* *, which, I doubt not, will delight the eye and sense of the fair, as long as that agreeable machine shall play in the hands of posterity. I am glad your fan is mounted so soon ; but I would have you varnish and glaze it at your leisure, and polish the sticks as much as you can. You may then cause it to be borne in the hands of both sexes, no less in Britain, than it is in China ; where it is ordinary for a Mandarine to fan himself cool after a debate, and a statesman to hide his face with it when he tells a grave lie.

I am, &c.

LETTER IV.

Dear Mr GAY,   *Sept.* 23. 1714.

WElcome to your native soil † ! welcome to your friends ! thrice welcome to me ! whe-ther returned in glory, blessed with court-interest, the love and familiarity of the great, and filled with agreeable hopes ; or melancholy with dejection, contemplative of the changes of fortune, and doubt-ful for the future : Whether returned a triumphant

---

* A poem of Mr Gay's so entitled.
† In the beginning of this year Mr Gay went over to Hano-ver with the Earl of Clarendon, who was sent thither by Q. Anne. On her death they returned to England : and it was on this occasion that Mr Pope met him with this friendly welcome.

Whig,

Whig, or a defponding Tory, equally all hail ! e-
qually beloved and welcome to me! If happy, I
am to partake in your elevation ; if unhappy, you
have ftill a warm corner in my heart, and a retreat
at Binfield in the worft of times at your fervice. If
you are a Tory, or thought fo by any man, I know
it can proceed from nothing but your gratitude to a
few people who endeavoured to ferve you, and whofe
politics were never your concern If you are a Whig,
as I rather hope, and, as I think, your principles
and mine (as brother-poets) had ever a bias to the
fide of liberty, I know you will be an honeft man,
and an inoffenfive one. Upon the whole, I know
you are incapable of being fo much of either party
as to be good for nothing. Therefore once more,
whatever you are, or in whatever ftate you are, all
hail !

One or two of your old friends complained they
had heard nothing from you fince the queen's
death ; I told them no man living loved Mr Gay
better than I, yet I had not once written to him in
all his voyage. This I thought a convincing proof,
how truly one may be a friend to another without
telling him fo every month. But they had reafons
too themfelves to allege in your excufe ; as 'men
who really value one another, will never want fuch
as make their friends and themfelves eafy. The late
univerfal concern in public affairs threw us all into
a hurry of fpirits : even I, who am more a philofopher than to expect any thing from any reign, was
borne away with the current, and full of the expectation of the fucceffor : during your journeys I
knew not whither to aim a letter after you ; that
was a fort of fhooting flying : add to this the demand Homer had upon me, to write fifty verfes
a-day, befides learned notes, all which are at a conclufion for this year. Rejoice with me, O my friend,
that my labour is over ; come and make merry with
me in much feafting : we will feed among the lilies
(by the lilies I mean the ladies.) Are not the Ro-
                                        falinda's

falinda's of Britain as charming as the Bloufalinda's of
the Hague? or have the two great paftoral poets of
our nation renounced love at the fame time ? for Philips, immortal Philips hath deferted, yea, and in a
ruftic manner kicked, his Rofalind. Dr Parnelle and
I have been infeparable ever fince you went. We
are now at the Bath, where (if you are not, as I
heartily hope better engaged) your coming would be
the greateft pleafure to us in the world. Talk not of
expenfes: Homer fhall fupport his children. I beg
a line from you directly to the poft-houfe in Bath.
Poor Parnelle is in an ill ftate of health.

Pardon me if I add a word of advice in the poetical way. Write fomething on the King, or Prince,
or Princefs. On whatfoever foot you may be with
the court, this can do no harm.—I fhall never know
where to end, and am confounded in the many
things I have to fay to you, though they all amount
but to this, that I am entirely, as ever,

Your, &c.

LETTER V.

London, Nov. 8. 1717.

I AM extremely glad to find by a letter of yours
to Mr Fortefcue, that you have received one
from me ; and I beg you to keep, as the greateft of
curiofities, that letter of mine which you received, and
I never writ.

But the truth is, that we were made here to expect
you in a fhort time, that I was upon the ramble moft
part of the fummer, and have concluded the feafon
in grief, for the death of my poor father.

I fhall not enter into a detail of my concerns and
troubles, for two reafons ; becaufe I am really afflicted and need no airs of grief, and becaufe they are
not the concerns and troubles of any but myfelf.
But I think you (without too great a compliment)
enough my friend, to be pleafed to know he died
eafily, without a groan, or the ficknefs of two minutes ;

nutes; in a word, as filently and peacefully as he lived.

Sic mihi contingat vivere, ficque mori!

I am not in the humour to fay gay things, nor in the affectation of avoiding them. I cannot pretend to entertain either Mr Pulteney or you, as you have done both my Lord Burlington and me, by your letter to Mr Lowndes *. I am only forry you have no greater quarrel to Mr Lowndes, and wish you paid fome hundreds a-year to the land-tax. That gentleman is lately become an inoffenfive perfon to me too; fo that we may join heartily in our addreffes to him, and (like true patriots) rejoice in all that good done to the nation and government, to which we contribute nothing ourfelves.

I fhould not forget to acknowledge your letter fent from Aix; you told me then that writing was not good with the waters, and, I find fince, you are of my opinion, that it is as bad without the waters. But, I fancy, it is not writing, but thinking, that is fo bad with the waters; and then you might write without any manner of prejudice, if you writ like our brother-poets of thefe days.

The Duchefs, Lord Warwick, Lord Stanhope, Mrs Bellenden, Mrs Lepell, and I cannot tell who elfe, had your letters: Dr Arbuthnot and I expect to be treated like friends. I would fend my fervices to Mr Pulteney, but that he is out of favour at court; and make fome compliment to Mrs Pulteney, if fhe were not a Whig. My Lord Burlington tells me fhe has much outfhined all the French ladies, as fhe did the Englifh before: I am forry for it, becaufe it will be detrimental to our holy religion, if heretical women fhould eclipfe thofe nuns and orthodox beauties, in whofe eyes alone lie all the hopes we

* A poem, entitled, *To my ingenious and worthy friend W. Lowndes, Efq*; author of that celebrated treatife in folio, called the LAND-TAX BILL.

can have, of gaining fuch fine gentlemen as you to
our church.

Your, &c.

I wifh you joy of the birth of the young prince,
becaufe he is the only prince we have, from whom
you have had no expectations and no difappointments.

LETTER VI.

From Mr G A Y *to Mr* F—.

Stanton-Harcourt, Aug. 9. 1718.

THE only news that you can expect to have
from me here, is news from heaven; for I am
quite out of the world, and there is fcarce any thing
can reach me except the noife of thunder, which undoubtedly you have heard too. We have read in old
authors of high towers levelled by it to the ground,
while the humble valleys have efcaped : the only
thing that is proof againlt it is the laurel ; which,
however, I take to be no great fecurity to the brains
of modern authors, but to let you fee that the contrary to this often happens, I mult acquaint you,
that the higheft and molt extravagant heap of towers
in the univerfe, which is in this neighbourhood,
ftand ftill undefaced, while a cock of barley, in our
next field, has been confumed to afhes. Would to
God that this heap of barley had been all that had
perifhed ! for unhappily beneath this little fhelter
fat two much more conftant lovers than ever were
found in romance under the fhade of a beech-tree.
John Hewet was a well-fet man of about five and
twenty ; Sarah Drew might be rather called comely
than beautiful, and was about the fame age. They
had paffed through the various labour of the year together, with the greateft fatisfaction ; if fhe milked,
it was his morning and evening care, to bring the
cows to her hand ; it was but laft fair that he bought
her

her a prefent of green filk for her ftraw hat, and the
pofie on her filver ring was of his chufing. Their love'
was the talk of the whole neighbourhood ; for fcandal'
never affirmed, that they had any other views than
the lawful poffeffion of each other in marriage. It
was that very morning that he had obtained the confent of her parents, and it was but till the next week
that they were to wait to be happy. Perhaps in the
intervals of their work they were now talking of the
wedding-cloaths, and John was fuiting feveral forts
of poppies and field-flowers to her complexion, to
chufe her a knot for the wedding-day. While they
were thus bufied, (it was on the laft of July between
two or three in the afternoon), the clouds grew black,
and fuch a ftorm of lightning and thunder enfued,
that all the labourers made the beft of their way to
what fhelter the trees and hedges afforded. Sarah
was frighted, and fell down in a fwoon on a heap of
barley. John, who never feparated from her, fat
down by her fide, having raked together two or
three heaps, the better to fecure her from the ftorm.
Immediately there was heard fo loud a crack, as if
heaven had fplit afunder ; every one was now foli-
licitous for the fafety of his neighbour, and called to
one another throughout the field : no anfwer being
returned to thofe who called to our lovers, they ftept
to the place where they lay ; they perceived the
barley all in a fmoke, and then fpied this faithful
pair : John with one arm about Sarah's neck, and the
other held over her, as to fcreen from the lightning.
They were ftruck dead, and ftiffened in this tender
pofture. Sarah's left eye-brow was finged, and
there appeared a black fpot on her breaft : her lover
was all over black, but not the leaft figns of life were
found in either. Attended by their melancholy
companions, they were conveyed to the town, and
the next day were interred in Stanton-Harcourt
church-yard. My Lord Harcourt, at Mr Pope's
and my requeft, has caufed a ftone to be placed over

them,

them, upon condition that we furnished the epitaph, which is as follows;

When Eaſtern lovers feed the fun'ral fire,
On the ſame pile the faithful pair expire :
Here pitying Heav'n that virtue mutual found,
And blaſted both, that it might neither wound.
Hearts ſo ſincere th' Almighty ſaw well pleas'd,
Sent his own lightning, and the victims ſeiz'd.

But my Lord is apprehenſive the country-people will not underſtand this, and Mr Pope ſays he will make one with ſomething of ſcripture in it, and with as little of poetry as Hopkins and Sternhold *.

Your, &c.

L E T T E R   VII.

Dear Gay,   *Sept.* 11. 1722.

I Thank you for remembering me ; I would do my beſt to forget myſelf, but that, I find, your idea is ſo cloſely connected to me, that I muſt forget both together, or neither. I am ſorry I could not have a glimpſe either of you, or of the ſun (your father) be-

* The epitaph was this,
　　　Near this place lie the bodies of
　　　JOHN HEWET and MARY DREW,
　　　　an induſtrious young man
　　　and virtuous maiden of this pariſh ;
　　　　Who being at harveſt-work
　　　　　(with ſeveral others)
　　　were in one inſtant killed by lightning
　　　the laſt day of July 1718.

　　Think not, by rig'rous judgment ſeiz'd,
　　　A pair ſo faithful could expire ;
　　Victims ſo pure heav'n ſaw well pleas'd,
　　And ſnatch'd them in celeſtial fire.
　　Live well, and fear no ſudden fate ;
　　When God calls virtue to the grave,
　　　Alike 'tis juſtice ſoon or late,
　　　Mercy alike to kill or ſave.
　　Virtue unmov'd can hear the call,
　　And face the flaſh that melts the ball.

fore

fore you went for Bath : but now it pleafes me to fee
fim, and hear of you. Pray put Mr Congreve in
mind that he has one on this fide of the world who
loves him ; and that there are more men and women
in the univerfe than Mr Gay and my Lady Duchefs.
There are ladies in and about Richmond, that pretend to value him and yourfelf, and one of them at
leaft may be thought to do it without affectation,
namely, Mrs Howard.

Pray confult with Dr Arbuthnot and Dr Cheyne,
to what exact pitch your belly may be fuffered to
fwell, not to outgrow theirs, who are, yet, your
betters. Tell Dr Arbuthnot, that even pigeon-pies
and hogs-puddings are thought dangerous by our
governours ; for thofe that have been fent to the
Bifhop of Rochefter, are opened and profanely pried
into at the tower : it is the firft time dead pigeons
have been fufpected of carrying intelligence. To
be ferious, you, and Mr Congreve, and the Doctor
will be fenfible of my concern and furprife at his
commitment, whofe welfare is as much my concern,
as any friends 1 have. I think myfeif a moft unfortunate wretch : I no fooner love, and, upon
knowledge, fix my efteem to any man ; but he either
dies, like Mr Craggs, or is fent to imprifonment, like
the Bifhop. God fend him as well as I wifh him,
manifeft him to be as innocent as I believe him, and
make all his enemies know him as well as I do, that
they may think of him as well !

If you apprehend this period to be of any danger
in being addrefled to you, tell Mr Congreve or the
Doctor, it is writ to them. 1 am
Your, &c.

LETTER VIII.

July 13. 1722.

I Was very much pleafed, not to fay obliged, by
your kind letter, which fufficiently warmed my
heart to have anfwered it fooner, had I not been de-
I 3 ceived.

ceived (a way one often is deceived) by hearkening
to women ; who told me that both Lady Burlington
and yourfelf were immediately to return from Tunbridge, and that my Lord was gone to bring you
back. The world furnifhes us with too many examples of what you complain of in yours, and, I affure
you, none of them touch and grieve me fo much as
what relates to you. I think your fentiments upon
it are the very fame I fhould entertain, I wifh thofe
we call great men had the fame notions, but they are
really the moft little creatures in the world ; and the
moft interefted, in all but one point ; which is, that
they want judgment to know their greateft intereft,
to encourage and chufe honeft men for their friends.

I have not once feen the perfon you complain of,
whom I have of late thought to be, as the apoftle
admonifheth, one flefh with his wife.

Pray make my fincere compliments to Lord Burlington, whom I have long known to have a ftronger bent of mind to be all that is good and honourable,
than almoft any one of his rank.

I have not forgot yours to Lord Bolingbroke,
though I hope to have fpeedily a fuller opportunity,
he returning for Flanders and France next month.

Mrs Howard has writ you fomething or other in a
letter, which, fhe fays, fhe repents. She has as
much good nature as if fhe had never feen any ill nature, and had been bred among lambs and turtle-
doves, inftead of princes and court-ladies.

By the end of this week, Mr Fortefcue will pafs a
few days with me : we fhall remember you in our
potations, and wifh you a fifher with us, on my
grafs-plat. In the mean time we wifh you fuccefs as
a fifher of women at the Wells, a rejoicer of the
comfortlefs and widow, and a playfellow of the
maiden, I am

Your, &c.

L E T-

LETTER IX.

Sept. 11. 1722.

I Think it obliging in you to defire an account of my health. The truth is, I have never been in a worfe ftate in my life, and find whatever I have tried as a remedy fo ineffectual, that I give myfelf entirely over. I wifh your health may be fet perfectly right by the waters ; and, be affured, I not only wifh that, and every thing elfe for you, as common friends wifh, but with a zeal not ufual among thofe we call fo. I am always glad to hear of, and from you ; always glad to fee you, whatever accidents or amufements have intervened to make me do either lefs than ufual. I not only frequently think of you, but conftantly do my beft to make others do it, by mentioning you to all your acquaintance. I defire you to do the fame for me to thofe you are now with : do me what you think juftice in regard to thofe who are my friends, and if there are any, whom I have unwillingly deferved fo little of as to be my enemies, I do not defire you to forfeit their opinion, or your own judgment in any cafe. Let time convince thofe who know me not, that I am an inoffenfive perfon ; though (to fay truth) I do not care how little I am indebted to time, for the world is hardly worth living in, at leaft to one that is never to have health a week together. I have been made to expect Dr Arbuthnot in town this fortnight, or elfe I had written to him. If he, by never writing to me, feems to forget me, I confider I do the fame feemingly to him, and yet I do not believe he has a more fincere friend in the world than I am : therefore I will think him mine. I am his, Mr Congreve's, and

Your, &c.

LET.

LETTER X.

I Faithfully affure you, in the midft of that melancholy with which I have been fo long encompaffed, in an hourly expectation almoft of my mother's death; there was no circumftance that rendered it more infupportable to me, than that I could not leave her to fee you. Your own prefent efcape from fo imminent danger, I pray God may prove lefs precarious than my poor mother's can be; whofe life at beft can be but a fhort reprieve, or a longer dying. But I fear, even that it is more than God will pleafe to grant me; for thefe two days paft, her moft dangerous fymptoms are returned upon her; and, unlefs there be a fudden change, I muft in a few days, if not in a few hours, be deprived of her. In the afflicting profpect before me, I know nothing that can fo much alleviate it as the view now given me (heaven grant it may increafe!) of your recovery. In the fincerity of my heart, I am exceffively concerned, not to be able to pay you, dear Gay, any part of the debt, I very gratefully remember, I owe you on a like fad occafion, when you was here comforting me in her laft great illnefs. May your health augment as faft as, I fear, hers muft decline: I believe that would be very faft — may the life that is added to you be paffed in good fortune and tranquillity, rather of your own giving to yourfelf, than from any expectations or truft in others. May you and I live together, without wifhing more felicity or acquifitions than friendfhip can give and receive without obligations to Greatnefs. God keep you, and three or four more of thofe I have known as long, that I may have fomething worth the furviving my mother. Adieu, dear Gay, and believe me (while you live and while I live)

Your, &c.

As I told you in my laft letter, I repeat it in this:
do

do not think of writing to me. The Doctor, Mrs Howard, and Mrs Blount, give me daily accounts of you.

LETTER XI.

Sunday night.

I Truly rejoiced to fee your hand-writing, though I feared the trouble it might give you. I wish I had not known that you are still fo exceffively weak. Every day for a week paft I had hopes of being able in a day or two more to fee you. But my mother advances not at all, gains no ftrength, and feems but upon the whole to wait for the next cold day to throw her into a diarrhœa, that muft, if it return, carry her off. This being daily to be feared, makes me not dare to go a day from her, left that fhould prove to be her laft. God fend you a fpeedy recovery, and fuch a total one as, at your time of life, may be expected. You need not call the few words I writ to you, either kind, or good ; that was, and is, nothing. But whatever I have in my nature of kindnefs, I really have for you ; and whatever good I could do, I would, among the very firft, be glad to do to you. In your circumftance the old Roman farewell is proper, *Vive memor noftri.*

Your, &c.

I fend you a very kind letter of Mr. Digby, between whom and me two letters have paffed concerning you.

LETTER XII.

NO words can tell you the great concern I feel for you ; I affure you it was not, and is not leffened, by the immediate apprehenfion I have now every day lain under of lofing my mother. Be affured, no duty lefs than that fhould have kept me one day from attending your condition : I would come

come and take a room by you at Hampſtead, to be
with you daily, were ſhe not ſtill in danger of death.
I have conſtantly had particular accounts of you from
the Doctor, which have not ceaſed to alarm me
yet. God preſerve your life, and reſtore your
health. I really beg it for my own ſake ; for I feel
I love you more than I thought in health, though I
always loved you a great deal. If I am ſo unfortunate as to bury my poor mother, and yet have the
good fortune to have my prayers heard for you, I
hope we may live moſt of our remaining days together. If, as I believe, the air of a better clime, as
the ſouthern part of France, may be thought uſeful
for your recovery, thither I would go with you infallibly ; and it is very probable we might get the Dean
with us, who is in that abandoned ſtate already in
which I ſhall ſhortly be, as to other cares and duties.
Dear Gay, be as cheerful as your ſufferings will permit : God is a better friend than a court ; even any
honeſt man is a better. I promiſe you my entire
friendſhip in all events, heartily praying for your
recovery.

Your, &c.

Do not write, if you are ever ſo able : the Doctor
tells me all.

L E T T E R   XIII.

I AM glad to hear of the progreſs of your recovery,
and the oftener I hear it, the better, when it
becomes eaſy to you to give it me. I ſo well remember the conſolation you were to me in my mother's
former illneſs, that it doubles my concern at this
time not to be able to be with you, or you able to be
with me. Had I loſt her, I would have been no
where elſe but with you during your confinement.
I have now paſſed five weeks without once going from
home, and without any company but for three or
four of the days. Friends rarely ſtretch their kindneſs

nefs fo far as ten miles. My Lord Bolingbroke and
Mr Bethel have not forgotten to vifit me : the reft
(except Mrs Blount once) were contented to fend meffages. I never paffed fo melancholy a time, and now
Mr Congreve's death touches me nearly. It was
twenty years and more that I have known him : eve-
very year carries away fomething dear with it, till
we outlive all tenderneffes, and become wretched
individuals again as we begun. Adieu! This is my
birthday, and this is my reflection upon it.

With added days if life give nothing new,
But like a fieve, let every pleafure through;
Some joy ftill loft, as each vain year runs o'er,
And all we gain, fome fad reflection more!
Is this a birthday? — 'Tis, alas! too clear,
'Tis but the fun'ral of the former year.

Your, &c.

LETTER XIV.

To the Honourable Mrs ——

June 20.

WE cannot omit taking this occafion to congratulate you upon the increafe of your family,
for your cow is this morning very happily delivered
of the better fort, I mean a female calf; fhe is as like
her mother as fhe can ftare. All knights-errants
palfreys were diftinguifhed by lofty names: we fee
no reafon why a paftoral lady's fheep and calves
fhould want names of the fofter found; we have
therefore given her the name of Cæfar's wife, Cal-
phurnia: imagining, that as Romulus and Remus were
fuckled by a wolf, this Roman lady was fuckled by
a cow, from whence fhe took that name. In order
to celebrate this birthday, we had a cold dinner at
Marble-hill *. Mrs Sufan offered us wine upon the

* Mrs Howard's houfe.

occafion,

occafion, and upon fuch an occafion we could not refufe it.   Our entertainment confifted of flefh and fifh,
and the lettice of a Greek ifland called *Cos*.   We
have fome thoughts of dining there to-morrow, to
celebrate the day after the birthday, and on Friday
to celebrate the day after that, where we intend to
entertain Dean Swift; becaufe we think your hall
the moft delightful room in the world except that
where you are.   If it was not for you, we would
forfwear all courts; and really it is the moft mortifying thing in nature, that we can neither get into
the court to live with you, nor you get into the country to live with us; fo we will take up with what we
can get that belongs to you, and make ourfelves as
happy as we can, in your houfe.

I hope we fhall be brought into no worfe company, when you all come to Richmond: for whatever
our friend Gay may wifh as to getting into court, I
difclaim it, and defire to fee nothing of the court but
yourfelf, being wholly and folely

Your, &c.

LETTER XV.

July 21.

YOU have the fame fhare in my memory that
good things generally have; I always know
(whenever I reflect) that you fhould be in my mind;
only I reflect too feldom.   However, you ought to
allow me the indulgence I allow all my friends, (and
if I did not, they would take it) in confideration
that they have other avocations, which may prevent
the proofs of their remembering me, though they
preferve for me all the friendfhip and good-will which
I deferve from them.   In like manner I expect from
you, that my paft life of twenty years may be fet a-
gainft the omiffion of (perhaps) one month: and if
you complain of this to any other, it is you are in
the fpleen, and not I in the wrong.   If you think
this letter fplenetic, confider I have juft received the

news

news of the death of a friend, whom I efteemed all
moft as many years as you; poor Fenton. He died
at Eafthamftead, of indolence and inactivity; let it not
be your fate, but ufe exercife. I hope the Duchefs *
will take care of you in this refpect, and either make
you gallop after her, or teafe you enough at home to
ferve inftead of exercife abroad. Mrs Howard is fo
concerned about you, and fo angry at me for not writing to you, and at Mrs Blount for not doing the
fame, that I am piqued with jealoufy and envy at
you, and hate you as much as if you had a great
place at court; which you will confefs a proper caufe
of envy and hatred, in any poet militant or unpen-
fioned. But to fet matters even, I own I love you;
and own, I am, as I ever was and juft as I ever fhall
be,-

Your, &c.

LETTER XVI.

Dear SIR,   *Oct.* 6. 1727.

I Have many years ago magnified in my own
mind, and repeated to you, a ninth beatitude,
added to the eight in the fcripture; " Bleffed is he
" who expects nothing, for he fhall never be difap-
" pointed." I could find in my heart to congratulate you on this happy difmiffion from all court-de-
pendence; I dare fay I fhall find you the better and
the honefter man for it, many years hence: very
probably the healthfuller, and the cheerfuller into
the bargain. You are happily rid of many curfed
ceremonies, as well as of many ill and vitious habits, of which few or no men efcape the infection,
who are hackneyed and trammelled in the ways of a
court. Princes indeed, and peers (the lackies of
princes) and ladies (the fools of peers) will fmile on
you the lefs; but men of worth, and real friends
will look on you the better. There is a thing, the

* Of Queenfberry.

only thing which kings and queens cannot give you (for they have it not to give) liberty, and which is worth all they have; which, as yet, I thank God, Englifhmen need not afk from their hands. You will enjoy that, and your own integrity, and the fa- tisfactory confcioufnefs of having not merited fuch graces from courts as are beftowed only on the mean, fervile, flattering, interefted, and undeferving. The only fteps to the favour of the great are fuch com- placencies, fuch compliances, fuch diftant decorums, as delude them in their vanities, or engage them in their paffions. He is their greateft favourite, who is the falfeft: and when a man, by fuch vile gradations, arrives at the height of grandeur and power, he is then at beft but in a circumftance to be hated, and in a condition to be hanged, for ferving their ends: fo many a minifter has found it!

I believe you did not want advice, in the letter you fent by my Lord Grantham; I prefume you writ it not, without: and you could not have bet- ter, if I guefs right at the perfon who agreed to your doing it, in refpect to any decency you ought to ob- ferve: for I take that perfon to be a perfect judge of decencies and forms. I am not without fears even on that perfon's account. I think it a bad omen: but what have I to do with court-omens? —— Dear Gay, adieu. I can only add a plain uncourtly fpeech: while you are nobody's fervant, you may be any one's friend; and as fuch I embrace you, in all conditions of life. While I have a fhilling, you fhall have fix-pence, nay eight-pence, if I can con- trive to live upon a groat. I am faithfully

Your, &c.

LETTER   XVII.

From Mr GAY *to Mr* POPE.

Aug. 2. 1728.

IT was two or three weeks ago that I writ you a letter; I might indeed have done it fooner; I
thought

thought of you every poft-day upon that account,
and every other day upon fome account or other.   I
muft beg you to give Mrs B. my fincere thanks for
her kind way of thinking of me, which I have heard
of more than once from our friend at court, who
feemed in the letter fhe writ to be in high health
and fpirits. Confidering the multiplicity of pleafures
and delights that one is over-run with in thofe places, I wonder how any body hath health and fpirits
enough to fupport them : I am heartily glad fhe has,
and whenever I hear fo, I find it contributes to mine.
You fee I am not free from dependence, though I
have lefs attendance than I had formerly; for a great
deal of my own welfare ftill depends upon hers.
Is the widow's houfe to be difpofed of yet ? I have not
given up my pretenfions to the dean; if it was to be
parted with, I wifh one of us had it; I hope you wifh
fo too, and that Mrs Blount and Mrs Howard wifh
the fame, and for the very fame reafon that I wifh
it.   All I could hear of you of late hath been by ad-
vertifements in newfpapers, by which one would
think the race of Curls was multiplied ; and, by the
indignation fuch fellows fhow againft you, that you
have more merit than any body alive could have.
Homer himfelf hath not been worfe ufed by the
French.   I am to tell you that the Duchefs makes
you her compliments, and is always inclined to like
any thing you do ; that Mr Congreve admires, with
me, your fortitude ; and loves, not envies your
performance, for we are not dunces.   Adieu.

LETTER   XVIII.

April 18. 1730.

IF my friendfhip were as effectual as it is fincere,
you would be one of thofe people who would be
vaftly advantaged and enriched by it.   I ever honoured thofe popes who were moft famous for nepo-
tifm ; it is a fign that the old fellows loved fomebody,
which is not ufual in fuch advanced years.   And I

now honour Sir Robert Walpole for his extensive bounty and goodness to his private friends and relations. But it vexes me to the heart when I reflect, that my friendship is so much less effectual than theirs; nay so utterly uselefs that it cannot give you any thing, not even a dinner at this diftance, nor help the general whom I greatly love, to catch one fifh. My only confolation is to think you happier than myfelf, and to begin to envy you, which is next to hating you (an excellent remedy for love). How comes it that Providence has been fo unkind to me (who am a greater object of compaffion than any fat man alive), that I am forced to drink wine, while you riot in water, prepared with oranges by the hand of the Duchefs of Queenfberry ? that I am condemned to live by a high-way fide, like an old patriarch, receiving all guefts, where my portico (as Virgil has it)

Mane falutantum totis vomit ædibus undam ,

while you are wrapt into the Idalian groves, fprinkled with rofe-water, and live in burrage, balm, and burnet up to the chin, with the Duchfs of Queenfberry ? that I am doomed to the drudgery of dining at court with the ladies in waiting at Windfor, while you are happily banifhed with the Duchefs of Queenfberry ? So partial is fortune in her difpenfations! for I deferved ten times more to be banifhed than you, and I know fome ladies who merit it better than even her Grace. After this I muft not name any, who dare do fo much for you as to fend you their fervices. But one there is, who exhorts me often to write to you, I fuppofe, to prevent or excufe her not doing it herfelf; fhe feems (for that is all I will fay for a courtier) to wifh you mighty well. Another, who is no courtier, frequently mentions you, and does certainly wifh you well — I fancy after all, they both do fo.

I writ to Mr Fortefcue, and told him the pains you took to fee him. The dean is well; I have had

many

many accounts of him from Irifh evidence, but only
two letters thefe four months, in both which you are
mentioned kindly : he is in the north of Ireland,
doing I know not what, with I know not whom.
Mr Cleland always fpeaks of you : he is at Tunbridge, wondering at the fuperiour carnivoracity of
our friend : he plays now with the old Duchefs, nay
dines with her, after fhe has won all his money. O-
ther news I know not, but that Counfellor Bickford
has hurt himfelf, and has the ftrongeft walking-ftaff
I ever faw. He intends fpeedily to make you a vifit
with it at Amefbury. I am my Lord Duke's, my Lady Duchefs's, Mr Dormer's, General Dormer's, and
Your, &c.

LETTER XIX.

Sept. 11. 1730.

I May with great truth return your fpeech, that I
think of you daily ; oftener indeed than is confiftent with the character of a reafonable man, who
is rather to make himfelf eafy with the things and
men that are about him, than uneafy for thofe which
he wants. And you, whofe abfence is in a manner
perpetual to me, ought rather to be remembered as
a good man gone, than breathed after as one living.
You are taken from us here, to be laid up in a more
blefled ftate with fpirits of a higher kind : fuch I
reckon his Grace and her Grace, fince their banifhment from an earthly court to a heavenly one, in
each other and their friends ; for, I conclude, none
but true friends will confort or affociate with them
afterwards. I cannot but look upon myfelf (fo unworthy as a man of Twitnam feems, to be ranked
with fuch rectified and fublimated beings as you) as
a feparated fpirit too from courts and courtly foppe-
ries. But, I own, not altogether fo divefted of ter-
rene matter, nor altogether fo fpiritualized, as to be
worthy admiffion to your depths of retirement and
contentment. I am tugged back to the world and

K 3   its

its regards too often; and no·wonder, when my retreat is but ten miles from the capital. I am within
ear-fhot of reports, within the vortex of lies and cenfures. I hear fometimes of the lampooners of beauty, the calumniators of virtue, the jokers at reafon
and religion. I prefume thefe are creatures and
things as unknown to you, as we of this dirty orb
are to the inhabitants of the planet Jupiter; except
a few fervent prayers reach you on the wings of the
poft, from two or three ·of your zealous votaries at
this diftance; as one Mrs H. who lifts up her heart
now and then to you, from the midft of the collu-
vies and fink of human greatnefs at W——r; one
Mrs B. that fancies you may remember her while
you lived in your mortal and too tranfitory ftate at
Peterfham; one Lord B. who admired the Duchefs
before fhe grew a goddefs; and a few others.

To defcend now to tell you what are our wants,
our complaints, and our miferies here; I muft ferioufly fay, the lofs of any one good woman is too
great to be borne eafily: and poor Mrs Rollinfon,
though a private woman, was fuch. Her hufband
is gone into Oxfordfhire very melancholy, and
thence to the Bath, to live on, for fuch is our fate,
and duty. Adieu. Write to me as often as you
will, and (to encourage you) I will write as feldom
as if you did not. Believe me

Your, &c.

LETTER ·XX.

DEAR SIR,   Oct. 1. 1730.

I AM fomething like the fun at this feafon, withdrawing from the world, but meaning it mighty
well, and refolving to fhine whenever I·can again.
But I fear the clouds of a long winter will overcome
me to fuch a degree, that any body will take a farthing candle for a better guide, and more ferviceable
companion. My friends may remember my bright-
er days, but will think (like the Irifhman) that the

moon

moon is a better thing when once I am gone. I do
not fay this with any allufion to my poetical capacity as a fon of Apollo, but in my companionable one
(if you will fuffer me to ufe a phrafe of the Earl of
Clarendon's), for I fhall fee or be feen of few of you
this winter. I am grown too faint to do any good,
or to give any pleafure. I not only, as Dryden finely fays, feel my notes decay as a poet, but feel my
fpirits flag as a companion, and fhall return again to
where I firft began, my books. I have been putting
my library in order, and enlarging the chimney in
it, with equal intention to warm my mind and body
(if I can) to fome life. A friend (a woman-friend,
God help me!) with whom I have fpent three or four
hours a-day thefe fifteen years, advifed me to pafs
more time in my ftudies : I reflected, fhe muft have
found fome reafon for this admonition, and concluded fhe would complete all her kindneffes to me by returning me to the employment I am fitteft for; converfation with the dead, the old, and the worm-
eaten.

Judge therefore if I might not treat you as a bea-
tified fpirit, comparing your life with my ftupid
ftate. For as to my living at Windfor with the ladies, &c. it is all a dream ; I was there but two
nights, and all the day out of that company. I
fhall certainly make as little court to others as they
do to me ; and that will be none at all. My fair-
weather friends of the fummer are going away for
London, and I fhall fee them and the butterflies together, if I live till next year ; which I would not
defire to do, if it were only for their fakes. But we
that are writers, ought to love pofterity, that pofterity may love us ; and I would willingly live to fee
the children of the prefent race, merely in hope
they may be a little wifer than their parents.

I am, &c.

LET.

L E T T E R XXI.

IT' is true that I write to you very feldom, and
have no pretence of writing which fatisfies me,
becaufe I have nothing to fay that can give you
much pleafure : only merely that I am in being,
which in truth is of little confequence to one from
whofe converfation I am cut off by fuch accidents or
engagements as feparate us. I continue, and ever
fhall, to wifh you all good and happinefs : I wifh
that fome lucky event might fet you in a ftate of eafe
and independency all at once! and that I might live
to fee you as happy, as this filly world and fortune
can make any one. Are we never to live together
more, as once we did ? I find my life ebbing apace,
and my affections ftrengthening as my age increafes ;
not that I am worfe, but better, in my health than
laft winter ; but my mind finds no amendment nor
improvement, nor fupport to lean upon, from thofe
about me : and fo I feel myfelf leaving the world,
as faft as it leaves me. Companions I have enough,
friends few, and thofe too warm in the concerns of
the world, for me to bear pace with ; or elfe fo divided from me, that they are but like the dead whofe
remembrance I hold in honour. Nature, temper,
and habit, from my youth made me have but one
ftrong defire ; all other ambitions, my perfon, education, conftitution, religion, &c. confpired to remove far from me. That defire was, to fix and preferve a few lafting, dependable friendfhips : and the
accidents which have difappointed me in it, have put
a period to all my aims. So I am funk into an idlenefs, which makes me neither care nor labour to be
noticed by the reft of mankind ; I propofe no re-
wards to myfelf, and why fhould I take any fort of
pains ? here I fit and fleep, and probably here I fhall
fleep till I fleep for ever, like the old man of Verona.
I hear of what paffes in the bufy world with fo little
attention, that I forget it the next day : and as to
the

the learned world, there is nothing pafles in it. I have
no more to add, but that I am, with the fame truth
as ever,

Your, &c.

LETTER XXII.

Oct. 23. 1730.

YOur letter is a very kind one, but I cannot fay
fo pleafing to me as many of yours have been,
through the account you give of the dejection of
your fpirits. I wifh the too conftant ufe of water
does not contribute to it; I find Dr Arbuthnot and
another very knowing phyfician of that opinion. I
alfo wifh you were not fo totally immerfed in the
country; I hope your return to town will be a prevalent remedy againft the evil of too much recollec-
tion. I wifh it partly for my own fake. We have
lived little together of late, and we want to be phyficians for one another. It is a remedy that agreed
very well with us both, for many years, and I fancy
our conftitutions would mend upon the old medicine
of *ftudiorum fimilitudo*, &c. I believe we both of
us want whetting; there are feveral here who will
do you that good office, merely for the love of wit,
which feems to be bidding the town a long and laft
adieu. I can tell of you of no one thing worth
reading, or feeing; the whole age feems refolved to
juftify the Dunciad, and it may ftand for a public
epitaph or monumental infcription like that at Ther-
mopylæ, on a *whole people perifhed!* There may indeed be a wooden image or two of poetry fet up, to
preferve the memory that there once were bards in
Britain; and (like the giants at Guildhall) fhow the
bulk and bad tafte of our anceftors: at prefent the
poor Laureat * and Stephen Duck ferve for this purpofe; a drunk fot of a *parfon* holds forth the em-
blem of *infpiration*, and an honeft induftrious

* Eufden,

threfher

threfher not unaptly reprefents *pains* and *labour*. I
hope this phænomenon of Wiltfhire has appeared at
Amefbury, or the Duchefs will be thought infenfible
to all bright qualities and exalted geniufes, in court
and country-alike. But he is a harmlefs man, and
therefore I am glad.

This is all the news talked of at court, but it will
pleafe you better to hear that Mrs Howard talks
of you, though not in the fame breath with the
Threfher, as they do of me. By the way, have you
feen or converfed with Mr Chubb, who is a wonder-
ful phænomenon of Wiltfhire ? I have read through
his whole volume * with admiration of the writer ;
though not always with approbation of the doctrine.
I have paffed juft three days in London in four
months, two at Windfor, half an one at Richmond,
and have not taken one excurfion into any other
country. Judge now whether I can live in my library. Adieu. Live mindful of one of your firft
friends, who will be fo till the laft. Mrs Blount deferves your remembrance, for fhe never forgets you,
and wants nothing of being a friend †.

I beg the Duke and her Grace's acceptance of my
fervices : the contentment you exprefs in their company pleafes me, though it be the bar to my own, in
dividing you from us. I am ever very truly

Your, &c.

* This was his 4to volume, written before he had given any
figns of thofe extravagancies which have fince rendered him fo
famous. As the court fet up Mr Duck for the rival of Mr
Pope, the city at the fame time confidered Chubb, as one who
would eclipfe Locke. The modefty of the court-poet kept him
fober in a very intoxicating fituation, while the vanity of this
new-fafhioned philofopher affifted his fage admirers in turning
his head.

† Alluding to thofe lines in the epiftle *on the characters of wo-
men*, verf. 159. 160. vol. 2.
" With ev'ry pleafing, ev'ry prudent part,
" Say what can Cloe want ?—She wants a heart."

LET-

LETTER XXIII.

Oct. 2. 1732.

SIR Clem. Cottrel tells me you will shortly come to town. We begin want to comfort in a few friends about us, while the winds whistle, and the waters roar. The sun gives us a parting look, but it is but a cold one; we are ready to change those distant favours of a lofty beauty, for a grofs material fire that warms and comforts more. I wish you could be here till your family come to town : you will live more innocently, and kill fewer harmlefs creatures, nay none, except by your proper deputy the butcher. It is fit for confcience fake, that you should come to town, and that the Duchefs should stay in the country, where no innocents of another fpecies may fuffer by her. I hope she never goes to church : the Duke should lock you both up, and lefs harm would be done. I advife you to make man your game, hunt and beat about here for coxcombs, and trufs up rogues in fatire : I fancy they will turn to a good account, if you can produce them frefh, or make them keep : and their relations will come, and buy their bodies of you.

The death of Wilks leaves Cibber without a colleague, abfolute and perpetual dictator of the stage, though indeed while he lived he was but as Bibulus to Cæfar. However, ambition finds fomething to be gratified with in a mere name ; or elfe, God have mercy upon poor ambition ! Here is a dead vacation at prefent, no politics at court, no trade in town, nothing stirring but poetry. Every man, and every boy, is writing verfes on the royal hermitage: I hear the Queen is at a lofs which to prefer; but for my own part, I like none fo well as Mr Poyntz's in Latin. Yon would oblige my Lady Suffolk if you tried your Mufe on this occafion. I am fure I would do as much for the Duchefs of Queenfberry, if she defired it. Several of your friends affure me it is
expected

expected from you : one should not bear in mind, all one's life, any little indignity one receives from a court; and therefore I am in hopes, neither her Grace will hinder you, nor you decline it.

The volume of miscellanies is just published, which concludes all our fooleries of that kind. All your friends remember you, and, I assure you, no one more than

Your, &c.

LETTER XXIV.

From Mr GAY *to Mr* POPE.

Oct. 7. 1732.

I AM at last returned from my Somersetshire expedition, but since my return I cannot so much boast of my health as before I went; for I am frequently out of order with my colical complaints, so as to make me uneasy and dispirited, though not to any violent degree. The reception we met with, and the little excursions we made were every way agreeable. I think the country abounds with beautiful prospects. Sir William Wyndham is at present amusing himself with some real improvements, and a great many visionary castles. We were often entertained with sea-views and sea-fish, and were at some places in the neighbourhood, among which l was mightily pleased with Dunster castle near Minehead. It stands upon a great eminence, and hath a prospect of that town, with an extensive view of the Bristol channel, in which are seen two small islands called the *Steep Holms* and *Flat Holms*, and on the other side we could plainly distinguish the divisions of fields in the Welch coast. All this journey I performed on horseback, and I am very much disappointed that at present I feel myself so little the better for it. I have indeed followed riding and exercise for three months successively, and really think I was as well without it ; so that I begin to fear the illness I have

fo

fo long and fo often complained of, is inherent in my conftitution, and that I have nothing for it but patience *.

As to your advice about writing panegyric, it is what I have not frequently done. I have indeed done it fometimes againft my judgment and inclinations, and I heartily repent of it. And at prefent, as I have no defire of reward, and fee no juft reafon of praife, I think I had better let it alone. There are flatterers good enough to be found, and I would not interfere in any gentleman's profeffion. I have feen no verfes on thefe fublime occafions; fo that I have no emulation: let the patrons enjoy the authors, and the authors their patrons, for I know myfelf unworthy.

I am, &c.

LETTER XXV.

Mr CLELAND *to* Mr GAY †.

Dec. 16. 1731.

I AM aftonifhed at the complaints occafioned by a late epiftle to the Earl of Burlington; and I fhould be afflicted were there the leaft juft ground for them. Had the writer attacked Vice, at a time when it is not only tolerated but triumphant, and fo far from being concealed as a defect, that it is proclaimed with oftentation as a merit; I fhould have been apprehenfive of the confequence: had he fatirized gamefters of a hundred thoufand pounds fortune, acquired by fuch methods as are in daily practice, and almoft univerfally encouraged; had he over warmly defended the religion of his country, againft fuch books as come from every prefs, are publicly

* Mr Gay died the November following at the Duke of Queenfberry's houfe in London, aged 46 years.——See Mr Pope's epitaph on him, vol. 2.
† This was written by the fame hand that wrote the *letter to the publifher*, prefixed to the Dunciad, vol. 2.

vended

vended in every fhop, and grcedily bought by almoft
every rank of men ; or had he called our excellent
weekly writers by the fame names which they openly beftow on the greateft men in the miniftry, and
out of the miniftry, for which they are all unpunifh-
ed, and moft rewarded : in any of thefe cafes, indeed, ·I might have judged him too prefumptuous,
and perhaps have trembled for his rafhnefs.

   I could not but hope better for this fmall and modeft epiftle, which attacks no vice whatfoever;
which deals only in folly, and not folly in general,
but a fingle fpecies of it ; that only branch, for the
oppofite excellency to which, the Noble Lord to
whom it is written muft neceffarily be celebrated.   I
fancied it might efcape cenfure, efpecially feeing
how tenderly thefe follies are treated, and really lefs
accufed than apologifed for.

> *Yet hence the poor are clôth'd, the hungry fed,*
> *Health to himfelf, and to his infants bread,*
> *The lab'rer bears.*

Is this fuch a crime, that to impute it to a man muft
be a grievous offence ? It is an innocent folly, and
much more beneficent than the want of it ; for ill
tafte employs more hands, and diffufes expenfe more
than a good one.   Is it a moral defect ? No, it is
but a natural one, a want of tafte.   It is what the
beft good man living may be liable to.   The wor-
thieft Peer may live exemplarily in an ill-favoured
houfe, and the beft-reputed citizen be pleafed with
a vile garden.   I thought (I fay) the author had the
common liberty to obferve a defect, and to compliment a friend for a quality that diftinguifhes him :
which I know not how any quality fhould do, if we
were not to remark that it was wanting in others. But,
they fay, the fatire is perfonal.   I thought it could
not be fo, becaufe all its reflections are on things.
His reflections are not on the man, but his houfe,
garden, &c.   Nay, he refpects (as one may fay) the
perfons of the Gladiator, the Nile, and the Triton :
                                           he

he is only forry to fee them (as he might be to fee
any of his friends) ridiculous by being in the wrong
place, and in bad company. Some fancy, that to
fay a thing is perfonal, is the fame as to fay it is
unjult, not confidering, that nothing can be juft
that is not perfonal. I am afraid that " all fuch
" writings and difcourfes as touch no man, will
" mend no man." The good-natured, indeed, are
apt to be alarmed at any thing like fatire ; and the
guilty readily concur with the weak for a plain reafon, becaufe the vitious look upon folly as their
frontier :

Jam proximus ardet
Ucalegon.

No wonder thofe who know ridicule belongs to
them, find an inward confolation in moving it from
themfelves as far as they can ; and it is never fo far,
as when they can get it fixed on the beft charafters.
No wonder thofe who are food for fatirifts fhould rail
at them as creatures of prey ; every beaft born for
our ufe would be ready to call a man fo.

I know no remedy, unlefs people in our age would
as little frequent the theatres, as they begin to do
the churches ; unlefs comedy were forfaken, fatire
filent, and every man left to do what feems good in
his own eyes, as if there were no kings, no prieft,
no poet, in Ifrael.

But I find myfelf obliged to touch a point, on
which I muft be more ferious ; it well deferves I
fhould : I mean the malicious application of the character of Timon, which, I will boldly fay, they
would impute to the perfon the moft different in the
world from a man-hater, to the perfon whofe tafte
and encouragement of wit have often been fhewn in
the righteft place. The author of that epiftle muft
certainly think fo, if he has the fame opinion of his
own merit as authors generally have ; for he has been
diftinguifhed by this very perfon.

Why, in God's name, muft a portrait, apparent-

L 2

ly

ly collected from twenty different men, be applied
to one only ? Has it his eye ? no, it is very unlike.
Has it his nofe or mouth ? no, they are totally dif-
fering. What then, I befeech you ? Why, it has
the mole on his chin. Very well; but muft the
picture therefore be his, and has no other man that
blemifh ?

Could there be a more melancholy inftance how
much the tafte of the public is vitiated, and turns
the moft falutary and feafonable phyfic into poifon,
than if amidft the blaze of a thoufand bright qualities in a great man, they fhould only remark there is
a fhadow about him ; as what eminence is without ?
I am confident the author was incapable of imputing
any fuch to one, whofe whole life (to ufe his own expreffion in print of him) is a *continued feries* of *good*
and *generous actions.*

I know no man who would be more concerned, if
he gave the leaft pain or offence to any innocent perfon ; and none who would be lefs concerned, if the
fatire were challenged by any one at whom he
would really aim at. If ever that happens, I dare
engage, he will own it, with all the freedom of
one whofe cenfures are juft, and who fets his name
to them.

L E T T E R XXIV.

To the Earl of BURLINGTON.

MY LORD,   *March* 7. 1731.

THE clamour raifed about my epiftle to you *
could not give me fo much pain, as I received
pleafure in feeing the general zeal of the world in
the caufe of a great man who is beneficent, and the
particular warmth of your Lordfhip in that of a private man who is innocent.

It was not the poem that deferved this from you ;
for as I had the honour to be your friend, I could

* The 4th ethic epiftle, vol. 2.

not

not treat you quite like a poet : but fure the writer deferved more candour, even from thofe who knew him not, than to promote a report, which, in regard to that noble perfon, was impertinent ; in regard to me, villanous. Yet I had no great caufe to wonder, that a character belonging to twenty fhould be applied to one ; fince, by that means, nineteen would efcape the ridicule.

I was too well content with my knowledge of that noble perfon's opinion in this affair, to trouble the public about it. But fince Malice and Miftake are fo long a-dying, I have taken the opportunity of a third edition to declare his belief, not only of my innocence, but of their malignity ; of the former of which my own heart is as confcious, as, I fear, fome of theirs muft be of the latter. His humanity feels a concern for the injury done to me, while his greatnefs of mind can bear with indifference the in-fult offered to himfelf *.

However, my Lord, I own, that critics of this fort can intimidate me, nay half incline me to write no more : that would be making the town a compliment which, I think, it deferves ; and which fome, I am fure, would take very kindly. This way of fatire is dangerous, as long as flander raifed by fools of the loweft rank, can find any countenance from thofe of a higher. Even from the conduct fhewn on this occafion, I have learned there are fome who would rather be wicked than ridiculous ; and therefore it may be fafer to attack vices than follies. I will therefore leave my betters in the quiet poffef-fion of their idols, their groves, and their high-places ; and change my fubject from their pride to their meannefs, from their vanities to their miferies : and, as the only certain way to avoid mifconftruc-tions, to leffen offence, and not to multiply ill-natu-red applications, I may probably, in my next,

* Alludes to the letter the Duke of Ch** wrote to Mr Pope on this occafion.

L 3 make

make ufe of real names inftead of fictitious ones. I am,

My Lord,

Your moft affectionate, &c.

L E T T E R   XXVII *.

Cirencefter.

IT is a true faying, that misfortunes alone prove one's friendfhips; they fhew us not only that of other people for us, but our own for them. We hardly know ourfelves any otherwife. I feel my be- ing forced to this Bath-journey as a misfortune; and to follow my own welfare preferably to thofe I love, is indeed a new thing to me: my health has not ufually got the better of my tenderneffes and affec- tions. I fet out with a heavy heart, wifhing I had done this thing the laft feafon; for every day I defer it, the more I am in danger of that accident, which I dread the moft, my mother's death, (efpecially fhould it happen while I am away.) And another reflection pains me, that I have never, fince I knew you, been fo long feparated from you, as I now muft be. Methinks we live to be more and more ftrangers, and every year teaches you to live without me: this abfence may, I fear, make my return lefs welcome and lefs wanted to you, than once it feemed, even after but a fortnight. Time ought not in reafon to diminifh friendfhip, when it confirms the truth of it by experience.

The journey has a good deal difordered me, not- withftanding my refting-place at Lord Bathurft's. My Lord is too much for me, he walks, and is in fpirits all day long; I rejoice to fee him fo. It is a right diftinction, that I am happier in feeing my friends fo many degrees above me, be it in fortune, health, or pleafures, than I can be in fharing either with them: for in thefe fort of enjoyments I cannot

* To Mrs B.

keep

keep pace with them, any more than I can walk
with a ftronger man. I wonder to find 1 am a companion for none but old men, and forget that I am
not a young fellow myfelf. The worlt is, that read-
ng and writing, which I have ftill the greateft relifh
for, are growing painful to my eyes. But if I can
preferve the good opinion of one or two friends, to
fuch a degree, as to have their indulgence to my
weakneffes, I will not complain of life; and if I
could live to fee you confult your eafe and quiet, by
becoming independent on thofe who will never help
you to either, I doubt not of finding the latter part
of my life pleafanter than the former, or prefent.
My uneafineffes of body I can bear ; my chief uneafinefs of mind is in your regard. You have a temper
that would make you *eafy* and *beloved*, (which is all
the happinefs one needs to wifh in this world), and
content with moderate things. All your point is not
to lofe that temper by facrificing yourfelf to others,
out of a miftaken tendernefs, which hurts you, and
profits not them. And this you muft do foon, or
it will be too late : habit will make it as hard for
you to live independent, as for L— to live out of a
court.

You muft excufe me for obferving what I think
any defect in you : you grow too indolent, and give
things up too eafily : which would be otherwife,
when you found and felt yourfelf your own : fpirits
would come in, as ill ufage went out. While you
live under a kind of perpetual dejection and oppreffion, nothing at all belongs to you, not your own
humour, nor your own *fenfe*.

You cannot conceive how much you would find
refolution rife, and cheerfulnefs grow upon you; if
you would once try to live independent for two or
three months. I never think tenderly of you but
this comes acrofs me, and thefore excufe my repeating it, for whenever 1 do not, I diffemble half that I
think of you. Adieu, pray write, and be particular
about your health.

L E T-

L E T T E R   XXVIII. *

Y Our letter, dated at nine o'clock on Tuefday
(night, I fuppofe) has funk me quite. Yefterday I hoped ; and yefterday I fent you a line or two
for our poor friend Gay, inclofed in a few words to
you ; about twelve or one o'clock you fhould have
had it. I am troubled about that, though the prefent caufe of our trouble be fo much greater †. Indeed I want a friend, to help me to bear it better.
We want each other. I bear a hearty fhare with
Mrs Howard, who has loft a man of a moft honeft
heart ; fo honeft an one, that I wifh her mafter had
none lefs honeft about him. The world after all is
a little pitiful thing ; not performing any one promife it makes us, for the future, and every day taking away and annulling the joys of the paft. Let
us comfort one another, and, if poffible, ftudy to
add as much more friendfhip to each other, as death
has deprived us of in him : I promife you more and
more of mine, which will be the way to deferve
more and more of yours.

I purpofely avoid faying more. The fubject is
beyond writing upon, beyond cure or eafe by reafon
or reflection, beyond all but one thought, that it is
the will of God.

So will the death of my mother be ! which now I
tremble at, now refign to, now bring clofe to me,
now fet farther off: every day alters, turns me a-
bout, and confufes my whole frame of mind. Her
dangerous diftemper is again returned, her fever coming onward again, though lefs in pain ; for which
laft however I thank God.

I am unfeignedly tired of the world, and receive
nothing to be called a pleafure in it, equivalent to
countervail either the death of one I have fo long li-

* To the fame.
† Mr Gay's death, which happened in Nov. 1732, at the
Duke of Queenfberry's houfe in London, aged 46.

ved

ved with, or of one I have fo long lived for. I have
nothing left but to turn my thoughts to one comfort; the laft we ufually think of, though the only
one we fhould in wifdom depend upon, in fuch a dif-
appointing place as this. I fit in her room, and fhe
is always prefent before me, but when I fleep. I
wonder I am fo well: I have fhed many tears, but
now I weep at nothing. I would above all things
fee you, and think it would comfort you to fee me
fo equal-tempered and fo quiet. But pray dine here;
you may, and fhe know nothing of it, for fhe dozes
much, and we tell her of no earthly thing, left it
run in her mind, which often trifles have done. If
Mr Bethel had time, I wifh he were your companion
hither. Be as much as you can with each other: be
affured I love you both, and be farther affured, that
friendfhip will increafe as I live on.

LETTER XXIX.

To HUGH BETHEL, Efq;

July 12. 1723.

I Affure you unfeignedly any memorial of your
good-nature and friendlinefs is moft welcome to
me, who knew thofe tenders of affection from you
are not like the common traffic of compliments and
profeffions, which moft people only give that they
may receive; and is at beft a commerce of vanity,
if not of falfehood. I am happy in not immediately
wanting the fort of good offices you offer: but if I
did want them, I fhould not think myfelf unhappy
in receiving them at your hands: this really is fome
compliment, for I would rather moft men did me a
fmall injury, than a kindnefs. I know your humanity, and, allow me to fay, I love and value you
for it: it is a much better ground of love and value,
than all the qualities I fee the world fo fond of: they
generally admire in the wrong place, and generally
moft admire the things they do not comprehend, or
the

the things they can never be the better for. Very
few can receive pleafure or advantage from wit which
they feldom tafte, or learning which they feldom
underftand ; much lefs from the quality, high birth,
or fhining circumftances of thofe to whom they profefs efteem, and who will always remember how
much they are their inferiours. But humanity and fo-
ciable virtues are what every creature wants every
day, and ftill wants more the longer he lives, and
moft the very moment he dies. It is ill travelling either in a ditch or on a terrace ; we fhould walk in the
common way, where others are continually paffing
on the fame level, to make the journey of life fupportable by bearing one another company in the
fame circumftances. Let me know how I may convey over the Odyffeys for your amufement in your
journey, that you may compare your own travels
with thofe of Ulyffes : I am fure yours are underta-
ken upon a more difinterefted, and therefore a more
heroic motive. Far be the omen from you, of returning as he did, alone, without faving a friend.

There is lately printed a book * wherein all human virtue is reduced to one teft, that of truth, and
branched out in every inftance of our duty to God
and man. If you have not feen it, you muft, and I
will fend it together with the Odyffey. The very
women read it, and pretend to be charmed with that
beauty which they generally think the leaft of. They
make as much ado about truth, fince this book appeared, as they did about health when Dr Cheyne's
came out ; and will doubtlefs be as conftant in the
purfuit of one, as of the other. Adieu.

* Mr Wollafton's book of *the religion of nature delineated.*
The Queen was fond of it ; and that made the reading of it,
and the talking of it, fafhionable.

L E T-

LETTER XXX.

To the fame.

Aug. 9. 1726.

I Never am unmindful of thofe I think fo well of as yourfelf; their number is not fo great as to confound one's memory. Nor ought you to decline writing to me, upon an imagination, that I am much employed by other people. For though my houfe is like the houfe of a patriarch of old, ftanding by the highway-fide, and receiving all travellers, neverthe-lefs I feldom go to bed without the reflection, that one's chief bufinefs is to be really at home : and I agree with you in your opinion of company, amufe-ments, and all the filly things which mankind would fain make pleafures of, when in truth they are la-bour and forrow.

I condole with you on the death of your relation, the Earl of C. as on the fate of a mortal man : e-fteem I never had for him, but concern and humanity I had : the latter was due to the infirmity of his laft period, though the former was not due to the tri-umphant and vain part of his courfe. He certainly knew himfelf beft at laft, and knew beft the little value of others, whofe neglect of him, whom they fo grofsly followed and flattered in the former fcene of his life, fhewed them as worthlefs as they could imagine him to be, were he all that his worft enemies believed of him : for my own part, I am forry for his death, and wifh he had lived long enough to fee fo much of the faithleffnefs of the world, as to have been above the mad ambition of governing fuch wretches as he muft have found it to be compofed of.

Though you could have no great value for this great man, yet acquaintance itfelf, the cuftom of feeing the face, or entering under the roof, of one that walks along with us in the common way of the world,

world, is enough to create a wifh at leaft for his being above ground, and a degree of uneafinefs at his
removal. It is the lofs of an object familiar to us :
I fhould hardly care to have an old poft pulled up,
that I remembered ever fince I was a child. And
add to this the reflection (in the cafe of fuch as were
not the beft of their fpecies) what their condition in
another life may be, it is yet a more important motive for our concern and compaffion. To fay the
truth, either in the cafe of death or life, almoft every body and every thing is a caufe or object for humanity, even profperity itfelf, and health itfelf;
fo many weak pitiful incidentals attend on them.

I am forry any relation of yours is ill, whoever
it be, for you do not name the perfon. But I conclude it is one of thofe to whofe houfes, you tell me,
you are going ; for I know no invitation with you
is fo ftrong as when any one is in diftrefs, or in want
of your affiftance : the ftrongeft proof in the world of
this, was your attendance on the late Earl.

I have been very melancholy for the lofs of Mr
Blount. Whoever has any portion of good nature
will fuffer on thefe occafions : but a good mind re-
wards its own fufferings. I hope to trouble you as
little as poffible, if it be my fate to go before you.
I am of old Ennius's mind, *Nemo me decorat lachry-
mis.* — I am but a *lodger* here : this is not an abiding
city, I am only to ftay out my leafe : for what has
perpetuity and mortal man to do with each other ?
But I could be glad you would take up with an inn
at Twitenham, as long as I am hoft of it : if not,
I would take up freely with any inn of yours. — A-
dieu, dear Sir : let us while away this life : and (if
we can) meet in another.

L E T.

LETTER XXXI.

To the fame.

June 24. 1727.

YOU are too humane and confiderate (things few people can be charged with). Do not fay you will not expect letters from me; upon my word, I can no more forbear writing fometimes to you, than thinking of you. I know the world too well, not to value you who are an example of acting, living, and thinking, above it, and contrary to it.

I thank God for my mother's unexpected recovery, though my hope can rife no higher than from reprieve to reprieve, the fmall addition of a few days to the many fhe has already feen. Yet fo fhort and tranfitory as this light is, it is all I have to warm or fhine upon me; and when it is out, there is nothing elfe that will live for me, or confume itfelf in my fervice. But I would have you think this is not the chief motive of my concern about her : gratitude is a cheap virtue, one may pay it very punctually, for it cofts us nothing, but our memory of the good done: And I owe her more good than ever I can pay, or fhe at this age receive, if I could. I do not think the tranquillity of the mind ought to be difturbed for many things in this world : but thofe offices that are neceffary duties either to our friends or ourfelves, will hardly prove any breach of it; and as much as they take away from our indolence and eafe of body, will contribute to our peace and quiet of mind by the content they give. They often afford the highest pleafure; and thofe who do not feel that, will hardly ever find another to match it, let them love themfelves ever fo dearly. At the fame time, it muft be owned, one meets with cruel difappointments in feeing fo often the beft endeavours ineffectual to make others happy, and very often (what is moft cruel of all)

all) through their own means *. But ftill, I affirm, thofe very difappointments of a virtuous man are greater pleafures than the utmoft gratifications and fucceffes of a mere felf-lover.

The great and fudden event which has juft now happened †, puts the whole world (I mean this whole world) into a new ftate. The only ufe I have, fhall, or wifh to make of it, is, to obferve the difparity of men from themfelves in a week's time : the defultory leaping and catching of new motions, new modes, new meafures; and that ftrange fpirit and life, with which men broken and difappointed refume their hopes, their folicitations, their ambitions! It would be worth your while, as a philofopher, to be bufy in thefe obfervations, and to come hither to fee the fury and buftle of the bees this hot feafon, without coming fo near as to be ftung by them.

Your, &c.

L E T T E R   XXXII.

To the fame.

June 17. 1728.

AFter the publifhing of my boyifh letters to Mr Cromwell, you will not wonder if I fhould forfwear writing a letter again while I live ; fince I do not correfpond with a friend upon the terms of any other free fubject of this kingdom. But to you I can never be filent, or referved ; and, I am fure, my opinion of your heart is fuch, that I could open mine to you in no manner which I could fear the whole world fhould know. I could publifh my own heart too, I will venture to fay, for any mifchief or malice there is in it: but a little too much folly or weaknefs might (I fear) appear, to make fuch a fpectacle either inftructive or agreeable to others.

* See letter 27. from Cirencefter.
† The death of K. George I. which happened the 11th of June 1727.

I

I am reduced to beg of all my acquaintance to fecure me from the like ufage for the future, by returning me any letters of mine which they may have preferved ; that I may not be hurt, after my death, by
that which was the happinefs of my life, their partiality and affection to me.

I have nothing of myfelf to tell you, only that I
have had but indifferent health. I have not made a
vifit to London : curiofity and the love of diffipation
die apace in me. I am not glad nor forry for it, but
I am very forry for thofe who have nothing elfe to
live on.

I have read much, but writ no more. I have fmall
hopes of doing good, no vanity in writing, and little
ambition to pleafe a world not very candid or deferving. If I can preferve the good opinion of a few
friends, it is all I can expect, confidering how little
good I can do even to them to merit it. Few people
have your candour, or are fo willing to think well of
another from whom they receive no benefit, and gratify no vanity. But of all the foft fenfations, the
greateft pleafure is to give and receive mutual truft.
It is by belief and firm hope, that men are made happy in this life, as well as in the other. My confidence in your good opinion, and dependence upon
that of one or two more, is the chief cordial drop I
tafte, amidft the infipid, the difagreeable, the cloy-
ing, or the dead-fweet, which are the common
draughts of life. Some pleafures are too pert, as
well as others too flat, to be relifhed long ; and vivacity in fome cafes is worfe than dulnefs. Therefore indeed for many years I have not chofen my
companions for any of the qualities in fafhion, but
almoft entirely for that which is the moft out-of-
fafhion, fincerity. Before I am aware of it, I am
making your panegyric, and perhaps my own too ;
for next to poffeffing the beft of qualities is the
efteeming and diftinguifhing thofe who poffefs them.
I truly love and value you, and fo I ftop fhort.

L E T T E R   XXXIII.

To the Earl of PETERBOROW.

My LORD,   Aug. 24. 1728.

I Prefume you may before this time be returned, from the contemplation of many beauties, animal and vegetable, in gardens; and poffibly fome rational, in ladies; to the better enjoyment of your own at Bevis-Mount. I hope, and believe, all you have feen will only contribute to it. I am not fo fond of making compliments to ladies as I was twenty years ago, or I would fay there are fome very reafonable, and one in particular there. I think you happy, my Lord, in being at leaft half the year almoft as much your own mafter as I am mine the whole year; and with all the difadvantageous incumbrances of quality, parts, and honour, as mere a gardener, loiterer, and labourer, as he who never had titles, or from whom they are taken. I have an eye in the laft of thefe glorious appellations to the ftyle of a Lord degraded or attainted: methinks they give him a better title than they deprive him of, in calling him *labourer*. *Agricultura*, fays Tully, *proxima fapientiæ*; which is more than can be faid, by moft modern nobility, of Grace, or Right Honourable, which are often *proxima ftultitiæ*. The great Turk, you know, is often a gardener, or of a meaner trade: and are there not (my Lord) fome circumftances in which you would refemble the great Turk? The two paradifes are not ill connected, of gardens and gallantry; and fome there are (not to name my Lord B.) who pretend they are both to be had, even in this life, without turning Muffulmen.

We have as little politics here within a few miles of the court (nay perhaps at the court) as you at Southampton: and our minifters, I dare fay, have lefs to do. Our weekly hiftories are only full of the feafts given to the Queen and Royal family by their

fervants, and the long and laborious walks her Majefty takes every morning. Yet if the graver hiftorians hereafter fhall be filent of this year's events, the
amorous and anecdotical may make pofterity fome
amends, by being furnifhed with the gallantries of
the great at home ; and it is fome comfort, that if
the men of the next age do not read of us, the women may.

From the time you have been abfent, I have not
been to wait on a certain great man, through modefty, through idlenefs, and through refpect. But for
my comfort, I fancy, that any great man will as foon
forget one that does him no harm, as he can one
that has done him any good. Believe me, my Lord,
yours.

LETTER XXXIV.

From the Earl of PETERBOROW.

I Muft confefs, that, in going to Lord Cobham's, I
was not led by curiofity. I went thither to fee
what I had feen, and what I was fure to like.

I had the idea of thofe gardens fo fixed in my imagination by many defcriptions, that nothing furprifed
me ; immenfity and Van Brugh appear in the whole,
and in every part. Your joining in your letter animal and vegetable beauty, makes me ufe this expreffion : I confefs the ftately Sacharifsa at Stow, but am
content with my little Amoret.

I thought you indeed more knowing upon the fubject, and wonder at your miftake : why will you imagine women infenfible to praife, much lefs to yours ?
I have feen them more than once turn from their lover to their flatterer. I am fure the farmerefs at Bevis in her higheft mortifications in the middle of her
Lent *, would feel emotions of vanity, if fhe knew
you gave her the character of a reafonable woman.

* The Countefs of Peterborow, a Roman Catholic.

M 3   You

You have been guilty again of another miftake, which hindered me fhowing your letter to a friend; when you join two ladies in the fame compliment, though you gave to both the beauty of Venus and the wit of Minerva, you would pleafe neither.

If you had put me into the Dunciad, I could not have been more difpofed to criticife your letter. What, Sir, do you bring it in as a reproach, or as a thing uncommon to a court, to be without politics? With politics indeed the Richlieu's, and fuch folks, have brought about great things in former days; but what are they, Sir, who, without policy, in our times, can make ten treaties in a year, and fecure everlaft-ing peace?

I can no longer difagree with you, though in jeft. Oh how heartily I join with you in your contempt for Excellency and Grace, and in you refteem of that moft noble title, *Loiterer*. If I were a man of many plums, and a good Heathen, I would dedicate a temple to Lazinefs. No man fure could blame my choice to fuch a deity, who confiders, that, when I have been fool enough to take pains, I always met with fome wife man able to undo my labours.

Your, &c.

LETTER XXXV.

YOU were in a very polemic humour when you did me the honour to anfwer my laft. I al-ways underftood, like a true controvertift, that to anfwer is only to cavil and quarrel: however, I forgive you, you did it (as all polemics do) to fhew your parts. Elfe was it not very vexatious, to deny me to commend two women at a time? It is true, my Lord, you know women as well as men: but fince you certainly love them better, why are you fo uncharitable in your opinion of them? Surely one lady may allow another to have the thing fhe herfelf leaft values, reafon, when beauty is uncontefted. Venus herfelf could allow Minerva to be goddefs of

wit,

wit, when Paris gave her the apple (as the fool herfelf thought) on a better account. I do fay, that
Lady P** is a reafonable woman ; and I think, fhe
will not take it amifs, if I fhould infift upon efteeming her, inftead of toafting her, like a filly thing I
could name, who is the Venus of thefe days. I fee
you had forgot my letter, or would not let her know
how much I thought of her in this reafonable way :
but I have been kinder to you, and have fhewn your
letter to one who will take it candidly.

But, for God's fake, what have you faid about
politicians ? you made me a great compliment in
the truft you repofed in my prudence, or what mifchief might not I have done you with fome that affect that denomination ? Your Lordfhip might as
fafely have fpoken of heroes. What a blufter would
the god of the winds have made, had one that we
know puffed againft Æolus, or (like Xerxes) whip-
ped the feas ? They had dialogued it in the language
of the Rehearfal,

> *I'll give him flafh for flafh—*
> *I'll give him dafh for dafh—*

But all now is fafe ; the poets are preparing fongs of
joy, and halcyon days are the word.

I hope, my Lord, it will not be long before your
dutiful affection brings you to town. I fear it will a
little raife your envy to find all the Mufes employed
in celebrating a royal work *, which your own partiality will think inferiour to Bevis-Mount. But if
you have any inclination to be even with them, you
need but put three or four wits into any hole in your
garden, and they will out-rhyme all Eaton and
Weftminfter. I think, Swift, Gay, and I could un-
dertake it, if you do not think our heads too expenfive : but the fame hand that did the others, will do
them as cheap. If all elfe fhould fail, you are
fure at leaft of the head, hand, and heart of your
fervant.

* The Hermitage,

Why

Why fhould you fear any difagreeable news to reach us at Mount Bevis? Do as I do even within ten miles of London, let no news whatever come near you. As to public affairs, we never knew a deader feafon : it is all filent, deep tranquillity. Indeed, they fay, it is fometimes fo juft before an earthquake. But whatever happens, cannot we obferve the wife neutrality of the Dutch, and let all all about us fall by the ears? or if you, my Lord, fhould be pricked on by any old-fafhioned notions of honour and romance, and think it neceffary for the general of the marines to be in action, when our fleets are in motion ; meet them at Spithead, and take me along with you. I decline no danger where the glory of Great Britain is concerned ; and will contribute to empty the largeft bowl of punch that fhall be rigged out on fuch an occafion. Adieu, my Lord, and may as many years attend you as may be happy and honourable !

LETTER XXXVI.

From the Earl of PETERBOROW.

YOU muft receive my letters with a juft impartiality, and give grains of allowance for a gloomy or rainy day ; I fink grievoufly with the weather-glafs, and am quite fpiritlefs when oppreffed with the thoughts of a birthday or a return.

Dutiful affection was bringing me to town, but undutiful lazinefs, and being much out of order, keep me in the country ; however, if alive, I muft make my appearance at the birthday. Where you fhowed one letter, you may fhew the other ; fhe that never was wanting in any good office in her power, will make a proper excufe, where a fin of omiffion, I fear, is not reckoned as a venial fin.

I confent you fhall call me polemic, or affociate me to any fect or corporation, provided you do not join me to the charitable rogues or to the pacific politicians of the prefent age. I have read over Barclay

clay * in vain, and find, after a ftroke given on the left, I cannot offer the right cheek for another blow : all I can bring myfelf to, is, to bear mortification from the fair fex with patience.

You feem to think it vexatious that I fhall allow you but one woman at a time, either to praife, or love. If I difpute with you upon this point, I doubt every jury will give a verdict againft me. So, Sir, with a Mahometan indulgence, I allow you pluralities, the favourite privilege of our church.

I find you do not mend upon correction : again I tell you, you muft not think of women in a reafon-able way; you know we always make goddeffes of thofe we adore upon earth ; and do not all the good men tell us, we muft lay afide reafon in what relates to the Deity ?

It is well the poets are preparing fongs of joy ; it is well to lay in antidotes of foft rhyme, againft the rough profe they may chance to meet with at Weft-minfter. I fhould have been glad of any thing of Swift's : pray, when you write to him next, tell him I expect him with impatience, in a place as odd and as much out of the way as himfelf.

Yours.

LETTER XXXVII.

From the fame.

WHenever you apply as a good Papift to your female mediatrix, you are fure of fuccefs ; but there is not a full affurance of your entire fub-miffion to mother-church, and that abates a little of your authority. However, if you will accept of country-letters, fhe will correfpond from the hay-cock, and I will write to you upon the fide of my wheelbarrow : furely fuch letters might efcape exa-mination.

* Barclay's apology for the Quakers.

Your

Your idea of the golden age is, that every fhep-herd might pipe where he pleafed. As I have lived longer, I am more moderate in my wifhes, and would be content with the liberty of not piping where I am not pleafed.

Oh how I wifh, to myfelf and my friends, a free-dom which Fate feldom allows, and which we often refufe ourfelves! why is our fhepherdefs * in volun-tary flavery? why muft our Dean fubmit to the co-lour of his coat, and live abfent from us? and why are you confined to what you cannot relieve?

I feldom venture to give accounts of my journeys beforehand, becaufe I take refolutions of going to London, and keep them no better than quarrelling lovers do theirs. But the devil will drive me thither about the middle of next month, and I will call up-on you to be fprinkled with holy water, before I enter the place of corruption.

Your, &c.

LETTER XXXVIII.

From the fame.

1732.

I AM under the greateft impatience to fee Dr Swift at Bevis-Mount, and muft fignify my mind to him by another hand, it not being permit-ted me to hold correfpondence with the faid dean, for no letter of mine can come to his hands.

And whereas it is apparent, in this Proteftant land, moft efpecially under the care of divine provi-dence, that nothing can fucceed or come to a happy iffue but by bribery; therefore let me know what he expects to comply with my defires, and it fhall be remitted unto him.

For though I would not corrupt any man for the whole world, yet a benevolence may be given with-out any offence to confcience; every one muft con-

* Mrs H.

fefs,

fefs, that gratification and corruption are two diſtinct terms; nay at worſt many good men hold, that, for a good end, ſome very naughty meaſures may be made uſe of.

But, Sir, I muſt give you ſome good news in re-lation to myſelf, becauſe, I know, you wiſh me well; I am cured of ſome diſeaſes in my old age, which tormented me very much in my youth.

I was poſſeſſed with violent and uneaſy paſſions, ſuch as a peeviſh concern for truth *, and a ſaucy love for my country.

When a Chriſtian prieſt preached againſt the ſpirit of the goſpel, when an Engliſh judge determined againſt Magna Charta, when the miniſter acted againſt common ſenſe, I uſed to fret.

Now, Sir, let what will happen, I keep myſelf in temper: as I have no flattering hopes, ſo I baniſh all uſeleſs fears; but as to the things of this world, I find myſelf in a condition beyond expectation; it being evident from a late parliamentary inquiry, that I have as much ready money, as much in the funds, and as great a perſonal eſtate, as Sir Robert S-tt-n.

If the tranſlator of Homer find fault with this unheroic diſpoſition, or (what I more fear) if the Draper of Ireland accuſe the Engliſhman of want of ſpirit: I ſilence you both with one line out of your own Horace. *Quid te exempta juvat ſpinis e pluribus una?* For I take the whole to be ſo corrupted, that a cure in any part would be of little avail.

Your, &c.

LETTER XXXIX.

Dr SWIFT *to the Earl of* PETERBOROW.

MY LORD,

I Never knew or heard of any perſon ſo volatile, and ſo fixed as your Lordſhip: you, while your

---

* As may be ſeen from his tranſactions with Fenwick in the year 1696-7.

imagination

imagination is carrying you through every corner of
the world, where you have or have not been, can at
the fame time remember to do offices of favour and
kindnefs to the meaneft of your friends ; and in all
the fcenes you have paffed, have not been able to
attain that one quality peculiar to a great man, of
forgetting every thing but injuries. Of this I am
a living witnefs againft you ; for being the moft in-
fignificant of all your old humble fervants, you
were fo cruel as never to give me time to afk a favour, but prevented me in doing whatever you
thought I defired, or could be for my credit or advantage.

I have often admired at the capricioufnefs of fortune in regard to your Lordfhip. She hath forced
courts to act againft their oldeft, and moft conftant
maxims ; to make you a general becaufe you had
courage and conduct; an ambaffador, becaufe you
had wifdom and knowledge in the interefts of Europe ; and an admiral on account of your fkill in ma-
ritime affairs : whereas, according to the ufual method of court-proceedings, I fhould have been at
the head of the army, and you of the church, or rather a curate under the Dean of St Patrick's.

The Archbifhop of Dublin laments that he did
not fee your Lordfhip till he was juft upon the point
of leaving the Bath : I pray God you may have
found fuccefs in that journey, elfe I fhall continue to
think there is a fatality in all your Lordfhip's undertakings, which only terminate in your own honour,
and the good of the public, without the leaft advantage to your health or fortune.

I remember Lord Oxford's miniftry ufed to tell me,
that not knowing where to write to you, they were
forced to write at you. It is fo with me ; for you
are in one thing an evangelical man, that you know
not where to lay your head, and, I think, you have
no houfe. Pray, my Lord, write to me, that I may
have the pleafure, in this fcoundrel-country, of going
about

about, and fhewing my depending parfons a letter
from the Earl of Peterborow,

I am, &c.

LETTER XL.

To * * * * †.

Sept. 13.

I Believe you are by this time immerfed in your
vaft wood ; and one may addrefs to you as to a
very abftracted perfon, like Alexander Selkirk, or
the felf-taught philofopher ‡. I fhould be very curious to know what fort of contemplations employ
you. I remember the latter of thofe I mentioned,
gave himfelf up to a devout exercife of making his
head giddy with various circumrotations, to imitate
the motions of the celeftial bodies. I do not think it
at all impoffible that Mr L * * may be far advanced
in that exercife, by frequent turns towards the feveral
afpects of the heavens, to which you may have been
pleafed to direct him in fearch of profpects and new
avenues. He will be tractable in time, as birds are
tamed by being whirled about; and doubtlefs come
not to defpife the meaneft fhrubs or coppice-wood,
though naturally he feems more inclined to admire
God, in his greater works, the tall timber : for, as
Virgil has it, *Non omnes arbufta juvant, humilefque
myricæ*. I wifh myfelf with you both, whether you
are in peace or at war, in violent argumentation
or fmooth confent, over Gazettes in the morning,
or over plans in the evening. In that laft article,
I am of opinion, your Lordfhip has a lofs of me;
for generally after the debate of a whole day we ac-
quiefced at night in the beft conclufion of which human reafon feems capable in all great matters, to
fall faft a fleep ! And fo we ended, unlefs immediate

† Lord Bathurft.
‡ The title of an Arabic treatife of the life of Hai Ebn
Yocktan.

revelation (which ever muſt overcome human reaſon) ſuggeſted ſome new lights to us, by a viſion in bed. But laying aſide theory, I am told, you are going directly to practice. Alas, what a fall will that be? A new building is like a new church; when once it is ſet up, you muſt maintain it in all the forms, and with all the inconveniencies; then ceaſe the pleaſant luminous days of inſpiration, and there is an end of miracles at once!

That this letter may be all of a piece, I will fill the reſt with an account of a conſultation lately held in my neighbourhood about deſigning a princely garden. Several critics were of ſeveral opinions: one declared he would not have too much art in it; for my notion (ſaid he) of gardening is, that it is only ſweeping nature *: another told them that gravel walks were not of a good taſte, for all the fineſt abroad were of looſe ſand: a third adviſed peremptorily there ſhould not be one lime-tree in the whole plantation: a fourth made the ſame excluſive clauſe extend to horſe-cheſnuts, which he affirmed not to be trees, but weeds: Dutch elms were condemned by a fifth; and thus about half the trees were proſcribed, contrary to the paradiſe of God's own planting, which is expreſsly ſaid to be planted with *all trees.* There were ſome who could not bear ever-greens, and called them never-greens; ſome, who were angry at them only when cut into ſhapes, and gave the modern gardeners the name of ever-green tailors; ſome, who had no diſlike to cones and cubes, but would have them cut in foreſt-trees; and ſome who were in a paſſion againſt any thing in ſhape, even againſt clipt-hedges, which they called green walls. Theſe (my Lord) are our men of taſte, who pretend to prove it by taſting little or nothing. Sure ſuch a taſte is like ſuch a ſtomach, not a good one, but a weak one. We have the ſame ſort of critics in poetry; one is fond of nothing but

* An expreſſion of Sir T. H.

heroics,

heroics, another cannot relish tragedies, another hates paftorals, all little wits delight in epigrams. Will you give me leave to add, there are the fame in divinity; where many leading critics are for rooting up more than they plant, and would leave the Lord's vineyard either very thinly furnished, or very oddly trimmed.

I have lately been with my Lord * * who is a zealous, yet a charitable planter, and has fo bad a tafte, as to like all that is good. He has a difpofition to wait on you in his way to the Bath, and, if he can go and return to London in eight or ten days, I am not without a hope of feeing your Lordship with the delight I always fee you. Every where I think of you, and every where I wifh for you.

I am, &c.

LETTER XLI.

To Mr C———

Sept. 2. 1732.

I Affure you I am glad of your letter, and have long wanted nothing but the permiffion you now give me, to be plain and unreferved upon this head. I wrote to you concerning it long fince; but a friend of yours and mine was of opinion, it was taking too much upon me, and more than I could be entitled to by the mere merit of long acquaintance, and goodwill. I have not a thing in my heart relating to any friend, which I would not, in my own nature, declare to all mankind. The truth is what you guefs; I could not efteem your conduct to an object of mifery fo near you as Mrs ———, and I have often hinted it to yourfelf. The truth is, I cannot yet efteem it for any reafon I am able to fee. But this I promife, I acquit you as far as your own mind acquits you. I have now no further caufe of complaint, for the unhappy lady gives me now no farther pain ; fhe is no longer an object either of yours or my compaffion :

N 2.   the

the hardſhips done her are lodged in the hands of God, nor has any man more to do in them, except the perſons concerned in occaſioning them.

As for the interruption of our correſpondence, I am ſorry you ſeem to put the teſt of my friendſhip upon that, becauſe it is what I am diſqualified from toward my other acquaintance, with whom I cannot hold any frequent commerce. I will name you the obſtacles which I cannot ſurmount; want of health, want of time, want of good eyes, and one yet ſtronger than them all, I write not upon the terms of other men. For however glad I might be of expreſſing my reſpect, opening my mind, or venting my concerns, to my private friends, I hardly dare while there are Curlls in the world. If you pleaſe to reflect either on the impertinence of weak admirers, the malice of low enemies, the avarice of mercenary bookſellers, or the ſilly curioſity of people in general, you will confeſs I have ſmall reaſon to indulge correſpondencies; in which too I want materials, as I live altogether out of town, and have abſtracted my mind (I hope) to better things than common news. I wiſh my friends would ſend me back thoſe forfeitures of my diſcretion, commit to my juſtice what I truſted only to their indulgence, and return me at the year's end thoſe trifling letters, which can be to them but a day's amuſement, but to me may prove a diſcredit as laſting and extenſive as the aforeſaid weak admirers, mean enemies, mercenary ſcribblers, or curious ſimpletons, can make it.

I come now to a particular you complain of, my not anſwering your queſtion about ſome party-papers, and their authors. This indeed I could not tell you, becauſe I never was, or will be privy to ſuch papers: and if by accident, through my acquaintance with any of the writers, I had known a thing they concealed, I ſhould certainly never be the reporter of it.

For my waiting on you at your country-houſe, I have often wiſhed it; it was my compliance to a ſuperiour duty that hindered me, and one which you
are

are too good a Chriftian to wifh I fhould have broken, having never ventured to leave my mother (at
her great age) for more than a week, which is too
little for fuch a journey.

Upon the whole, I muft acquit myfelf of any act
or thought, in prejudice to the regard I owe you, as
fo long and obliging an acqnaintance and correfpondent. I am fure I have all the good wifhes for yourfelf and your family, that become a friend : there is
no accident that can happen to your advantage, and
no action that can redound to your credit, which I
fhould not be ready to extol, or to rejoice in. And
therefore I beg you to be affured, I am in difpofition
and will, though not fo much as I would be in teftimonies or writing, .

Yours, &c.

LETTER XLII.

To Mr RICHARDSON.

Jan. 13. 1732.

I Have at laft got my mother fo well, as to allow
myfelf to be abfent from her for three days. As
Sunday is one of them, I do not know whether I
may propofe to you to employ it in the manner you
mentioned to me once. Sir Godfrey called employing the pencil, the prayer of a painter ; and affirmed
it to be his proper way of ferving God, by the talent
he gave him. I am fure, in this inftance, it is ferving your friend ; and, you know, we are allowed to
do that (nay even to help a neighbour's ox or afs)
on the Sabbath ; which though it may feem a general precept, yet in one fenfe particularly applies to
you, who have helped many a human ox, and many
a human afs, to the likenefs of man, not to fay of
God.

Believe me, dear Sir, with all good wifhes for yourfelf and your family, (the happinefs of which ties I
N 3   know

know by experience, and have learned to value from the late danger of lofing the beft of mine),

Your, &c..

LETTER XLIII.

To the fame.

Twickenham, June 10. 1733.

AS I know you and I mutually defire to fee one another, I hoped that this day our wifhes would have met, and brought you hither. And this for the very reafon which poffibly might hinder your coming, that my poor mother is dead *: I thank God, her death was as eafy as her life was innocent; and as it coft her not a groan, or even a figh, there is yet upon her countenance fuch an expreffion of tranquillity, nay, almoft of pleafure, that it is even amiable to behold it. It would afford the fineft image of a faint expired, that ever painting drew; and it would be the greateft obligation which even that obliging art could ever beftow on a friend, if you could come and fketch it for me. I am fure, if there be no very prevalent obftacle, you will leave any common bufinefs to do this; and I hope to fee you this evening, as late as you will, or to-morrow morning as early, before this winter-flower is faded. I will defer her interment till to-morrow night. I know you love me, or I could not have written this— I could not (at this time) have written at all—Adieu! May you die as happily!

Your, &c.

LETTER XLIV.

To the fame.

IT is hardly poffible to tell you the joy your pencil gave me, in giving me another friend, fo much

* Mrs Pope died the 7th of June 1733, aged 93.

the

the fame ! and which (alas for mortality !) will outlaſt
the other. Poſterity will, through your means, ſee
the man whom it will for ages honour *, vindicate,
and applaud, when envy is no more, and when (as I
have already ſaid in the Eſſay to which you are ſo
partial)

The ſons ſhall bluſh their fathers were his foes.

That Eſſay has many faults, but the poem you ſent
me has but one, and that I can eaſily forgive. Yet
I would not have it printed for the world, and yet I
would not have it kept unprinted neither—but all in
good time. I am glad you publiſh your Milton.
B—ly will be angry at you, and at me too ſhortly,
for what I could not help, a ſatirical poem on verbal
criticiſm, by Mr Mallet, which he has inſcribed to
me, but the poem itſelf is good (another cauſe of anger to any critic). As for myſelf, I reſolve to go on
in my quiet, calm, moral courſe, taking no ſort of
notice of man's anger, or woman's ſcandal, with
virtue in my eyes, and truth upon my tongue.
Adieu.

LETTER XLV.

To Mr BETHEL.

Aug. 9. 1733.

YOU might well think me negligent or forgetful
of you, if true friendſhip and ſincere eſteem
were to be meaſured by common forms and compliments. The truth is, I could not write then, without ſaying ſomething of my own condition, and of
my loſs of ſo old and ſo deſerving a parent, which
really would have troubled you ; or I muſt have kept
a ſilence upon that head, which would not have ſuited that freedom and ſincere opening of the heart
which is due to you from me. I am now pretty
well, but my home is uneaſy to me ſtill, and I am

* Lord Bolingbroke.

therefore

therefore wandering about all this fummer. I was
but four days at Twickenham fince the occafion that
made it fo melancholy. I have been a fortnight in
Effex, and am now at Dawley (whofe mafter is your
fervant), and going to Cirencefter to Lord Bathurft.
I fhall alfo fee Southampton with Lord Peterborow.
The court and Twit'nam I fhall forfake together. I
wifh I did not leave our friend *, who deferves more
quiet, and more health. and happinefs, than can be
found in fuch a family. The reft of my acquaintance are tolerably happy in their various ways of life,
whether court, country, or town ; and Mr Cleland
is as well in the park as if he were in Paradife. I
heartily hope Yorkfhire is the fame to you ; and that
no evil, moral or phyfical, may come near you.

I have now but too much melancholy leifure, and
no other care but to finifh my Effay on Man. There
will be in it one line that may offend you, (I fear),
and yet I will not alter or omit it, unlefs you come
to town and prevent me before I print it, which will
be in a fortnight in all probability. In plain truth,
I will not deny myfelf the greateft pleafure I am capable of receiving, becaufe another may have the modefty not to fhare it. It is all a poor poet can do, to
bear teftimony to the virtue he cannot reach : befides, that, in this age, I fee too few good examples, not to lay hold on any I can find. You fee,
what an interefted man I am. Adieu.

L E T T E R XLVI.

To ————†

Sept. 7. 1733.

YOU cannot think how melancholy this place
makes me; every part of this wood puts into
my mind poor Mr Gay, with whom I paffed once a
great deal of pleafant time in it, and another friend
who is near dead, and quite loft to us, Dr Swift. I

* Mrs B.   † Mrs E.

really

really can find no enjoyment in the place; the fame
fort of uneafinefs as I find at Twit'nam, whenever
I pafs near my mother's room.

I have not yet writ to Mrs **. I think I fhould,
but have nothing to fay that will anfwer the character they confider me in, as a wit; befides, my eyes
grow very bad, (whatever is the caufe of it), I will
put them out for no body but a friend; and, I proteft, it brings tears into them almoft to write to you,
when I think of your ftate and mine. I long to write
to Swift, but cannot. The greateft pain I know, is
to fay things fo very fhort of one's meaning, when
the heart is full.

I feel the going out of life faft enough, to have
little appetite left to make compliments, at beft ufelefs, and for the moft part unfelt fpeeches. It is but
in a very narrow circle that Friendfhip walks in this
world, and I care not to tread out of it more than I
needs muft; knowing well, it is but to two or three
(if quite fo many) that any man's welfare or memory·
can be of confequence: the reft, I believe, I may·
forget, and be pretty certain they are already even,
if not beforehand with me.

Life, after the firft warm heats are over, is all
down-hill: and one almoft wifhes the journey's end,
provided we were fure but to lie down eafy, whenever the night fhall overtake us.

I dreamed all laft night of —— She has dwelt (a
little more than perhaps is right) upon my fpirits: I
faw a very deferving gentleman in my travels, who
has formerly, I have heard, had much the fame mif-
fortune; and (with all his good breeding and fenfe)
ftill bears a cloud and melancholy caft, that never
can quite clear up, in all his behaviour and converfation. I know another, who, I believe, could promife, and eafily keep his word, never to laugh in his
life. But one muft do one's beft, not to be ufed by
the world as that poor lady was by her fifter, and
not feem too good, for fear of being thought affected,
or whimfical.

It

It is a real truth, that to the laſt of my moments,. the thought of you, and the beſt of my wiſhes for you, will attend you, told or untold : I could wiſh you had once the conſtancy and reſolution to act for yourſelf, whether before or after I leave you, (the only way I ever ſhall leave you), you muſt determine; but reflect, that the firſt would make me, as well as yourſelf, happier ; the latter could make you only ſo. Adieu.

L E T T E R   XLVII.

From Dr A R B U T H N O T.

Hampſtead, July 17. 1734..

I Little doubt of your kind concern for me, nor of that of the lady you mention. I have nothing to repay my friends with at preſent, but prayers and good wiſhes. I have the ſatisfaction to find that I. am as officiouſly ſerved by my friends, as he that has thouſands to leave in legacies ; beſides the aſſurance of their ſincerity. God almighty has made my bo· dily diſtreſs as eaſy as a thing of that nature can be.. I have found ſome relief, at leaſt ſometimes, from the air of this place. My nights are bad, but many poor creatures have worſe.

As for you, my good friend, I think ſince our. firſt acquaintance there have not been any of thoſe little ſuſpicions or jealouſies, that often affect the ſincereſt friendſhips : I am ſure, not on my ſide. I muſt be ſo ſincere as to own, that though I could not help valuing you for thoſe talents which the world prizes, yet they were not the foundation of my friendſhips ;. they were quite of another ſort ; nor ſhall I at preſent offend you by enumerating them : and I make it my laſt requeſt, that you will continue that noble diſdain and abhorrence of vice which you ſeem naturally endued with ; but ſtill with a due regard to your own ſafety ; and ſtudy more to reform than chaſtiſe, though the one cannot be effected without the other..

Lord·

Lord Bathurſt I have always honoured, for every good quality that a perſon of his rank ought to have : pray, give my reſpects and kindeſt wiſhes to the family. My veniſon-ſtomach is gone, but I have thoſe about me, and often with me, who will be very glad of his preſent. If it is left at my houſe, it will be tranſmitted ſafe to me.

A recovery in my caſe, and at my age, is impoſſible ; the kindeſt wiſh of my friends is Euthanaſia. Living or dying, I ſhall always be

Yours, &c.

LETTER XLVIII.

To Dr ARBUTHNOT.

July 26. 1734.

I Thank you for your letter, which has all thoſe genuine marks of a good mind by which I have ever diſtinguiſhed yours, and for which I have ſo long loved you. Our friendſhip has been conſtant ; becauſe it was grounded on good principles, and therefore not only uninterrupted by any diſtruſt, but by any vanity, much leſs any intereſt.

What you recommend to me with the ſolemnity of a laſt requeſt, ſhall have its due weight with me. That diſdain and indignation againſt vice, is (I thank God) the only diſdain and indignation I have : it is ſincere, and it will be a laſting one. But ſure it is as impoſſible to have a juſt abhorrence of vice, without hating the vitious, as to bear a true love for virtue, without loving the good. To reform and not to chaſtiſe, I am afraid, is impoſſible ; and that the beſt precepts, as well as the beſt laws, would prove of ſmall uſe, if there were no examples to enforce them. To attack vices in the abſtract, without touching perſons, may be ſafe fighting indeed, but it is fighting with ſhadows. General propoſitions are obſcure, miſty, and uncertain, compared with plain, full, and home examples : precepts only apply to

our

our reafon, which in moft men is but weak : exam--
ples are pictures, and ftrike the fenfes, nay, raife the
pallions, and call in thofe (the ftrongeft and moft general of all motives) to the aid of reformation. Every
vitious man makes the cafe his own, and that is the
only way by which fuch men can be affected, much
lefs deterred. So that to chaftife is to reform. The
only fign by which I found my writings ever did any
good,. or had any weight,. has been that they raifed
the anger of bad men. And my greateft comfort,
and encouragement to proceed, has been to fee, that
thofe who have no fhame, and no fear of any thing
elfe, have appeared touched by my fatires.

As to your kind concern for my fafety, I can guefs
what occafions it at this time. Some characters * I
have drawn are fuch, that if there be any who deferve them, it is evidently a fervice to mankind to
point thofe men out; yet fuch as, if all the world
gave them, none, I think, will own they take to
themfelves. But if they fhould, thofe of whom all
the world think in fuch a manner, muft be men I
cannot fear. Such in particular as have the meannefs to do mifchiefs in the dark, have feldom the
courage to juftify them in the face of day ; the talents that make a cheat or a whifperer, are not the
fame that qualify a man for an infulter ; and as to
private villany, it is not fo fafe to join in an aflafli-
nation, as in a libel †. I will confult my fafety fo
far as I think becomes a prudent man ; but not fo
far as to omit any thing which I think becomes an
honeft one. As to perfonal attacks beyond the law,
every man is liable to them : as for danger within
the law, I am not guilty enough to fear any. For
the good opinion of all the world, I know, it is not
to be had : for that of worthy men, I hope, I fhall
not forfeit it: for that of the great, or thofe in
power, I may wifh I had it; but if, through mifre-

* The character of Sporus in the epiftle to Dr Arbuthnot,
vol. 2.
† See the following letter to a Noble Lord.

prefentations

reprefentations (too common about perfons in that flation) I have it not, I fhall be forry, but not miferable in the want of it.

It is certain, much freer fatirifts than I have enjoyed the encouragement and protection of the princes under whom they lived. Auguftus and Mæcenas made Horace their companion, though he had been in arms on the fide of Brutus : and, allow me to remark, it was out of the fuffering party too, that they favoured and diftinguifhed Virgil. You will not fufpect me of comparing myfelf with Virgil and Horace, nor even with another court-favourite, Boileau *. I have always been too modeft to imagine my panegyrics were incenfe worthy of a court ; and that, I hope, will be thought the true reafon why I have never offered any. I would only have obferved, that it was under the greateft princes and beft minifters, that moral fatirifts were moft encouraged ; and that then poets exercifed the fame jurifdiction over the follies, as hiftorians did over the vices of men. It may alfo be worth confidering, whether Auguftus himfelf makes the greater figure, in the writings of the former, or of the latter? and whether Nero and Domitian do not appear as ridiculous for their falfe tafte and affectation, in Perfius and Juvenal, as odious for their bad government in Tacitus and Suetonius ? In the firft of thefe reigns it was, that Horace was protected and careffed ; and in the latter that Lucan was put to death, and Juvenal banifhed.

I would not have faid fo much, but to fhew you my whole heart on this fubject; and to convince you, I am deliberately bent to perform that requeft which you make your laft to me, and to perform it with temper, juftice, and refolution. As your approbation (being the teftimony of a found head and an honeft heart) does greatly confirm me herein, I wifh you may live to fee the effect it may hereafter

* See letter 104. to Mr Warburton,

.have upon me, in fomething more deferving of that
approbation. But if it be the will of God, (which,
.I know, will alfo be yours), that we muſt feparate,
I hope it will be better for you than it can be for me.
You are fitter to live, or to die, then any man I
know. Adieu, my dear friend ! and may God pre-
.ferve your life eafy, or make your death happy *.

[We find by letter xix. that the Duchefs of Buckinghamſhire would have had Mr Pope to draw her
hufband's character. But though he refufed this
.office, yet in his epiſtle *on the Charaƈters of Women,*
.thefe lines,

To heirs unknown defcends th' unguarded ſtore,
Or wanders, heav'n-directed, to the poor.
Vol. 2. ver. 149. 150.

are fuppofed to mark her out in fuch a manner as not
to be miſtaken for another ; and having faid of himfelf, that *he held a lie in profe and verfe to be the
fame :* all this together gave a handle to his enemies,
fince his death, to publiſh the following paper, (entitled, *The Charaƈter of Katharine,* &c.), as written
by him. To which (in vindication of the deceafed
poet) we have fubjoined a letter to a friend, that
will let the reader fully into the hiſtory of the
writing and *publication* of this extraordinary CHA-
RACTER.]

The C H A R A C T E R of KATHARINE
late Duchefs of Buckinghamſhire and Normanby.

By the late Mr POPE.

SHE was the daughter of James II. and of the
Countefs of Dorcheſter, who inherited the inte-

* This excellent perfon died Feb. 27. 1734-5.

grity

grity and virtue of her father with happier fortune.
She was married firſt to James Earl of Angleſey;
and ſecondly to John Sheffield Duke of Buckinghamſhire and Normanby; with the former ſhe exer-
ciſed the virtues of *patience* and *ſuffering*, as long as
there was any hopes of doing good by either; with
the latter all other *conjugal virtues*. The man of fineſt
ſenſe and ſharpeſt diſcernment, ſhe had the happineſs
to pleaſe; and in that found her only pleaſure.
When he died, it ſeemed as if his ſpirit was only
breathed into her, to fulfil what he had begun, to
perform what he had concerted, and to preſerve and
watch over what he had left, *his only ſon*; in the
care of whoſe health, the forming of whoſe mind,
and the improvement of whoſe fortune, ſhe acted
with the conduct and ſenſe of the father, ſoftened,
but not overcome, with the tenderneſs of the mother.
Her underſtanding was ſuch as muſt have made a
figure, had it been in a man; but the modeſty of her
ſex threw a veil over its luſtre, which neverthelefs
ſuppreſſed only the expreſſion, not the exertion of it;
for her ſenſe was not ſuperiour to her reſolution,
which, when once ſhe was in the right, preſerved
her from making it only a tranſition to the wrong,
the frequent weakneſs even of the beſt women. She
often followed wiſe counſel, but ſometimes went before it, always with ſucceſs. She was poſſeſſed of a
ſpirit, which aſſiſted her to get the better of thoſe
accidents which admitted of any redreſs, and enabled her to ſupport outwardly, with decency and
dignity, thoſe which admitted of none; yet melted
inwardly through almoſt her whole life, at a ſucceſ-
ſion of melancholy and affecting objects, the loſs of
all her children, the misfortunes of *relations and*
friends, public and private, and the death of thoſe
who were deareſt to her. Her heart was as compaſſionate as it was great: her affections warm even to
ſolicitude: her friendſhip not violent or jealous, but
rational and perſevering: her gratitude equal and
conſtant to the living; to the dead boundleſs and he-

roical. What perfon foever fhe found worthy of her
efteem, fhe would not give up for any power on
earth; and the greateft on earth whom fhe could not
efteem, obtained from her no farther tribute than decency. Her good-will was wholly directed by merit,
not by accident; not meafured by the regard they
profeffed for her own defert, but by her idea of
theirs: and as there was no merit which fhe was not
able to imitate, there was none which fhe could envy: therefore her converfation was as free from detraction, as her opinions from prejudice or prepoffef-
fion. As her thoughts were her own, fo were her
words; and fhe was as fincere in uttering her
judgment, as impartial in forming it. She was a
fafe companion, many were ferved, none ever fuffered by her acquaintance: inoffenfive, when unpro-
voked; when provoked, not ftupid: but the moment her enemy ceafed to be hurtful, fhe could ceafe
to act as an enemy. She was therefore not a bitter,
but confiftent enemy: (though indeed, when forced
to be fo, the more a finifhed one for having been
long a-making.) And her proceeding with ill people was more in a calm and fteady courfe, like Juftice, than in quick and paffionate onfets, like Revenge. As for thofe of whom fhe only thought ill,
fhe confidered them not fo much as once to wifh them
ill; of fuch, her contempt was great enough to put
a ftop to all other other paffions that could hurt them.
Her love and averfion, her gratitude and refentment,
her efteem and neglect were equally open and ftrong;
and alterable only from the alteration of the perfons
who created them. Her mind was too noble to be
infincere, and her heart too honeft to ftand in need of
it; fo that fhe never found caufe to repent her conduct either to a friend or an enemy. There remains
only to fpeak of her perfon, which was moft amia-
bly majeftic, the niceft eye could find no fault in the
outward lineaments of her face or proportion of her
body; it was fuch, as pleafed where-ever fhe had a
defire it fhould; yet fhe never envied that of any
other,

other, which might better pleafe in general : in the
fame manner, as being content that her merits were
efteemed where fhe defired they fhould, fhe never
depretiated thofe of any other that were efteemed
or preferred elfewhere. For fhe aimed not at a general love or a general efteem where fhe was not
known ; it was enough to be poffeffed of both
where-ever fhe was. Having lived to the age of
fixty-two years ; not courting regard, but receiving
it from all who knew her ; not loving bufinefs; but
difcharging it fully wherefoever duty or friendfhip
engaged her in it; not following greatnefs, but not
declining to pay refpect; as far as was due from independency and difintereft ; having honourably ab-
folved all the parts of life, fhe forfook this world,
where fhe had left no act of duty or virtue undone,
for that where alone fuch acts are rewarded, on the
13th day of March 1742-3 *:

Mr. POPE *to* JAMES MOYSER, *of Beverly,*
Efq;

DEAR SIR,   *Bath,* *July* 11. 1743.

I AM always glad to hear of you; and where I can,
I always inquire of you. But why have you
omitted to tell me one word of your own health ?
The account of our friend's † is truly melancholy,
added to the circumftance of his being detained (I
fear, without much hope) in a foreign country,
from the comfort of feeing (what a good man moft
defires and beft deferves to fee to the laft hour) his
friends about him. The public news ‡ indeed give
every Englifhman a reafonable joy, and I truly feel
it with you, as a national joy, not a party one ;

---

* " The above character was written by Mr Pope foma
" years before her Grace's death." So the printed edition.
† Mr Bethel.
‡ The victory at Dettingen.

nay as a general joy to all nations where bloodshed
and misery must have been introduced, had the ambition and perfidy of —— prevailed.

I come now to answer your friend's question.
The whole of what he has heard of my writing
the character of the old Duke of Buckingham is untrue *. I do not remember ever to seen it in MS.
nor have I ever seen the pedigree he mentions other-
wise than after the Duchess had printed it with the
will, and sent one to me, as, I suppose, she did to
all her acquaintance. I do not wonder it should be
reported I writ that character, after a story which I
will tell you in your ear, and to yourself only.
There was another *character written of her Grace*
by herself, (with what help, I know not) ; but she
shewed it me in her blots, and pressed me, by all the
adjurations of friendship, to give her my sincere
opinion of it. I acted honestly, and did so. She seemed to take it patiently, and, upon many exceptions
which I made, engaged me to take the whole, and
to select out of it just as much as I judged might
stand, and return her the copy. I did so. Immediately she picked a quarrel with me, and we never saw each other in five or six years. In the mean
time, she shewed this character (as much as was ex-
tracted of it in my hand-writing) as a composition
of my own, in her praise. And very probably it is
now in the hands of Lord Hervey. Dear Sir, I sincerely wish you, and your whole family, (whose welfare is so closely connected), the best health and
truest happiness ; and am (as is also the master of
this place)

Your, &c.

* He says *the old Duke*, because he wrote a a very fine epitaph
for the son, vol. 2.

A

A LETTER, &c. 163

A LETTER * to a Noble Lord.

On occasion of some libels written and propagated at court, in the year 1732-3.

My Lord, Nov. 30. 1733.

YOur Lordship's † epistle has been published some days, but I had not the pleasure and pain of seeing it till yesterday : pain, to think your Lordship should attack me at all; pleasure, to find that you can attack me so weakly. As I want not the humility, to think myself in every way but one your inferiour, it seems but reasonable that I should take the only method either of self-defence or retaliation, that is left me, against a person of your quality and power. And as by your choice of this weapon, your pen, you generously (and modestly too, no doubt) meant to put yourself upon a level with me ; I will as soon believe that your Lordship would give a wound to a man unarmed, as that you would deny me the use of it in my own defence.

I presume you will allow me to take the same liberty, in my answer to so candid, polite, and ingenious a nobleman, which your Lordship took in yours,

* This letter (which was first printed in the year 1733) bears the same place in our author's prose that the epistle to Dr Arbuthnot does in his poetry. They are both apologetical, repelling the libellous slanders on his reputation : with this difference, that the epistle to Dr Arbuthnot, his friend, was chiefly directed against Grubstreet writers; and this letter to the Noble Lord, his enemy, against court-scribblers. For the rest, they are both master-pieces in their kinds; that in verse, more grave, moral, and sublime ; this in prose, more lively, critical, and pointed; but equally conducive to what he had most at heart, the vindication of his moral character : the only thing he thought worth his care in literary altercations; and the first thing he would expect from the good offices of a surviving friend.

† Entitled, An epistle to a Doctor of Divinity from a Nobleman at Hampton-court, Aug. 28. 1733, and printed the November following for J. Roberts. Fol.

to

to fo *grave*, *religious*, and *refpectable* a clergyman *: as you anfwered his *Latin* in *Englifh*, permit me to anfwer your *verfe* in *profe*. And though your Lord-fhip's realons for not writing in *Latin*, might be ftronger than mine for not writing in 'verfe, yet 'I may plead *two good* ones, for this conduct: the one, that I want the talent of fpinning *a thoufand lines in a* day †, (which, I think, is as much *time* as this fubject deferves); and the other, that I take your Lord-fhip's *verfe* to be as much *profe* as this letter. But no doubt it was your choice, in writing to a friend,' to renounce all the pomp of poetry, and give us this excellent model of the familiar.

When I confider the *great difference* betwixt the rank your *Lordfhip* holds in the *world*, and the rank which your *writings* are like to hold in the *learned world*, I prefume that diftinction of ftyle is but ne-ceffary, which you will fee obferved through this let-ter. When I fpeak of *you*, my Lord, it will be with all the deference due to the inequality which fortune has made between you and myfelf: but when I fpeak of your *writings*, my Lord, I muft, I can do nothing but trifle.

I fhould be obliged indeed to leffen this *refpect*, if all the nobility (and efpecially the elder brothers) are but fo many hereditary fools ‡, if the privilege of Lords be to want brains ||, if noblemen can hardly write or read ⊣, if all their bufinefs is but to drefs and vote ⊦⊦, and all their employment in court, to tell lies, flatter in public, flander in private, be falfe to each other, and follow nothing but felf-intereft =,'

Blefs

* Dr S.
† And *Pope* with juftice of fuch lines may fay,
His Lordfhip fpins a thoufand in a day. *Epift. p.* 6:
‡ That to good blood by old prefcriptive rules
Gives right hereditary to be fools.
|| Nor wonder that my brain no more affords,
But recollect the privilege of lords.
⊣ And when you fee me fairly write my name;
For *England*'s fake wifh all could do the fame.
⊦⊦ Whilft all our bus'nefs is to drefs and vote.
= Courts are only larger families,
The growth of each, few truths, and many lies

Blefs me, my Lord, what an account is this you give
of them? and what would have been faid of me, had
I immolated, in this manner, the whole body of the
nobility, at the ftall of a well-fed prebendary?
  Were it the mere *excefs* of your Lordfhip's *wit*,
that carried you thus triumphantly over all the bounds
of decency, I might confider your Lordfhip on your
Pegafus, as a fprightly hunter on a mettled horfe;
and while you were trampling down all our works,
patiently fuffer the injury, in pure admiration of the
noble fport. But fhould the cafe be quite otherwife,
fhould your Lordfhip be only like a *boy* that is *run a-
way with*; and run away with by a *very foal*; really common charity, as well as refpect for a noble family, would oblige me to ftop your career, and to
help you down from *this Pegafus*.
  Surely the little praife of a *writer* fhould be a
thing below your ambition: you, who were no fóon-
er born, but in the lap of the Graces; no fooner at
fchool, but in the arms of the Mufes; no fooner in
the world, but you practifed all the fkill of it; no
fooner in the court, but you poffeffed all the art of it!
Unrivalled as you are, in making a figure, and in making a fpeech, methinks, my Lord, you may well
give up the poor talent of turning a diftich. And
why this fondnefs for poetry? Profe admits of the
two excellencies you moft admire, diction and fiction:
it admits of the talents you chiefly poffefs, a moft
fertile invention, and moft florid expreffion; it is
with profe, nay the plaineft profe, that you beft
could teach our nobility to vote, which, you juftly
obferve, is half at leaft of their bufinefs * : and give
me leave to prophefy, it is to your talent in profe,
and not in verfe, to your fpeaking, not your writing,
to your art at court, not your art of poetry, that
your Lordfhip muft owe your future figure in the
world.

in private fatirize, in public flatter,
Few to each other, all to one point true;
Which one I fhan't, nor need explain. Adieu, *p. rh.*
* All their bus'nefs is to drefs, and vote.

My

My Lord, whatever you imagine, this is the advice of a friend, and one who remembers he formerly had the honour of some profession of friendship
from you : whatever was his *real share* in it, whether small or great, yet as your Lordship could never have had the least *loss* by continuing it, or the
least *interest* by withdrawing it ; the misfortune of
losing it, I fear, must have been owing to his own
deficiency or *neglect*. But as to any *actual fault* which
deserved to forfeit it in such a degree, he protests he
is to this day guiltless and ignorant. It could at
most be but a fault of *omission* ; but indeed by omis-
sions, men of your Lordship's uncommon merit may
sometimes think themselves so injured, as to be capable of an inclination to injure another ; who,
though very much below their quality, may be a-
bove the injury.

I never heard of the least displeasure you had conceived against me, till I was told that an imitation
I had made of * *Horace* had offended some persons,
and among them your Lordship. I could not have
apprehended that a few *general strokes* about a *Lord
scribbling carelesly* †, a *pimp*, or a *spy* at court, a *sharp-
er* in a gilded chariot, &c. that these, I say, should
be ever applied as they have been, by *any malice* but
that which is the greatest in the world, *the malice of
ill people to themselves.*

Your Lordship so well knows (and the whole court
and town through your means so well know) how
far the resentment was carried upon that imagination,
not only in the *nature* of the *libel* ‡ you propagated
against me, but in the extraordinary *manner*, *place*,
and presence in which it was propagated ‖ ; that I
shall

---

* The first satire of the second book, printed in 1732,
vol. 1.

† He should have added, thathe called this nobleman who
scribbled so carelesly, Lord *Fanny*.

‡ *Verses to the imitator of Horace*, afterwards printed by J. Roberts 1732. fol.

‖ It was for this reason that this letter, as soon as it was
printed, was communicated to the Q.

ſhall only ſay, it ſeemed to me to exceed the bounds of juſtice, common ſenſe, and decency.

I wonder yet more, how a *lady*, of great wit, beauty, and fame for her poetry, (between whom and your Lordſhip there is a *natural*, a *juſt*, and a *well-grounded eſteem)*, could be prevailed upon to take a part in that proceeding. Your reſentments againſt me indeed might be equal, as my offence to you both was the ſame; for neither had I the leaſt miſunder-ſtanding with that lady till after I was the *author* of my own misfortune in diſcontinuing her acquaint-ance. I may venture to own a truth, which cannot be unpleaſing to either of you I aſſure you my reaſon for ſo doing, was merely that you had both *too much wit* for me * ; and that I could not do, with *mine*, many things which you could with *yours*. The in-jury done you in withdrawing myſelf could be but ſmall, if the value you had for me was no greater than you have been pleaſed ſince to profeſs. But ſurely, my Lord, one may ſay, neither the revenge, nor the language you held, bore any *proportion* to the pretended offence : the appellations of † *fce* to *humankind*, an *enemy* like the *devil* to all that have *being* ; *ungrateful*, *unjuſt*, deſerving to be *whipt*, *blanketed*, *kicked*, nay *killed* ; a *monſter*, an *aſſaſſin*, whoſe converſation every man ought to *ſhun*, and a-gainſt whom *all doors* ſhould be ſhut ; I beſeech you, my Lord, had you the leaſt right to give, or to en-courage or juſtify any other in giving ſuch language as this to me ? Could I be treated in terms more ſtrong or more atrocious, if, during my acquaintance with you, I had been a *betrayer*, a *backbiter*, a *whi-ſperer*, an *eaves-dropper*, or an *informer ?* Did I in all that time ever throw *a falſe dye*, or palm *a foul card* upon you ? Did I ever *borrow*, *ſteal*, or accept, ei-

Once, and but once, his heedleſs youth was bit,
And lik'd that dang'rous thing, a female wit.
* See the letter to Dr Arbuthnot amongſt the variations, vol. 1.
† See the aforeſaid *Verſes to the imitator of Horace.*

ther

ther *money, wit*, or *advice* from you ? Had I ever the
honour to join with either of you in one *ballad, fatire, pamphlet*, or *epigram*, on any person *living* or
dead ? Did I ever do you fo great an *injury* as to put
off *my own verfes* for *yours*, efpecially on *thofe perfons* whom they might *moft offend*? I am confident
you cannot anfwer in the affirmative ; and I can truly affirm, that ever fince I loft the happinefs of your
converfation, I have not publifhed or written one
fyllable of, or to either of you ; never hitched your
names in a *verfe*, or trifled with your *good names in
company*. Can I be honeftly charged with any other
crime but an *emiffion* (for the word *neglect*, which I
ufed before, flipped my pen unguardedly) to continue
my admiration of you all my life, and ftill to contemplate, face to face, your many excellencies and
perfections ? I am perfuaded you can reproach me
truly with no great *faults*, except my *natural ones*,
which I am as ready to own, as to do all juftice to
the contrary *beauties* in you. It is true, my Lord, I
am fhort, not well fhaped, generally ill-dreffed, if
not fometimes dirty : your Lordfhip and Ladyfhip
are ftill in bloom ; your figures fuch, as rival the *A-
pollo* of *Belvedere*, and the *Venus* of *Medicis* ; and
your faces fo finifhed, that neither ficknefs or paffion can deprive them of *colour* ; I will allow your
own in particular to be the fineft that ever *man* was
bleffed with : preferve it, my Lord, and reflect, that
to be a critic, would coft it too many *frowns*, and
to be a ftatefman, too many *wrinkles!* I further
confefs, I am now fomewhat old ; but fo your Lordfhip and this excellent lady, with all your beauty,
will (I hope) one day be. I know your genius and
hers fo perfectly *tally*, that you cannot but join in
admiring each other, and by confequence in the contempt of all fuch as myfelf. You have both, in my
regard, been like — (your Lordfhip, I know, loves
a *fimile*, and it will be one fuitable to your *quality)*
you have been like *two princes*, and I like a *poor a-
nimal* facrificed between them to cement a lafting
                                                    league :

league: I hope I have not bled in vain; but that fuch an amity may endure for ever! For though it be what common *underſtandings* would hardly conceive, two *wits* however may be perſuaded, that it is in friendſhip as in enmity, The more *danger*, the more *honour*.

Give me the liberty, my Lord, to tell you, why I never replied to thoſe *verſes* on the *imitator* of *Horace?* They regarded nothing but my *figure*, wh.ch I ſet no value upon; and my *morals*, which, I knew, needed no defence: Any honeſt man has the pleaſure to be confcious, that it is out of the power of the *wittieſt*, nay the *greateſt perſon* in the kingdom, to leſſen him *that way*, but at the expenſe of his own *truth*, *honour*, or *juſtice*.

But though I declined to explain myſelf juſt at the time when I was fillily threatened, I ſhall now give your Lordſhip a frank account of the offence you imagined to be meant to you. *Fanny* (my Lord) is the plain Engliſh of *Fannius*, a real perſon, who was a fooliſh critic, and an enemy of *Horace:* perhaps a noble one, for ſo (if your Latin be gone in earneſt *) I muſt acquaint you, the word *Beatus* may be conſtrued.

> *Beatus Fannius! ultro*
> *Delatis capſis et* imagine.

This *Fannius* was, it ſeems, extremely fond both of his *poetry* and his *perſon*, which appears by the pictures and *ſtatues* he cauſed to be made of himſelf, and by his great diligence to propagate *bad verſes* at *court*, and get them admitted into the library of *Auguſtus*. He was moreover of a delicate or *effeminate complexion*, and conſtant at the aſſemblies and opera's of thoſe days, where he took it into his head to *ſlander poor Horace*.

> *Ineptus*
> Fannius, *Hermogenis* lædat *conviva Tigelli*.

* all I learn'd from Dr *Freind* at fchool,
Has quite deſerted this poor John Trot-head,
And left plain native Engliſh in its ſtead,   *Epiſt. p. 2.*

till it provoked him at laſt juſt to *name* him, give him a *laſh*, and ſend him whimpering to the *ladies*. :

Diſcipularum *inter jubeo plorare cathedras*. '

So much for *Fanny*, my Lord. The word *ſpins* (as Dr *Freind* or even Dr *Sherwin* could aſſure you) was the literal tranſlation of *deduci* ; a metaphor taken from a *ſilk-worm*, my Lord, to ſignify any *ſlight*, *ſilken*, (or as your Lordſhip and the Ladies call it) * *flimzy* piece of work. I preſume your Lordſhip has enough of this, to convince you there was nothing *perſonal* but to *that Fannius*, who (with all his fine accompliſhments) had never been heard of, but for *that Horace* he injured.

In regard to the Right Honourable Lady, your Lord-ſhip's friend, I was far from deſigning a perſon of her condition by a name ſo derogatory to her, as that of *Sappho* ; a name proſtituted to every infamous crea-ture that ever wrote verſe or novels. I proteſt I ne-ver *applied* that name to her in any verſe of mine, *public* or *private* ; and (I firmly believe) not in any *letter* or *converſation*. Whoever could invent a falſe-hood to ſupport an accuſation, I pity ; and whoever can believe ſuch a character to be theirs, I pity ſtill more. God forbid the court or town ſhould have the complaiſance to *join* in that opinion ! Certainly I meant it only of ſuch modern *Sappho's*, as imitate much more the *lewdneſs* than the *genius* of the an-cient one ; and upon whom their wretched brethren frequently beſtow both the *name* and the *qualifica-tion* there mentioned †.

There was another reaſon why I was ſilent as to that paper — I took it for a *lady*'s (on the printer's word in the title-page), and thought it too preſuming, as well as indecent, to contend with one of that *ſex* in *altercation* : for I never was ſo mean a creature as

---

* Weak texture of his *flimzy* brain. *p.* 6.
† From furious Sappho ſcarce a milder fate,
 Pox'd by her love, or libell'd by her hate.
                          1 Sat. b. ii. *Hor.*

to

to commit my anger againſt, a *lady to paper*, though but in a *private letter*. But ſoon after, her denial of it was brought to me by a noble perſon of *real honour* and *truth*. Your Lordſhip indeed ſaid you had it from a lady; and the lady ſaid it was your Lordſhip's; ſome thought the beautiful by-blow had *two fathers*, or (if one of them will hardly be allowed a man) *two mothers*; indeed I think *both ſexes* had a ſhare in it, but which was *uppermoſt*, I know not: I pretend not to determine the exact method of this *witty fornication:* and if I call it *yours*, my Lord, it is only becauſe, whoever *got* it, you *brought it forth*.

Here, my Lord, allow me to obſerve the different proceeding of the *ignoble poet*, and his *noble enemies.* What he has written of *Fanny*, *Adonis*, *Sappho*, or who you will, he owned he publiſhed, he ſet his name to: what they have *publiſhed* of him, they have denied to have *written*; and what they have *written* of him, they have denied to have *publiſhed*. One of theſe was the caſe in the paſt libel, and the other in the preſent. For though the parent has owned it to a few choice friends, it is ſuch as he has been obliged to deny in the moſt particular terms, to the great perſon whoſe opinion *concerned him moſt*.

Yet, my Lord, this epiſtle was a piece not written in *haſte*, or in a *paſſion*, but many months after all pretended provocation; when you was at *full leiſure* at Hampton-court, and I the object *ſingled*, like a *deer cut of ſeaſon*, for ſo ill-timed, and ill-placed a diverſion. It was a *deliberate* work, directed to a *reverend perſon* *, of the moſt *ſerious* and *ſacred* character, with whom you are known to cultivate a *ſtrict correſpondence*, and to whom it will not be doubted, but you open your *ſecret ſentiments*, and deliver your *real judgment* of men and things. This, I ſay, my Lord, with ſubmiſſion, could not but awaken all my *reflection* and *attention*. Your Lordſhip's opinion of me as a *poet*, I cannot help; it is

* Dr. S.

yours,

yours, my Lord, and that were enough to mortify
a poor man ; but it is not yours *alone*, you muſt be
content to ſnare it with the *gentlemen* of the *Dunciad*,
and (it may be) with many *more innocent* and *ingenious
men*. If your Lordſhip deſtroys my *poetical* character,
they will claim their part in the glory ; but, give me
leave to ſay, if my *moral* character be ruined, it muſt
be *wholly* the work of *your Lordſhip* ; and will be
hard even for you to do, unleſs I *myſelf co-operate*.

How can you talk (my moſt worthy Lord) of all
Pope's works as ſo many *libels*, affirm, that *he has
no invention* but in *defamation* *, and charge him
with *ſelling another man's labours printed with his
own name* † ? Fie, my Lord, you forget yourſelf.
He printed not his name before a line of the perſon's
you mention ; that perſon himſelf has told you and
all the world in the book itſelf, what part he had in
it, as may be ſeen at the concluſion of his notes to
the Odyſſey. I can only ſuppoſe your Lordſhip
(not having at that time *forgot your Greek)* deſpiſed
to look upon the *tranſlation* ; and ever ſince entertained too mean an opinion of the tranſlator to caſt
an eye upon it. Beſides, my Lord, when you ſaid
he *ſold* another man's works, you ought in juſtice to
have added that he *bought* them, which very much
alters the caſe... What he gave him was five hundred
pounds : his receipt can be produced to your Lordſhip : I dare not affirm he was as *well paid* as *ſome
writers* (much his inferiours) have been ſince ; but
your Lordſhip will reflect that I am no man of quality, either to *buy* or *ſell* ſcribbling ſo high : and that
I have neither *place, penſion*, nor *power* to reward
for *ſecret ſervices*. It cannot be, that one of your
rank can have the leaſt *envy* to ſuch an author as I :
but were that *poſſible*, it were much better gratified
by employing *not your own*, but ſome of *thoſe low
and ignoble pens* to do you this *mean office*. I dare en-

---

* to his eternal ſhame,
Prov'd he can ne'er invent but to defame..
† And ſold Broom's labours printed with Pope's name. *p*. 7.

gage

gage you will have them for lefs than I gave Mr
Broom, if your friends have not raifed the mar-
ket : let them drive the bargain for you, my Lord;
and you may depend on feeing, every day in the
week, as many (and now and then as pretty) verfes,
as thefe of your Lordfhip.

And would it not be full as well, that my poor
perfon fhould be abufed by them, as by one of your
rank and quality? Cannot *Curl* do the fame? nay
has he not done it before your Lordfhip, in the fame
kind of language, and almoft the *fame words?* I cannot but think the worthy and *difcreet clergyman*
himfelf will agree, it is *improper,* nay *unchriftian,* to
expofe the *perfonal* defects of our brother : that both
fuch perfect forms as yours, and fuch unfortunate
ones as mine, proceed from the hand of the fame
maker, who *fafhioneth his veffels* as he pleafeth, and
that it is not from their *fhape* we can tell whether
they are made for *honour* or *difhonour.* In a word,
he would teach you charity to your greateft enemies;
of which number, my Lord, I cannot be reckoned,
fince, though a poet, I was never your flatterer.

Next, my Lord, as to the *obfcurity* * *of my birth*
(a reflection copied alfo from Mr *Curl* and his brethren), I am forry to be obliged to fuch a prefump-
tion as to name my *family* in the fame leaf with
your Lordfhip's : but my father had the honour in
one inftance to refemble you, for he was a *younger
brother.* He did not indeed think it a happinefs to
bury his *elder brother,* though he had one, who wanted fome of thofe good qualities which *yours* poffeffed.
How fincerely glad could I be, to pay to that young
nobleman's memory the debt I owed to his friendfhip, whofe early death deprived your family of as
much *wit* and *honour* as he left behind him in
any branch of it. But as to my father, I could affure you, my Lord, that he was no mechanic (neither
a hatter, nor, which might pleafe your Lordfhip yet
better, a cobler), but in truth, of a very tolerable fa-

* Hard as thy heart, and as thy birth obfcure.

P 3
mily;

mily : and my mother of an ancient one, as well born and educated as that *lady* whom your Lordſhip made choice of to be the *mether of your own children*; whoſe merit, beauty, and vivacity (if tranſmitted to your poſterity) will be a *better preſent* than even the noble blood they derive *only* from *you*. A mother, on whom I was never obliged ſo far to reflect, as to ſay, ſhe *ſpoiled me* *. And a father, who never found himſelf obliged to ſay of me that he *diſapproved my conduct*. In a word, my Lord, I think it enough, that my parents, ſuch as they were, never coſt me a *bluſh*; and that their ſon, ſuch as he is, never coſt them a *tear*.

I have purpoſely omitted to conſider your Lordſhip's criticiſms on my *poetry*. As they are exactly the ſame with thoſe of the *forementioned authors*, I apprehend they would juſtly charge me with partiality, if I gave to *you* what belongs to *them* ; or paid more diſtinction to the *ſame things* when they are in your mouth, than when they were in theirs. It will be ſhewing both them and you (my Lord) a *more particular reſpect*, to obſerve how much they are honoured by *your imitation of them*, which indeed is carried through your whole epiſtle. I have read ſomewhere at *ſchool* (though I make it no *vanity* to have forgot where) that *Tully* naturalized a few phraſes at the inſtance of ſome of his friends. Your Lordſhip has done more in honour of theſe gentlemen ; you have authoriſed not only their *aſſertions*, but their *ſtyle*. For example, *A* flow *that* wants ſkill *to reſtrain its* ardour,—*a* dictionary *that gives us nothing at* its own expenſe,—*As luxuriant branches* bear *but little fruit, ſo wit unpruned* is *but raw fruit* —*While you* rehearſe ignorance, *you ſtill* know enough *to do it in verſe*—*Wits* are *but glittering* ignorance.—The *account of* how *we paſs our time*— and, *the weight on Sir R. W*—'*s* brain. *You can* ever *receive from* no *head more than ſuch a head* (as

---

* A noble father's heir ſpoil'd by his mother.
    His Lordſhip's account of himſelf. **p. 7.**

no head) *has to give :* Your Lordſhip would have
ſaid *never* receive inſtead of *ever*, and *any head* inſtead of *no head :* but all this is perfectly new, and
has greatly enriched our language.

You are merry, my Lord, when you ſay *Latin*
and *Greek*

Have quite deſerted your poor John Trot-head,
And left plain native Engliſh in their ſtead.

for (to do you juſtice) this is nothing leſs than *plain
Engliſh.* And as for your *John Trot-head,* I cannot
conceive why you ſhould give it that name ; for by
ſome papers * I have ſeen ſigned with that name, it is
certainly a head *very different* from your Lordſhip's.

Your Lordſhip ſeems determined to fall out with
every thing you have learned at ſchool : you complain next of a *dull dictionary,*

*That gives us nothing at its own expenſe,
But a few modern words for ancient ſenſe.*

Your Lordſhip is the firſt man that ever carried the
love of wit ſo far, as to expect a *witty dictionary.* A
dictionary that gives us *any thing but words,* muſt
not only be an *expenſive,* but a very *extravagant dictionary* †. But what does your Lordſhip mean by its
giving us but *a few modern words* for *ancient ſenſe ?*
If by *ſenſe* (as I ſuſpect) you mean *words (a miſtake
not unuſual),* I muſt do the dictionary the juſtice to
ſay, that it gives us *juſt as many modern words as
ancient ones.* Indeed, my Lord, you have more
need to complain of a bad grammar, than of a dull
dictionary.

Doctor Freind, I dare anſwer for him, never
taught you to talk

* See ſome treatiſes printed in the appendix to the Craftſman,
about that time.

† Yet we have ſeen many of theſe *extravagant* dictionaries,
and are likely to ſee many more, in an age ſo abounding in
ſcience, that the ordinary vehicles of it prove inſufficient to diftribute it abroad.

of

of Sapphic, Lyric, and Iambic odes.

Your Lordſhip might as well bid your preſent tutor, your tailor, make you a *coat, ſuit of cloaths,* and *breeches* ; for you muſt have forgot your logic, as well as grammar, not to know, that Sapphic and Iambic are both included in Lyric ; that being the *genus,* and thoſe the *ſpecies.*

> *For all cannot invent who can* tranſlate,
> *No more than thoſe who* clothe *us, can* create.

Here your Lordſhip ſeems in labour for a meaning. Is it that you would have tranſlations, *originals?* for it is the common opinion, that the *buſineſs* of a tranſlator is to *tranſlate,* and not to *invent,* and of a tailor to *clothe,* and not to *create.* But why ſhould you, my Lord, of all mankind, abuſe a tailor ? not to ſay *blaspheme* him ; if he can (as ſome think) at leaſt go halves with God almighty in the formation of a *beau.* Might not Dr Sherwin rebuke you for this, and bid you *remember your* Creator *in the days of your youth?*

From a *tailor,* your Lordſhip proceeds (by a beautiful gradation) to a *ſilkman.*

> *Thus P—pe we find*
> *The gaudy* Hinchcliff *of a beauteous mind.*

Here too is ſome ambiguity. Does your Lordſhip uſe *Hinchcliff* as a *proper name?* or as the ladies ſay a *hinchcliff* or a *colmar,* for a *ſilk* or a *fan?* I will venture to affirm, no critic can have a perfect taſte of your Lordſhip's works, who does not underſtand both your *male phraſe* and your *female phraſe.*

Your Lordſhip, to finiſh your climax, advances up to a *hatter* ; a mechanic, whoſe employment, you inform us, is not (as was generally imagined) to *cover people's heads,* but to *dreſs their brains*.* A moſt uſeful mechanic indeed ! I cannot help wiſhing

---

* For this mechanic's, like the hatter's pains,
Are but for dreſſing other people's brains.

to have been one, for fome people's fake.—But this too may be only another *lady-phrafe :* Your Lordfhip and the ladies may take a *head-drefs* for a *head,* and underfland, that to *adorn the head* is the fame thing as to *drefs the brains.*

Upon the whole, I may thank your Lordfhip for this high panegyric: for if I have but *dreſſed* up *Homer,* as your *tailor,* *filkman,* and *hatter* have *equipped your Lordfhip,* I muft be owned to have dreffed him *marvellouſly indeed,* and no wonder if he is *admired by the ladies* *.

After all, my Lord, I really wifh you would learn your *grammar.* What if you put yourfelf a while under the tuition of your friend *W——m?* May not I with all refpect fay to you, what was faid to *another noble poet* by Mr Cowley, *Pray, Mr* Howard †, *if you did read your* grammar, *what harm would it do you?* You yourfelf wifh all Lords would *learn to write* ‡; though I do not fee of what ufe it could be, if their whole bufinefs is to *give their votes* ||; it could only be ferviceable *in figning their protefts.* Yet furely this fmall portion of learning might be indulged to your Lordfhip, without any breach of that *privilege* ‡ you fo generoufly affert to all thofe of your rank, or too great an infringement of that *right.* ✝ which you claim as *hereditary,* and for which, no doubt, your noble father will thank you. Surely, my Lord, no man was ever fo bent upon depretiating himfelf!

All your readers have obferved the following lines :

* By girls admir'd. *p.* 6.
† The Honourable Mr Edward Howard, celebrated for his poetry.
‡ And when you fee me fairly write my name,
For England's fake wifh all Lords did the fame,.
|| —All our bufinefs is to drefs and vote. *p.* 4.
‡ The want of brains. *ib.*
✝ To be fools. *ib.*

Horw

How oft we hear some witling pert and dull,-
By fashion coxcomb, and by nature fool,
With hackney maxims, in dogmatic strain,
Scoffing religion and the marriage-chain ?
Then from his common-place-book he repeats,
The lawyers all are rogues, and parsons cheats,
That vice and virtue's nothing but a jest,
And all morality deceit well drest ;
That life itself is like a wrangling game, &c.

The whole town and court (my good Lord) have
heard *this witling*; who is so much every body's acquaintance but his own, that I will engage *they all*
name the *same person.* But to hear *you* say that this
is only— *of whipt cream* a *frothy store,* is a sufficient
proof, that never mortal was endued with so humble
an opinion both of himself and his own wit, as your
Lordship : for, I do assure you, these are by much
the best verses in your whole poem.

How unhappy is it for me, that a person of your
Lordship's *modesty* and *virtue,* who manifests so tender a regard to *religion, matrimony,* and *morality*;.
who, though an ornament to the court; cultivate an
exemplary correspondence with the *clergy* ; nay, who
disdain not charitably to converse with, and even assist,
some of the very worst of writers ; (so far as to cast
a few *conceits,* or drop a few *antitheses* even among
the *dear joys* of the *Courant)* ; that you, I say, should
look upon me alone as reprobate and unamendable !
Reflect what *I was,* and what *I am.* I am even
annihilated by your anger : for in these verses you
have robbed me of *all power to think* [*], and, in your
others, of the very *name* of a *man !* Nay, to shew
that this is wholly your own doing, you have told us
that before I wrote my *last epistles,* (that is, before I
unluckily mentioned *Fanny* and *Adonis,* whom, I
protest, I knew not to be your Lordship's relations),
I might have lived and died in glory [†].

[*] *R—r,* who ne'er could think. *p.* 7.
[†] In glory then he might have liv'd and dy'd. *ib.*

What

What would I not do to be well with your Lordfhip ? Though, you obferve, I am a mere *imitator*
of *Homer, Horace, Boileau, Garth,* &c. (which I
have the lefs caufe to be afhamed of, fince they were
imitators of one another), yet what if I fhould folemnly engage never to imitate *your* Lordfhip ? May it
not be one ftep towards an accommodation, that
while you remark my *ignorance in Greek,* you are fo
good as to fay, you have *forgot your own.?* What if
I fhould confefs I tranflated from *D'Acier ?* That
furely could not but oblige your Lordfhip, who are
known to prefer *French* to all the learned languages.
But allowing that in the fpace of *twelve years* acquaintance with *Homer,* I might unhappily contract
as much *Greek,* as your Lordfhip did in *two* at the
univerfity, why may I not forget it again, as happily ?

Till fuch a reconciliation take effect, I have but
one thing to entreat of your Lordfhip. It is, that
you will not decide of my *principles* on the fame
grounds as you have done of my *learning :* nor give
the fame account of my *want of grace,* after you
have loft all acquaintance with my *perfon,* as you do
of my *want of Greek,* after you have confeffedly loft
all acquaintance with the *language.* You are too
generous, my Lord, to follow the *gentlemen* of the
Dunciad quite fo far, as to feek my *utter perdition ;*
as *Nero* once did *Lucan*'s, merely for prefuming to
be a *poet,* while one of fo much greater quality was
a *writer.* I therefore make this humble requeft to
your Lordfhip, that the next time you pleafe *to write
of me, fpeak of me,* or even *whifper of me* *, you will
recollect it is full *eight years* fince I had the honour
of *any converfation* or *correfpondence* with your Lordfhip, except *juft half an hour* in a lady's lodgings at
court, and then I had the happinefs of her being
prefent all the time. It would therefore be difficult

* The *whifper,* that, to greatnefs ftill too near,
Perhaps yet vibrates on his fovereign's ear.
Epift. to Dr Arbuthnot, vol. 2.

even

even for your Lordſhip's penetration to tell, to what, or from what *principles, parties*, or *ſentiments*, moral, political, or theological, I may have been converted, or perverted in all that time.   I beſeech your Lordſhip to conſider the injury a man of your *high rank* and *credit* may do to a *private perſon* under *penal laws* and many other difadvantages, not for want of *honeſty* or *conſcience*, but merely perhaps for having too *weak a head*, or too *tender a heart* *.   It is by *theſe alone* I have hitherto lived excluded from all *poſts* of *profit* or *truſt :* as I can interfere with the *views* of *no man*, do not deny me, my Lord, *all that is left*, a little *praiſe*, or the common encouragement due, if not to my *genius*, at leaſt to my *induſtry*.

Above all, your Lordſhip will be careful not to wrong my *moral character* with THOSE † under whoſe *protection* I live, and through whoſe *lenity* alone I can live with comfort.   Your Lordſhip, I am confident, upon conſideration, will think, you inadvertently went a little *too far* when you recommended to THEIR peruſal, and ſtrengthened by the weight of your approbation, a *libel*, mean in its reflections upon my poor *figure*, and ſcandalous in thoſe on my *honour* and *integrity :* wherein I was repreſented as " *an enemy* to human race, a *murderer* of repu-" tations, and a *monſter* marked by God like *Cain*, " deſerving to wander accurſed through the world."

A ſtrange picture of a man, who had the good fortune to enjoy many friends, who will be always remembered as the firſt ornaments of their age and country ; and no enemies that ever contrived to be heard of, except Mr *John Dennis*, and your Lordſhip : a man who never wrote a line in which the *religion* or *government* of his country, the *royal family*, or their *miniſtry* were difreſpectfully mentioned ; the animoſity of any one party gratified at the expenſe of another ; or any cenſure paſſed, but upon

* See letter to Biſhop Atterbury, let. iv.
† The K. and Q.

known

known vice, acknowledged folly, or *aggreffing impertinence*. It is with infinite pleaſure he finds, that *ſome
men* who ſeem *aſhamed* and *afraid* of *nothing elſe*, are
ſo very ſenſible of *his ridicule :* and it is for that very
reaſon he reſolves, (by the grace of God, and your
Lordſhip's good leave),

> *That, while he breathes, no rich or noble knave
> Shall walk the world in credit to his grave.*

This, he thinks, is rendering the beſt ſervice he can
to the public, and even to the good government of
his country; and for this, at leaſt, he may deſerve
ſome countenance, even from the GREATEST PER-
SONS in it. Your Lordſhip knows OF WHOM I ſpeak.
Their NAMES I ſhould be as ſorry, and as much a-
ſhamed, to place near *yours*, on ſuch an occaſion, as
I ſhould be to ſee *you*, my Lord, placed ſo near *their*
PERSONS, if you could ever make ſo ill an uſe of
their ear * as to aſperſe or miſrepreſent any one innocent man.

This is all I ſhall ever aſk of your Lordſhip, except your pardon for this tedious letter. I have the
honour to be, with equal *reſpect* and *concern*,

My LORD,

Your truly devoted ſervant,

A. POPE.

* Cloſe at the ear of Eve, *Ep. to Dr Arbuth,* vol. 1.

LETTERS to and from Dr SWIFT.

From the year 1713 to 1737.

LETTER I.

Mr POPE *to* Dr SWIFT *.

SIR,   *Binfield, Dec.* 8. 1713.

NOT to trouble you at prefent with a recital of all my obligations to you, I fhall only mention two things, which I take particularly kind of you : your defire that I fhould write to you ; and your propofal of giving me twenty guineas to change my religion ; which laft you muft give me leave to make the fubject of this letter.

Sure, no clergyman ever offered fo much out of his own purfe for the fake of any religion. It is almoft as many pieces of gold, as an apoftle could get of filver from the priefts of old, on a much more valuable confideration. I believe it will be better worth my while to propofe a change of my faith by fubfcription, than a tranflation of Homer. And to convince you how well difpofed I am to the reformation, I fhall be content, if you can prevail with my Lord Treafurer and the miniftry to rife to the fame fum, each of them, on this pious account, as my Lord Halifax has done on the profane one. I am afraid there is no being at once a poet and a good Chriftian ; and I am very much ftraitened between two, while the Whigs feem willing to contribute as

---

* This letter was wrote by Mr Pope in anfwer to one from Dr Swift, wherein he had jocofely made an offer to his friend of a fum of money, *ex caufa religionis,* or, in plain Englifh, to induce Mr Pope to change his religion.——It was never inferted in any former edition of Pope's works.

much,

much, to continue me the one, as you would, to make me the other. But if you can move every man in the government, who has above ten thousand pounds a-year, to fubfcribe as much as yourfelf, I fhall become a convert as moft men do, when the Lord turns it to my intereft. I know they have the truth of religion fo much at heart, that they would certainly give more to have one good fubject tranflated from Popery to the church of England, than twenty Heathenifh authors out of any unknown tongue into ours. I therefore commiffion you, Mr DEAN, with full authority, to tranfact this affair in my name, and to propofe as follows. Firft, That as to the head of our church, the Pope, I may engage to renounce his power, whenfoever I fhall receive any particular indulgences from the head of your church, the Queen.

As to communion in one kind, I fhall alfo promife to change it for communion in both, as foon as the miniftry will allow me.

For invocations to faints, mine fhall be turned to dedications to finners, when I fhall find the great ones of this world as willing to do me any good, as I believe thofe of the other are.

You fee I fhall not be obftinate in the main points. But there is one article I muft referve, and which you feemed not unwilling to allow me, prayer for the dead. There are people to whofe fouls I wifh as well as to my own; and I muft crave leave humbly to lay before them, that though the fubfcriptions above mentioned will fuffice for myfelf, there are neceffary perquifites and additions, which I muft demand on the fcore of this charitable article. It is alfo to be confidered, that the greater part of thofe whofe fouls I am moft concerned for, were unfortunately heretics, fchifmatics, poets, painters, or perfons of fuch lives and manners, as few or no churches are willing to fave. The expenfe will therefore be the greater to make an effectual provifion for the faid fouls.

Q 2   Old

Old Dryden, though a Roman Catholic, was a poet; and it is revealed in the visions of some ancient saints, that no poet was ever saved under some hundred of masses. I cannot set his delivery from purgatory at less than fifty pounds Sterling.

Walsh was not only a Socinian, but (what you will own is harder to be saved) a Whig. He cannot modestly be rated at less than an hundred.

L'Estrange being a Tory, we compute him but at twenty pounds; which I hope no friend of the party can deny to give, to keep him from damning in the next life, considering they never gave him sixpence to keep him from starving in this.

All this together amounts to one hundred and seventy pounds.

In the next place, I must desire you to represent, that there are several of my friends yet living, whom I design, God willing, to outlive, in consideration of legacies; out of which it is a doctrine in the reformed church, that not a farthing shall be allowed to save their souls who gave them.

There is one **** who will die within these few months, with ***** one Mr Jervas, who hath grievously offended in making the likeness of almost all things in heaven above and earth below; and one Mr Gay, an unhappy youth, who writes pastorals during the time of divine service; whose case is the more deplorable, as he hath miserably lavished away all that silver he should have reserved for his soul's health, in buttons and loops for his coat.

I cannot pretend to have these people honestly saved under some hundred pounds, whether you consider the difficulty of such a work, or the extreme love and tenderness I bear them, which will infallibly make me push this charity as far as I am able. There is but one more whose salvation I insist upon, and then I have done: but indeed it may prove of so much greater charge than all the rest, that I will only lay the case before you and the ministry, and

leave

leave to their prudence and generofity, what fum they fhall think fit to beftow upon it.

The perfon I mean, is Dr Swift, a dignified clergyman, but one, who, by his own confeffion, has compofed more libels than fermons. If it be true, what I have heard often affirmed by innocent people, That too much wit is dangerous to falvation, this unfortunate gentleman muft certainly be damned to all eternity. But I hope his long experience in the world, and frequent converfation with great men, will caufe him (as it has fome others) to have lefs and lefs wit every day. Be it as it will, I fhould not think my own foul deferved to be faved, if I did not endeavour to fave his; for I have all the obligations in nature to him. He has brought me into better company than I cared for, made me merrier when I was fick than I had a mind to be, and put me upon making poems, on purpofe that he might alter them, &c.

I once thought I could never have difcharged my debt to his kindnefs; but have lately been informed, to my unfpeakable comfort, that I have more than paid it all. For Monf. de Montagne has affured me, " that the perfon who receives a benefit, " obliges the giver :" for fince the chief endeavour of one friend is to do good to the other, he who adminifters both the matter and occafion, is the man who is liberal. At this rate it is impoffible Dr Swift fhould be ever out of my debt; as matters ftand already: and for the future, he may expect daily more obligations from.

His moft faithful, affectionate,

humble fervant,

A. POPE.

I have finifhed the *Rape of the Lock;* but I believe I may ftay here till Chriftmas, without hinderance of bufinefs.

L E T T E R   II.

Mr POPE *to Dr* SWIFT.

June 18. 1714.

WHatever apologies it might become me to make at any other time for writing to you, I shall ufe none now, to a man who has owned himfelf as frenetic as a cat in the country. In that circumftance, I know by experience a letter is a very ufeful, as well as amufing thing : if you are too bufied in ftate-affairs to read it, yet you may find entertainment in folding it into divers figures, either doubling it into a pyramidical, or twifting it into a ferpentine form : or, if your difpofition fhould not be fo mathematical, in taking it with you to that place where men of ftudious minds are apt to fit longer than ordinary ; where, after an abrupt divifion of the paper, it may not be unpleafant to try to fit and rejoin the broken lines together. All thefe amufements I am no ftranger to in the country, and doubt not but (by this time) you begin to relifh them, in your prefent contemplative fituation.

I remember a man, who was thought to have fome knowledge in the world, ufed to affirm, that no people in town ever complained they were forgotten by their friends in the country : but my increafing experience convinces me he was miftaken ; for I find a great many here grievoufly complaining of you, upon this fcore. I am told farther, that you treat the few you correfpond with in a very arrogant ftyle, and tell them you admire at their infolence in difturbing your meditations, or even inquiring of your * retreat : but this I will not pofitively affert, becaufe I never received any fuch infulting e-

---

* Some time before the death of Queen Anne, when her minifters were quarrelling, and the Dean could not reconcile them he retired to a friend's houfe in Berkfhire, and never faw them after.

piftle from you. My Lord Oxford fays you have
not written to him once fince you went: but this
perhaps may be only policy, in him or you : and I,
who am half a Whig, muft not entirely credit any
thing he affirms. At Button's it is reported you are
gone to Hanover, and that Gay goes only on an em-
baffy to you. Others apprehend fome dangerous˙
ftate-treatife from your retirement; and a wit, who
affects to imitate Balfac, fays, that the miniftry now
are like thofe Heathens of old, who received their
oracles from the woods. The gentlemen of the Roman-Catholic perfuafion are not unwilling to credit
me, when I whifper, that you are gone to meet fome
Jefuits commiffioned from the court of Rome, in
order to fettle the moft convenient methods to be
taken for the coming of the pretender. Dr Arbuthnot is fingular in his opinion, and imagines your only defign is to attend at full leifure to the life and adventures of Scriblerus *. This indeed muft be
granted of greater importance than all the reft; and
I wifh I could promife fo well of you. The top of
my own ambition is to contribute to that great work,
and I fhall tranflate Homer by the by. Mr Gay has
acquainted you what progrefs I have made in it. I
cannot name Mr Gay, without all the acknowledgments which I fhall ever owe you, on his account.
If I writ this in verfe, I would tell you, you are like
the fun, and while men imagine you to be retired or
abfent, are hourly exerting your indulgence, and
bringing things to maturity for their advantage. Of
all the world, you are the man (without flattery)
who ferve your friends with the leaft oftentation; it
is almoft ingratitude to thank you, confidering your

* This project (in which the principal perfons engaged were
Dr Arbuthnot, Dr Swift, and Mr Pope, was, to write a complete fatire in profe upon the abufes in every branch of fcience,
comprifed in the hiftory of the life and writings of Scriblerus;
of which only fome detached parts and fragments were done,
fuch as the *Memoirs of Scriblerus*, the *Travels of Gulliver*, the
Treatife of the Profund, the literal criticifms on *Virgil, &c.*

temper ;

temper ; and this is the period of all my letter which
I fear you will think the most impertinent. I am,
with the trueft affection,

Yours, &c.

L E T T E R   III.

From Dr S W.I F T *to Mr* P O P E.

Dublin, June 28. 1715.

MY Lord Bishop of Clogher* gave me your kind
letter full of reproaches for my not writing.
I am naturally no very exact correfpondent ; and
when I leave a country without probability of returning, I think as feldom as I can of what I loved or
efteemed in it, to avoid the *defiderium* which of all
things makes life moft uneafy. But you muft give
me leave to add one thing, that you talk at your
eafe, being wholly unconcerned in public events :
for, if your friends the Whigs continue, you may
hope for fome favour ; if the Tories return, you are
at leaft fure of quiet. You know how well I loved
both Lord Oxford and Bolingbroke, and how dear
the Duke of Ormond is to me : do you imagine I
can be eafy while their enemies are endeavouring to
take off their heads ? *I nunc, & verfus tecum medita-
re canoros.* — Do you imagine I can be eafy when I
think of the probable confequences of thefe proceedings, perhaps upon the very peace of the nation, but
certainly of the minds of fo many hundred thoufand
good fubjects ? Upon the whole, you may truly at-
tribute my filence to the eclipfe, but it was that
eclipfe which happened on the firft of Auguft.

I borrowed your Homer from the Bishop (mine is
not yet landed), and read it out in two evenings. If it
pleafeth others as well as me, you have got your

---

* Dr *St George Afh,* formerly a fellow of *Trinity college, Dublin,* (to whom the Dean was a pupil), afterwards Bishop of
Clogher, and tranflated to the fee of Derry in 1716-17.

end

end in profit and reputation : yet I am angry at fome
bad rhymes and triplets, and pray in your next do
not let me have fo many unjuftifiable rhymes to *war*
and *gods*.   I tell you all the faults I know, only in
one or two places you are a little obfcure; but I expected you to be fo in one or two and twenty.   I
have heard no foul talk of it here, for indeed it
is not come over ; nor do we very much abound in
judges, at leaft I have not the honour to be acquainted with them.   Your notes are perfectly good, and
fo are your preface and effay.   You were pretty bold
in mentioning Lord Bolingbroke in that preface.
I faw the key to the Lock but yefterday : I think
you have changed it a good deal, to adapt it to the
prefent times.

God be thanked I have yet no parliamentary bufinefs, and if they have none with me, I fhall never
feek their acquaintance.   I have not been very fond
of them for fome years paft, not when I thought
them tolerably good ; and therefore if I can get leave
to be abfent, I fhall be much inclined to be on that
fide, when there is a parliament on this : but truly
I muft be a little eafy in my mind before I can think
of Scriblerus.

You are to underftand that I live in the corner of
a vaft unfurnifhed houfe ; my family confifts of a
fteward, a groom, a helper in the ftable, a footman,
and an old maid, who are all at board-wages ; and
when I do not dine abroad, or make an entertainment (which laft is very rare), I eat a mutton-pye,
and drink half a pint of wine : my amufements are
defending my fmall dominions againft the Archbifhop,
and endeavouring to reduce my rebellious choir.
Perditur hæc inter mifero lux.   I defire you will prefent my humble fervice to Mr Addifon, Mr Congreve,
and Mr Rowe, and Gay.   I am, and will be always, extremely yours, &c.

L E T T E R IV.

Mr P O P E *to Dr* S W I F T.

June 20. 1716.

I Cannot fuffer a friend to crofs the Irifh feas without bearing a teftimony from me of the conftant efteem and affection I am both obliged and inclined to have for you. It is better he fhould tell you than I, how often you are in our thoughts and in our cups, and how I learn to fleep lefs * and drink more, whenever you are named among us. I look upon a friend in Ireland as upon a friend in the other world, whom (popifhly fpeaking) I believe conftantly well difpofed towards me, and ready to do me all the good he can, in that ftate of feparation, though I hear nothing from him, and make addreffes to him but very rarely. A Proteftant divine cannot take it amifs that I treat him in the fame manner with my patron faint.

I can tell you no news, but what you will not fufficiently wonder at, that I fuffer many things as an author militant; whereof, in your days of probation, you have been a fharer, or you had not arrived to that triumphant ftate you now defervedly enjoy in the church. As for me, I have not the leaft hopes of the cardinalet, though I fuffer for my religion in almoft every weekly paper. I have begun to take a pique at the pfalms of David (if the wicked may be credited, who have printed a fcandalous one † in my name). This report I dare not difcourage too much, in a profpect I have at prefent of a poft under the Marquis de Langallerie ‡, wherein if I can but do fome fignal fervice againft the Pope, I may be confiderably advanced by the Turks, the only religious

---

* Alluding to his conftant cuftom of fleeping after dinner.
† In Curl's collection.
‡ One who made a noife then, as Count Bonneval has done fince.

people

people I dare confide in. If it should happen hereafter that I should write for the holy law of Maho-
.met, I hope it may make no breach between you and
me; every one muſt live, and I beg you will not be
the man to manage the controverſy againſt me. The
church of Rome I judge (from many modern ſymp-
toms, as well as ancient prophecies) to be in a declining condition; that of England will in a ſhort time
be ſcarce able to maintain her own family: ſo
churches ſink as generally as banks in Europe, and
for the ſame reaſon; that religion and trade, which
at firſt were open and free, have been reduced into
the management of companies, and the roguery of
directors.

I do not know why I tell you all this, but that I
always loved to talk to you; but this is not a time
for any man to talk to the purpoſe. Truth is a
kind of contraband commodity, which I would not
venture to export, and therefore the only thing
tending that dangerous way which I ſhall ſay, is,
that I am, and always will be, with the utmoſt ſincerity,

Yours, &c.

LETTER V.

From Dr S W I F T *to Mr* P O P E.

Aug. 30. 1716.

I Had the favour of yours by Mr F. of whom, before any other queſtion relating to your health or
fortune, or ſucceſs as a poet, I inquired your principles in the common form, " Is he a Whig or a To-
" ry?" I am ſorry to find they are not ſo well tallied
to the preſent juncture as I could wiſh. I always
thought the terms of *facto* and *jure* had been introduced by the poets, and that poſſeſſion of any ſort in
kings was held an unexceptionable title in the courts
of Parnaſſus. If you do not grow a perfect good
ſubject in all its preſent latitudes, I ſhall conclude
you

you are become rich, and able to live without dedications to men in power, whereby one great inconvenience will follow, that you, and the world, and
posterity will be utterly ignorant of their virtues.
For, either your brethren have miserably deceived us
these hundred years past, or power confefs virtue, as
naturally as five of your Popish facraments do grace.
—You fleep lefs and drink more—But your mafter
Horace was *Vini fomnique benignus :* and, as I take
it, both are proper for your trade. As to mine, there
are a thoufand poetical texts to confirm the one ; and
as to the other, I know it was anciently the cuftom
to fleep in temples for thofe who would confult
the oracles, " Who dictates to me flumbering *,"
&c.

    You are an ill Catholic, or a worfe geographer;
for I can affure you, Ireland is not paradife, and I
appeal even to any Spanifh divine, whether addreffes
were ever made to a friend in hell, or purgatory ?
And who are all thefe enemies you hint at ? I can
only think of Curl, Gildon, Squire Burnet, Black-
more, and a few others whofe fame I have forgot;
tools, in my opinion, as neceffary for a good writer,
as pen, ink, and paper.   And befides, I would fain
know whether every draper doth not fhew you three
or four damned pieces of fluff to fet off his good one?
However, I will grant, that one thorough bookfell-
ing-rogue is better qualified to vex an author, than
all his contemporary fcribblers in critic or fatire, not
only by ftolen copies of what was incorrect or unfit
for the public, but by downright laying other mens
dulnefs at your door.   I had a long defign upon the
ears of that Curl, when I was in credit; but the
rogue would never allow me a fair ftroke at them, although my penknife was ready drawn and fharp. I
can hardly believe the relation of his being poifoned,
although the hiftorian pretends to have been an eye-
witnefs: but I beg pardon, fack might do it, although rats-bane would not.   I never faw the thing

  * Milton.

you mention as falsely imputed to you ; but I think
the frolics of merry hours, even when we are guilty,
fhould not be left to the mercy of our beft friends,
until Curl and his refemblers are hanged.

With fubmiffion to the better judgment of you and
your friends, I take your project of an employment
under the Turks to be idle and unneceffary. Have
a little patience, and you will find more merit and
encouragement at home by the fame methods. You
are ungrateful to your country ; quit but your own
religion, and ridicule ours, and that will allow you
a free choice for any other, or for none at all, and
pay you well into the bargain. Therefore pray do
not run and difgrace us among the Turks, by telling
them you were forced to leave your native home, becaufe we would oblige you to be a Chriftian ; whereas we will make it appear, to all the world, that we
only compelled you to be a Whig.

There is a young ingenious Quaker in this town
who writes verfes to his miftrefs, not very correct,
but in a ftrain purely what a poetical Quaker fhould
do, commending her look and habit, &c. It gave
me a hint that a fet of Quaker paftorals might fucceed, if our friend Gay * could fancy it, and I
think it a fruitful fubject ; pray hear what he fays.
I believe further, the paftoral ridicule is not ex-
haufted ; and that a porter, footman, or † chair-
man's paftoral might do well. Or what think you
of a Newgate paftoral, among the whores and thieves
here ?

Laftly, to conclude, I love you never the worfe
or feldom writing to you. I am in an obfcure
fcene, where you know neither thing nor perfon.
can only anfwer yours, which I promife to do after
a fort whenever you think fit to employ me. But I
can affure you, the fcene and the times have depreff-

* Gay wrote a paftoral of this kind, which is publifhed in
his works.
† Swift himfelf wrote one of this kind, entitled, *Dermot and
Sheelah.*

ed me wonderfully; for I will impute no defect to thofe two paltry years which have flipped by fince I had the happinefs to fee you. I am, with the trueft efteem,

Yours, &c.

LETTER VI. *

From Dr SWIFT *to* Mr POPE.

Dublin, *Jan.* 10. 1721.

A Thoufand things have vexed me of late years, upon which I am determined to lay open my mind to you. I rather chufe to appeal to you than to my Lord Chief Juftice Whitfhed, under the fituation I am in. For I take this caufe properly to lie before you : you are a much fitter judge of what concerns the credit of a writer, the injuries that are done him, and the reparations he ought to receive. Befides, I doubt whether the arguments I could fuggeft to prove my own innocence would be of much weight from the gentlemen of the long robe to thofe in furs, upon whofe decifion about the difference of ftyle or fentiments, I fhould be very unwilling to leave the merits of my caufe.

Give me leave then to put you in mind, (although you cannot eafily forget it), that, about ten weeks before the Queen's death, I left the town, upon occafion of that incurable breach among the great men at court, and went down to Berkfhire, where you may remember that you gave me the favour of a vifit. While I was in that retirement, I writ a difcourfe which I thought might be ufeful in fuch a juncture of affairs, and fent it up to London ; but, upon fome difference in opinion between me and a certain great minifter now abroad, the publifhing of it was deferred fo long that the Queen died, and I recalled my

---

* This letter Mr Pope never received, nor did he believe it was ever fent.

copy,

copy, which hath been ever fince in fafe hands. In
a few weeks after the lofs of that excellent princefs,
I came to my ftation here ; where I have continued
ever fince in the greateft privacy, and utter ignorance
of thofe events which are moft commonly talked of
in the world. I neither know the names nor number of the royal family which now reigns, further
than the prayer-book informs me. I cannot tell who
is chancellor, who are fecretaries, nor with what nations we are in peace or war. And this manner of
life was not taken up out of any fort of affectation,
but merely to avoid giving offence, and for fear of
provoking party-zeal.

I had indeed written fome memorials of the four
laft years of the Queen's reign, with fome other informations, which I received, as neceffary materials
to qualify me for doing fomething in an employment
then defigned me * : but, as it was at the difpofal of
a perfon who had not the fmalleft fhare of fteadinefs
or fincerity, I difdained to accept it.

Thefe papers, at my few hours of health and leifure, I have been digefting + into order by one fheet
at a time ; for I dare not venture any further, left
the humour of fearching and feizing papers fhould
revive; not that I am in pain of any danger to myfelf, (for they contain nothing of prefent times or
perfons, upon which I fhall never lofe a thought
while there is a cat or a fpaniel in the houfe), but to
preferve them from being loft among meffengers and
clerks.

I have written, in this kingdom, a ‡ difcourfe to
perfuade the wretched people to wear their own manufactures inftead of thofe from England. This
treatife foon fpread very faft, being agreeable to the
fentiments of the whole nation, except of thofe gen-

---

* Hiftoriographer.

† Thefe papers were never publifhed, though faid to be yet in
being. Swift is reported to have faid, that it was the beft work
he had ever written.——They are now publifhed in 8vo.

‡ A propofal for the univerfal ufe of Irifh manufactures.

R 2   tlemen

tlemen who had employments, or were expectants.
Upon which a perfon in great office here immediately
took the alarm : he fent in hafte for the chief juftice,
and informed him of a feditious, factious, and viru-
lent pamphlet, lately publifhed, with a defign of
fetting the two kingdoms at variance ; directing at
the fame time that the printer fhould be profecuted
with the utmoft rigour of law.   The chief juftice
had fo quick an underftanding, that he refolved, if
poffible, to outdo his orders.   The grand juries of
the county and city were practifed effectually with
to reprefent the faid pamphlet with all aggravating
epithets, for which they had thanks fent them from
England, and their prefentments publifhed for feveral weeks in all the newfpapers.   The printer was
feized, and forced to give great bail :   after his trial
the jury brought him in not guilty, although they
had been culled with the utmoft induftry ;   the chief
juftice fent them back nine times, and kept them
eleven hours, until, being perfectly tired out, they
were forced to leave the matter to the mercy of the
judge, by what they call a fpecial verdict.   During
the trial, the chief juftice, among other fingularities,
laid his hand on his breaft, and protefted folemnly
that the author's defign was to bring in the pretender ; although there was not a fingle fyllable of
party in the whole treatife, and although it was
known that the moft eminent of thofe who profeffed
his own principles, publicly difallowed his proceedings.   But the caufe being fo very odious and
impopular, the trial of the verdict was deferred from
one term to another, until upon the Duke of G—ft-n
the Lord Lieutenant's arrival, his Grace, after ma-
ture advice, and permiffion from England, was pleafed to grant a *Noli profequi.*
   This is the more remarkable, becaufe it is faid
that the man is no ill decider in common cafes of
property, where party is out of the queftion ;   but
when that intervenes, with ambition at heels to pufh
it forward, it muft needs confound any man of little
fpirit,

spirit, and low birth, who hath no other endowment than that fort of knowledge, which, however poffeffed in the higheft degree, can poffibly give no one good quality to the mind.

It is true, I have been much concerned, for feveral years paft, upon account of the public as well as for myfelf, to fee how ill a tafte for wit and fenfe prevails in the world, which politics, and South-fea, and party, and opera's, and mafquerades have introduced. For, befides many infipid papers which the malice of fome hath entitled me to, there are many perfons appearing to wifh me well, and pretending to be judges of my ftyle and manner, who have yet afcribed fome writings to me, of which any man of common fenfe and literature would be heartily afhamed. I cannot forbear inftancing a treatife called a *Dedication upon dedications*, which many would have to be mine, although it be as empty, dry, and fervile a compofition, as I remember at any time to have read. But above all, there is one circumftance which makes it impoffible for me to have been author of a treatife, wherein there are feveral pages containing a panegyric on King George, of whofe character and perfon I am utterly ignorant, nor ever had once the curiofity to inquire into either, living at fo great a diftance as I do, and having long done with whatever can relate to public matters.

Indeed I have formerly delivered my thoughts very freely, whether I were afked or no; but never affected to be a counfellor, to which I had no manner of call. I was humbled enough to fee myfelf fo far outdone by the Earl of Oxford in my own trade as a fcholar, and too good a courtier not to difcover his contempt of thofe who would be men of importance out of their fphere. Befides, to fay the truth, although I have known many great minifters ready enough to hear opinions, yet I have hardly feen one that would ever defcend to take advice; and this pedantry arifeth from a maxim themfelves do not believe at the fame time they practife by it, that there is something profound in politics, which men of plain honest fenfe cannot arrive to.

I only wifh my endeavours had fucceeded better in the great point I had at heart, which was that of reconciling the minifters to each other. This might have been done, if others, who had more concern and more influence, would have acted their parts; and, if this had fucceeded, the public intereft both of church and ftate would not have been the worfe, nor the Proteftant fucceffion endangered.

But, whatever opportunities a conftant attendance of four years might have given me for endeavouring to do good offices to particular perfons, I deferve at leaft to find tolerable quarter from thofe of the other party; for many of which I was a conftant advocate with the Earl of Oxford, and for this I appeal to his Lordfhip: he knows how often I preffed him in favour of Mr Addifon, Mr Congreve, Mr Rowe, and Mr Steele; although I freely confefs that his Lordfhip's kindnefs to them was altogether owing to his generous notions, and the efteem he had for their wit and parts, of which I could only pretend to be a remembrancer. For I can never forget the anfwer he gave to the late Lord Halifax, who upon the firft change of the miniftry interceded with him to fparc Mr Congreve: it was by repeating thefe two lines of Virgil,

Non obtufa adeo geftamus pectora Pœni,
Nec tam averfus equos Tyria fol jungit ab urbe.

Purfuant to which, he always treated Mr Congreve with the greateft perfonal civilities, affuring him of his conftant favour and protection, and adding, that he would ftudy to do fomething better for him.

I remember it was in thofe times a ufual fubject of raillery towards me among the minifters, that I never came to them without a Whig in my fleeve: which I do not fay with any view towards making

my

my court: for the new principles * fixed to thofe
of that denomination, I did then, and do now from
my heart abhor, deteft, and abjure, as wholly dege-
nerate from their predeceffors. I have converfed in
fome freedom with more minifters of ftate of all parties than ufually happens to men of my level ; and,
I confefs, in their capacity as minifters, I look upon them as a race of people whofe acquaintance no
man would court otherwife than upon the fcore of
vanity or ambition. The firft quickly wears off,
(and is the vice of low minds, for a man of fpirit is
too proud to be vain), and the other was not my
cafe. Befides, having never received more than one
fmall favour, I was under no neceffity of being a
flave to men in power, but chofe my friends by their
perfonal merit, without examining how far their notions agreed with the politics then in vogue. I frequently converfed with Mr Addifon, and the others
I named, (except Mr Steele), during all my Lord
Oxford's miniftry ; and Mr Addifon's friendfhip to
me continued inviolable, with as much kindnefs as
when we ufed to meet at my Lord Sommers † or
Halifax, who were leaders of the oppofite party.

I would infer from all this, that it is with great
injuftice I have thefe many years been pelted by your
pamphleteers, merely upon account of fome regard
which the Queen's laft minifters were pleafed to have
for me : and yet in my confcience I think I am a
partaker in every ill defign they had againft the Proteftant fucceffion, or the liberties and religion of their
country ; and can fay with Cicero, " that I fhould
" be proud to be included with them in all their
" actions, *tanquam in equo Trojano.*" But if I have
never difcovered by my words, writings, or actions,

---

* He means particularly the principle at that time charged
upon them, by their enemies, of an intention *to prefcribe the
Tories.*

† Lord Sommers had very warmly recommended Dr Swift to
the favour of Lord Wharton, when he went the Queen's Lieutenant into Ireland, in the year 1709.

any

any party-virulence *, or dangerous defigns againſt the prefent powers ; if my friendſhip and converſation were equally ſhewn among thoſe who liked or difapproved the proceedings then at court, and that. I was known to be a common friend of all deſerving perfons of the latter fort, when they were in diſtrefs ; I cannot but think it hard, that I am not ſuffered to run quietly among the common herd of people, whoſe opinions unfortunately differ from thoſe which lead to favour and preferment. -

I ought to let you know, that the thing we called a Whig in England is a creature altogether different from thoſe of the fame denomination here ; at leaſt it was ſo during the reign of her late Majeſty. Whether thoſe on your ſide have changed or no, it hath not been my bufinefs to inquire. I remember my excellent friend Mr Addiſon, when he firſt came over hither fecretary to the Earl of Wharton then Lord Lieutenant, was extremely offended at the conduct and difcourfe of the chief managers here : he told me they were a fort of people who feemed to think that the principles of a Whig confiſted in nothing elfe but damning the church, reviling the clergy, abetting the diſſenters, and ſpeaking contemptibly of revealed religion.

I was difcourfing fome years ago with a certain miniſter about that whiggiſh or fanatical genius, ſo prevalent among the Engliſh of this kingdom : his Lordſhip accounted for it by that number of Cromwell's foldiers, adventurers eſtabliſhed here, who were all of the foureſt leaven, and the meaneſt birth, and whoſe poſterity are now in poſſeſſion of their lands and their principles. However, it muſt be confeſſed, that of late fome people in this country are grown weary of quarrelling, becaufe intereſt, the great motive of quarrelling, is at an end ; for it is hardly worth contending who ſhall be an excifeman,

---

* The *Examiners* were not then publiſhed amongſt the Dean's works.

a country-vicar, a crier in the courts, or an under-clerk.

You will perhaps be inclined to think, that a per-fon fo ill treated as I have been, muft at fome time or other have difcovered very dangerous opinions in government; in anfwer to which, I will tell you what my political principles were in the time of her late glorious Majefty, which I never contradicted by any action, writing. or difcourfe.

Firft, I always declared myfelf againft a Popifh fucceffor to the crown, whatever title he might have by the proximity of blood : neither did I ever re-gard the right line, except upon two accounts : firft, as it was eftablifhed by law ; and fecondly, as it hath much weight in the opinions of the people. For ne-ceffity may abolifh any law, but cannot alter the fen-timents of the vulgar ; right of inheritance being perhaps the moft popular of all topics : and there-fore in great changes when that is broke, there will remain much heartburning and difcontent among the meaner people ; which (under a weak prince and corrupt adminiftration) may have the worft confe-quences upon the peace of any ftate.

As to what is called a *revolution-principle*, my opinion was this ; That whenever thofe evils which ufually attend and follow a violent change of govern-ment, were not in probability fo pernicious as the grievance we fuffer under a prefent power, then the public good will juftify fuch a revolution. And this I took to have been the cafe in the Prince of Orange's expedition, although in the confequences it produced fome very bad effects, which are likely to ftick long enough by us.

I had likewife in thofe days a mortal antipathy a-gainft ftanding armies in times of peace : becaufe I always took ftanding armies to be only fervants hi-red by the mafter of the family for keeping his own children in flavery ; and becaufe I conceived, that a prince, who could not think himfelf fecure without mercenary troops, muft needs have a feparate intereft

reft from that of his fubjects. Although I am not
ignorant of thofe artificial neceffities which a corrupted miniftry.can create, for keeping up forces to
fupport a faction againft the public intereft.

As to parliaments, I adored the wifdom of that
Gothic inftitution, which made them annual: and
I was confident our liberty could never be placed
upon a firm foundation, until that ancient law were
reftored among us. For who fees not, that, while
fuch affemblies are permitted to have a longer dura-
tion, there grows up a commerce of corruption between the miniftry and the deputies, wherein they
both find their accounts, to the manifeft danger of
liberty? which traffic would neither anfwer the
defign nor expenfe, if parliaments met once a-year.

I ever abominated that fcheme of politics, (now
about thirty years old), of fetting up a moneyed intereft in oppofition to the landed. For I conceived,
there could not be a truer maxim in our government
than this, That the poffeffors of the foil are the beft
judges of what is for the advantage of the kingdom.
If others had thought the fame way, funds of credit
and South-fea projects would neither have been felt
nor heard of.

I could never difcover the neceffity of fufpending
any law upon which the liberty of the moft innocent
perfons depended; neither do I think this practice
hath made the tafte of arbitrary power fo agreeable,
as that we fhould defire to fee it repeated. Every
rebellion fubdued and plot difcovered, contribute to
the firmer eftablifhment of the prince: in the latter
cafe, the knot of confpirators is entirely broke, and
they are to begin their work anew under a thoufand
difadvantages; fo that thofe diligent inquiries into
remote and problematical guilt, with a new power
of enforcing them by chains and dungeons to every
perfon whofe face a minifter thinks fit to diflike, are
not only oppofite to that maxim, which declareth it
better that ten guilty men fhould efcape, than one
innocent fuffer; but likewife leave a gate wide o-

pen to the whole tribe of informers, the moſt accurſed, and proſtitute, and abandoned race, that
God ever permitted to plague mankind.

It is true, the Romans had a cuſtom of chuſing a
dictator, during whoſe adminiſtration the power of
other magiſtrates was ſuſpended; but this was done
upon the greateſt emergencies; a war near their
doors, or ſome civil diſſenſion : for armies muſt be
governed by arbitrary power. But when the virtue
of that commonwealth gave place to luxury and ambition, this very office of dictator became perpetual
in the perſons of the Cæſars and their ſucceſſors,
the moſt infamous tyrants that have any where appeared in ſtory.

Theſe are ſome of the ſentiments I had, relating
to public affairs, while I was in the world : what
they are at preſent, is of little importance either to
that or myſelf; neither can I truly ſay I have any at
all, or, if I had, I dare not venture to publiſh
them : for however orthodox they may be while I
am now writing, they may become criminal enough
to bring me into trouble before midſummer. And
indeed I have often wiſhed for ſome time paſt, that a
political catechiſm might be publiſhed by authority
four times a-year, in order to inſtruct us how we are
to ſpeak, write, and act, during the current quarter.
I have by experience felt the want of ſuch an inſtruc-
tor.: for, intending to make my court to ſome people on the prevailing ſide by advancing certain old
whiggiſh principles, which, it ſeems, had been ex-
ploded about a month before, I have paſſed for a
diſaffected perſon. I am not ignorant how idle a
thing it is, for a man in obſcurity to attempt defending his reputation as a writer, while the ſpirit of
faction hath ſo univerſally poſſeſſed the minds of
men, that they are not at leiſure to attend to any
thing elſe. They will juſt give themſelves time to
libel and accuſe me, but cannot ſpare a minute to
hear my defence. So in a plot-diſcovering age, I
have often known an innocent man ſeized and im-
priſoned,

prifoned, and forced to lie feveral months in chains, while the minifters were not at leifure to hear his petition, until they had profecuted and hanged the number they propofed.

All I can reafonably hope for by this letter, is to convince my friends, and others who are pleafed to wifh me well, that I have neither been fo ill a fubject nor fo ftupid an author, as I have been reprefented by the virulence of libeliers, whofe malice hath taken the fame train in both, by fathering dangerous principles in government upon me, which I never maintained, and infipid productions, which I am not capable of writing. For, however I may have been foured by perfonal ill-treatment, or by melancholy profpects for the public, I am too much a politician to expofe my own fafety by offenfive words. And, if my genius and fpirit be funk by increafing years, I have at leaft enough difcretion left, not to miftake the meafure of my own abilities, by attempting fubjects where thofe talents are neceffary, which perhaps I may have loft with my youth.

LETTER VII.

Dr SWIFT to Mr GAY.

Dublin, Jan. 8. 1722-3.

COming home after a fhort Chriftmas ramble, I found a letter upon my table, and little expected when I opened it to read your name at the bottom. The beft and greateft part of my life, until thefe laft eight years, I fpent in England; there I made my friendfhips, and there I left my defires. I am condemned for ever to another country; what is in prudence to be done? I think, to be *oblitufque meorum, oblivifcendus et illis.* What can be the defign of your letter but malice, to wake me out of a fcurvy fleep, which however is better than none? I am towards nine years older fince I left you, yet that is the leaft of my alterations; my bufinefs, my diverfions,

verfions, my converfations, are all entirely changed
for the worfe, and fo are my ftudies and my amufements in writing; yet, after all, this humdrum way
of life might be paffable enough, if you would let me
alone. I fhall not be able to relifh my wine, my
parfons, my horfes, nor my garden, for three months,
until the fpirit you have raifed fhall be difpoffefed.
I have fometimes wondered that I have not vifited
you; but I have been ftopped by too many reafons,
befides years and lazinefs, and yet thefe are very good
ones. Upon my return after half a year amongft
you, there would be to me *defiderio nec pudor nec
modus.* I was three years reconciling myfelf to the
fcene, and the bufinefs, to which fortune hath condemned me, and ftupidity was what I had recourfe
to. Befides, what a figure fhould I make in London, while my friends are in poverty, exile, diftrefs,
or imprifonment, and my enemies with rods of iron?
Yet I often threaten myfelf with the journey, and am
every fummer practifing to get health to bear it.
The only inconvenience is, that I grow old in the
experiment. Although I care not to talk to you as a
divine, yet I hope you have not been author of your
colic. Do you drink bad wine, or keep bad company? Are you not as many years older as I? It will
not be always, *Et tibi quos mihi dempferit apponet annos.* I am heartily forry you have any dealings with
that ugly diftemper, and I believe our friend Arbuthnot will recommend you to temperance and exercife. I wifh they could have as good an effect upon the giddinefs I am fubject to, and which this moment I am not free from. I fhould have been glad if
you had lengthened your letter by telling me the
prefent condition of many of my old acquaintance,
Congreve, Arbuthnot, Lewis, &c. but you mention
only Mr Pope, who I believe is lazy, or elfe he might
have added three lines of his own. I am extremely
glad he is not in your cafe of needing great mens favour, and could heartily wifh that you were in his. I
have been confidering why poets have fuch ill fuccefs

in making their court, fince they are allowed to be
the greateft and beft of all flatterers. The defect is,
that they flatter only in print or in writing, but not
by word of mouth : they will give things under
their hand which they make a confcience of fpeaking.
Befides, they are too libertine to haunt antechambers,
too poor to bribe porters and footmen, and too proud
to cringe to fecond-hand favourites in a great family.
Tell me, are you not under original fin by the dedication of your eclogues to Lord Bolingbroke? I am
an ill judge at this diftance; and befides, am, for
my eafe, utterly ignorant of the commoneft things
that pafs in the world; but if all courts have a fame-
nefs in them (as the parfons phrafe it), things may be
as they were in my time, when all employments
went to parliament-mens friends, who had been ufeful in elections, and there was always a huge lift of
names in arrears at the treafury, which would at leaft
take up your feven years expedient to difcharge even
one half. I am of opinion, if you will not be offended,
that the fureft courfe would be to get your friend who
lodgeth in your houfe, to recommend you to the next
chief governour who comes over here for a good civil
employment, or to be one of his fecretaries, which
your parliament-men are fond enough of, when there
is no room at home. The wine is good and reafonable; you may dine twice a-week at the deanery-
houfe; there is a fet of company in this town fufficient for one man; folks will admire you, becaufe
they have read you, and read of you; and a good
employment will make you live tolerably in London,
or fumptuoufly here; or if you divide between both
places, it will be for your health.

I wifh I could do more than fay I love you. I left
you in a good way both for the late court, and the
fucceffors; and, by the force of too much honefty or
too little fublunary wifdom, you fell between two
ftools. Take care of your health and money; be lefs
modeft and more active; or elfe turn parfon and get

FROM DR SWIFT, &c. 207

a bithopric here: Would to God they would fend us
as good ones from your fide!
I am ever, &c.

LETTER VIII.

Mr POPE *to Dr* SWIFT.

Jan. 12. 1723.

I Find a rebuke in a late letter of yours, that both
ftings and pleafes me extremely. Your faying
that I ought to have writ a poftfcript to my friend
Gay's, makes me not content to write lefs than a
whole letter; and your feeming to take his kindly,
gives me hopes you will look upon this as a fincere
effect of friendfhip. Indeed as I cannot but own the
lazinefs with which you tax me, and with which I
may equally charge you, for both of us have had
(and one of us hath both had and given *) a furfeit
of writing; fo I really thought you would know
yourfelf to be fo certainly entitled to my friendfhip,
that it was a poffeffion you could not imagine ftood in
need of any further deeds or writings to affure you
of it.

Whatever you feem to think of your withdrawn
and feparate ftate at this diftance, and in this abfence, Dean Swift lives ftill in England, in every
place and company where he would chufe to live,
and I find him in all the converfations I keep, and in
all the hearts in which I defire any fhare.

We have never met thefe many years without mention of you. Befides my old acquaintance, I have
found that all my friends of a later date are fuch as
were yours before: Lord Oxford, Lord Harcourt,
and Lord Harley may look upon me as one entailed
upon them by you: Lord Bolingbroke is now returned (as I hope) to take me with all his other hereditary rights: and, indeed, he feems grown fo
much a philofopher, as to fet his heart upon fome of

* Alluding to his large work on Homer.

S 2. them

them as little, as upon the poet you gave him. It is sure my ill fate, that all those I moſt loved, and with whom I moſt lived, muſt be baniſhed. After both of you left England, my conſtant hoſt was the Biſhop of * Rocheſter. Sure this is a nation that is curſedly afraid of being over-run with too much po-liteneſs, and cannot regain one great genius, but at the expenſe of another. I tremble for my Lord Peterborow (whom I now lodge with) ; he has too much wit, as well as courage, to make a ſolid gene-ral † : and if he eſcapes being baniſhed by others, I fear he will baniſh himſelf. This leads me to give you ſome account of the manner of my life and con-verſation, which has been infinitely more various and diſſipated, than when you knew me and cared for me ; and among all ſexes, parties, and profeſſions. A glut of ſtudy and retirement in the firſt part of my life caſt me into this ; and this, I begin to ſee, will throw me again into ſtudy and retirement.

The civilities I have met with from oppoſite ſets of people, have hindered me from being violent or four to any party ; but at the ſame time the obſerva-tions and experiences I cannot but have collected, have made me leſs fond of, and leſs ſurpriſed at any : I am therefore the more afflicted and the more angry at the violences and hardſhips I ſee practiſed by ei-ther. The merry vein you knew me in, is ſunk into a turn of reflection, that has made the world pretty indifferent to me ; and yet I have acquired a quiet-neſs of mind which by fits improves into a certain degree of cheerfulneſs, enough to make me juſt ſo

* Dr Atterbury.
† This Mr Walſh ſeriouſly thought to be the caſe, where, in a letter to Mr Pope, he ſays,—" When we were in the north " my Lord Wharton ſhewed me a letter he had received from a " certain great general in Spain ; [Lord Peterb.] I told him, I " would by all means have that general recalled, and ſet to wri- " ting here at home ; for it was impoſſible that a man with ſo " much wit as he ſhewed, could be fit to command an army, o " do any other buſineſs."

good-humoured as to wifh that world well. My friendfhips are increafed by new ones, yet no part of the warmth I felt for the old is diminifhed. Averfions I have none, but to knaves (for fools I have learned to bear with), and fuch I cannot be commonly civil to ; for I think thofe men are next to knaves who converfe with them. The greateft man in power of this fort fhall hardly make me bow to him, unlefs I had a perfonal obligation, and that I will take care not to have. The top pleafure of my life is one I learned from you both how to gain and how to ufe ; the freedom of friendfhip with men, much my fuperiours. To have pleafed great men, according to Horace, is a praife ; but not to have flattered them, and yet not have difpleafed them, is a greater. I have carefully avoided all intercourfe with poets and fcribblers, unlefs where by great chance I have found a modeft one. By thefe means I have had no quarrels with any perfonally ; none have been enemies, but who were alfo ftrangers to me ; and as there is no great need of an eclairciffement with fuch, whatever they writ or faid I never retaliated, not only never feeming to know, but often really never knowing, any thing of the matter. There are very few things that give me the anxiety of a wifh ; the ftrongeft I have would be to pafs my days with you, and a few fuch as you : but fate has difperfed them all about the world ; and I find to wifh it is as vain, as to wifh to fee the millennium and the kingdom of the juft upon earth.

If I have finned in my long filence, confider there is one to whom you yourfelf have been as great a finner. As foon as you fee his hand, you will learn to do me juftice, and feel in your heart how long a man may be filent to thofe he truly loves and refpects.

LETTER IX.

Lord BOLINGBROKE *to* Dr SWIFT.

I AM not fo lazy as Pope, and therefore you muft
not expect from me the fame indulgence to lazinefs; in defending his own caufe he pleads yours,
and becomes your advocate while he appeals to you
as his judge : you will do the fame on your part;
and I, and the reft of your common friends, fhall
have great juftice to expect from two fuch righteous
tribunals ! You refemble perfectly the two alehoufe-
keepers in Holland, who were at the fame time
burgomafters of the town, and taxed one another's
bills alternately. I declare beforehand I will not
ftand to the award; my title to your friendfhip is
good, and wants neither deeds nor writings to
confirm it : but annual acknowledgments at leaft
are neceffary to preferve it: and I begin to fufpect by your defrauding me of them, that you hope
in time to difpute it, and to urge prefcription
againft me. I would not fay one word to you
ab ut myfelf (fince it is a fubject on which you appear to have no curiofity), was it not to try how far
the contraft between Pope's fortune and manner of
life, and mine, may be carried.

I have been, then, infinitely more uniform and lefs
diffipated than when you knew me and cared for me.
That love which I ufed to fcatter with fome profu-
fion among the female kind, has been thefe many
years devoted to one object. A great many misfortunes (for fo they are called, though fometimes very
improperly), and a retirement from the world, have
made that juft and nice difcrimination between my
acquaintance and my friends, which we have feldom
fagacity enough to make for ourfelves; thofe infects
of various hues, which ufed to hum and buz about
me while I ftood in the funfhine, have difappeared
fince I lived in the fhade. No man comes to a hermitage

mitage but for the fake of the hermit ; a few philofophical friends come often to mine, and they are
fuch as you would be glad to live with, if a dull
climate and duller company have not altered you extremely from what you was nine years ago.

The hoarfe voice of party was never heard in this
quiet place ; gazettes and pamphlets are banifhed
from it, and if the lucubrations of Ifaac Bickerftaff
be admitted, this diftinction is owing to fome ftrokes
by which it is judged that this illuftrious philofopher
had (like the Indian Fohu, the Grecian Pythagoras,
the Perfian Zoroafter, and others his precurfors a-
mong the Zabians, Magians, and the Egyptian
feers) both his outward and his inward doctrine, and
that he was of no fide at the bottom. When I am
there, I forget I ever was of any party myfelf ; nay,
I am often fo happily abforbed by the abftracted reafon of things, that I am ready to imagine there never was any fuch monfter as Party. Alas, I am foon
awakened from that pleafing dream by the Greek
and Roman hiftorians, by Guicciardine, by Machia-
vel, and Thuanus ; for I have vowed to read no hiftory of our own country, till that body of it which
you promifed to finifh, appears *.

I am under no apprehenfion that a glut of ftudy
and retirement fhould caft me back into the hurry of
the world ; on the contrary, the fingle regret which
I ever feel, is that I fell fo late into this courfe of
life ; my philofophy grows confirmed by habit, and
if you and I meet again, I will extort this approbation from you : *Jam non confilio bonus, fed more eo
perductus, ut non tantum recte facere poffim, fed nifi
recte facere non poffim.* The little incivilities I have
met with from oppofite fets of people, have been fo
far from rendering me violent or four to any, that I
think myfelf obliged to them all ; fome have cured
me of my fears, by fhewing me how impotent the
malice of the world is ; others have cured me of my

* See the firft note on lett, 6, above,

hopes,

hopes, by fhewing how precarious popular friendfhips are ; all have cured me of furprife : in driving
me out of party, they have driven me out of curfed company ; and in ftripping me of titles, and
rank, and eftate, and fuch trinkets, which every
man that will may fpare, they have given me that
which no man can be happy without.

Reflection and habit have rendered the world fo
indifferent to me, that I am neither afflicted nor rejoiced, angry nor pleafed at what happens in it, any
farther than perfonal friendfhips intereft me in the
affairs of it, and this principle extends my cares but
a little way. Perfect tranquillity is the general tenour of my life : good digeftions, ferene weather,
and fome other mechanic fprings, wind me above it
now and then, but I never fall below it ; I am fometimes gay, but I am never fad. I have gained new
friends, and have loft fome old ones ; my acquifitions
of this kind give me a good deal of pleafure, becaufe they have not been made lightly : I know no
vows fo folemn as thofe of friendfhip, and therefore
a pretty long noviciate of acquaintance fhould methinks precede them : my loffes of this kind give me
but little trouble, I contributed nothing to them,
and a friend who breaks with me unjuftly, is not
worth preferving. As foon as I leave this town
(which will be in a few days), I fhall fall back into
that courfe of life, which keeps knaves and fools at
a great diftance from me : I have an averfion to
them both, but in the ordinary courfe of life I
think I can bear the fenfible knave better than the
fool. One muft indeed with the former be in fome
or other of the attitudes of thofe wooden men whom
I have feen before a fword-cutler's fhop in Germany,
but even in thefe conftrained poftures the witty
rafcal will divert me ; and he that diverts me does
me a great a deal of good, and lays me under an
obligation to him, which I am not obliged to pay
him in another coin : the fool obliges me to be almoft as much upon my guard as the knave, and he
                                                    makes

makes me no amends; he numbs me like the tor-
por, or he teafes me like the fly. This is the picture of an old friend, and more like him than that
will be which you once afked, and which he will
fend you, if you continue ftill to defire it.—Adieu,
dear Swift, with all thy faults I love thee entirely ;
make an effort, and love me on with all mine.

LETTER X.

From Dr SWIFT.

Dublin, Sept. 20. 1723.

REturning from a fummer-expedition of four
months on account of my health, I found a
letter from you, with an appendix longer than yours
from Lord Bolingbroke. I believe there is not a
more miferable malady than an unwillingnefs to
write letters to our beft friends, and a man might be
philofopher enough in finding out reafons for it.
One thing is clear, that it fhews a mighty difference
betwixt friendfhip and love, for a lover (as I have
heard) is always fcribbling to his miftrefs. If I could
permit myfelf to believe what your civility makes
you fay, that I am ftill remembered by my friends in
England, I am in the right to keep myfelf here—
Non fum qualis eram. I left you in a period of life
when one year does more execution than three at
yours, to which if you add the dulnefs of the air,
and of the people, it will make a terrible fum. I
have no very ftrong faith in you pretenders to retirement; you are not of an age for it, nor have gone
through either good or bad fortune enough to go into a corner, and form conclufions *de contemptu mundi et fuga fæculi*, unlefs a poet grows weary of too
much applaufe, as minifters do of too much weight
of bufinefs.

Your happinefs is greater than your merit, in
chufing your favourites fo indifferently among either
party ; this you owe partly to your education, and
partly

partly to your genius employing you in an art in which faction has nothing to do, for I fuppofe Virgil and Horace are equally read by Whigs and Tories. You have no more to do with the conftitution of church and ftate, than a Chriftian at Conftantinople; and you are fo much the wifer and the happier, becaufe both parties will approve your poetry as long as you are known to be of neither.

Your notions of friendfhip are new to me * : I believe every man is born with his *quantum*, and he cannot give to one without robbing another. I very well know to whom I would give the firft places in my friendfhip, but they are not in the way: I am condemned to another fcene, and therefore I diftribute it in pennyworths to thofe about me, and who difpleafe me leaft; and fhould do the fame to my fellow-prifoners, if I were condemned to jail. I can likewife tolerate knaves much better than fools, becaufe their knavery does me no hurt in the commerce I have with them, which however I own is more dangerous, though not fo troublefome, as that of fools. I have often endeavoured to eftablifh a friendfhip among all men of genius, and would fain have it done : they are feldom above three or four contemporaries, and if they could be united, would drive the world before them. I think it was fo among the poets in the time of Auguftus : but envy, and party, and pride, have hindered it among us. I do not include the fubalterns, of which you are feldom without a large tribe. Under the name of poets and fcribblers I fuppofe you mean the fools you are content to fee fometimes, when they happen to be modeft; which was not frequent among them while I was in the world.

I would defcribe to you my way of living, if any method could be called fo in this country. I chufe my companions among thofe of leaft confequence and moft compliance : I read the moft trifling books

* Yet they are the Chriftian notions.

I

I can find, and whenever I write, it is upon the moft trifling fubjects : but riding, walking, and fleeping take up eighteen of the twenty-four hours. I pro-craftinate more than I did twenty years ago, and have feveral things to finifh which I put off to twenty years hence : *Hæc eft vita folutorum*, &c. I fend you the compliments of a friend of yours, who hath paff-ed four months this fummer with two grave acquaint-ance at his country-houfe, without ever once going to Dublin, which is but eight miles diftant ; yet when he returns to London, I will engage you fhall find him as deep in the court of requefts, the park, the opera's, and the coffeehoufe, as any man there. I am now with him for a few days.

You muft remember me with great affection to Dr Arbuthnot, Mr Congreve, and Gay.—I think there are no more *eodem tertio's* between you and me, ex-cept Mr Jervas, to whofe houfe I addrefs this, for want of knowing where you live : for it was not clear from your laft, whether you lodge with Lord Peterborow, or he with you ?

I am ever, &c.

LETTER XI.

Sept. 14, 1725.

I Need not tell you, with what real delight I fhould have done any thing you defired, and in particu-lar any good offices in my power towards the bearer of your letter, who is this day gone for France. Perhaps it is with poets as with prophets, they are fo much better liked in another country than their own, that your gentleman, upon arriving in Eng-land, loft his curiofity concerning me. However, had he tried, he had found me his friend ; I mean he had found me yours. I am difappointed at not knowing better a man whom you efteem, and com-fort myfelf only with having got a letter from you,

with

with which (after all) I fit down a gainer; fince to my great pleafure it confirms my hope of once more feeing you. After fo many difperfions and fo many divifions, two or three of us may yet be gathered to-gether : not to plot, not to contrive filly fchemes of ambition, or to vex our own or other's hearts with bufy vanities (fuch as perhaps at one time of life or o-ther take their tour in every man), but to divert our-felves, and the world too if it pleafes ; or at worft, to laugh at others as innocently and as unhurtfully as at ourfelves. Your travels * I hear much of; my own I promife you fhall never more be in a ftrange land, but a diligent, I hope ufeful, inveftigation of my own territories †. I mean no more tranflations, but fomething domeftic, fit for my own country, and for my own time.

If you come to us, I will find you elderly ladies e-nough that can halloo, and two that can nurfe, and they are too old and feeble to make too much noife ; as you will guefs, when I tell you they are my own mother, and my own nurfe. I can alfo help you to a lady who is as deaf, though not fo old, as your-felf; you will be pleafed with one another, I will en-gage, though you do not hear one another ; you will converfe like fpirits by intuition. What you will moft wonder at, is, fhe is confiderable at court, yet no party-woman ; and lives in court, yet would be eafy, and make you eafy.

One of thofe you mention, (and I dare fay always will remember), Dr Arbuthnot, is at this time ill of a very dangerous diftemper, an impofthume in the bowels ; which is broke, but the event is very un-certain. Whatever that be (he bids me tell you, and I write this by him); he lives or dies your faithful friend ; and one reafon he has to defire a little long-er life, is the wifh to fee you once more.

He is gay enough in this circumftance to tell you, he would give you (if he could) fuch advice as might

* Gulliver.   † The Effay on Man.

cure

cure your deafnefs; but he would not advife you, if you were cured, to quit the pretence of it; becaufe you may by that means hear as much as you will, and anfwer as little as you pleafe. Believe me

Yours, &c.

LETTER XII.

From Dr SWIFT.

Sept. 29. 1725.

I Am now returning to the noble fcene of Dublin, into the grand monde, for fear of burying my parts; to fignalize myfelf among curates and vicars, and correct all corruptions crept in relating to the weight of bread and butter, through thofe dominions where I govern. I have employed my time (befides ditching) in finifhing, correcting, amending, and tranfcribing my * travels, in four parts complete, newly augmented, and intended for the prefs when the world fhall deferve them, or rather when a printer fhall be found brave enough to venture his ears. I like the fcheme of our meeting after diftreffes and difperfions: but the chief end I propofe to myfelf in all my labours, is to vex the world, rather than divert it; and if I could compafs that defign without hurting my own perfon or fortune, I would be the moft indefatigable writer you have ever feen, without reading. I am exceedingly pleafed that you have done with tranflations. Lord Treafurer Oxford often lamented, that a rafcally world fhould lay you under a neceffity of mifemploying your genius for fo long a time. But fince you will now be fo much better employed, when you think of the world, give it one lafh the more at my requeft. I have ever hated all nations, profeffions, and communities; and all my love is towards individuals. For inftance, I hate the tribe of lawyers; but I love Counfellor fuch

* Gulliver's travels.

a one, and Judge fuch a one. It is fo with phyficians, (I will not fpeak of my own trade), foldiers,
Englifh, Scotch, French, and the reft. But principally I hate and deteft that animal called *man*, although I heartily love John, Peter, Thomas, and fo.
forth. This is the fyftem upon which I have governed myfelf many years (but do not tell), and fo I
fhall go on till I have done with them. I have got
materials towards a treatife, proving the falfity of
that definition *animal rationale*, and to fhew it fhould
be only *rationis capax*. Upon this great foundation
of mifanthropy (though not in Timon's manner) the
whole building of my travels is erected ; and I never
will have peace of mind, till all honeft men are o:
my opinion. By confequence you are to embrace i'
immediately, and procure that all who deferve my
efteem may do fo too. The matter is fo clear, tha
it will admit of no difpute ; nay, I will hold a hundred pounds that you and I agree in the point.

I did not know your Odyffey was finifhed, being
yet in the country, which I fhall leave in three days
I thank you kindly for the prefent, but fhall like i
three fourths the lefs, for the mixture you mentio:
of other hands ; however, I am glad you faved your
felf fo much drudgery.—I have been long told b
Mr Ford of your great achievements in building an
planting, and efpecially of your fubterranean paffag
to your garden, whereby you turned a blunder int
a beauty, which is a piece of *ars poetica*.

I have almoft done with Harridans, and fhall foo
become old enough to fall in love with girls of fou
teen. The lady whom you defcribe to live at cour
to be deaf, and no party-woman, I take to be my
thology, but know not how to moralize it. Si
cannot be Mercy ; for Mercy is neither deaf, n
lives at court : Juftice is blind, and perhaps dea
but neither is fhe a court-lady : Fortune is bo
blind and deaf, and a court-lady ; but then fhe is
moft damnable party-woman, and will never mal
me eafy, as you promife. It muft be riches, whi
                                              anfwe.

answers all your defcription. I am glad fhe vifits
you ; but my voice is fo weak, that I doubt fhe will
never hear me.

Mr Lewis fent me an account of Dr Arbuthnot's
llnefs; which is a very fenfible affliction to me, who,
by living fo long out of the world, have loft that
hardnefs of heart contracted by years and general
converfation. I am daily lofing friends, and neither
feeking nor getting others. Oh, if the world had but
a dozen of Arbuthnots in it, I would burn my travels! But however he is not without fault. There is
a paffage in Bede, highly commending the piety and
learning of the Irifh in that age, where, after abundance of praifes, he overthrows them all, by lament-
ing that, alas ! they kept Eafter at a wrong time of
the year. So our Doctor has every quality and virtue
that can make a man amiable or ufeful ; but, alas, he
hath a fort of flouch in his walk ! I pray God protect
him, for he is an excellent Chriftian, though not a
Catholic.

I hear nothing of our friend Gay, but I find the
court keeps him at hard meat. I advifed him to
come over here with a Lord Lieutenant. Philips
writes little flams (as Lord Leicefter called thofe fort
of verfes) on Mifs Carteret. A Dublin blackfmith,
a great poet, hath imitated his manner in a poem to
the fame Mifs. Philips is a complainer; and on this
occafion I told Lord Carteret, that complainers never fucceeded at court, though railers do.

Are you altogether a country-gentleman, that I
muft addrefs to you out of London, to the hazard of
your lofing this precious letter, which I will now
conclude, although fo much paper is left? I have an
ill name, and therefore fhall not fubfcribe it ; but
you will guefs it comes from one who efteems and
loves you about half as much as you deferve, I mean
as much as he can.

I am in great concern at what I am juft told is
in fome of the newfpapers, that Lord Bolingbroke is
much hurt by a fall in hunting. I am glad he has

fo much youth and vigour left, (of which he hath
not been thrifty); but I wonder he has no more difcretion.

LETTER XIII.

Oct. 15. 1725.

I Am wonderfully pleafed with the fuddennefs of
your kind anfwer. It makes me hope you are
coming towards us, and that you incline more and
more to your old friends, in proportion as you draw
nearer to them, and are getting into our vortex.
Here is one, who was once a powerful planet, but
has now (after long experience of all that comes of
fhining) learned to be content, with returning to his
firft point, without the thought or ambition of fhining at all. Here is another, who thinks one of the
greateft glories of his father was to have diftinguifhed
and loved you, and who loves you hereditarily. Here
is Arbuthnot, recovered from the jaws of death, and
more pleafed with the hope of feeing you again, than
of reviewing a world; every part of which he has long
defpifed, but what is made up of a few men like
yourfelf. He goes abroad again, and is more cheerful than even health can make a man; for he has a
good confcience into the bargain, (which is the moft
catholic of all remedies, though not the moft univerfal.) I knew it would be a pleafure to you to
hear this, and in truth that made me write fo foon
to you.

I am forry poor P. is not promoted in this age;
for certainly if his reward be of the next, he is of
all poets the moft miferable. I am alfo forry for another reafon; if they do not promote him, they will
fpoil the conclufion of one of my fatires, where,
having endeavoured to correct the tafte of the town
in wit and criticifm, I end thus,

But

But what avails to lay down rules for sense?
In —'s reign these fruitless lines were writ,
When Ambrose Philips was preferr'd for wit!

Our friend Gay is used as the friends of Tories are
by Whigs, (and generally by Tories too.) Because
he had humour, he was supposed to have dealt with
Dr Swift: in like manner as when any one had learning formerly, he was thought to have dealt with the
devil. He puts his whole trust at court in that lady
whom I described to you, and whom you take to be
an allegorical creature of fancy. I wish she really
were riches for his sake; though as for yours, I question whether (if you knew her) you would change
her for the other.

Lord Bolingbroke had not the least harm by his
fall. I wish he had received no more by his other
fall. Lord Oxford had none by his. But Lord Bolingbroke is the most improved mind since you saw
him, that ever was improved, without shifting into a
new body, or being: *paullo minus ab angelis.* I
have often imagined to myself, that if ever all of us
meet again, after so many varieties and changes,
after so much of the old world and of the old man
in each of us has been altered, that scarce a single
thought of the one, any more than a single atom of
the other, remains just the same; I have fancied, I
say, that we should meet like the righteous in the
Millennium, quite in peace, divested of all our former passions, smiling at our past follies, and content
to enjoy the kingdom of the just in tranquillity. But
I find you would rather be employed as an avenging
angel of wrath, to break your vial of indignation
over the heads of the wretched creatures of this
world; nay, would make them *eat your book*, which
you have made (I doubt not) as bitter a pill for them
as possible.

I will not tell you what designs I have in my head
(besides writing a set of maxims in opposition to all
Rochefoucault's principles) till I see you here, face

T 3. to

to face. Then you fhall have no reafon to complain of me, for want of a generous difdain of this world, though I have not loft my ears in yours and their fervice. Lord Oxford too (whom I have now the third time mentioned in this letter, and he deferves to be always mentioned in every thing that is addreff-ed to you, or comes from you) expects you: that ought to be enough to bring you hither; it is a bet-ter reafon than if the nation expected you. For I really enter as fully as you can defire, into your prin-ciple of love of individuals: and I think the way to have a public fpirit is firft to have a private one: for who can believe (faid a friend of mine) that any man can care for a hundred thoufand people, who never cared for one? No ill-humoured man can ever be a patriot, any more than a friend.

I defigned to have left the following page for Dr Arbuthnot to fill; but he is fo touched with the pe-riod in yours to me concerning him, that he intends to anfwer it by a whole letter. He too is bufy about a book, which I guefs he will tell you of. So adieu —What remains worth telling you? Dean Berkley is well, and happy in the profecution of his fcheme. Lord Oxford and Lord Bolingbroke in health; Duke Difney fo alfo; Sir William Wyndham better; Lord Bathurft well. Thefe and fome others preferve their ancient honour and ancient friendfhip. Thofe who do neither, if they were d—d, what is it to a Prote-ftant prieft, who has nothing to do with the dead? I anfwer for my own part as a Papift, I would not pray them out of purgatory.

My name is as bad an one as yours, and hated by all bad poets, from Hopkins and Sternhold, to Gildon and Cibber. The firft prayed againft me with the Turk; and a modern imitator of theirs (whom I leave you to find out) has added the Chri-ftian to them, with proper definitions of each in this manner.

The Pope's the whore of Babylon,
The Turk he is a Jew;   •

The

LETTER. XIV.

From Dr. S W I F T.

Nov. 26. 1725.

I Should fooner have acknowledged yours, if a fe-
verish diforder, and the relics of it, had not difabled me for a fortnight. I now begin to make excufes, becaufe I hope I am pretty near feeing you,
and therefore I would cultivate an acquaintance; becaufe if you do not know me when we meet, you
need only keep one of my letters, and compare it
with my face, for my face and letters are counter-
parts of my heart. I fear I have not expreffed that
right; but I mean well, and I hate blots. I look in
your letter, and in my confcience you fay the fame
thing, but in a better manner. Pray tell my Lord
Bolingbroke, that I wifh he were banifhed again; for
then I fhould hear from him, when he was full of
philofophy, and talked *de contemptu mundi.* My
Lord Oxford was fo extremely kind as to write to me
immediately an account of his fon's birth: which I
immediately acknowledged; but before my letter
could reach him, I wifhed it in the fea. I hope I was
more afflicted than his Lordfhip It is hard that
parfons and beggars fhould be over-run with brats,
while fo great and gocd a family wants an heir to
continue it. I have received his father's picture,
but I lament *(fub figillo confeffionis)* that it is not fo
true a refemblance as I could wifh. Drown the
world! I am not content with defpifing it, but I
would anger it, if I could with fafety. I wifh there
were an hofpital built for its defpifers, where one
might act with fafety; and it need not be a large
building, only I would have it well endowed.
P * * is *fort çhancellant,* whether he fhall turn parfon
or

or no. But all employments here are engaged, or in reverfion. Caft wits and caft beaux have a proper fanctuary in the church : yet we think it a fevere judgment, that a fine gentleman, and fo much the finer for hating ecclefiaftics, fhould be a domeftic humble retainer to an Irifh prelate. He is neither; fecretary nor gentleman-ufher, yet ferves in both capacities. He hath publifhed feveral reafons why he : never came to fee me ; but the beft is, that I have not waited on his Lordfhip. We have had a poem fent from London in imitation of that on Mifs Carteret. It is on Mifs Harvey of a day old ; and we fay and think it is yours. I wifh it were not, becaufe I am againft monopolies.—You might have fpared me a few more lines of your fatire, but I hope in a few months to fee it all. To hear boys like you talk of Millenniums and tranquillity ! I am older by thirty years, Lord Bolingbroke by twenty, and you but by ten, than when we laft were together ; and we fhould differ more than ever, you coquetting a maid of honour, my Lord looking on to fee how the gamefters play, and I railing at you both. I defire you and all my friends will take a fpecial care, that my difaffection to the world may not be imputed to my age ; for I have credible witneffes ready to depofe, that it hath never varied from the twentyfirft to the f—ty-eighth year of my life, (pray fill that blank charitably.) I tell you after all, that I do not hate mankind : it is *vous autres* who hate them, becaufe you would have them reafonable animals, and are angry at being difappointed. I have always rejected that definition, and made another of my own. I am no more angry with—than I was with the kite that laft week flew away with one of my chickens ; and yet I was pleafed when one of my fervants fhot him two days after. This I fay, becaufe you are fo hardy as to tell me of your intentions to write maxims in oppofition to Rochefoucault, who is my favourite, becaufe I found my whole character in him :

him * : however, I will read him again, becaufe it is poffible I may have fince undergone fome alteration.—Take care the bad poets do not out-wit you, as they have ferved the good ones in every age, whom they have provoked to tranfmit their names to pofterity. Mævius is as well known as Virgil, and Gildon will be as well known as you, if his name gets into your verfes : and as to the difference between good and bad fame, it is a perfect trifle. I afk a thoufand pardons, and fo leave you for this time, and will write again, without concerning myfelf whether you write or no.

I am, &c.

LETTER XV.

Dec. 10. 1725.

I Find myfelf the better acquainted with you for a long abfence, as men are with themfelves for a long affliction. Abfence does but hold off a friend, to make one fee him the more truly. I am infinitely more pleafed to hear you are coming near us, than at any thing you feem to think in my favour ; an opinion which has perhaps been aggrandifed by the diftance or dulnefs of Ireland, as objects look larger through a medium of fogs : and yet I am infinitely pleafed with that too. I am much the happier. for finding (a better thing than our wits) our judgments jump in the notion, that all fcribblers fhould be paffed by in filence. To vindicate one's felf againft fuch nafty flander, is much as wife as it was in your countryman, when the people imputed a ftink to him, to prove the contrary by fhewing his backfide. So let Gildon and Philips reft in peace ! What Virgil had to do with Mævius, that he fhould wear him upon his fleeve to all eternity, I do not know. I have been the longer upon this, that I may prepare you

* This, methinks, is no great compliment to his own heart,

for

for the reception both you and your works may poffibly meet in England. We your true acquaintance
will look upon you as a good man, and love you ;
others will look upon you as a wit, and hate you.
So you know the worft ; unlefs you are as vindica-
tive as Virgil, or the aforefaid Hibernian.

I wifh as warmly as you for an hofpital in which
to lodge the defpifers of the world ; only I fear it
would be filled wholly, like Chelfea, with maimed
foldiers, and fuch as had been difabled in its fervice.
I would rather have thofe, that, out of fuch generous principles as you and I, defpife it, fly in its
face, than retire from it. Not that I have much
anger againft the great ; my fpleen is at the little
rogues of it. It would vex one more to be knocked
on the head with a pifs-pot, than by a thunderbolt.
As to great oppreffors, they are like kites or eagles ;
one expects mifchief from them : but to be fquirted
to death (as poor Wycherley faid to me on his deathbed) by apothecaries apprentices, by the underftrap-
pers of under-fecretaries to fecretaries who were no
fecretaries — this would provoke as dull a dog as
Ph——s himfelf.

So much for enemies : now for friends. Mr L——
thinks all this indifcreet : the Doctor not fo ; he loves
mifchief the beft of any good-natured man in England. Lord B. is above trifling. When he writes of
any thing in this world, he is more than mortal : *if
ever he trifles, it muft be when he turns a divine.*
Gay is writing tales for Prince William. I fuppofe
Mr Philips will take this very ill, for two reafons ;
one, that he thinks all childifh things belong to him ;
and the other, becaufe he will take it ill to be taught
that one may write things to a child without being
childifh. What have I more to add ; but that Lord
Oxford defires earneftly to fee you ; and that many
others whom you do not think the worft of, will be
gratified by it? None more, be affured, than yours,
&c.,

P. S. Pope

P. S. Pope and you are very great wits, and I
think very indifferent philofophers. If you defpifed
the world as much as you pretend, and perhaps believe, you would not be fo angry with it. The
founder of your fect, that noble original whom you
think it fo great an honour to refemble *, was a
flave to the worft part of the world, to the court;
and all his big words were the language of a flight-
ed lover, who defired nothing fo much as a reconciliation, and feared nothing fo much as a rupture. I
believe the world hath ufed me as fcurvily as moft
people; and yet I could never find in my heart to be
thoroughly angry with the fimple, falfe, capricious
thing. I fhould blufh alike, to be difcovered fond
of the world, or piqued at it. Your definition of
animal rationis capax, inftead of the common one
animal rationale, will not bear examination. Define
but reafon, and you will fee why your diftinction
is no better than that of the pontiff Cotta, between *mala ratio*, and *bona ratio*. But enough of
this. Make us a vifit, and I will fubfcribe to any
fide of thefe important queftions which you pleafe.
We differ lefs than you imagine perhaps, when
you wifhed me banifhed again: but I am not lefs
true to you and to philofophy in England, than I was
in France.

Yours, &c. B.

LETTER XVI.

From Dr SWIFT.

London, May 4. 1726.

I Had rather live in forty Irelands than under the
frequent difquiets of hearing you are out of order. I always apprehend it moft after a great dinner; for the leaft tranfgreffion of yours, if it be only two bits and one fup more than your ftint, is a

* Seneca.

great

great debauch ; for which you certainly pay more
thon thofe fots who are carried dead drunk to bed.
My Lord Peterborow fpoiled every body's dinner,
but efpecially mine, with telling us that you were
detained by ficknefs. Pray let me have three lines
under any hand or pot-hook that will give me a better account of your health ; which concerns me
more than others, becaufe I love and efteem you for
reafons that moft others have little to do with, and
would be the fame although you had never touched
a pen, further than with writing to me.

I am gathering up my luggage, and preparing
for my journey. I will endeavour to think of you as
little as I can ; and when I write to you, I will ftrive
not to think of you. This I intend in return to your
kindnefs ; and further, I know nobody has dealt
with me fo cruelly as you ; the confequences of
which ufage I fear will laft as long as my life ; for
fo long fhall I be (in fpite of my heart) entirely
yours.

LETTER XVII.

Aug. 22. 1726.

MAny a fhort figh you coft me the day I left
you, and many more you will coft me, till
the day you return. I really walked about like a
man banifhed ; and when I came home, found it no
home. It is a fenfation like that of a limb lopped
off ; one is trying every minute unawares to ufe it,
and finds it is not. I may fay you have ufed me
more cruelly than you have done any other man ;
you have made it more impoffible for me to live at
eafe without you. Habitude itfelf would have done
that, if I had lefs friendfhip in my nature than I
have. Befides my natural memory of you, you
have made a local one, which prefents you to me in
every place I frequent. I fhall never more think of
Lord Cobham's, the woods of Ciceter, or the pleafing profpect of Byberry, but your idea muft be
joined

joined with them; nor fee one feat in my own garden, or one room in my own houſe, without a phantom of you, ſitting or walking before me. I travelled with you to Cheſter, I felt the extreme heat of the weather, the inns, the roads, the confinement and cloſeneſs of the uneaſy coach, and wiſhed a hundred times I had either a deanery or a horſe in my gift. In real truth, I have felt my ſoul peeviſh ever ſince with all about me, from a warm uneaſy deſire after you. I am gone out of myſelf to no purpoſe, and cannot catch you. *Inhiat in pedes*, was not more properly applied to a poor dog after a hare, than to me with regard to your departure. I wiſh I could think no more of it, but lie down and ſleep till we meet again, and let that day (how far ſoever off it be) be the morrow. Since I cannot, may it be my amends that every thing you wiſh may attend you where you are, and that you may find every friend you have there in the ſtate you wiſh him or her; ſo that your viſits to us may have no other effect, than the progreſs of a rich man to a remote eſtate, which he finds greater than he expected; which knowledge only ſerves to make him live happier where he is, with no diſagreeable proſpect if ever he ſhould chuſe to remove. May this be your ſtate till it become what I wiſh. But indeed I cannot expreſs the warmth with which I wiſh you all things, and myſelf you. Indeed you are ingraved elſewhere than on the cups you ſent me, (with ſo kind an inſcription), and I might throw them into the Thames without injury to the giver. I am not pleaſed with them, but take them very kindly too: and had I ſuſpected any ſuch uſage from you, I ſhould have enjoyed your company leſs than I really did; for at this rate I may ſay,

Nec tecum poſſum vivere, nec ſine te.

I will bring you over juſt ſuch another preſent, when I go to the deanery of St Patrick's; which I promiſe you to do, if ever I am enabled to return your kindneſs. *Donarem pateras*, &c. Till then I will

drink (or Gay fhall drink) daily healths to you, and
I will add to your infcription the old Roman vow
for years to come, VOTIS X. VOTIS XX.
My mother's age gives me authority to hope it for
yours. Adieu.

LETTER XVIII.

Sept. 3. 1726.

YOurs to Mr Gay gave me greater fatisfaction
than that to me, (though that gave me a great
deal); for to hear that you were fafe at your journey's
end, exceeds the account of your fatigues while in the
way to it : otherwife believe me, every tittle of each
is important to me, which fets any one thing before
my eyes that happens to you. I writ you a long
letter, which I guefs reached you the day after your
arrival. Since then I had a conference with Sir
———, who expreffed his defire of having feen you
again before you left us. He faid he obferved a willingnefs in you to live among us ; which I did not
deny ; but at the fame time told him, you had no
fuch defign in your coming this time, which was
merely to fee a few of thofe you loved : but that indeed all thofe wifhed it, and particularly Lord Peterborow and myfelf, who wifhed you loved Ireland
lefs, had you any reafon to love England more. I
faid nothing but what I think would induce any man
to be as fond of you as I, plain truth, did they
know either it, or you. I cannot help thinking (when
I confider the whole fhort lift of our friends) that
none of them except you and I are qualified for the
mountains of Wales. The Doctor goes to cards,
Gay to court ; one lofes money, ones lofes his
time : another of our friends labours to be unambi
tious, but he labours in an unwilling foil. One
lady you like has too much of France to be fit for
Wales : another is too much a fubject to princes and
potentates, to relifh that wild tafte of liberty and
poverty. Mr Congreve is too fick to bear a thin air
and

and she that leads him too rich, to enjoy any thing.
Lord Peterborow can go to any climate, but never
stay in any. Lord Bathurst is too great a husband-
man to like barren hills, except they are his own to
improve. Mr Bethel indeed is too good and too honest to live in the world, but yet it is fit, for its example, he should. We are left to ourselves in my
opinion, and may live where we please, in Wales,
Dublin, or Bermudas: and for me, I assure you I
love the world so well, and it loves me so well, that I
care not in what part of it I pass the rest my of days.
I see no sunshine but in the face of a friend.

I had a glimpse of a letter of yours lately, by
which I find you are (like the vulgar) apter to think
well of people out of power, than of people in
power; perhaps it is a mistake, but however there is
something in it generous. Mr *** takes it extreme
kindly, I can perceive, and he has a great mind to
thank you for that good opinion, for which I believe
he is only to thank his ill fortune : for, if I am
not in an errour, he would rather be in power, than
out.

To shew you how fit I am to live in the mountains, I will with great truth apply to myself an old
sentence : " Those that are in, may abide in ;
" and those that are out, may abide out : yet to
" me, those that are in shall be as those that are out,
" and those that are out shall be as those that are
" in."

I am indifferent as to all those matters, but I miss
you as much as I did the first day, when (with a
short sigh) I parted. Where-ever you are, (or on the
mountains of Wales, or on the coast of Dublin,

Tu mihi, seu magni superas jam saxa Timavi,
Sive oram Illyrici legis æquoris—),

I am, and ever shall be yours, &c.

L E T T E R XIX.

Mr G A Y *to Dr* S W I F T.

Nov. 17. 1726.

ABout ten days ago a book was publifhed here of the travels of one Gulliver, which hath been the converfation of the whole town ever fince: the whole impreffion fold in a week; and nothing is more diverting than to hear the different opinions people give of it, though all agree in liking it extremely It is generally faid that you are the author; but I am told, the bookfeller declares, he knows not from what hand it came. From the higheft to the loweft it is univerfally read, from the cabinet-council to the nurfery. The politicians to a man agree, that it is free from particular reflections, but that the fatire on general focieties of men is too fevere. Not but we now and then meet with people of greater perfpicuity, who are in fearch for particular applications in every leaf; and it is highly probable we fhall have keys publifhed to give light into Gulliver's defign. Lord —— is the perfon who leaft approves it, blaming it as a defign of evil confequence to depretiate human nature, at which it cannot be wondered that he takes moft offence, being himfelf the moft accomplifhed of his fpecies, and fo lofing more than any other of that praife which is due both to the dignity and virtue of a man *. Your friend, my Lord Harcourt, commends it very much, though he thinks in fome places the matter too far carried. The Duchefs-dowager of Marlborough is in raptures at it; fhe fays fhe can dream of nothing elfe fince fhe read it: fhe declares, that fhe hath now found out, that her whole life hath been loft in

---

* It is no wonder a man of worth fhould *condemn* a fatire on his fpecies; as it injures virtue and violates truth: and as little, that a corrupt man fhould *approve* it, becaufe it juftifies his principles, and tends to excufe his practice.

carefling

careffing the worft part of mankind, and treating the
beft as her foes; and that if fhe knew Gulliver,
though he had been the worft enemy fhe ever had,
fhe would give up her prefent acquaintance for his
friendfhip. You may fee by this, that you are not
much injured by being fuppofed the author of this
piece. If you are, you have difobliged us, and two
or three of your beft friends, in not giving us the
leaft hint of it while you were with us ; and in particular Dr Arbuthnot, who fays it is ten thoufand pi-
ties he had not known it, he could have added fuch
abundance of things upon every fubject. Among la-
dy-critics, fome have found out that Mr Gulliver
had a particular malice to maids of honour. Thofe
of them who frequent the church, fay, his defign is
impious, and that it is depretiating the works of the
Creator. Notwithftanding, I am told the Princefs
hath read it with great pleafure. As to other critics,
they think the flying ifland is the leaft entertaining ;
and fo great an opinion the town have of the impoffibility of Gulliver's writing at all below himfelf, it
is agreed that part was not writ by the fame hand,
though this hath its defenders too. It hath paffed
Lords and Commons, *nemine contradicente* ; and the
whole town, men, women, and children, are quite
full of it.

Perhaps I may all this time be talking to you of
a book you have never feen, and which hath not
yet reached Ireland ; if it hath not, I believe what
we have faid will be fufficient to recommend it to
your reading, and that you will order me to fend it
to you.

But it will be much better to come over yourfelf,
and read it here, where you will have the pleafure
of variety of commentators, to explain the difficult
paffages to you.

We all rejoice that you have fixed the precife time
of your coming to be *cam hirundine prima* ; which we
modern naturalifts pronounce ought to be reckoned,
contrary to Pliny, in this northern latitude of fifty

two degrees, from the end of February, ſtyl. Greg.
at fartheſt. But to us your friends, the coming of
ſuch a black ſwallow as you, will make a ſummer in
the worſt of ſeaſons. We are no leſs glad at your
mention of Twickenham and Dawley ; and in town
you know you have a lodging at court.

The Princeſs is clothed in Iriſh ſilk ; pray give our
ſervice to the weavers. We are ſtrangely ſurpriſed to
hear that the bells in Ireland ring without your money. I hope you do not write the thing that is not.
We are afraid that B— hath been guilty of that
crime, that you (like Honynhnm) have treated him
as a Yahoo, and diſcarded him your ſervice. I fear
you do not underſtand theſe modiſh terms, which e-
very creature now underſtands but yourſelf.

You tell us your wine is bad, and that the clergy
do not frequent your houſe, which we look upon to
be tautology. The beſt advice we can give you, is,
to make them a preſent of your wine, and come away
to better.

You fancy we envy you, but you are miſtaken ;
we envy thoſe you are with, for we cannot envy the
man we love. Adieu.

LETTER XX.

I Have reſolved to take time ; and in ſpite of all
misfortunes and demurs, which ſickneſs, lameneſs, or diſability of any kind can throw in my way,
to write you (at intervals) a long letter. My two
leaſt fingers of one hand hang impediments to the o-
thers *, like uſeleſs dependents, who only take up

---

* This was occaſioned by a bad accident as he was returning
home in a friend's chariot ; which in paſſing a bridge was overturned, and thrown with the horſes into the river. The glaſſes
being up, and Mr Pope unable to break them, he was in immediate danger of drowning ; when the poſtilion, who had juſt recovered himſelf, beat the glaſs, which lay uppermoſt, to pieces : a
fragment of which cut one of Mr Pope's hands very dangerouſly.

room,

room, and never are active or affiftant to our wants. I
fhall never be much the better for them.—I congratulate you firft upon what you call your coufin's won-
derful book, which is *publica trita manu* at prefent,
and I prophefy will be hereafter the admiration of ail
men. That countenance with which it is received
by fome ftatefmen, is delightful; I wifh I could tell
you how every fingle man looks upon it, to obferve
which has been my whole diverfion this fortnight. I
have never been a night in London fince you left me,
till now for this very end; and indeed it has fully anfwered my expectations.

I find no confiderable man very angry at the book.
Some indeed think it rather too bold, and too general a fatire: but none, that I hear of, accufe it of
particular reflections; (I mean no perfons of confequence, or good judgment; the mob of critics, you
know, always are defirous to apply fatire to thofe
they envy for being above them): fo that you needed not to have been fo fecret upon this head. Motte
received the copy (he tells me) he knew not from
whence, nor from whom, dropped at his houfe in the
dark, from a hackney-coach. By computing the time,
I found it was after you left England; fo, for my
part, I fufpend my judgment.

I am pleafed with the nature and quality of your
prefent to the Princefs. The Irifh ftuff you fent to
Mrs H. her R. H. laid hold of, and has made up for
her own ufe. Are you determined to be national in
every thing, even in your civilities? You are the
greateft politician in Europe at this rate; but as you
are a rational politician, there is no great fear of you,
you will never fucceed.

Another thing in which you have pleafed me, was
what you fay to Mr P. by which it feems to me that
you value no man's civility above your own dignity,
or your own reafon. Surely, without flattery, you
are now above all parties of men; and it is high time
to be fo, after twenty or thirty years obfervation of
the great world.

Nullius

Nullius addictus jurare in verba magistri.

I question not, many men would be of your intimacy, that you might be of their interest : but God forbid any honest or witty man should be of any, but that of his country. They have scoundrels enough to write for their paffions and their designs ; let us write for truth, for honour, and for posterity. If you muft needs write about politics at all, (but perhaps it is full as wife to play the fool any other way), furely it ought to be fo as to preferve the dignity and integrity of your character with thofe times to come, which will moft impartially judge of you.

I wifh you had writ to Lord Peterborow ; no man is more affectionate toward you. Do not fancy none but Tories are your friends ; for at that rate I muft be, at moft, but half your friend, and fincerely I am wholly fo. Adieu, write often, and come foon ; for many wifh you well, and all would be glad of your company.

L E T T E R XXI.

From Dr S w i f t.

Dublin, Nov. 17. 1726.

I Am juft come from anfwering a letter of Mrs H —'s, writ in fuch myftical terms, that I fhould never have found out the meaning, if a book had not been fent me called *Gulliver's Travels,* of which you fay fo much in yours. I read the book over, and in the fecond volume obferve feveral paffages, which appear to be patched and altered *, and the ftyle of a different fort (unlefs I am much miftaken). Dr Arbuthnot likes the projectors leaft † ; others,

---

* This was the fact, which is complained of and redreffed in the late edition printed for A. Donaldfon.

† Becaufe he underftood it to be intended as a fatire on the *Royal Society.*

you

you tell me, the flying ifland : fome think it wrong
to be fo hard upon whole bodies or corporations; yet
the general opinion is, that reflections on particular
perfons are moft to be blamed : fo that, in thefe cafes,
I think the beft method is to let cenfure and opinion
take their courfe. A bifhop here faid, that book
was full of improbable lies, and for his part, he
hardly believed a word of it. And fo much for Gulliver.

Going to England is a very good thing, if it were
not attended with an ugly circumftance of returning
to Ireland. It is a fhame you do not perfuade your
minifters to keep me on that fide, if it were but by a
court-expedient of keeping me in prifon for a plot-
ter ; but at the fame time I muft tell you, that fuch
journeys very much fhorten my life; for a month
here is longer than fix at Twickenham.

How comes friend Gay to be fo tedious ? Another
man can publifh fifty thoufand lies fooner than he
can fifty fables.

I am juft going to perform a very good office; it
is to affift with the Archbifhop, in degrading a parfon who couples all our beggars ; by which I fhall
make one happy man ; and decide the great queftion
of an indelible character in favour of the principles
in fafhion. This I hope you will reprefent to the miniftry in my favour, as a point of merit ; fo farewell
till I return.

I am come back, and have deprived the parfon,
who by a law here is to be hanged the next couple
he marries. He declared to us, that he refolved to be
hanged ; only defired, that when he was to go to the
gallows, the Archbifhop would take off his excommu-
nication. Is not he a good Catholic ? and yet he is
but a Scotchman. This is the only Irifh event I ever
troubled you with, and I think it deferves notice. —
Let me add, that, if I were Gulliver's friend, I
would defire all my acquaintance to give out that his
copy was bafely mangled, and abufed, and added
to,

to, and blotted out by the printer; for fo to me it
feems, in the fecond volume particularly.

Adieu.

L E T T E R   XXII.

From Dr S w i f t.

Dec. 5. 1726,

I Believe the hurt in your hand affects me more
than it does yourfelf, and with reafon, becaufe
I may probably be a greater lofer by it. What have
accidents to do with thofe who are neither jockeys,
nor fox-hunters, nor bullies, nor drunkards? And
yet a rafcally groom fhall gallop a foundered. horfe
ten miles upon a caufey, and get home fafe.

I am very much pleafed that you approve what was
fent; becaufe I remember to have heard a great man
fay, that nothing required more judgment than
making a prefent; which when it is done to thofe of
high rank, ought to be of fomething that is not
readily got for money. You oblige me, and at the
fame time do me juftice in what you obferve as to
Mr P. Befides, it is too late in life for me to act o-
therwife, and therefore I follow a very eafy road to
virtue, and purchafe it cheap. If you will give me
leave to join us, is not your life and mine a ftate of
power, and dependence a ftate of flavery? We care
not threepence whether a prince or minifter will
fee us or no : we are not afraid of having ill offices done us, nor are at the trouble of guarding our
words for fear of giving offence. I do agree that
riches are liberty; but then we are to put into the
balance how long our apprenticefhip is to laft in acquiring them.

Since you have received the verfes, I moft earneftly entreat you to burn thofe which you do not approve, and in thofe few where you may not diflike
fome parts, blot out the reft, and fometimes (though

it be againſt the lazineſs of your nature) be ſo kind
to make a few corrections, if the matter will bear
them. I have ſome few of thoſe things I call thoughts
moral and diverting ; if you pleaſe, I will ſend the
beſt I can pick from them, to add to the new volume.
I have reaſon to chuſe the method you mention of
mixing the ſeveral verſes, and I hope thereby among
the bad critics to be entitled to more merit than is
my due.

This moment I am ſo happy to have a letter from
my Lord Peterborow, for which I entreat you will
preſent him with my humble reſpects and thanks,
though he all-to-be-Gullivers me by very ſtrong in-
ſinuations. Though you deſpiſe riddles, I am ſtrongly tempted to ſend a parcel to be printed by themſelves, and make a nine-penny job for the bookſeller. There are ſome of my own, wherein I exceed
mankind ; *mira poemata !* the moſt ſolemn that
were ever ſeen ; and ſome writ by others, admirable
indeed, but far inferiour to mine ; but I will not
praiſe myſelf. You approve that writer who laughs
and makes others laugh ; but why ſhould I who hate
the world, or you who do not love it, make it ſo
happy ? therefore I reſolve from henceforth to handle
only ſerious ſubjects, *niſi quid tu, docte Trebati, diſſen-
tis.*

Yours, &c.

LETTER XXIII.

March 8. 1726-7.

MR Stopford will be the bearer of this letter,
for whoſe acquaintance I am, among many
other favours, obliged to you : and I think the acquaintance of ſo valuable, ingenious, and unaffected
a man, to be none of the leaſt obligations.

Our miſcellany is now quite printed. I am pro-
digiouſly pleaſed with this joint volume ; in which
methinks we look like friends, ſide by ſide, ſerious

and

and merry by turns, conversing interchangeably, and
walking down hand in hand to posterity ; not in the
stiff forms of learned authors, flattering each other,
and setting the rest of mankind at nought ; but in a
free, unimportant, natural, easy manner, diverting
others just as we diverted ourselves. The third volume consists of verses; but I would chuse to print
none but such as have some peculiarity, and may be
distinguished for ours, from other writers. There is
no end of making books, Solomon said, and above
all of making miscellanies, which all men can make.
For unless there be a character in every piece, like
the mark of the elect, I should not care to be one
of the twelve thousand signed.

You received, I hope, some commendatory verses
from a horse and a Lilliputian, to Gulliver ; and an
heroic epistle of Mrs Gulliver. The bookseller
would fain have printed them before the second edition of the book, but I would not permit it without
your approbation : nor do I much like them. You
fee how much like a poet I write ; and yet if
you were with us, you would be deep in politics.
People are very warm, and very angry, very little to
the purpose ; but therefore the more warm and the
more angry. *Non nostrum est tantas componere lites.*
I stay at Twitnam, without so much as reading news-
papers, votes, or any other paltry pamphlets. Mr
Stopford will carry you a whole parcel of them,
which are sent for your diversion, but not imitation.
For my own part, methinks I am at Glubdubdrib,
with none but ancients and spirits about me.

I am rather better than I use to be at this season,
but my hand (though, as you see, it has not lost its
cunning) is frequently in very awkward sensations,
rather than pain. But to convince you it is pretty
well, it has done some mischief already, and just been
strong enough to cut the other hand, while it was
aiming to prune a fruit-tree.

Lady Bolingbroke has writ you a long, lively letter, which will attend this. She has very bad health,
he

e very good. Lord Peterborow has writ twice to
ou. We fancy some letters have been intercepted,
r loft by accident. About ten thoufand things I
vant to tell you : I wish you were as impatient to
iear them; for if fo, you would, you muft come ear-
y this fpring. Adieu. Let me have a line from you.
am vexed at lofing Mr Stopford as foon as I knew
iim : but I thank God I have known him no long-
r. If every man one begins to value. muft fettle in
reland, pray make me know no more of them, and
forgive you this one.

L E T T E R XXIV.

Oct. 2. 1727.

IT is a perfect trouble to me to write to you, and
your kind letter left for me at Mr Gay's affect-
:d me fo much, that it made me like a girl. I cannot tell what to fay to you ; I only feel that I wish
you well in every circumftance of life ; that it is almoft as good to be hated as to be loved, confidering
the pain it is to minds of any tender turn, to find
:hemfelves fo utterly impotent to do any good, or
give any eafe to thofe who deferve moft from us. I
would very fain know, as foon as you recover your
complaints, or any part of them. Would to God I
could eafe any of them, or had been able even to
have alleviated any ! I found I was not, and truly it
grieved me. I was forry to find you could think
yourfelf eafier in any houfe than in mine, though at
the fame time I can allow for a tendernefs in your
way of thinking, even when it feemed to want that
tendernefs. I cannot explain my meaning ; perhaps
you know it. But the beft way of convincing you of
my indulgence, will be, if I live, to vifit you in Ireland, and act there as much in my own way as you
did here in yours. I will not leave your roof, if I
am ill. To your bad health I fear there was added
fome difagreeable news from Ireland, which might

occafion your fo fudden departure : for the laſt time I
faw you, you aſſured me you would not leave us this
whole winter, unleſs your health grew better; and I
do not find it did fo. I never complied fo unwillingly in my life with any friend as with you, in ſtaying
fo entirely from you ; nor could I have had the conſtancy to do it, if you had not promiſed that before
you went, we ſhould meet, and you would fend to us
all to come. I have given your remembrances to
thoſe you mention in yours. We are quite forry for
you, I mean for ourſelves. I hope, as you do, that
we ſhall meet in a more durable and more ſatisfactory
ſtate : but the leſs fure I am of that, the more I
would indulge it in this. We are to believe, we
ſhall have fomething better than even a friend, there ;
but certainly here we have nothing fo good. Adieu
for this time. May you find every friend you go to
as pleaſed and happy, as every friend you went from
is forry and troubled.

Yours, &c.

LETTER XXV.

From Dr SWIFT.

Dublin, Oct. 12. 1727.

I Have been long reaſoning with myſelf upon the
condition I am in, and in concluſion have
thought it beſt to return to what fortune hath made
my home. I have there a large houſe, and fervants
and conveniencies about me. I may be worſe than
I am, and I have no where to retire. I therefore
thought it beſt to return to Ireland, rather than go
to any diſtant place in England. Here is my main-
tenance, and here my convenience. If it pleaſes
God to reſtore me to my health, I ſhall readily make
a third journey ; if not, we muſt part as all human
creatures have parted. You are the beſt and kindeſt
friend in the world, and I know nobody alive or
dead

ʋhom I am fo much obliged ; and if ever
ʒ me angry, it was for your too much care
ʒ. I have often wifhed that God almighty
fo eafy to the weaknefs of mankind, as to
iends be acquainted in another ftate ; and if
ıwrite an Utopia for heaven, that would be
ıy fchemes. This wildnefs you muft allow
ıufe I am giddy and deaf.
it more convenient to be fick here, without
ıion of making my friends uneafy ; yet my⸗
alone would not have done, if that unfo⸗ .
ımfortlefs deafnefs had not quite tired me.
ılieve I fhould have returned from the inn,
not feared it was only a fhort intermiffion,
year was late, and my licence expiring.
ıefides all other faults, I fhould be a very ill
ı doubt your friendfhip and kindnefs. But
ıleafed God that you are not in a ftate of
o-be mortified with the care and ficknefs of
Two fick friends never did well together ;
ıffice is fitter for fervants and humble com⸗
to whom it is wholly indifferent whether
ıhem trouble or no. The cafe would be quite
ʒ if you were with me ; you could refufe to
ıody ; and here is a large houfe, where we
hear each other if we were both fick. I
ıce of orderly elderly people of both fexes at
d, who are of no confequence, and have
per for attending us ; who can bawl when I
. and tread foftly when I am only giddy and⸗
ʒep.
another reafon for my hafte hither ; which
ıging my agent, the old one having terribly
my little affairs ; to which, however, I am
ı indifferent, that I believe I fhall lofe two
hundred pounds rather than plague my⸗
ı accounts ; fo that I am very well qua⸗
be a Lord, and put into Peter Walter's

God continue and increafe Mr Congreve's
amendment ;

amendment ; though he does not deferve it like you, having been too lavifh of that health which Nature gave him.

I hope my Whitehall landlord is nearer to a place than when I left him ; as the preacher faid, " the " day of judgment was nearer than ever it had been " before."

Pray God fend you health, *det falutem, det opes;; animam æquam tibi ipfe parabis.* You fee Horace wifhed for money, as well as health ; and I would hold a crown he kept a coach ; and I fhall never be a friend to the court, till you do fo too.

Yours, &c,

LETTER XXVI.

From Dr SWIFT,

October 30. 1727.

THE firft letter I writ after my landing was to Mr Gay ; but it would have been wifer to direct it to Tonfon or Lintot, to whom I believe his lodgings are better known than to the runners of the poft-office. In that letter you will find what a quick change I made in feven days from London to the deanery, through many nations and languages unknown to the civilized world. And I have often reflected, in how few hours, with a fwift horfe, or a ftrong gale, a man may come among a people as unknown to him as the antipodes. If I did not know you more by your converfation and kindnefs, than by your letter, I might be bafe enough to fufpect, that, in point of friendfhip, you acted like fome philofophers who writ much better upon virtue than they practifed it. In anfwer, I can only fwear, that you have taught me to dream ; which I had not done in twelve years, further than by inexpreffible nonfenfe : but now I can every night diftinctly fee Twickenham, and the grotto, and Dawley, and many other

et

et cetera's; and it is but three nights since I beat
Mrs Pope. I must needs confefs, that the pleasure I
take in thinking on you, is very much lessened by the
pain I am in about your health. You pay dearly for
the great talents God hath given you ; and for the
consequences of them in the esteem and distinction
you receive from mankind, unless you can provide
a tolerable stock of health : in which pursuit I cannot much commend your conduct, but rather entreat
you would mend it, by following the advice of my
Lord Bolingbroke, and your other physicians. When
you talked of cups and impressions, it came into my
head to imitate you in quoting scripture, not to
your advantage. I mean what was said to David by
one of his brothers ; *I knew thy pride, and the
naughtiness of thy heart.* I remember when it grieved
your soul to see me pay a penny more than my club
at an inn, when you had maintained me three
months at bed and board ; for which, if I had dealt
with you in the Smithfield way, it would have coft
me a hundred pounds ; for I live worse here upon
more. Did you ever confider, that I am for life almoft twice as rich as you, and pay no rent, and
drink French wine twice as cheap as you do Port,
and have neither coach, chair, nor mother ? As to
the world, I think you ought to fay to it with St
Paul, *If we have fown unto you fpiritual things, is it
a great thing if we fhall reap your carnal things ?*
This is more proper ftill, if you confider the French
word *fpiritual*, in which fenfe the world ought to
pay you better than they do. If you made me a
present of a thoufand pound, I would not allow myfelf to be in your debt ; and if I made you a prefent
of two, I would not allow myfelf to be out of it.
But I have not half your pride. Witnefs what Mr
Gay fays in his letter, that I was cenfured for begging prefents, though I limited them to ten fhillings.
I fee no reafon (at leaft my friendfhip and vanity fee
none) why you fhould not give me a vifit, when you
fhall happen to be difengaged. I will fend a perfon

to Chester to take care of you; and you shall be
used by the best folks we have here, as well as civility and good-nature can contrive. I believe local
motion will be no ill physic; and I will have your
coming inscribed on my tomb, and recorded in ne-
ver-dying verse.

I thank Mrs Pope for her prayers; but I know
the mystery. A person of my acquaintance, who
used to correspond with the last Great Duke of Tuf-
cany, shewing one of the Duke's letters to a friend,
and professing great sense of his Highness's friendship, read this passage out of the letters, *I would
give one of my fingers to procure your real good.* The
person to whom this was read, and who knew the
Duke well, said, the meaning of *real good* was only,
that the other might turn a good Catholic. Pray ask
Mrs Pope whether this story is applicable to her and
me? I pray God bless her; for I am sure she is a
good Christian, and (which is almost as rare) a good
woman.

Adieu.

LETTER XXVII.

Mr G A Y *to* Dr S W I F T.

Oct. 22. 1727.

THE Queen's family is at last settled, and in the
list I was appointed gentleman-usher to the
Princess Louisa, the youngest Princess; which, upon
account that I am so far advanced in life, I have declined accepting; and have endeavoured, in the best
manner I could, to make my excuses by a letter to
her Majesty. So now all my expectations are va-
nished; and I have no prospect, but in depending
wholly upon myself, and my own conduct. As I am
used to disappointments, I can bear them; but as I
can have no more hopes, I can no more be disappointed; so that I am in a blessed condition.—You
remember

remember you were advifing me to go into Newgate to finifh my fcenes the more correctly.—I now think I fhall, for I have no attendance to hinder me.; but my opera is already finifhed. I leave the reft of this paper to Mr Pope.

Gay is a free-man, and I writ him a long congratulatory letter upon it. Do you the fame. It will mend him, and make him a better man than a court could do. Horace might keep his coach in Auguftus's time, if he pleafed ; but I will not in the time of our Auguftus. My poem, (which it grieves me that I dare not fend you a copy of, for fear of the Curls and Dennis's of Ireland, and ftill more for fear of the worft of traitors, our friends and, admirers), my poem, I fay, will fhew what a diftinguifhing age we lived in. Your name is in it, with fome others, under a mark of fuch ignominy as you will not much grieve to wear in that company. Adieu, and God blefs you, and give you health and fpirits,

Whether thou chufe Cervantes' ferious air,
Or laugh and fhake in Rab'lais' eafy chair,
Or in the graver gown inftruct mankind,
Or, filent, let thy morals tell thy mind.

Thefe two verfes are over and above what I have faid of you in the poem. Adieu.

LETTER XXVIII.

Dr SWIFT *to* Mr GAY.

Dublin, Nov. 23. 1727.

I Entirely approve your refufal of that employment, and your writing to the Queen. I am perfectly confident you have a keen enemy in the miniftry. God forgive him, but not till he puts himfelf in a ftate to be forgiven. Upon reafoning with myfelf, I fhould hope they are gone too far to difcard

difcard you quite, and that they will give you fomething ; which, although much lefs than they ought,
will be (as far as it is worth) better circumftantia-
ted : and fince you already juft live, a middling help
will make you juft tolerable. Your latenefs in life
(as you fo foon call it) might be improper to begin
the world with, but almoft the eldeft men may hope
to fee changes in a court. A minifter is always
feventy : you are thirty years younger; and confider,
Cromwell himfelf did not begin to appear till he
was older than you. I beg you will be thrifty,
and learn to value a fhilling, which Dr Birch faid
was a ferious thing. Get a ftronger fence about your
1000 l. and throw the inner fence into the heap, and
be advifed by your Twickenham landlord and me
about an annuity. You are the moft refractory, honeft, good-natured man I ever have known. I could
argue out this paper. — I am very glad your opera is
finifhed, and hope your friends will join the readier
to make it fucceed, becaufe you are ill-ufed by
others.

I have known courts. thefe thirty-fix years, and
know they differ ; but in fome things they are extremely conftant. Firft, in the trite old maxim of a
minifter's never forgiving thofe he hath injured.
Secondly, in the infincerity of thofe who would be
thought the beft friends. Thirdly, in the love of
fawning, cringing, and tale-bearing. Fourthly, in
facrificing thofe whom we really wifh well, to a point
of intereft, or intrigue. Fifthly, in keeping every
thing worth taking, for thofe who can do fervice or
differvice.

Now, why does not Pope publifh his dulnefs * ?
The rogues he marks will die of themfelves in peace,
and fo will his friends, and fo there will be neither
punifhment nor reward.—Pray inquire how my Lord
St John does ? There is no man's health in England I
am more concerned about than his.—I wonder whe-

* The Dunciad.   ,

ther

ther you begin to taſte the pleaſure of independency ? or whether you do not ſometimes leer upon the
court, *oculo retorto*. Will you not think of an annuity, when you are two years older, and have doubled
your purchaſe-money ? Have you dedicated your
opera, and got the uſual dedication-fee of twenty
guineas ? How is the Doctor ? does he not chide that
you never called upon him for hints ? Is my Lord
Bolingbroke, at the moment I am writing, a pl nter,
a philoſopher, or a writer ? Is Mr Pultney in expectation of a ſon, or my Lord Oxford of a new old
manuſcript ?

I bought your opera to-day for ſixpence ; a curſed
print. I find there is neither dedication nor preface,
both which wants I approve ; it is in the *grand
gout*.

We are as full of it, *pro modulo noſtro*, as London
can be ; continually acting, and houſes crammed,
and the Lord Lieutenant ſeveral times there laughing his heart out. I did not underſtand that the
ſcene of Locket and Peachum's quarrel was an imitation of one between Brutus and Caſſius, till I was
told it. I wiſh Mackheath, when he was going to
be hanged, had imitated Alexander the Great when
he was dying. I would have had his fellow-rogues
deſire his commands about a ſucceſſor, and he to anſwer, Let it be the moſt worthy, &c. We hear a million of ſtories about the opera, of the applauſe at
the ſong, *That was levell'd at me*, when two great
miniſters were in a box together, and all the world
ſtaring at them. I am heartily glad your opera hath
mended your purſe, though perhaps it may ſpoil your
court.

Will you deſire my Lord Bolingbroke, Mr Pultney, and Mr Pope, to command you to buy an annuity with two thouſand pounds, that you may
laugh at courts, and bid miniſters———

Ever preſerve ſome ſpice of the alderman, and
prepare againſt age, and dulneſs, and ſickneſs, and
coldneſs or death of friends. A where has a reſource
                                                left,

left, that fhe can turn bawd; but an old decayed
poet is a creature abandoned, and at mercy, when he
can find none.. Get me likewife Polly's mezzotin-
to. Lord, how the fchoolboys at Weftminfter, and
univerfity-lads adore you at this juncture ! Have .
you made as many men laugh, as minifters can make
weep ?

I will excufe Sir ——— the trouble of a letter.
When ambaffadors came from Troy to condole with
Tiberius upon the death of his nephew, after two
years ; the Emperor anfwered, that he likewife con-
doled with them for the untimely death of Hector. .
I always loved and refpected him very much, and do
ftill as much as ever : and it is a return fufficient, if
he pleafes to accept the offers of my moft humble :
fervice.

The Beggar's opera hath knocked down Gulliver;
I hope to fee Pope's Dulnefs knock down the
Beggar's opera, but not till it hath fully done its.
job.

To expofe vice, and make people laugh with innocence, does more public fervice than all the minifters of ftate from Adam to Walpole ; and fo
adieu.

LETTER XXIX.

Lord BOLINGBROKE *to Dr* SWIFT.

POpe charges himfelf with this letter. He has
been here two days; he is now hurrying to
London ; he will hurry back to Twickenham in two
days more ; and, before the end of the week, he will
be, for ought I know, at Dublin. In the mean time,
his *Dulnefs* * grows and flourifhes, as if he was there
already. It will indeed be a noble work. The many
will ftare at it, the few will fmile, and all his patrons, from Bickerftaff to Gulliver, will rejoice, to fee
themfelves adorned in that immortal piece.

* The Dunciad.

I,

I hear that you have had fome return of your illnefs, which carried you fo fuddenly from us, (if indeed it was your own illnefs which made you in fuch
hafte to be at Dublin). Dear Swift, take care of
your health. I will give you a receipt for it, *à la*
Montagne, or, which is better, *à la Bruyere*. *Nou-*
rirer bien votre corps ; ne le fatiguer jamais : laiffer
rouiller l'efprit, meuble inutil, voire outil dangereux :
laiffer fonner vos cloches le matin, pour eveiller les cha-
noines, et pour faire dormir le Doyen d'un fommeil
doux et profond, qui lui procure de beaux fonges :
lever vous tard, et aller à l'églife, pour vous faire
payer d'avoir bien dormi et bien dejeuné. As to myfelf, (a perfon about whom I concern myfelf very
little), I muft fay a word or two out of complaifance
to you. I am in my farm, and here I fhoot ftrong
and tenacious roots. I have caught hold of the earth,
(to ufe a gardener's phrafe), and neither my enemies
nor my friends will find it an eafy matter to tranf-
plant me again. Adieu. Let me hear from you, at
leaft of you. I love you for a thoufand things ; for
none more than for the juft efteem and love which
you have for all the fons of Adam.

P. S. According to Lord Bolingbroke's account,
I fhall be at Dublin in three days. I cannot help
adding a word, to defire you to expect my foul there
with you by that time ; but as for the jade of a body that is tacked to it, I fear there will be no drag-
ging it after. I affure you I have few friends here
to detain me, and no powerful one at court abfolutely to forbid my journey. I am told the gynocracy
are of opinion, that they want no better writers
than Cibber and the Britifh journalift ; fo that we
may live at quiet, and apply ourfelves to our more
abftrufe ftudies. The only courtiers I know, or have
the honour to call my friends, are John Gay and
Mr Bowry. The former is at prefent fo employed
in the elevated airs of his opera, and the latter in
the exaltation of his high dignity, (that of her Majefty's

jefly's waterman), that I can fcarce obtain a categorical anfwer from either to any thing I fay to them. But the opera fucceeds extremely, to yours and my extreme fatisfaction, of which he promifes this poft to give you a full account. I have been in a worfe condition of health than ever, and think my immortality is very near out of my enjoyment : fo it muft be in you, and in pofterity, to make me what amends you can for dying young. Adieu. While I am, I am yours. Pray love me, and take care of yourfelf.

LETTER XXX.

March 23. 1727-8.

I Send you a very odd thing, a paper printed in Bofton in New-England, wherein you will find a real perfon, a member of their parliament, of the name of *Jonathan Gulliver*. If the fame of that traveller has travelled thither, it has travelled very quick to have folks chriftened already by the name of the fuppofed author. But if you object, that no child fo lately chriftened could be arrived at years of maturity to be elected into parliament ; I reply, (to folve the riddle), that the perfon is an *Anabaptift*, and not chriftened till full age, which fets all right. However it be, the accident is very fingular, that their two names fhould be united.

Mr Gay's opera has been acted near forty days running, and will certainly continue the whole feafon. So he has more than a fence about his thoufand pound : he will foon be thinking of a fence about his two thoufand. Shall no one of us live as we would wifh each other to live ? Shall he have no annuity, you no fettlement on this fide, and I no profpect of getting to you on the other ? This world is made for Cæfar,—as Cato faid ; for ambitious, falfe, or flattering people, to domineer in. Nay they would not, by their good-will, leave us our very books, thoughts, or words, in quiet. I defpife the
world

world yet, I affure you, more than either Gay or you, and the court more than all the reft of the world. As for thofe fcribblers for whom you apprehend I would fupprefs my *Dulnefs*, (which by the way, for the future, you are to call by a more pompous name, *The Dunceiad*), how much that neft of hornets are my regard, will eafily appear to you, when you read the treatife of the Bathos.

At all adventures, yours and my name fhall ftand linked as friends to pofterity, both in verfe and profe, and (as Tully calls it) *in confuetudine ftudiorum*. Would to God our perfons could but as well, and as furely, be infeparable! I find my other ties dropping from me : fome worn off, fome torn off, others relaxing daily : my greateft, both by duty, gratitude, and humanity, time is fhaking every moment, and it now hangs but by a thread ! I am many years the older, for living fo much with one fo old ; much the more helplefs, for having been fo long helped and tended by her; much the more confiderate and tender, for a daily commerce with one who required me juftly to be both to her ; and confequently the more melancholy and thoughtful ; and the lefs fit for others, who want only in a companion or a friend, to be amufed or entertained. My conftitution too has had its fhare of decay, as well as my fpirits, and I am as much in the decline at forty, as you at fixty. I believe we fhould be fit to live together, could I get a little more health, which might make me not quite infupportable. Your deafnefs would agree with my dulnefs ; you would not want me to fpeak when you could not hear. But God forbid you fhould be as deftitute of the focial comforts of life, as I muft when I lofe my mother ; or that ever you fhould lofe your more ufeful acquaintance fo utterly, as to turn your thoughts to fuch a broken reed as I am, who could fo ill fupply your wants. I am extremely troubled at the returns of your deafnefs ; you cannot be too particular in the accounts of your health to me ; every thing you do or fay in this kind obliges me, nay, delights me, to fee the juftice you do me, in thinking me concerned in all your concerns ; fo that though the pleafanteft thing you can tell me be that you are better or eafier, next to that it pleafes me, that you make me the perfon you would complain to.

As the obtaining the love of valuable men is the happieft end I know of this life, fo the next felicity is, to get rid of fools and fcoundrels ; which I cannot but own to you was one part of my defign in falling upon thefe authors, whofe incapacity is not greater than their infincerity, and of whom I have always found, (if I may quote myfelf),

That each bad author is as bad a friend.

This poem will rid me of thofe infects.

Cedite, Romani fcriptores, cedite, Graii ;
Nefcio quid *majus nafcitur Iliade* ;

I mean than *my Iliad* ; and I call it *Nefcio quid,* which is a degree of modefty ; but however; if it fi- lence thefe fellows *, it muft be fomething greater than any Iliad in Chriftendom.

Adieu.

LETTER XXXI.

From Dr SWIFT.

Dublin, May 10. 1728.

I Have with great pleafure fhewn the New-England newfpaper with the two names *Jonathan Gulli- ver* ; and I remember Mr Fortefcue fent you an ac- count from the affizes of one *Lemuel Gulliver,* who had a caufe there, and loft it on his ill reputation of being a liar. Thefe are not the only obfervations I have made upon odd ftrange accidents in trifles, which in things of great importance would have been

* It did, in a litle time, effectually filence them.

matter for hiftorians. Mr Gay's opera hath been
acted here twenty times ; and my Lord Lieutenant *
tells me, it is very well performed ; he hath feen it
often, and approves it much.

You give a moft melancholy account of yourfelf,
and which I do not approve. I reckon, that a man
fubject like us to bodily infirmities, fhould only occafionally converfe with great people, notwithftanding all their good qualities, eafineffes, and kindneffes.
There is another race which I prefer before them, as
beef and mutton for conftant diet before partridges :
I mean a middle kind both for underftanding and
fortune, who are perfectly eafy, never impertinent,
complying in every thing, ready to do a hundred
little offices that you and I may often want, who dine
and fit with me five times for once that I go to them,
and whom I can tell without offence, that I am o-
therwife engaged at prefent. This you cannot expect from any of thofe that either you, or I, or both
are acquainted with on your fide ; who are only fit
for our healthy feafons, and have much bufinefs of
their own. God forbid I fhould condemn you to
Ireland (*quanquam O !*) ; and for England I defpair ;
and indeed a change of affairs would come too late
at my feafon of life, and might probably produce
nothing on my behalf. You have kept Mrs Pope
longer, and have had her care beyond what from nature you could expect ; not but her lofs will be very
fenfible, whenever it fhall happen. I fay one thing,
that both fummers and winters are milder here than
with you ; all things for life in general better for a
middling fortune : you will have an abfolute command of your company, with whatever obfequiouf-
nefs or freedom you may expect or allow. I have an
elderly houfekeeper †, who hath been my W—lp—le
above thirty years, whenever I lived in this kingdom. I have the command of one or two villas near
this town : you have a warm apartment in this houfe,
and two gardens for amufement. I have faid enough,

* Lord Carteret.   † Mrs Brent.

Y 2.   yet

yet not half. Except abſence from friends, I confeſs
freely that I have no diſcontent at living here ; beſides what ariſes from a ſilly ſpirit of liberty, which
as it neither ſours my drink, nor hurts my meat, nor
ſpoils my ſtomach farther than in imagination, ſo I
reſolve to throw it off. .

   You talk of this Dunciad ; but I am impatient to
have it *volare per ora* ; — there is now a vacancy for
fame. The Beggar's opera hath done its taſk ; *diſce-
dat, uti conviva ſatur.*

Adieu.

LETTER XXXII.

From Dr SWIFT.

June 1. 1728.

I Look upon my Lord Bolingbroke and us two, as
a peculiar triumvirate, who have nothing to expect, or to fear ; and ſo far fitteſt to converſe with
one another. Only he and I are a little ſubject to
ſchemes ; and one of us (I will not ſay which) upon
very weak appearances; and this you have nothing to
do with. I do profeſs without affectation, that your
kind opinion of me as a patriot (ſince you call it ſo)
is what I do not deſerve ; becauſe what I do is owing
to perfect rage and reſentment, and the mortifying
ſight of ſlavery, folly, and baſeneſs about me, among
which I am forced to live. And I will take my oath,
that you have more virtue in an hour, than I in ſeven
years : for you deſpiſe the follies and hate the vices
of mankind, without the leaſt ill effect on your temper ; and with regard to particular men, you are inclined always rather to think the better; whereas
with me it is always directly contrary. I hope, however, this is not in you from a ſuperiour principle of
virtue, but from your ſituation, which hath made all
parties and intereſts indifferent to you, who can be
under no concern about high and low church, Whig
and Tory, or who is firſt miniſter.——Your long letter

ter was the laſt I received till this by Dr Delany, although you mention another ſince. The Doctor told
me your ſecret about the Dunciad; which does not
pleaſe me, becauſe it defers gratifying my vanity in
the moſt tender point, and perhaps may wholly diſap-
point it. As to one of your inquiries, I am eaſy enough
in great matters, but have a thouſand paltry vexations in my little ſtation; and the more contemptible,
the more vexatious. There might be a Lutrin writ
upon the tricks uſed by my chapter to teaſe me. I
do not converſe with one creature of ſtation or title,
but I have a ſet of eaſy people whom I entertain
when I have a mind. I have formerly deſcribed
them to you; but, when you come, you ſhall have
the honours of the country as much as you pleaſe,
and I ſhall on that account make a better figure as long
as I live. Pray God preſerve Mrs Pope for your ſake
and eaſe; I love and eſteem her too much to wiſh it
for her own. If I were five and twenty, I would wiſh
to be of her age, to be as ſecure as ſhe is of a better
life. Mrs P. B. has writ to me, and is one of the
beſt letter-writers I know; very good ſenſe, civility,
and friendſhip, without any ſtiffnefs or conſtraint.
The Dunciad has taken wind here; but if it had
not, you are as much known here as in England, and
the univerſity-lads will croud to kiſs the hem of your
garment. I am grieved to hear that my Lord Bolingbroke's ill health forced him to the Bath. Tell
me, is not Temperance a neceſſary virtue for great
men, ſince it is the parent of Eaſe and Liberty? ſo
neceſſary for the uſe and improvement of the mind,
and which philoſophy allows to be the greateſt feli-
cities of life? I believe, had health ben given ſo liberally to you, it would have been better huſbanded
without ſhame to your parts.

LETTER XXXIII.

Dawley, *June* 28. 1728.

I Now hold the pen for my Lord Bolingbroke, who is reading your letter between two haycocks; but his attention is fomewhat diverted by cafting his eyes on the clouds, not in admiration of what you fay, but for fear of a fhower. He is pleafed with your placing him in the triumvirate, between yourfelf and me; though he fays that he doubts he fhall fare like Lepidus, while one of us runs away with all the power like Auguftus, and another with all the pleafures like Anthony. It is upon a forefight of this, that he has fitted up his farm, and you will agree, that this fcheme of retreat at leaft is not founded upon weak appearances. Upon his return from the Bath, all peccant humours, he finds, are purged out of him; and his great temperance and œconomy are fo fignal, that the firft is fit for my conftitution, and the latter would enable you to lay up fo much money as to buy a bifhopric in England. As to the return of his health and vigour, were you here, you might inquire of his haymakers; but as to his temperance, I can anfwer, that (for one whole day) we have had nothing for dinner but mutton-broth, beans, and bacon, and a barn-door fowl.

Now his Lordfhip is run after his cart, I have a moment left to myfelf to tell you, that I overheard him yefterday agree with a painter for 200 *l.* to paint his country-hall with trophies of rakes, fpades, prongs, &c. and other ornaments, merely to countenance his calling this place a farm.—Now turn over a new leaf.—

He bids me affure you, he fhould be forry not to have more fchemes of kindnefs for his friends, than of ambition for himfelf. There, though his fchemes may be weak, the motives at leaft are ftrong. And

he fays further, if you could bear as great a fall,
and decreafe of your revenues, as he knows by experience he can, you would not live in Ireland an
hour.

The Dunciad is going to be printed in all pomp,
with the infcription, which makes me proudeft. It
will be attended with *Proeme, Prolegomena, Teftimo-
nia Scriptorum, Index Authorum*, and notes *variorum*.
As to the latter, I defire you to read over the text,
and make a few in any way you like beft *, whether
dry raillery, upon the ftyle and way of commenting
of trivial critics ; or humorous, upon the authors
in the poem ; or hiftorical, of perfons, places, times ;
or explanatory; or collecting the parallel paffages of
the ancients. Adieu. I am pretty well, my mother not ill ; Dr Arbuthnot vexed with his fever
by intervals. I am afraid he declines, and we fhall
lofe a worthy man. I am troubled about him very
much.

I am, &c.

L E T T E R   XXXIV.

From Dr S W I F T.

July 16. 1728.

I Have often run over the *Dunciad* in an Irifh edition, (I fuppofe full of faults), which a gentleman
fent me. The notes I could wifh to be very large,
in what relates to the perfons concerned.; for I have
long obferved, that twenty miles from London nobody underftands hints, initial letters, or town facts
and paffages ; and in a few years not even thofe who
live in London. I would have the names of thofe
fcribblers printed indexically at the beginning or end
of the poem, with an account of their works, for the
reader to refer to. I would have all the parodies (as

* Dr Swift did fo.

they

they are called) referred to the author they imitate.—
When I began this long paper, I thought I fhould
have filled it with fetting down the feveral paffages I
had marked in the edition I had ; but I find it unneceffary, fo many of them falling under the fame rule.
After twenty times reading the whole, I never in my
opiniun faw fo much gocd fatire, or more good fenfe,
in fo many lines. How it paffes in Dublin, I know
not yet ; but I am fure it will be a great difadvan-
tage to the poem, that the perfons and facts will not
be underftood, till an explanation comes out, and a
very full one. I imagine it is not to be publifhed
till towards winter, when folks begin to gather in
town. Again I infift, you muft have your afterifks
filled up with fome real names of real dunces.

I am now reading your preceding letter, of June
28. and find that all I have advifed above is mentioned there. I would be glad to know whether the
quarto edition is to come out anonymoufly, as publifhed by the commentator, with all his pomp of
prefaces, &c. and among many complaints of fpurious editions. I am thinking whether the editor
fhould not follow the old ftyle of this excellent author, &c. and refine in many places when you meant
no refinement ; and into the bargain take all the load
of naming the dunces, their qualities, hiftories, and
performances.

As to yourfelf, I doubt you want a fpurrer-on to
exercife and to amufements ; but to talk of decay at
your feafon of life, is a jeft. But you are not fo regular as I. You are the moft temperate man God-ward,
and the moft intemperate your felf-ward, of moft I
have known. I fuppofe Mr Gay will return from
the Bath with twenty pounds more flefh, and two
hundred lefs in money. Providence never defigned
him to be above two and twenty, by his thought-
leffnefs and cullibility. He hath as little forefight
of age, ficknefs, poverty, or lofs of admirers, as a
girl at fifteen. By the way, I muft obferve, that
my Lord Bolingbroke (from the effects of his kindnefs

nefs to me) argues moft fophiftically : the fall from
a million to a hundred thoufand pounds is not fo
great, as from eight hundred pounds a-year to one :
befides, he is a controller of fortune, and poverty
dares not look a great minifter in the face under his
loweft declenfion. I never knew him live fo great
and expenfively as he hath done fince his return from
exile ; fuch mortals have refources that others are
not able to comprehend.. But God blefs you, whofe
great genius has not fo tranfported you as to leave
you to the courtefy of mankind ; for wealth is liberty, and liberty is a blefling fitteft for a philofopher,
— and Gay is a flave juft by two thoufand pounds
too little. — And Horace was of my mind, and let
my Lord contradict him, if he dares. ——

L E T T E R XXXV.

Bath, Nov. 12: 1728.

I Have paffed fix weeks in queft of health, and found
it not; but I found the folly of folicitude about
it in a hundred inftances.; the contrariety of opinions
and practices, the inability of phyficians, the blind
obedience of fome patients, and as blind rebellion
of others. I believe at a certain time of life, men
are either fools, or phyficians for themfelves, and
zealots, or divines for themfelves.

It was much in my hopes that you intended us a
winter's vifit; but laft week I repented that wifh,
having been alarmed with a report of your lying ill
on the road from Ireland ; from which I am juft relieved, by an affurance that you are ftill at Sir A—'s
planting and building : two things that I envy you
for, befides a third, which is the fociety of a valuable lady. I conclude, (though I know nothing of
it), that you quarrel with her, and abufe her every
day, if fhe is fo. I wonder I hear of no lampoons
upon her, either made by yourfelf, or by others, becaufe you efteem her. I think it a vaft pleafure, that
whenever

whenever two people of merit regard one another, fo many fcoundrels envy and are angry at them : it is bearing teftimony to a merit they cannot reach ; and if you knew the infinite content I have received of late, at the finding yours and my name conftantly united in any filly fcandal, I think you would go near to fing *Io triumphe !* and celebrate my happinefs in verfe ; and, I believe, if you will not, I fhall. The infcription to the Dunciad is now printed, and inferted in the poem. Do you care I fhould fay any thing farther how much that poem is yours ? fince certainly without you it had never been. Would to God we were together for the reft of our lives ! The whole weight of fcribblers would juft ferve to find us amufement, and not more. I hope you are too well employed to mind them. Every ftick you plant, and every ftone you lay, is to fome purpofe ; but the bufinefs of fuch lives as theirs is but to die daily, to labour, and raife nothing. I only wifh we could comfort each other under our bodily infirmities ; and let thofe who have fo great a mind to have more wit than we, win it and wear it. Give us but eafe, health, peace, and fair weather ! I think it is the beft wifh in the world, and you know whofe it was. If I lived in Ireland, I fear the wet climate would endanger more than my life ; my humour, and health ; I am fo atmofpherical a creature.

I muft not omit acquainting you, that what you heard of the words fpoken of you in the drawing-room, was not true. The fayings of princes are generally as ill related as the fayings of wits. To fuch reports little of our regard fhould be given, and lefs of our conduct influenced by them.

L E T-

Dublin, Feb. 13. 1728.

I Lived very eafily in the country. Sir A. is a man
of fenfe, and a fcholar, has a good voice, and
my Lady a better; fhe is perfectly well bred, and
defirous to improve her underftanding, which is very
good, but cultivated too much like a fine lady. She
was my pupil there, and feverely chid when fhe
read wrong. With that, and walking, and making
twenty little amufing improvements, and writing fa-
mily-verfes of mirth, by way of libels on my Lady,
my time paffed very well, and in very great order; infinitely better than here, where I fee no creature but
my fervants, and my old Prefbyterian houfekeeper,
denying myfelf to every body, till I fhall recover
my ears.

The account of another Lord Lieutenant was
only in a common newfpaper, when I was in the
country; and if it fhould have happened to be true, I
would have defired to have had accefs to him, as the
fituation I am in requires. But this renews the grief
for the death of our friend Mr Congreve, whom I
loved from my youth, and who furely, befides his
other talents, was a very agreeable companion. He
had the misfortune to fquander away a very good
conftitution in his younger days; and I think a man
of fenfe and merit like him, is bound in confcience
to preferve his health for the fake of his friends, as
well as of himfelf. Upon his own account I could
not much defire the continuance of his life under fo
much pain, and fo many infirmities. Years have not
yet hardened me; and I have an addition of weight
on my fpirits fince we loft him; though I faw him
fo feldom; and poffibly if he had lived on, fhould
never have feen him more. I do not only wifh, as

you

you afk me, that I was unacquainted with any deferving perfon, but almoft that I never had a friend.
Here is an ingenious good-humoured phyfician *, a
fine gentleman, an excellent fcholar, eafy in his fortunes, kind to every body, hath abundance of
friends, entertains them often and liberally, they
pafs the evening with him at cards, with plenty of
good meat and wine, eight or a dozen together; he
loves them all, and they him. He has twenty of
thefe at command; if one of them dies, it is no more
than poor Tom! he gets another, or takes up with
the reft, and is no more moved than at the lofs of his
cat: he offends nobody, is eafy with every body.
—Is not this the true happy man? I was defcribing
him to my Lady A——, who knows him too; but fhe
hates him mortally by my character, and will not
drink his health. I would give half my fortune for
the fame temper; and yet I cannot fay I love it; for
I do not love my Lord,—who is much of the
Doctor's nature. I hear Mr Gay's fecond opera †,
which you mention, is forbid; and then he will
be once more fit to be advifed, and reject your advice. Adieu.

L E T T E R XXXVII.

Dr SWIFT to Lord BOLINGBROKE.

Dublin, March 21. 1729.

YOU tell me you have not quitted the defign of
collecting, writing, &c. This is the anfwer
of every finner who defers his repentance. I wifh
Mr Pope were as great an urger as I; who long for
nothing more than to fee truth under your hands,
laying all detraction in the duft.—I find myfelf difpofed every year, or rather every month, to be more
angry and revengeful; and my rage is fo ignoble,

* Dr Helfham.   † Polly.

that

that it defcends even to refent the folly and bafenefs
of the enflaved people among whom I live. I knew
an old Lord in Leicefterfhire, who amufed himfelf
with mending pitchforks and fpades for his tenants
gratis. Yet I have higher ideas left, if I were nearer
to objects on which I might employ them ; and con-
temning my private fortune, would gladly crofs the
channel and ftand by, while my betters were driving
the boars out of the garden, if there be any probable
expectation of fuch an endeavour. When I was of
your age, I often thought of death ; but now after a
dozen years more, it is never out of my mind, and
terrifies me lefs. I conclude, that Providence hath
ordered our fears to decreafe with our fpirits : and
yet I love *la bagatelle* better than ever ; for finding
it troublefome to read at night, and the company
here growing taftelefs, I am always writing bad
profe, or worfe verfes, either of rage or raillery,
whereof fome few efcape to give offence or mirth,
and the reft are burnt.

They print fome Irifh trafh in London, and charge
it on me, which you will clear me of to my friends ;
for all are fpurious except one paper *, for which
Mr Pope very lately chid me. I remember your
Lordfhip ufed to fay, that a few good fpeakers would
in time carry any point that was right ; and that the
common method of a majority, by calling, To the
queftion, would never hold long when reafon was on
the other fide. Whether politics do not change like
gaming by the invention of new tricks, I am ignorant. But I believe in your time, you would never, as a minifter, have fuffered an act to pafs through
the H. of C——s, only becaufe you were fure of a
majority in the H. of L——s to throw it out : becaufe
it would be unpopular, and confequently a lofs of
reputation. Yet this, we are told, hath been the
cafe in the qualification-bill relating to penfioners.
It fhould feem to me, that corruption, like avarice,

---

* Entitled, *A Libel on Dr Delany, and a certain great Lord.*

hath

hath no bounds. I had opportunities to know the proceedings of your miniſtry better than any other man of my rank; and having not much to do, I have often compared it with theſe laſt ſixteen years of a profound peace all over Europe; and we running ſeven millions in debt. I am forced to play at ſmall game, to ſet the beaſts here a-madding, merely for want of better game. *Tentanda via eſt qua me quoque poſſim*, &c.—The d--- take thoſe politics, where a dunce might govern for a dozen years together. I will come in perſon to England, if I am provoked, and ſend for the dictator from the plough. I diſdain to ſay, O *mihi praeteritos* — but *cruda deo viridiſque ſenectus*. Pray, my Lord, how are the gardens? have you taken down the mount, and removed the yew-hedges? Have you not bad weather for the ſpring-corn? Has Mr Pope gone farther in his ethic poems? and is the head-land ſown with wheat? and what ſays Polybius? and how does my Lord St John * ? which laſt queſtion is very material to me, becauſe I love Burgundy, and riding between Twickenham and Dawley.—I built a wall five years ago; and when the maſons played the knaves, nothing delighted me ſo much as to ſtand by, while my ſervants threw down what was amiſs. I have likewiſe ſeen a monkey overthrow all the diſhes and plates in a kitchen, merely for the pleaſure of ſeeing them tumble, and hearing the clatter they made in their fall. I wiſh you would invite me to ſuch another entertainment. But you think, as I ought to think, that it is time for me to have done with the world; and ſo I would, if I could get into a better before I was called into the beſt; and not die here in a rage, like a poiſoned rat in a hole. I wonder you are not aſhamed to let me pine away in this kingdom, while you are out of power.

I come from looking over the *Melange* above written, and declare it to be a true copy of my

---

* Lord St John of Batterſea, father to Lord Bolingbroke.

prefent difpofition; which muſt needs pleaſe you, ſince nothing was ever more diſpleaſing to myſelf. I deſire you to prefent my moſt humble reſpects to my Lady.

L E T T E R XXXVIII.

D<small>r</small> S<small>W I F T</small> *to Lord* B<small>O L I N G B R O K E</small>.

Dublin, April 5. 1729.

I Do not think it could be poſſible for me to hear better news than that of your getting over your ſcurvy ſuit, which always hung as a dead weight on my heart. I hated it in all its circumſtances, as it affected your fortune and quiet, and in a ſituation of life that muſt make it every way vexatious. And as I am infinitely obliged to you for the juſtice you do me in ſuppoſing your affairs do at leaſt concern me as much as my own; ſo I would never have pardoned your omitting it. But before I go on, I cannot forbear mentioning what I read laſt ſummer in a newſpaper, that you were writing the hiſtory of your own times. I ſuppoſe ſuch a report might ariſe from what was not ſecret among your friends, of your intention to write another kind of hiſtory; which you often promiſed Mr. Pope and me to do. I know he deſires it very much; and I am ſure I deſire nothing more, for the honour and love I bear you, and the perfect knowledge I have of your public virtue. My Lord, I have no other notion of Oeconomy, than that it is the parent of Liberty and Eaſe; and I am not the only friend you have who hath chid you in his heart for the neglect of it, though not with his mouth, as I have done. For there is a ſilly errour in the world, even among friends, otherwiſe very good, not to intermeddle with mens affairs in ſuch nice matters. And, my Lord, I have made a maxim, that ſhould be writ in letters of diamonds, That a wiſe man ought to have mo-

ney,

ney in his head,. but not in his heart. Pray, my
Lord, inquire whether your prototype, my Lord
Digby, after the reſtoration, when he was at Briſtol,
did not take ſome care of his fortune, notwithſtanding that quotation I once ſent you out of his ſpeech
- to the H. of Commons? In my conſcience, I believe
Fortune, like other drabs, values a man gradually
leſs for every year he lives. I have demonſtration
for it; becauſe if I play at piquet for ſixpence with
a man or a woman two years younger than myſelf,
I always loſe : and there is a young girl of twenty,.
who never fails of winning my money at backgammon, though ſhe is a bungler, and the game be ec-
cleſiaſtic. As to the public, I confeſs nothing could
cure my itch of meddling with it but theſe frequent
returns of deafneſs, which have hindered me from
paſſing laſt winter in London : yet I cannot but conſider the perfidiouſneſs of ſome people, who, I
thought, when I was laſt there, upon a change that
happened, were the moſt impudent in forgetting their
profeſſions that I have ever known. Pray, will you
pleaſe' to take your pen, and blot me out that political maxim from whatever book it is in, That *res.
nolunt diu male adminiſtrari*; the commonneſs makes
me not know who is the author, but ſure he muſt be
ſome modern.

• I am ſorry for Lady Bolingbroke's ill health : but
I proteſt I never knew a very deſerving perſon of
that ſex, who had not too much reaſon to complain
of ill health. I never wake without finding life a
more inſignificant thing than it was the day before;
which is one great advantage I get by living in this
country, where there is nothing I ſhall be ſorry to
loſe. But my greateſt miſery is recollecting the
ſcene of twenty years paſt; and then all on a ſudden
dropping into the preſent. I remember, when I was
a little boy, I felt a great fiſh at the end of my line,
which I drew up almoſt on the ground, but it dropt
in, and the diſappointment vexes me to this very
day ; and I believe, it was the type of all my future
                                    diſappointments.

difappointments. I fhould be afhamed to fay this to
you, if you had not a fpirit fitter to bear your own
misfortunes, than I have to think of them. Is there
patience left to reflect, by what qualities wealth and
greatnefs are got, and by what qualities they are
loft? I have read my friend Congreve's verfes to
Lord Cobham, which end with a vile and falfe moral; and I remember is not in Horace to Tibullus,
which he imitates, "that all times are equally vir-
" tuous and vitious;" wherein he differs from all
poets, philofophers, and Chriftians, that ever writ.
It is more probable that there may be an equal quan-
tity of virtues always in the world; but fometimes
there may be a peck of it in Afia, and hardly a
thimble-full in Europe. But if there be no virtue,
there is abundance of fincerity; for I will venture all
I am worth, that there is not one human creature in
power, who will not be modeft enough to confefs
that he proceeds wholly upon a principle of corruption. I fay this, becaufe I have a fcheme, in-fpite of
your notions, to govern England upon the principles
of virtue; and when the nation is ripe for it, I defire
you will fend for me. I have learned this by living
like a hermit; by which I am got backwards about
nineteen hundred years in the æra of the world, and
begin to wonder at the wickednefs of men. I dine
alone upon half a difh of meat; mix water with my
wine; walk ten miles a-day; and read Baronius.
*Hic explicit epiftola ad Dom. Bolingbroke, et incipit
ad amicum Pope.*

Having finifhed my letter to Ariftippus, I now begin to you. I was in great pain about Mrs Pope, having heard from others that fhe was in a very dangerous way, which made me think it unfeafonable to
trouble you. I am afhamed to tell you, that, when
I was very young, I had more defire to be famous
than ever fince; and fame, like all things elfe in
this life, grows with me every day more a trifle.
But you, who are fo much younger, although you

want that health you deserve, yet your spirits are as
vigorous as if your body were sounder. I hate a
croud, where I have not an easy place to see and be
seen. A great library always makes me melancholy,
where the best author is as much squeezed, and as
obscure, as a porter at a coronation. In my own
little library, I value the compilements of Grævius
and Gronovius, which make thirty-one volumes in
folio, (and were given me by my Lord Bolingbroke), more than all my books besides ; because,
whoever comes into my closet, casts his eyes immediately upon them, and will not vouchsafe to
look upon Plato or Xenophon. I tell you, it is almost incredible how opinions change by the decline
or decay of spirits ; and I will further tell you, that
all my endeavours from a boy to distinguish myself,
were only for want of a great title and fortune, that
I might be used like a lord by those who have an
opinion of my parts ; whether right or wrong, it is
no great matter ; and so the reputation of wit or
great learning does the office of a blue riband, or
of a coach and six horses. To be remembered for
ever on the account of our friendship, is what would
exceedingly please me ; but yet I never loved to
make a visit, or be seen walking with my betters ;
because they get all the eyes and civilities from me.
I no sooner writ this than I corrected myself, and remembered Sir Fulk Grevil's epitaph, " Here lies,
" &c. who was friend to Sir Philip Sidney." And
therefore I most heartily thank you for your desire
that I would record our friendship in verse ; which if
I can succeed in, I will never desire to write one
more line in poetry while I live. You must present
my humble service to Mrs Pope, and let her know
I pray for her continuance in the world, for her own
reason, that she may live to take care of you.

L E T-

LETTER XXXIX.

From Dr SWIFT.

Aug. 11. 1729.

I AM very fenfible, that in a former letter I talked very weakly of my own affairs, and of my
imperfect wifhes and defires ; which, however, I find
with fome comfort do now daily decline, very fuitable to my ftate of health for fome months paft. For
my head is never perfectly free from giddinefs, and
efpecially towards night. Yet my diforder is very
moderate, and I have been without a fit of deafnefs
this half-year ; fo I am like a horfe, which, though
off his mettle, can trot on tolerably ; and this comparifon puts me in mind to add, that I am returned
to be a rider, wherein I wifh you would imitate me.
As to this country, there have been three terrible
years dearth of corn, and every place ftrowed with
beggars ; but dearths are common in better climates,
and our evils here lie much deeper. Imagine a nation, the two thirds of whofe revenues are fpent out
of it ; and who are not permitted to trade with the
other third, and where the pride of women will not
fuffer them to wear their own manutactures, even
where they excel what come from abroad. This is
the true ftate of Ireland in a very few words.
Thefe evils operate more every day, and the kingdom is abfolutely undone, as I have been telling often in print thefe ten years paft.
　What I have faid requires forgivenefs, but I had
a mind for once to let you know the ftate of our affairs, and my reafon for being more moved than
perhaps becomes a clergyman, and a piece of a philofopher : and perhaps the increafe of years and diforders may hope for fome allowance to complaints,
efpecially when I may call myfelf a ftranger in a
ftrange land. As to poor Mrs Pope, (if fhe be ftill
alive), I heartily pity you and pity her. Her great
piety

piety and virtue will infallibly make her happy in a
better life, and her great age hath made her fully
ripe for heaven and the grave, and her beft friends
will moft wifh her eafed of her labours, when
fhe hath fo many good works to follow them. The
lofs you will feel by the want of her care and kindnefs, I know very well; but fhe has amply done
her part, as you have yours. One reafon why I
would have you in Ireland when you fhall be at your
own difpofal, is, that you may be mafter of two or
three years revenues, *provifæ frugis in annos copia*,
fo as not to be pinched in the leaft when years increafe, and perhaps your health impairs : and when
this kingdom is utterly at an end, you may fupport
me for the few years I fhall happen to live ; and who
knows but you may pay me exorbitant intereft for
the fpoonful of wine, and fcraps of a chicken it will
coft me to feed you ? I am confident you have too
much reafon to complain of ingratitude ; for I never
yet knew any perfon one tenth part fo heartily difpofed as you are to do good offices to others, without the leaft private view.

Was it a gafconade to pleafe me, that you faid
your fortune was increafed 100 *l.* a-year fince I left
you ? you fhould have told me how. Thofe *fubfidia
fenectuti* are extremely defirable, if they could be
got with juftice, and without avarice; of which
vice, though I cannot charge myfelf yet, nor feel
any approaches towards it, yet no ufurer more wifhes
to be richer, (or rather to be furer of his rents). But
I am not half fo moderate as you ; for I declare I
canot live eafily under double to what you are fatif-
fied with.

I hope Mr Gay will keep his 3000 *l.* and live on
the intereft, without decreafing the principal one
penny ; but I do not like your feldom feeing him. I
hope he is grown more difengaged from his intent-
nefs on his own affairs, which I ever difliked, and is
quite the reverfe to you, unlefs you are a very dex-
trous difguifer. I defire my humble fervice to Lord
Oxford,

Oxford, Lord Bathurſt, and particularly to Mrs B——,
but to no lady at court. God bleſs you for being a
greater dupe than I. I love that character too myſelf, but I want your charity. Adieu.

LETTER XL.

Oct. 9. 1729.

IT pleaſes me, that you received my books at laſt :
but you have never once told me if you approve
the whole, or diſapprove not of ſome parts of the
commentary, &c. It was my principal aim in the
entire work to perpetuate the friendſhip between us,
and to ſhew that the friends or the enemies of one
were the friends or enemies of the other. If in any
particular any thing be ſtated or mentioned in a different manner from what you like, pray tell me
freely, that the new editions now coming out here,
may have it rectified. You will find the octavo rather more correct than the quarto, with ſome additions to the notes and epigrams caſt in, which I wiſh
had been increaſed by your acquaintance in Ireland. I
rejoice in hearing that Drapiers-hill is to emulate Parnaſſus. I fear the country about it is as much impo-
veriſhed. I truly ſhare in all that troubles you, and
wiſh you removed from a ſcene of diſtreſs, which I
know works your compaſſionate temper too ſtrongly.
But if we are not to ſee you here, I believe I ſhall
once in my life ſee you there. You think more for
me, and about me, than any friend I have, and you
think better for me. Perhaps you will not be contented, though I am, that the additional 100 *l.* a-
year is only for my life. My mother is yet living,
and I thank God for it : ſhe will never be troubleſome to me, if ſhe be not ſo to herſelf. But a melancholy object it is, to obſerve the gradual decays both
of body and mind, in a perſon to whom one is tied
by the links of both. I cannot tell whether her
death itſelf would be ſo afflicting.

You are too careful of my worldly affairs. I am
rich

rich enough, and I can afford to give away 100 *l.* a-year. Do not be angry : I will not live to be very old ; I have revelations to the contrary. I would not crawl upon the earth without doing a little good when I have a mind to do it. I will enjoy the pleasure of what I give, by giving it alive, and seeing another enjoy it. When I die, I should be ashamed to leave enough to build me a monument, if there were a wanting friend above ground.

Mr Gay assures me his 3000 *l.* is kept entire and sacred ; he seems to languish after a line from you, and complains tenderly. Lord Bolingbroke has told me ten times over he was going to write to you. Has he, or not ? The Doctor is unalterable, both in friendship and quadrille : his wife has been very near death last week : his two brothers buried their wives within these six weeks. Gay is sixty miles off, and has been so all this summer, with the Duke and Duchess of Queensberry. He is the same man : so is every one here that you know. Mankind is unamendable. *Optimus ille qui minimis urgetur.*— Poor Mrs * * is like the rest ; she cries at the thorn in her foot, but will suffer nobody to pull it out. The court-lady I have a good opinion of ; yet I have treated her more negligently than you would do, because you like to see the inside of a court, which I do not. I have seen her but twice. You have a desperate hand at dashing out a character by great strokes, and at the same time a delicate one at fine touches. God forbid you should draw mine, if I were conscious of any guilt : but if I were conscious only of folly, God send it ! for as nobody can detect a great fault so well as you, nobody would so well hide a small one. But, after all, that lady means to do good, and does no harm, which is a vast deal for a courtier. I can assure you that Lord Peterborow always speaks kindly of you, and certainly has as great a mind to be your friend as any one. I must throw away my pen ; it cannot, it will never tell you what I inwardly am to you. *Quod nequeo monstrare, et sentio tantum.*

LETTER XLI.

Lord BOLINGBROKE *to Dr* SWIFT.

Bruffels, Sept. 27. 1729.

I Have brought your French acquaintance * thus
far on her way into her own country, and confiderably better in health than fhe was when fhe
went to Aix. I begin to entertain hopes that fhe
will recover fuch a degree of health as may render
old age fupportable. Both of us have clofed the
tenth luftre, and it is high time to determine how we
fhall play the laft act of the farce. Might not my
life be entitled much more properly a *What-d'ye-
call-it*, than a *farce?* Some comedy, a great deal of
tragedy, and the whole interfperfed with fcenes of
Harlequin, Scaramouch, and Dr Baloardo, the prototype of your hero. — I ufed to think fometimes
formerly of old age and of death : enough to prepare
my mind ; not enough to anticipate forrow, to dafh
the joys of youth, and to be all my life a-dying. I
find the benefit of this practice now, and find it more
as I proceed on my journey : little regret when I
look backwards, little apprehenfion when I look forward. You complain grievoufly of your fituation in
Ireland : I would complain of mine too in England,
but I will not, nay, I ought not ; for I find by long
experience, that I can be unfortunate without being
unhappy. I do not approve your joining together
the *figure of living*, and the *pleafure of giving*,
though your old-prating friend Montagne does fomething like it in one of his rhapfodies. To tell you my
reafons would be to write an eflay, and I fhall hardly have time to write a letter ; but if you will come
over, and live with Pope and me, I will fhew you in
an inftant why thofe two things fhould not *aller de
pair* ; and that forced retrenchments on both may be

* Lady Bolingbroke.

made,

made, without making us even uneafy. You know
that I am too expenfive, and all mankind knows,
that I have been cruelly plundered; and yet I feel
in my mind, the power of defcending without anxiety, two or three ftages more. In fhort, Mr Dean,
if you will come to a certain farm in Middlefex, you
fhall find that I can live frugally without growling
at the world, or being peevifh with thofe whom fortune has appointed to eat my bread, inftead of appointing me to eat theirs: and yet I have naturally
as little difpofition to frugality as any man alive.
You fay you are no philofopher, and I think you are
in the right to diflike a word which is fo often abufed; but I am fure you like to follow reafon, not
cuftom, (which is fometimes the reafon, and oftener
the caprice of others, of the mob of the world.)
Now. to be fure of doing this, you muft wear your
philofophical fpectacles as conftantly as the Spaniards
ufed to wear theirs. You muft make them part of
your drefs, and fooner part with your broad-brim-
med beaver, your gown, your fcarf, or even that
emblematical veftment, your furplice. Through this
medium you will fee few things to be vexed at, few
perfons to be angry at: and yet there will frequently
be things which we ought to wifh altered, and perfons whom we ought to wifh hanged.

In your letter to Pope, you agree, that a regard
for fame becomes a man more towards his exit, than
at his entrance into life; and yet you confefs, that
the longer you live, the more you grow indifferent
about it. Your fentiment is true and natural; your
reafoning, I am afraid, is not fo upon this occafion:
Prudence will make us defire fame, becaufe it gives
us many real and great advantages in all the affairs
of life. Fame is the wife man's means; his ends are
his own good, and the good of fociety. You poets
and orators have inverted this order; you propofe
fame as the end; and good, or at leaft great actions,
as the means. You go further: you teach our felf-
love

love to anticipate the applaufe which we fuppofe will be paid by pefterity to our names ; and with idle notions of immortality you turn other heads befides your own : I am afraid this may have done fome harm in the world.

Fame is an objeæt which men purfue fuccefsfully by various, and even contrary courfes. Your doctrine leads them to look on this end as. effential, and on the means as indifferent ; fo that Fabricius and Craffus, Cato and Cæfar, preffed forward to the fame goal. After all, perhaps it may appear, from a confideration of the depravity of mankind, that you could do no better, nor keep up virtue in the world, without calling this paffion, or this direction of felflove, in to your aid. Tacitus has crouded this excufe for you, according to his manner, into a maxim, Contemptu famæ, contemni virtutes. But now, whether we confider fame as an ufeful inftrument in all the occurrences of private and public life, or whether we confider it as the caufe of that pleafure which our felf-love is fo fond of ; methinks, our entrance into life, or (to fpeak more properly) our youth, not our old age, is the feafon when we ought to defire it moft, and therefore when it is moft becoming to defire it with ardour. If it is ufeful, it is to be defired moft when we have, or may hope to have, a long fcene of action open before us. Towards our exit, this fcene of action is or fhould be clofed ; and then, methinks, it is unbecoming to grow fonder of a thing which we have no longer occafion for. If it is pleafant, the fooner we are in poffeffion of fame, the longer we fhall enjoy this pleafure. When it is acquired early in life, it may tickle us on till old age ; but when it is acquired late, the fenfation of pleafure will be more faint, and mingled with the regret of our not having tafted it fooner.

From my farm, Oct. 5.

I am here ; I have feen Pope, and one of my firft inquiries was after you. He tells me a thing I am

forry to hear: You are building, it feems, on a piece
of land you have acquired for that purpofe, in fome
county of Ireland *. Though I have built in a part
of the world, which I prefer very little to that where
you have been thrown and confined by our ill fortune
and yours, yet I am forry you do the fame thing. I
have repented a thoufand times of my refolution, and
I hope you will repent of yours before it is executed.
Adieu, my old and worthy friend. May the phyfical
evils of life fall as eafily upon you, as ever they did
on any man who lived to be old; and may the moral evils which furround us, make as little impreffion
on you, as they ought to make on one who has fuch
fuperiour fenfe to eftimate things by, and fo much
virtue to wrap himfelf up in.

My wife defires not to be forgotten by you. She
is faithfully your fervant, and zealoufly your admi-
rer. She will be concerned and difappointed not to
find you in this ifland at her return, which hope both
fhe and I had been made to entertain before I went
abroad.

L E T T E R   XLII.

Dr Swift to Lord Bolingbroke.

Dublin, Oct. 31. 1729.

I Received your Lordfhip's travelling letter of feveral dates, at feveral ftages, and from different
nations, languages, and religions. Neither could
any thing be more obliging than your kind remembrance of me in fo many places. As to your ten
luftres, I remember, when I complained in a letter
to Prior, that I was fifty years old, he was half angry in jeft, and anfwered me out of Terence, *Ifta
commemoratio eft quafi exprobratio.* How then ought
I to rattle you, when I have a dozen years more to
anfwer for, all monaftically paffed in this country of
liberty, and delight, and money, and good company!

* In the county of Armagh, called *Drapier's Hill.*

I go on anfwering your letter. It is you were my
hero, but the other * never was : yet if he were, it
was your own fault, who taught me to love him, and
often vindicated him, in the beginning of your miniftry, from my accufations. But I granted he had
the greateft inequalities of any man alive, and his
whole fcene was fifty times more a What-d'ye-call-
it, than yours : for, I declare, yours was *unie* ; and
I wifh you would fo order it, that the world may be
as wife as I upon that article. Mr Pope wifhes it
too ; and I believe there is not a more honeft man in
England, even without wit. But you regard us
not. —— I was † forty-feven years old when I began
to think of death ; and the reflections upon it now
begin when I wake in the morning, and end when I
am going to fleep. ——I writ to Mr Pope, and not
to you. My birth, although from a family not un-
diftinguifhed in its time, is many degrees inferiour
to yours ; all my pretenfions from perfon and parts
infinitely fo ; I a younger fon of younger fons ; you
born to a great fortune : yet I fee you, with all your
advantages, funk to a degree that you could never
have been without them : but yet I fee you as much
efteemed, as much beloved, as much dreaded, and
perhaps more, (though it be almoft impoffible), than
ever you were in your higheft exaltation ; — only I
grieve like an alderman that you are not fo rich.
And yet, my Lord, I pretend to value money as little as you ; and I will call five hundred witneffes (if
you will take Irifh witneffes) to prove it. I renounce your whole philofophy, becaufe it is not your
practice. By the *figure of living*, (if I ufed that expreffion to Mr Pope), I do not mean the parade, but
a fuitablenefs to your mind ; and as for the *pleafure
of giving*, I know your foul fuffers when you are
debarred of it. Could you, when your own generofity and contempt of outward things, (be not offended, it is no ecclefiaftical, but an Epictetian phrafe),
could you, when thefe have brought you to it, come

* Lord Oxford.   † The year of Queen Anne's death.

over and live with Mr Pope and me at the deanery? I could almoſt wiſh the experiment were tried. — No, God forbid, that ever ſuch a ſcoundrel as Want ſhould dare to approach you. But, in the mean time, do not brag, retrenchments are not your talent. But, as old Weymouth ſaid to me in his lordly Latin, *Philoſopha verba, ignava opera*; I wiſh you could learn arithmetic, that three -and two make five, and will never make more. My philoſophical ſpectacles which you adviſed me to, will tell me that I can live on 50 *l.* a-year, (wine excluded, which my bad health forces me to); but I cannot endure that *otium* ſhould be *ſine dignitate.* — My Lord, what I would have ſaid of fame, is meant of fame which a man enjoys in his life; becauſe I cannot be a great Lord, I would acquire what is a kind of *ſub-ſidium*; I would endeavour that my betters ſhould ſeek me by the merit of ſomething diſtinguiſhable, inſtead of my ſeeking them. The deſire of enjoying it in after-times, is owing to the ſpirit and folly of youth : but with age we learn to know the houſe is ſo full, that there is no room for above one or two at moſt in an age, through the whole world. My lord, I hate and love to write to you ; it gives me pleaſure, and kills me with melancholy. The d— take ſtu-pidity, that it will not come to ſupply the want of philoſophy.

LETTER XLIII.

From Dr S w i f t.

Oct. 31. 1729.

YOU were ſo careful of ſending me the Dunciad, that I have received five of them, and have pleaſed four friends. I am one of every body who approve every part of it, text and comment; but am one abſtracted from every body, in the happineſs of being recorded your friend, while wit, and humour, and politeneſs ſhall have any memorial among us.

As

As for your octavo edition, we know nothing of it; for we have an octavo of our own, which hath fold wonderfully, confidering our poverty, and dulnefs, the confequence of it.

I writ this poft to Lord B; and told him in my letter, that, with a great deal of lofs for a frolic, I will fly as foon as build; I have neither years, nor fpirits, nor money, nor patience for fuch amufements. The frolic is gone off, and I am only 100 *l.* the poorer. But this kingdom is grown fo exceffively poor, that we wife men muft think of nothing but getting a little ready money. It is thought there are not two hundred thoufand pounds of fpecie in the whole ifland; for we return thrice as much to our abfentees, as we get by trade, and fo are all inevitably undone; which I have been telling them in print thefe ten years, to as little purpofe as if it came from the pulpit. And this is enough for Irifh politics, which I only mention, becaufe it fo nearly touches myfelf. I muft repeat what, I believe, I have faid before, that I pity you much more than Mrs Pope. Such a parent and friend hourly declining before your eyes, is an object very unfit for your health, and duty, and tender difpofition; and I pray God it may not affect you too much. I am as much fatisfied that your additional 100 *l. per annum* is for your life as if it were for ever. You have enough to leave your friends, I would not have them glad to be rid of you; and I fhall take care that none but my enemies will be glad to get rid of me. You have embroiled me with Lord B—— about the figure of living, and the pleafure of giving. I am under the neceffity of fome little paltry figure in the ftation I am: but I make it as little as poffible. As to the other part, you are bafe, becaufe I thought myfelf as great a giver as ever was of my ability; and yet in proportion you exceed, and have kept it till now a fecret even from me, when I wondered how you were able to live with your whole little revenue. Adieu.

L—— C——, who doth his duty of a 'good governour in inflaving this kingdom as much as he can, talks to me of you in the manner he ought.

L E T T E R   XLIV.

Lord BOLINGBROKE *to Dr* SWIFT.

Nov. 19. 1729.

I Find that you have laid afide your project of building in Ireland, and that we fhall fee you in this ifland *cum zephyris, et hirundine prima.* I know not whether the love of fame increafes as we advance in age; fure I am that the force of friendfhip does. I loved you almoft twenty years ago, I thought of you as well as I do now; better was beyond the power of conception, or, to avoid an equivoque, beyond the extent of my ideas. Whether you are more obliged to me for loving you as well when I knew you lefs, or for loving you as well after loving you fo many years, I fhall not determine. What I would fay is this : Whilft my mind grows daily more independent of the world, and feels lefs need of leaning on external objects, the ideas of friendfhip return oftener, they bufy me, they warm me more. Is it that we grow more tender as the moment of our great feparation approaches? or is it that they who are to live together in another ftate, (for *vera amicitia non nifi inter bonos*), begin to feel more ftrongly that divine fympathy which is to be the great band of their future fociety? There is no one thought which fooths my mind like this. I encourage my imagination to purfue it, and am heartily afflicted when another faculty of the intellect comes boifteroufly in, and wakes me from fo pleafing a dream, if it be a dream. I will dwell no more on œconomics than I have done in my former letter. Thus much only I will fay, that *otium cum dignitate* is to be had with 500 *l.* a-year as well as with 5000 : the difference will be found in the value of the man, and not in that of the eftate.

eftate. I do affure you, that I have never quitted the
defign of collecting, revifing, improving, and extend-
ing feveral materials which are ftill in my power; and
I hope that the time of fetting myfelf about this laft
work of my life is not far off. Many papers of much
curiofity and importance are loft, and fome of them in
a manner which would furprife and anger you. However, I fhall be able to convey feveral great truths to
pofterity, fo clearly and fo authentically, that the Bur-
nets and the Oldmixons of another age may rail, but
not be able to deceive. Adieu, my friend. I have taken up more of this paper than belongs to me, fince
Pope is to write to you. No matter: for, upon re-
collection, the rules of proportion are not broken;
he will fay as much to you in one page, as I have
faid in three. Bid him talk to you of the work he is
about, I hope in good earneft; it is a fine one; and
will be, in his hands, an original *. His fole complaint is, that he finds it too eafy in the execution.
This flatters his lazinefs; it flatters my judgment, who
always thought, that (univerfal as his talents are) this
is eminently and peculiarly his, above all the writers
I know living or dead; I do not except Horace.

Adieu,

LETTER XLV.

Nov. 28. 1729.

THis letter (like all mine) will be a rhapfody;
it is many years ago fince I wrote as a wit †.
How many occurrences or informations muft one
omit, if one determined to fay nothing that one
could not fay prettily? I lately received from the
widow of one dead correfpondent, and the father of
another, feveral of my own letters of about fifteen
and twenty years old; and it was not unentertaining
to myfelf to obferve, how and by what degrees I
ceafed to be a witty writer; as either my experience

---

* *Effay on Man.*
† He ufed to value himfelf on this particular.

grew

grew on the one hand, or my affection to my corre-
spondents on the other. Now, as I love you better
than moſt I have ever met with in the world, and
eſteem you too the more, the longer I have compared
you with the reſt of the world ; ſo inevitably I write
to you more negligently, that is, more openly, and
what all but ſuch as love one another will call writing worſe. I ſmile to think how Curll would be-
bit, were our epiſtles to fall into his hands, and how
glorioufly they would fall ſhort of every ingenious
reader's expectations ?

You cannot imagine what a vanity it is to me to
have ſomething to rebuke you for in the way of œconomy. I love the man that builds a houſe *ſubito in-*
genic, and makes a wall for a horſe ; then cries, " We-
" wiſe men muſt think of nothing but getting ready
" money." I am glad you approve my annuity ;
all we have in this world is no more than an annuity,
as to our own enjoyment ; but I will increaſe your regard for my wiſdom, and tell you, that this annuity includes alſo the life of another *, whoſe concern ought
to be as near me as my own, and with whom my
whole proſpects ought to finiſh. I throw my javelin
of hope no farther, *Cur brevi fortes jaculamur ævo*
——&c.

The ſecond (as it is called, but indeed the eighth)
edition of the Dunciad, with ſome additional notes
and epigrams, ſhall be ſent you, if I know any opportunity ; if they reprint it with you, let them by
all means follow that octavo edition.——The Drapier's letters are again printed here, very laudably as
to paper, print, &c. for you know I diſapprove Iriſh
politics, (as my commentator tells you), being a ſtrong
and jealous ſubject of England. The lady you mention, you ought not to complain of for not acknowledging your preſent, ſhe having lately received a
much richer preſent from Mr Knight of the S. Sea ;
and you are ſenſible ſhe cannot ever return it to one
in the condition of an outlaw. It is certain, as he

* His mother's.

can never expect any favour *, his motive muſt be
wholly diſintereſted. Will not this reflection make
you bluſh? Your continual deplorings of Ireland,
make me wiſh you were here long enough to forget
thoſe ſcenes that ſo afflict you: I am only in fear if
you were, you would grow ſuch a patriot here too,
as not to be quite at eaſe for your love of old England.——It is very poſſible, your journey, in the
time I compute, might exactly tally with my intended one to you; and if you muſt ſoon again go back,
you would not be unattended. For the poor woman
decays perceptibly every week; and the winter may
too probably put an end to a very long, and a very
irreproachable life. My conſtant attendance on her
does indeed affect my mind very much, and leſſen
extremely my deſires of long life, ſince I ſee the beſt
that can come of it is a miſerable benediction. I
look upon myſelf to be many years older in two
years ſince you ſaw me. The natural imbecillity of
my body, joined now to this acquired old age of the
mind, makes me at leaſt as old as you, and we are
the fitter to crawl down the hill together: I only deſire I may be able to keep pace with you. My firſt
friendſhip at ſixteen was contracted with a man of
ſeventy, and I found him not grave enough or con-
ſiſtent enough for me, though we lived well to his
death. I ſpeak of old Mr Wycherley; ſome letters
of whom (by the by) and of mine, the bookſellers
have got and printed, not without the concurrence of
a noble friend of mine and yours †. I do not much
approve of it, though there is nothing for me to be
aſhamed of, becauſe I will not be aſhamed of any
thing I do not do myſelf, or of any thing that is not
immoral, but merely dull, (as for inſtance, if they
printed this letter I am now writing, which they eaſily may, if the underlings at the poſt-office pleaſe to

* He was miſtaken in this. Mr Knight was pardoned, and
came home in the year 1742.
† See the occaſion in the ſecond and third paragraphs of the
preface to Pope's letters, in vol. 3.

take

take a copy of it). I admire, on this confideration, your fending your laft to me quite open, without a feal, wafer, or any clofure whatever, manifefting the utter opennefs of the writer. I would do the fame by this, but fear it would look like affectation to fend two letters fo together.——I will fully reprefent to our friend, (and, I doubt not, it will touch his. heart), what you fo feelingly fet forth as to the bad-nefs of your Burgundy, &c. He is an extreme ho-neft man, and indeed ought to be fo, confidering how very indifcreet and unreferved he is. But I do not approve this part of his character, and will ne-ver join with him in any of his idlenefies in the way of wit. You know my maxim to keep as clear of all offence, as I am clear of all intereft in either party. I was once difpleafed before at you for complaining to Mr ** of my not having a penfion, and am fo again at your naming it to a certain Lord. I have given proof in the courfe of my whole life, (from the time when I was in the friendfhip of Lord Bolingbioke and Mr Craggs, even to this· when I am civilly treated by Sir R. Walpole), that I never thought myfelf fo warm in any party's caufe as to deferve their money, and therefore would never have accepted it. But give me leave to tell you, that of all mankind the two perfons I would leaft have accepted any favour from, are thofe very two to whom you have unluckily fpoken of it. I defire you to take off any impreffions which that dia-logue may have left on his Lordfhip's mind, as if I ever had any thought of being beholden to him, or any other, in that way. And yet you know I am no enemy to the prefent conftitution; I believe, as fincere a wellwifher to it, nay, even to the church eftablifhed, as any minifter in or out of employment whatever, or any bifhop of England or Ireland. Yet am I of the religion of Erafmus, a Catholic : fo I live, fo I fhall die; and hope one day to meet you, Bifhop Atterbury, the younger Craggs, Dr Garth, Dean Berkeley, and Mr Hutchinfon, in that place, to·

which.

which God of his infinite mercy bring us, and every body!

Lord B's anfwer to your letter I have juſt received, and join it to this packet. The work he fpeaks of with fuch abundant partiality, is a fyſtem of ethics in the Horatian way.

LETTER XLVI.

April 14. 1730,

THis is a letter extraordinary, to do and fay nothing but recommend to you (as a clergyman, and a charitable one) a pious and a good work, and for a good and an honeſt man : moreover, he is above feventy, and poor, which you might think included in the word *honeſt*. I fhall think it a kindnefs done myfelf, if you can propagate Mr Weſtley's fubfcription for his commentary on Job, among your divines, (biſhops excepted, of whom there is no hope), and among fuch as are believers, or readers, of fcripture ; even the curious may find fomething to pleafe them, if they fcorn to be edified. It has been the labour of eight years of this learned man's life ; I call him what he is, a learned man, and I engage you will approve his profe more than you formerly could his poetry. Lord Bolingbroke is a favourer of it, and allows you to do your beſt to ferve an old Tory, and a fufferer for the church of England, though you are a Whig, as I am.

We have here fome verfes in your name, which I am angry at. Sure you would not ufe me fo ill as to flatter me. I therefore think it is fome other weak Iriſhman.

P. S. I did not take the pen out of Pope's hands, I proteſt to you. But fince he will not fill the remainder of the page, I think I may without offence. I feek no epiſtolary fame, but am a good deal pleafed to think that it will be known hereafter that you and I lived in the moſt friendly intimacy together.——

Pliny

Pliny writ his letters for the public ; fo did Seneca, fo did Balfac, Voiture, &c. Tully did not ; and therefore thefe give us more pleafure than any which have come down to us from antiquity. When we read them, we pry into a fecret which was intended to be kept from us. That is a pleafure. We fee Cato, and Brutus, and Pompey, and others, fuch as they really were, and not fuch as the gaping multitude of their own age took them to be, or as hiftorians and poets have reprefented them to ours. That is another pleafure. I remember to have feen a proceffion at Aix-la-Chapelle, wherein an image of Charlemagne is carried on the fhoulders of a man, who is hid by the long robe of the imperial faint. Follow him into the veftry, you fee the bearer flip from under the robe, and the gigantic figure dwindles into an image of the ordinary fize, and is fet by among other lumber.—I agree much with Pope, that our climate is rather better than that you are in, and perhaps your public fpirit would be lefs grieved, or oftener comforted, here than there. Come to us therefore on a vifit at leaft. It will not be the fault of feveral perfons here, if you do not come to live with us. But great good-will, and little power, produce fuch flow and feeble effects as can be acceptable to heaven alone, and heavenly men.——I know you will be angry with me, if I fay nothing to you of a poor woman *, who is ftill on the other fide of the water in a moft languifhing ftate of health. If fhe regains ftrength enough to come over, (and fhe is better within a few weeks), I fhall nurfe her in this farm † with all the care and tendernefs poffible. If fhe does not, I muft pay her the laft duty of friendfhip where-ever fhe is, though I break through the whole plan of life which I have formed in my mind. Adieu. I am moft faithfully and affectionately yours.

* Lady Bolingbroke.
† Lord Bolingbroke's feat at Dawley in Middlefex.

L E T-

LETTER XLVII.

Lord BOLINGBROKE *to* DR SWIFT.

Jan. 1730-31.

I Begin my letter, by telling you, that my wife has been returned from abroad about a month, and that her health, though feeble and precarious, is better than it has been thefe two years. She is much your fervant ; and as fhe has been her own phyfician with fome fuccefs, imagines fhe could be yours with the fame. Would to God you was within her reach She would, I believe, prefcribe a great deal of the *medicina animi*, without having recourfe to the books of Trifmegiftus. Pope and I fhould be her principal apothecaries in the courfe of the cure ; and though our beft botanifts complain, that few of the herbs and fimples which go to the compofition of thefe remedies, are to be found at prefent in our foil ; yet there are more of them here than in Ireland ; befides, by the help of a little chemiftry, the moft noxious juices may become falubrious, and rank poifon a fpecific.—Pope is now in my library with me, and writes to the world, to the prefent and to future ages, whilft I begin this letter which he is to finifh to you. What good he will do to mankind, I know not ; this comfort he may be fure of, he cannot do lefs than you have done before him. I have fometimes thought, that if preachers, hangmen, and moral writers keep vice at a ftand, or fo much as retard the progrefs of it, they do as much as human nature admits. A real reformation is not to be brought about by ordinary means ; it requires thofe extraordinary means which become punifhments as well as leffons. National corruption muft be purged by national calamities.——Let us hear from you. We deferve this attention, becaufe we defire it, and becaufe we believe that you defire to hear from us.

LETTER XLVIII.

Lord BOLINGBROKE *to* Dr SWIFT.

March 29.

I Have delayed feveral pofts anfwering your letter of January laft, in hopes of being able to fpeak to you about a projeft which concerns us both, but me the moft, fince the fuccefs of it would bring us together. It has been a good while in my head, and at my heart; if it can be fet a-going, you fhall hear more of it. I was ill in the beginning of the winter for near a week, but in no danger either from the nature of my diftemper, or from the attendance of three phyficians. Since that bilious intermitting fever, I have had, as I had before, better health than the regard I have paid to health deferves. We are both in the decline of life, my dear Dean, and have been fome years going down the hill; let us make the paffage as fmooth as we can. Let us fence a-gainft phyfical evil by care; and the ufe of thofe means which experience muft have pointed out to us: let us fence againft moral evil by philofophy. I renounce the alternative you propofe. But we may, nay, (if we will follow nature, and do not work up imagination againft her plaineft dictates), we fhall of courfe grow every year more indifferent to life, and to the affairs and interefts of a fyftem out of which we are foon to go. This is much better than ftupi-dity. The decay of paffion ftrengthens philofophy; for paffion may decay, and ftupidity not fucceed. *Paffions* (fays Pope, our divine, as you will fee one time or other) are the *gales* of life: let us not complain that they do not blow a ftorm. What hurt does age do us, in fubduing what we toil to fubdue all our lives? It is now fix in the morning. I recall the time, (and am glad it is over), when about this hour I ufed to be going to bed, furfeited with plea-fure, or jaded with bufinefs: my head often full of

fchemes,

fchemes, and my heart as often full of anxiety. Is it a misfortune, think you, that I rife at this hour refrefhed, ferene, and calm ? that the paft, and even the prefent affairs of life ftand like objects at a di-ftance from me, where I can keep off the difagreeable fo as not to be ftrongly affected by them, and from whence I can draw the others nearer to me ? Paffions in their force would bring all thefe, nay even future contingencies, about my ears at once, and reafon would but ill defend me in the fcuffle.

I leave Pope to fpeak for himfelf; but I muft tell you, how much my wife is obliged to you. She fays fhe would find ftrength enough to nurfe you, if you was here; and yet, God knows, fhe is extremely weak. The flow fever works under, and mines the conftitution; we keep it off fometimes; but ftill it returns, and makes new breaches before nature can repair the old ones. I am not afhamed to fay to you, that I admire her more every hour of my life. Death is not to her the King of Terrours; fhe beholds him without the leaft. When fhe fuffers much, fhe wifh-es for him as a deliverer from pain; when life is to-lerable, fhe looks on him with diflike; becaufe he is to feparate her from thofe friends to whom fhe is more attached, than to life itfelf. —You fhall not ftay for my next, as long as you have for this letter; and in every one, Pope fhall write fomething much better than the fcraps of old philofophers, which were the prefents, *munufcula*, that Stoical fop Se-neca ufed to fend in every epiftle to his friend Luci-lius.

P. S. My Lord has fpoken juftly of his Lady: why not I of my mother? Yefterday was her birthday, now entering on the ninety-firft year of her age; her memory much diminifhed, but her fenfes very little hurt; her fight and hearing good; fhe fleeps not ill, eats moderately, drinks water, fays her prayers; this is all fhe does. I have reafon to thank God for continuing fo long to me a very good and tender-pa-reat;

rent; and for allowing me to exercife for fome
years, thofe cares which are now as neceffary to her,
as hers have been to me. An object of this fort daily before one's eyes very much foftens the mind, but
perhaps may hinder it from the willingnefs of con-
tracting other ties of the like domeftic nature, when
one finds how painful it is even to enjoy the tender
pleafures. I have formerly made fome ftrong efforts
to get and to deferve a friend : perhaps it were wifer
never to attempt it, but live extempore, and look
upon the world only as a place to pafs through, juft
pay your hofts their due, difperfe a little charity,
and hurry on. Yet am I juft now writing (or rather
planning) a book, to make mankind look upon this
life with comfort and pleafure, and put morality in
good humour.— And juft now too I am going to fee
one I love very tenderly ; and to morrow to entertain
feveral civil people, whom if we call friends, it is by
the courtefy of England.— *Sic, fic juvat ire fub
umbras.* While we do live, we muft make the beft
of life,

Cantantes *licet ufque (minus via lædet) eamus,*

as the fhepherd faid in Virgil, when the road was
long and heavy. I am yours.

LETTER XLIX.

Lord BOLINGBROKE *to Dr* SWIFT.

YOU may affure yourfelf, that, if you come over
this fpring, you will find me not only got
back into the habits of ftudy, but devoted to that
hiftorical tafk, which you have fet me thefe many
years. I am in hopes of fome materials which will
enable me to work in the whole extent of the plan I
propofe to myfelf. If they are not to be had, I muft
accommodate my plan to this deficiency. In the mean
time Pope has given me more trouble than he or I
thought

thought of; and you will be furprifed to find that I
have been partly drawn by him, and partly by myfelf, to write a pretty large volume upon a very grave
and very important fubject; that I have ventured to
pay no regard whatever to any authority except facred authority; and that I have ventured to ftart a
thought, which muft, if it is pufhed as fuccefsfully
as I think it is, render all your metaphyfical theology both ridiculous and abominable. There is an expreffion in one of your letters to me, which makes
me believe you will come into my way of thinking
on this fubject; and yet I am perfuaded that divines
and freethinkers would both be clamorous againft it,
if it was to be fubmitted to their cenfure, as I do not
intend that it fhall. The paffage I mean, is that
where you fay that you told Dr ** the grand points
of Chriftianity ought to be taken as infallible revelations, &c.

It has happened, that, whilft I was writing this to
you, the Doctor came to make me a vifit from London, where I heard he was arrived fome time ago.
He was in hafte to return, and is, I perceive, in
great hafte to print. He left with me eight differtations *, a fmall part, as I underftand, of his work,
and defired me to perufe, confider, and obferve upon them againft Monday next, when he will come
down again. By what I have read of the two firft,
I find myfelf unable to ferve him. The principles
he reafons upon are begged in a difputation of this
fort, and the manner of reafoning is by no means
clofe and conclufive. The fole advice I could give
him in conference, would be that which he would
take ill, and not follow. I will get rid of this tafk
as well as I can; for I efteem the man, and fhould
be forry to difoblige him where I cannot ferve
him.

As to retirement and exercife, your notions are
true. The firft fhould not be indulged fo much as to

* Revelation examined with candour.

B b 3

'render

render us favage, nor the laft neglected fo as to impair health. But I know men who, for fear of being favage, live with all who will live with them ; and who, to preferve their health, faunter away half their time. Adieu. Pope calls for the paper.

P. S. I hope what goes before will be a ftrong motive to your coming. God knows if ever I fhall fee Ireland ; I fhall never defire it, if you can be got hither, or kept here. Yet I think I fhall be, tco foon, a free-man.—Your recommendations I conftantly give to thofe you mention ; though fome of them I fee but feldom, and am every day more retired. I am lefs fond of the world, and lefs curious about it; yet no way out of humour, difappointed, or angry; though in my way I receive as many injuries as my betters ; but I do not feel them ; therefore I ought not to vex other people, nor even to return injuries. I pafs almoft all my time at Dawley and at home. My Lord (of which I partly take the merit to myfelf) is as much eftranged from politics as I am. Let philofophy be ever fo vain, it is lefs vain now than politics, and not quite fo vain at prefent as divinity. I know nothing that moves ftrongly but fatire; and thofe who are afhamed of nothing elfe, are fo of being ridiculous. I fancy, if we three were together but for three years, fome good might be done even upon this age.

I know you will defire fome account of my health. It is as ufual, but my fpirits rather worfe. I write little or nothing. You know I never had either a tafte or talent for politics, and the world minds nothing elfe. I have perfonal obligations which I will ever preferve, to men of different fides ; and I wifh nothing fo much as public quiet, except it be my own quiet. I think it a merit, if I can take off any man from grating or fatirical fubjects, merely on the fcore of party : and it is the greateft vanity of my life, that I have contributed to turn my Lord Bolingbroke to fubjects moral, ufeful, and more worthy his pen.

pen. Dr ――――'s book is what I cannot commend
fo much as Dean Berkeley's *, though it has many
things ingenious in it, and is not deficient in the
writing part : but the whole book, though he meant
it *ad populum*, is, I think, purely *ad clerum*.

Adieu.

LETTERS of Dr SWIFT to Mr GAY, &c. †

From the year 1729 to 1732.

LETTER L.

Dublin, March 19. 1729.

I Deny it. I do write to you according to the old
ftipulation ; for, when you kept your old company, when I writ to one, I writ to all. But I am
ready to enter into a new bargain, fince you are got
into a new world, and will anfwer all your letters.
You are firft to prefent my moft humble refpects to
the Duchefs of Queenfberry, and let her know that
I never dine without thinking of her ; although it be
with fome difficulty that I can obey her when I dine
with forks that have but two prongs, and when the
fauce is not very confiftent. You muft likewife tell
her Grace, that fhe is a general toaft among all honeft
folks here ; and particularly at the deanery, even in
the face of my Whig-fubjects.—I will leave my
money in Lord Bathurft's hands ; and the management of it (for want of better) in yours : and pray
keep the intereft-money in a bag wrapt up and fealed

* A fine original work, called, *The Minute Philofopher.*
† Found among Mr Gay's papers, and returned to Dr Swift
by the Duke of Queenfberry and Mr Pope.

by

by itfelf, for fear of your own fingers under your
careleffnefs. Mr Pope talks of you as a perfect
ftranger: but the different purfuits, and manners, and
interefts of life, as Fortune hath pleafed to difpofe
them, will never fuffer thofe to live together, who
by their inclinations ought never to part. I hope
when you are rich enough, you will have fome little
œconomy of your own in town or country, and be
able to give your friend a pint of Port: for the domeftic feafon of life will come on. I had never
much hopes of your vampt play; although Mr Pope
feemed to have, and although it were ever fo good.
But you fhould have done like the parfons, and
changed your text; I mean the title, and the names
of the perfons. After all, it was an effect of idlenefs; for you are in the prime of life, when invention and judgment go together. I wifh you had
100 l. a-year more for horfes.—I ride and walk
whenever good weather invites; and am reputed the
beft walker in this town, and five miles round. I
writ lately to Mr Pope. I wifh you had a little vil-
lakin in his neighbourhood: but you are yet too
volatile; and any lady with a coach and fix horfes
would carry you to Japan.

L E T T E R LI.

Dublin, Nov. 10. 1730.

WHen my Lord Peterborow, in the Queen's
time, went abroad upon his embaffies; the
miniftry told me, that he was fuch a vagrant, they
were forced to write *at* him by guefs, becaufe they
knew not where to write *to* him. This is my cafe
with you; fometimes in Scotland, fometimes at
Ham-walks, fometimes God knows where. You
are a man of bufinefs, and not at leifure for infigni-
ficant correfpondence. It was I got you the employment of being my Lord Duke's *premier miniftre:* for
his Grace having heard how good a manager you
were

were of my revenue, thought you fit to be intrufted with ten talents. I have had twenty times a ftrong inclination to fpend a fummer near Salifbury-downs; having rode over them more than once; and with a young parfon of Salifbury reckoned twice the ftones of Stonehenge, which are either ninety-two or ninety-three. I defire to prefent my moft humble acknowledgments to my Lady Duchefs in return of her civility. I hear an ill thing, that fhe is *matre pulchra filia pulchrior*. I never faw her fince fhe was a girl, and would be angry fhe fhould excel her mother, who was long my principal goddefs. I defire you will tell her Grace, that the ill management of forks is not to be helped when they are only bidential, which happens in all poor houfes, efpecially thofe of poets. Upon which account a knife was abfolutely neceffary at Mr Pope's, where it was morally impoffible with a bidential fork to convey a morfel of beef, with the incumbrance of muftard and turnips, into your mouth at once. And her Grace hath coft me thirty pounds to provide tridents for fear of offending her; which fum I defire fhe will pleafe to return me.—I am fick enough to go to the Bath; but have not heard it will be good for my diforder. I have a ftrong mind to fpend my 200 *l.* next fummer in France. I am glad I have it; for there is hardly twice that fum left in this kingdom. You want no fettlement (I call the family where you live, and the foot you are upon, a fettlement) till you increafe your fortune to what will fupport you with eafe and plenty; a good houfe and a garden. The want of this I much dread for you. For I have often known a fhe-coufin of a good family and fmall fortune, paffing months among all her relations, living in plenty, and taking her circles, till fhe grew an old maid, and every body weary of her. Mr Pope complains of feldom feeing you: but the evil is unavoidable; for different circumftances of life have always feparated thofe whom friendfhip would join. God hath taken care of this, to prevent
vent

vent any progrefs towards real happinefs here ; which
would make life more defirable, and death too
dreadful. I hope you have now one advantage that
you always wanted before ; and the want of which
made your friends as uneafy as it did yourfelf: I
mean the removal of that folicitude about your own
affairs, which perpetually filled your thoughts, and
difturbed your converfation. For if it be true what
Mr Pope ferioufly tells me, you will have opportunity of faving every groat of the intereft you receive ;
and fo by the time he and you grow weary of each·
other, you will be able to pafs the reft of your wine-
lefs life, in eafe and plenty, with the additional
triumphal comfort of never having received a penny
from thofe taftelefs ungrateful people from whom
you deferved fo much ; and who deferve no better
geniufes than thofe by whom they are celebrated.———
If you fee Mr Cefar, prefent my humble fervice to
him, and let him know that the fcrub libel printed
againft me here, and reprinted in London, for which
he fhewed a kind concern to a friend of us both,,
was written by myfelf, and fent to a Whig-printer.
It was in the ftyle and genius of fuch fcoundrels,
when the humour of libelling ran in this ftrain a-
gainft a friend of mine whom you know.——But my
paper is ended.

LETTER LII.

Dublin, Nov. 19. 1730.

I Writ to you a long letter about a fortnight paft,
    concluding you were in London, from whence
I underftood one of your former was dated. Nor
did I imagine you were gone back to Aimfbury fo
late in the year ; at which feafon I take the country
to be only a fcene for thofe who have been ill ufed
by a court on account of their virtues : which is a
ftate of happinefs the more valuable, becaufe it is
not accompanied by envy ; although nothing deferves

ferves it more. I would gladly fell a dukedom to
lofe favour in the manner their Graces have done.
I believe my Lord Carteret, fince he is no longer
Lieutenant, may not wifh me ill; and I have told
him often, that I only hated him as Lieutenant. I
confefs he had a genteeler manner of binding the
chains of this kingdom than moft of his predeceffors ;
and I confefs at the fame time that he had fix times
a regard to my recommendation, by preferring fo
many of my friends in the church : the two laft acts
of his favour were to add to the dignities of Dr Delany and Mr Stopford ; the laft of whom was by you
and Mr Pope put into Mr Pultney's hands. I told
you in my laft, that a continuance of giddinefs
(though not in a violent degree) prevented my
thoughts of England at prefent. For in my cafe a
domeftic life is neceffary ; where I can, with the
centurion, fay to my fervant, Go, and he goeth ;
and, Do this, and he doth it. I now hate all people
whom I cannot command ; and confequently a
Duchefs is at this time the hatefulleft lady in the
world to me, one only excepted ; and I beg her
Grace's pardon for that exception ; for, in the way
I mean, her Grace is ten thoufand times more hate-
ful. I confefs I begin to apprehend you will fquander my money, becaufe I hope you never lefs wanted it : and if you go on with fuccefs for two years
longer, I fear I fhall not have a farthing of it left.
The Doctor hath ill informed me, who fays that
Mr Pope is at prefent the chief poetical favourite ;
yet Mr Pope himfelf talks like a philofopher, and one
wholly retired. But the vogue of our few honeft
folks here is, that Duck is abfolutely to fucceed
Eufden in the laurel ; the contention being between
Concanen or Theobald, or fome other hero of the
Dunciad. I never charged you for not talking ; but
the dubious ftate of your affairs in thofe days was
too much the fubject ; and I wifh the Duchefs had
been the voucher of your amendment. Nothing fo
much contributed to my eafe as the turn of affairs
after

after the Queen's death ; by which all my hopes
being cut off, I could have no ambition left, unless
I would have been a greater rascal than happened to
suit with my temper. I therefore sat down quietly
at my morsel, adding only thereto a principle of
hatred to all succeeding measures and ministries by
way of sauce to relish my meat. And I confess one
point of conduct in my Lady Duchess's life hath added much poignancy to it. There is a good Irish
practical bull towards the end of your letter ; where
you spend a dozen lines in telling me you must
leave off, that you may give my Lady Duchess
room to write ; and so you proceed to within two or
three lines of the bottom : though I would have remitted you my 2co l. to have left place for as many
more.

To the Duchess.

Madam,

My beginning thus low is meant as a mark of re-
spect, like receiving your Grace at the bottom of the
stairs. I am glad you know your duty ; for it hath
been a known and established rule above twenty
years in England, that the first advances have been
constantly made me by all ladies who aspired to my
acquaintance, and the greater their quality, the
greater were their advances. Yet, I know not by
what weakness, I have condescended graciously to
dispense with you upon this important article.
Though Mr Gay will tell you, that a nameless person * sent me eleven messages before I would yield to
a visit : I mean a person to whom he is infinitely obliged, for being the occasion of the happiness he now
enjoys, under the protection and favour of my Lord
Duke and your Grace. At the same time, I cannot
forbear telling you, Madam, that you are a little

* The Princess of Wales, afterwards Queen Caroline.

imperious

imperious in your manner of making your advances.
You fay, perhaps you fhall not like me : I affirm you
are miftaken, which I can plainly demonftrate ; for
I have certain intelligence, that another perfon dif-
likes me of late, with whofe likings yours have not
for fome time paft gone together.   However, if I
fhall once have the honour to attend your Grace, I
will, out of fear and prudence, appear as vain as I
can, that I may not know your thoughts of me.
This is your own direction, but it was needlefs : for
Diogenes himfelf would be vain, to have received
the honour of being one moment of his life in the
thoughts of your Grace.

L E T T E R   LIII.

Dublin, March 13. 1730-1.

YOur fituation is an odd one ; the Duchefs is
your treafurer, and Mr Pope tells me you are
the Duke's.   And I had gone a good way in fome
verfes on that occafion, prefcribing leffons to direct
your conduct, in a negative way ; not to do fo and
fo, &c. like other treafurers ; how to deal with fervants, tenants, or neighbouring fquires, which I take
to be courtiers, parliaments, and princes in alliance ;
and fo the parallel goes on, but grows too long to
pleafe me.   I prove that poets are the fitteft perfons
to be treafurers and managers to great perfons, from
their virtue, and contempt of money, &c. — Pray,
why did you not get a new heel to your fhoe ? unlefs you would make your court at St James's, by affecting to imitate the Prince of Lilliput. — But the
reft of your letter being wholly taken up in a very
bad character of the Duchefs, I fhall fay no more to
you, but apply myfelf to her Grace.

MADAM, Since Mr Gay affirms that you love to
have your own way, and fince I have the fame perfection,   I will fettle that matter immediately, to

prevent thofe ill confequences he apprehends. Your
Grace fhall have your own way, in all places except
your own houfe, and the domains about it. There,
and there only, I expect to have mine; fo that you
have all the world to reign in, bating only two or
three hundred acres, and two or three houfes in town
and country. I will likewife, out of my fpecial grace,
certain knowledge, and mere motion, allow you to
be in the right againft all human kind, except myfelf, and to be never in the wrong but when you differ from me. You fhall have a greater privilege in
the third article, of fpeaking your mind; which I
fhall gracioufly allow you now and then to do even
to myfelf, and only rebuke you when it does not
pleafe me.

Madam, I am now got as far as your Grace's letter; which having not read this fortnight, (having
been out of town, and not daring to truft myfelf
with the carriage of it), the prefumptuous manner in
which you begin had flipt out of my memory. But
I forgive you to the feventeenth line, where you begin to banifh me for ever, by demanding me to anfwer all the good character fome partial friends have
given me. Madam, I have lived fixteen years in
Ireland, with only an intermiffion of two fummers in
England; and confequently am fifty years older than
I was at the Queen's death, and fifty thoufand times
duller, and fifty million times more peevifh, perverfe,
and morofe; fo that, under thefe difadvantages, I can
only pretend to excel all your other acquaintance a-
bout fome twenty bars length. Pray, Madam, have
you a clear voice? and will you let me fit at your
left hand, at leaft within three of you? for of two
bad ears, my right is the beft. My groom tells me,
that he likes your park, but your houfe is too little.
Can the parfon of the parifh play at backgammon,
and hold his tongue? Is any one of your women a
good nurfe, if I fhould fancy myfelf fick for four
and twenty hours? How many days will you maintain me and my equipage? When thefe prelimina-
ries

ries are fettled, I muft be very poor, very fick, or
dead, or to the laft degree unfortunate, if I do not
attend you at Aimfbury. For, I profefs, you are
the firft Lady that ever I defired to fee, fince the firft
of Auguft 1714; and I have forgot the date when
that defire grew ftrong upon me; but I know I was
not then in England, elfe I would have gone on foot
for that happinefs, as far as to your houfe in Scotland. But I can foon recollect the time, by afking
fome ladies here the month, the day, and the hour
when I began to endure their company : which however I think was a fign of my ill judgment ; for I do
not perceive they mend in any thing, but envying
or admiring your Grace. I diflike nothing in your
letter but an affected apology for bad writing, bad
fpelling, and a bad pen, which you pretend Mr Gay
found fault with; wherein you affront Mr Gay, you
affront me, and you affront yourfelf. Falfe fpelling
is only excufable in a chambermaid, for I would
not pardon it in any of your waiting-women. ——
Pray God preferve your Grace and family, and give
me leave to expect that you will be fo juft to remember me among thofe who have the greateft regard for
virtue, goodnefs, prudence, courage, and generofity;
after which you muft conclude, that I am, with the
greateft refpect and gratitude, Madam, your Grace's,
moft obedient and moft humble fervant, &c.

To Mr GAY.

I have juft got yours of February 24. with a poftfcript by Mr Pope. I am in great concern for him.;
I find Mr Pope dictated to you the firft part, and
with great difficulty fome days after added the reft.
I fee his weaknefs by his hand-writing. How much
does his philofophy exceed mine ? I could not bear
to fee him : I will write to him foon.

LETTER LIV.

Dublin, June 29. 1731.

EVer fince I received your letter, I have been upon a balance about going to England, and landing at Briftol, to pafs a month at Aimfbury, as the Duchefs hath given me leave. But many difficulties have interfered ; firft, I thought I had done with my law-fuit, and fo did all my lawyers ; but my adverfary, after being in appearance a Proteftant thefe twenty years, hath declared he was always a Papift, and confequently, by the law here, cannot buy nor (I think) fell ; fo that I am at fea again, for almoft all I am worth. But I have ftill a worfe evil : for the giddinefs I was fubject to, inftead of coming feldom and violent, now conftantly attends me more or lefs, though in a more peaceable manner, yet fuch as will not qualify me to live among the young and healthy ; and the Duchefs, in all her youth, fpirit, and grandeur, will make a very ill nurfe, and her women not much better. Valetudinarians muft live where they can command, and fcold ; I muft have horfes to ride, I muft go to bed and rife when I pleafe, and live where all mortals are fubfervient to me. I muft talk nonfenfe when I pleafe, and all who are prefent muft commend it. I muft ride thrice a-week, and walk three or four miles befides, every day.

I always told you Mr ———— was good for nothing but to be a rank courtier. I care not whether he ever writes to me or no. He and you may tell this to the Duchefs ; and I hate to fee you fo charitable, and fuch a cully ; and yet I love you for it, becaufe I am one myfelf.

You are the fillieft lover in Chriftendom. If you like Mrs ————, why do you not command her to take you ? If fhe does not, fhe is not worth purfuing. You do her too much honour ; fhe hath neither

ther fenfe nor tafte, if fhe dares to refufe you, though
fhe had ten thoufand pounds. I do not remember
to have told you of thanks that you have not given,
nor do I underftand your meaning, and I am fure I
had never the leaft thoughts of any myfelf. If I am
your friend, it is for my own reputation, and from a
principle of felf-love; and I do fometimes reproach
you for not honouring me by letting the world know
we are friends.

I fee very well how matters go with the Duchefs
in regard to me. I heard her fay, Mr Gay, fill your
letter to the Dean, that there may be no room for me;
the frolic is gone far enough; I have writ thrice;
I will do no more; if the man has a mind to come,
let him come; what a clutter is here? pofitively I will
not write a fyllable more. She is an ungrateful
Duchefs, confidering how many adorers I have pro-
cured her here, over and above the thoufands fhe had
before. — I cannot allow you rich enough till you
are worth 7000 *l.* which will bring you 300 *per annum* ; and this will maintain you, with the perqui-
fite of fpunging while you are young; and when
you are old, will afford you a pint of Port at night,
two fervants, and an old maid, a little garden, and
pen and ink, — provided you live in the country.—
Have you no fcheme either in verfe or profe?
The Duchefs fhould keep you at hard meat, and by
that means force you to write; and fo I have done
with you.

MADAM,

SINCE I began to grow old, I have found all ladies become inconftant, without any reproach from
their confcience. If I wait on you, I declare, that
one of your women (which ever it is that has defigns upon a chaplain) muft be my nurfe, if I happen to be fick or peevifh at your houfe; and in that
cafe you muft fufpend your domineering claim till I
recover. Your omitting the ufual appendix to Mr
Gay's letters hath done me infinite mifchief here;

for while you continued them, you would wonder
how civil the ladies here were to me, and how much
they have altered. fince. I dare not confefs that I
have defcended fo low as to write to your Grace, after the abominable neglect you have been guilty of;
for if they but fufpected it, I fhould lofe them all.
One of them, who had an inkling of the matter, (your
Grace will hardly believe it), refufed to beg my pardon upon her knees, for once neglecting to make my
rice-milk.—Pray, confider this, and do your duty, or
dread the confequence. I promife you fhall have
your will fix minutes every hour at Aimfbury, and
feven in London, while I am in health: but if I
happen to be fick, I mult govern to a fecond. Yet,
properly fpeaking, there is no man alive with fo
much truth and refpect your Grace's moft obedient
and devoted fervant.

LETTER LV.

Aug. 28. 1731.

YOU and the Duchefs ufe me very ill; for I
profefs I cannot diftinguifh the ftyle or the
hand-writing of either. I think her Grace writes
more like you than herfelf; and that you write more
like her Grace than yourfelf. I would fwear the beginning of your letter writ by the Duchefs, though it
is to pafs for yours; becaufe there is a curfed lie in
it, that fhe is neither young nor healthy, and befides
it perfectly refembles the part fhe owns. I will likewife fwear, that what I mult fuppofe is written by the
Duchefs, is your hand: and thus I am puzzled and
perplexed between you; but I will go on in the in-
nocency of my own heart. I am got eight miles
from our famous metropolis, to a country-parfon's,
to whom I lately gave a city-living, fuch as an Englifh chaplain would leap at. I retired hither for
the public good, having two great works in hand:
one to reduce the whole politenefs, wit, humour,
and

and ſtyle of England into a ſhort fyſtem, for the uſe
of all perſons of quality, and particularly the maids
of honour *. The other is of almoſt equal importance ; I may call it the whole duty of ſervants, in
about twenty ſeveral ſtations, from the ſteward and
waiting-woman down to the ſcullion and pantry-
boy †.—I believe no mortal had ever ſuch fair invitations, as to be happy in the beſt company of England. I wiſh I had liberty to print your letter with
my own comments upon it. There was a.fellow in
Ireland, who from a ſhoe-boy grew to be ſeveral
times one of the chief governours, wholly illiterate,
and with hardly common ſenſe. A Lord Lieutenant
told the firſt King George, that he was the greateſt
ſubject he had in both kingdoms ; and truly this
character was gotten and preſerved by his never appearing in England ; which was the only wiſe thing
he ever did, except purchaſing ſixteen thouſand
pound-a-year—Why, you need not ſtare : it is eaſily applied : I muſt be abſent, in order to preſerve
my credit with her Grace.—Lo here comes in the
Ducheſs again, (I know her by her dd's ; but am a
fool for diſcovering my art), to defend herſelf againſt
my conjecture of what ſhe ſaid.—Madam, I will imitate your Grace, and write to you upon the ſame line.
I own it is a baſe unromantic ſpirit in me to ſuſpend
the honour of waiting at your Grace's feet, till I can
finiſh a paltry law-ſuit. It concerns indeed almoſt
all my whole fortune ; it is equal to half Mr Pope's,
and two thirds of Mr Gay's, and about ſix weeks rent
of your Grace's. This curſed accident hath drilled
away the whole ſummer. But, Madam, underſtand
one thing, that I take all your ironical civilities in a
literal ſenſe ; and whenever I have the honour to attend you, ſhall expect them to be literally perform-

* *Wagſtaff's Dialogues of polite converſation*, publiſhed in his
lifetime. See Swift's works, vol. 7.
† An imperfect thing of this kind, called *Directions to ſervants in general*, has been publiſhed ſince his death. See Swift's
works, vol. 7.

ed :

ed : though perhaps I fhall find it hard to prove
your hand-writing in a court of juftice ; but that will
not be much for your credit. How miferably hath
your Grace been miftaken in thinking to avoid envy
by running into exile, where it haunts you more than
ever it did even at court ? *Non te civitas, non regia
domus in exilium miferunt, fed tu utrafque.* So fays
Cicero (as your Grace knows), or fo he might have
faid.

I am told, that the Craftfman, in one of his papers,
is offended with the publifhers of (I fuppofe) the laft
edition of the Dunciad ; and I was afked whether
you and Mr Pope were as good friends to the new
difgraced perfon as formerly ? This I knew nothing
of, but fuppofe it was the confequence of fome miftake. As to writing, I look on you juft in the prime
of life for it, the very feafon when judgment and invention draw together. But fchemes are perfectly
accidental : fome will appear barren of hints and
matter, but prove to be fruitful, and others the contrary ; and what you fay is paft doubt, that every one
can beft find hints for himfelf ; though it is poffible
that fometimes a friend may give you a lucky one
juft fuited to your own imagination. But all this is
almoft paft with me : my invention and judgment
are perpetually at fifty-cuffs, till they have quite difabled each other ; and the mereft trifles I ever wrote
are ferious philofophical lucubrations, in comparifon
to what I now bufy myfelf about, as (to fpeak in the
author's phrafe) the world may one day fee *.

L E T T E R LVI.

Sept. 10. 1731.

IF your ramble was on horfeback, I am glad of it
on account of your health : but I know your arts
of patching up a journey between ftage-coaches and
friends coaches ; for you are as arrant a cockney as

*. His ludicrous prediction was fince his death, and very much
to his difhonour, ferioufly fulfilled.

any

any hofier in Cheapfide. One clean fhirt with two
cravats, and as many handkerchiefs, make up your
equipage ; and as for a night-gown, it is clear from
Homer, that Agamemnon rofe without one. I have
often had it in my head to put it into yours, that
you ought to have fome great work in fcheme, which
may take up feven years to finifh, befides two or
three under-ones, that may add another thoufand
pound to your ftock ; and then I fhall be in lefs pain
about you. I know you can find dinners ; but you
love twelve-penny coaches too well, without confidering that the intereft of a whole thoufand pounds
brings you but half a crown a-day. I find a greater
longing than ever to come amongft you ; and reafon
good, when I am teafed with dukes and duchefïes
for a vifit, all my demands complied with, and all
excufes cut off. You remember, " O happy Don
" Quixote! queens held his horfe, and duchefïes
" pulled off his armour," or fomething to that purpofe. He was a mean-fpirited fellow ; I can fay ten
times more ; O happy, &c. fuch a Duchefs was defigned to attend him, and fuch a Duke invited him
to command his palace. *Nam iftos reges ceteros me-
morare nolo, hominum mendicabula.* Go read your
Plautus, and obferve Strobilus vapouring after he
had found the pot of gold.———I will have nothing
to do with that lady : I have long hated her on
your account, and the more, becaufe you are fo forgiving as not to hate her : however, fhe has good
qualities enough to make her efteemed ; but not one
grain of feeling. I only wifh fhe were a fool.———
I have been feveral months writing near five hundred
lines on a pleafant fubjeft, only to tell what my
friends and enemies will fay on me after I am dead *.
I fhall finifh it foon ; for I add two lines every week,
and blot out four, and alter eight. I have brought
in you and my other friends, as well as enemies and
detraftors.———It is a great comfort to fee how cor-

* This has been publifhed, and is amongft the beft of his
poems. See Swift's works, vol. 6.

ruption and ill conduct are inſtrumental in uniting
virtuous perſons and lovers of their country of all
denominations ; Whig and Tory, High and Low
church, as ſoon as they are left to think freely, all
joining in opinion.   If this be diſaffection, pray God
ſend me always among the diſaffected ! and I heartily wiſh you joy of your ſcurvy treatment at court,
which hath given you leiſure to cultivate both public
and private virtue, neither of them likely to be ſoon
met with within the walls of St James's or Weſtminſter.——But I muſt here diſmiſs you, that I may pay
my acknowledgments to the Duke for the great honour he hath done me.

My Lord,
    I could have ſworn that my pride would be always
able to preſerve me from vanity, of which I have
been in great danger to be guilty for ſome months
paſt, firſt by the conduct of my Lady Duchefs, and
now by that of your Grace, which had like to finiſh
the work.   And I ſhould have certainly gone about
ſhewing my letters, under the charge of ſecrecy, to
every blab of my acquaintance, if I could have the
leaſt hope of prevailing on any of them to believe,
that a man in ſo obſcure a corner, quite thrown out
of the preſent world, and within a few ſteps of the
next, ſhould receive ſuch condeſcending invitations,
from two ſuch perſons to whom he is an utter ſtran-
ger, and who know no more of him than what they
have heard by the partial repreſentations of a friend.
But, in the mean time, I muſt deſire your Grace not
to flatter yourſelf, that I waited for your conſent to
accept the invitation. I muſt be ignorant indeed, not
to know, that the Duchefs, ever ſince you met, hath
been moſt politicly employed in increaſing thoſe
forces, and ſharpening thoſe arms, with which ſhe ſub-
dued you at firſt, and to which, the braver and the
wiſer you grow, you will more and more ſubmit.
Thus I knew myſelf on the ſecure ſide ; and it was
a mere piece of good manners to inſert that clauſe,

of

of which you have taken the advantage. But as I cannot forbear informing your Grace, that the Du-chefs's great fecret in her art of government hath been to reduce both your wills into one; fo I am content, in due obfervance to the forms of the world, to return my molt humble thanks to your Grace, for fo great a favour as you are pleafed to offer me, and which nothing but impoffibilities shall prevent me from receiving; fince I am, with the greatest reafon, truth, and refpect, my Lord, your Grace's molt obe-dient, &c.

MADAM,

I have confulted all the learned in occult fciences of my acquaintance, and have fat up eleven nights to difcover the meaning of thofe two hieroglyphical lines in your Grace's hands at the bottom of the laft Aimfbury letter; but all in vain. Only it is agreed, that the language is Coptic; and a very profound Behmift affures me, the ftyle is poetic, containing an invitation from a very great perfon of the female fex, to a ftrange kind of man whom she never faw : and this is all I can find; which, after fo many former in-vitations, will ever confirm me in that refpect, where-with I am, Madam, your Grace's molt obedient, &c.

LETTER LVII.

Mr GAY to Dr SWIFT.

Dec. 1. 1731.

YOU ufed to complain that Mr Pope and I would not let you fpeak : you may now be even with me, and take it out in writing. If you do not fend to me now and then, the poft-office will think me of no confequence, for I have no correfpondent but you. You may keep as far from us as you pleafe : you cannot be forgotten by thofe who ever knew you; and therefore pleafe me by fometimes shewing

that

that I am not forgot by you. I have nothing to take
me off from my friendſhip to you. ˙I ſeek no new acquaintance, and court no favour ; I ſpend no ſhil-
lings in coaches or chairs, to levees or great viſits ;
and, as I do not want the aſſiſtance of ſome that I
formerly converſed with, I will not ſo much as ſeem
to ſeek to be a dependent. As to my ſtudies, I have
not been entirely idle, though I cannot ſay that I
have yet perfected any thing. What I have done
is ſomething in the way of thoſe fables I have already publiſhed. All the money I get is by ſaving ;
ſo that by habit there may be ſome hopes (if I grow
richer) of my becoming a miſer. All miſers have
their excuſes ; the motive to my parſimony is independence. If I were to be repreſented by the Ducheſs (ſhe is ſuch a dowright niggard for me), this
character might not be allowed me ; but I really
think I am covetous enough for any who lives at the
court-end of the town, and who is as poor as myſelf :
for I do not pretend that I am equally ſaving with
S—k. Mr Lewis defired you might be told that he
hath five pounds of yours in his hands, which he
fancies you may have forgot ; for he will hardly
allow that a verſe-man can have a juſt knowledge of
his own affairs. When you got rid of your law-ſuit,
I was in hopes that you had got your own, and was
free from every vexation of the law ; but Mr Pope
tells me you are not entirely out of your perplexity,
though you have the ſecurity now in your own poſſeſſion. But ſtill your caſe is not ſo bad as Capt. Gulliver's, who was ruined by having a decree for him
with coſts. I have had an injunction for me againſt
pirating bookſellers ; which I am ſure to get nothing
by, and will, I fear, in the end, drain me of ſome
money. When I began this proſecution, I fancied
there would be ſome end of it ; but the law ſtill goes
on, and it is probable I ſhall ſome time or other ſee
an attorney's bill as long as the book. Poor Duke
Diſney is dead, and hath left what he had among his
friends ; among whom are, Lord Bolingbroke, 500 l. ;

Mr

Mr Pelham, 500 l.; Sir William Wyndham's young-
eft fon, 500 l.; Gen. Hill, 500 l. ; Lord Maſſam's
fon, 500 l.

You have the good wiſhes of thoſe I converſe
with. They know they gratify me, when they remember you; but I really think they do it purely for
your own fake. I am fatisfied with the love and
friendſhip of good men, and envy not the demerits
of thoſe who are moſt conſpicuouſly diſtinguiſhed.
Therefore, as I fet a juſt value upon your friendſhip,
you cannot pleaſe me more than letting me now and
then know that you remember me; the only fatiſ-
faction of diſtant friends!

P. S. Mr Gay's is a good letter, mine will be a
very dull one ; and yet what you will think the
worſt of it, is what ſhould be its excuſe, that I write
in a headach that has laſted three days.   I am never
ill but I think of your ailments, and repine that they
mutually hinder our being together : though in one
point I am apt to differ from you, for you ſhun your
friends when you are in thoſe circumſtances, and I
defire them ; your way is the more generous, mine
the more tender.   Lady — took your letter very
kindly, for I had prepared her to expect no anſwer
under a twelvemonth; but kindneſs perhaps is a
word not applicable to courtiers. However, ſhe is an
extraordinary woman there, who will do you common juſtice. For God's fake, why all this ſcruple a-
bout Lord B——'s keeping your horſes, who has a
park ; or about my keeping you on a pint of wine
a-day? We are infinitely richer than you imagine.
John Gay ſhall help me to entertain you, though you
come like King Lear with fifty knights.—Though
ſuch profpects as I wiſh, cannot now be formed for
fixing you with us, time may provide better before
you part again. The old Lord may die, the benefice
may drop, or, at worſt, you may carry me into Ireland.   You will fee a work of Lord B——'s, and
one of mine; which, with a juſt neglect of the pre-

fent age, confult only pofterity ; and, with a noble
fcorn of politics, afpire to philofophy.· I am glad
you refolve to meddle no more with the low concerns and interefts of parties, even of countries ; (for
countries are but larger parties). *Quid verum atque*
decens, curare, et rogare, noftrum fit. I am much
pleafed with your defign upon Rochefoucault's maxim ; pray finifh it *. I am happy whenever you
join our names together. So would Dr Arbuthnot
be : but at this time he can be pleafed with nothing ; for his darling fon is dying in all probability, by the melancholy account I received this
morning.

The paper you afk me about is of little value. It
might have been a feafonable fatire upon the fcandalous language and paffion with which men of condition have ftooped to treat one another. Surely
they facrifice too much to the people, when they facrifice their own characters, families, &c. to the diverfion of that rabble of readers. I agree with you
in my contempt of moft popularity, fame, &c.;
even as a writer I am cool in it ; and whenever you
fee what I am now writing, you will be convinced I
would pleafe but a few, and (if I could) make mankind lefs admirers, and greater reafoners †. I ftudy
much more to render my own portion of being eafy,
and to keep this peevifh frame of the human body
in good humour. Infirmities have not quite un-
manned me ; and it will delight you to hear they
are not increafed, though not diminifhed. I thank
God, I do not very much want people to attend me,
though my mother now cannot. When I am fick,
I lie down ; when I am better, I rife up. I am ufed,

* The poem on his own death, formed upon a maxim of
Rochefoucault. It is one of the beft of his performances, but
very characteriftic.

† The poem he means is the *Effay on Man*. But this point
he could never gain. His readers would *admire* his poetry in
fpite of him, and would not underftand his *reafoning* after all his
pains.

to the headach, &c. If greater pains arrive, (fuch as
my late rheumatifm), the fervants bathe and plafter
me, or the furgeon fcarifies me; and I bear it, becaufe I muft. This is the evil of nature, not of fortune. I am juft now as well as when you was here.
I pray God you were no worfe. I fincerely wifh my
life were paffed near you ; and, fuch as it is, I would
not repine at it.—All you mention remember you,
and wifh you here.

L E T T E R   LVIII.

Dr S W I F T to Mr G A Y.

Dublin, May 4. 1732.

I Am now as lame as when you writ your letter ;
and almoft as lame as your letter itfelf, for
want of that limb from my Lady Duchefs, which
you promifed, and without which I wonder how it
could limp hither. I am not in a condition to make
a true ftep even on Aimfbury downs ; and I declare,
that a corporeal falfe ftep is worfe than a political
one ; nay, worfe than a thoufand political ones : for
which I appeal to courts and minifters, who hobble
on and profper, without the fenfe of feeling. To
talk of riding and walking, is infulting me ; for I
can as foon fly as do either. It is your pride or
lazinefs, more than chair-hire, that makes the town
expenfive. No honour is loft by walking in the
dark. And in the day, you may beckon a black-
guard-boy under a gate, near your vifiting place ;
(experto crede), fave eleven pence, and get half a
crown's worth of health. The worft of my prefent
misfortune is, that I eat and drink, and can digeft
neither for want of exercife : and, to increafe my
mifery, the knaves are fure to find me at home, and
make huge void fpaces in my cellars. I congratulate
with you, for lofing your great acquaintance. In
fuch a cafe, philofophy teaches that we muft fubmit,

and be content with good ones. I like Lord Cornbury's refufing his penfion; but I demur at his being
elected for Oxford; which, I conceive, is wholly
changed, and entirely devoted to new principles.
So it appeared to me the two laft times I was
there.

I find, by the whole caft of your letter, that you
are as giddy and as volatile as ever; juft the reverfe
of Mr Pope, who hath always loved a domeftic life
from his youth. I was going to wifh you had fome
little place that you could call your own; but I profefs, I do not know you well enough to contrive any
one fyftem of life that would pleafe you. You pretend to preach up riding and walking to the Duchefs;
yet, from my knowledge of you after twenty years,
you always joined a violent defire of perpetually
fhifting places and company, with a rooted lazinefs,
and an utter impatience of fatigue. A coach and fix
horfes is the utmoft exercife you can bear; and this
only when you can fill it with fuch company as is
beft fuited to your tafte; and how glad would you
be if it could waft you in the air to avoid jolting?
while I, who am fo much later in life, can, or at
leaft could, ride 500 miles on a trotting horfe. You
mortally hate writing, only becaufe it is the thing
you chiefly ought to do; as well to keep up the
vogue you have in the world, as to make you eafy
in your fortune. You are merciful to every thing
but money, your beft friend, whom you treat with
inhumanity. Be affured, I will hire people to watch
all your motions, and to return me a faithful account. Tell me, have you cured your abfence of
mind? Can you attend to trifles? Can you at Aimfbury write domeftic libels to divert the family and
neighbouring fquires for five miles round? or venture fo far on horfeback, without apprehending a
ftumble at every ftep? Can you fet the footmen a-
laughing as they wait at dinner? and do the Duchefs's
women admire your wit? In what efteem are you
with the vicar of the parifh? Can you play with him
at

at backgammon ? Have the farmers found out that you cannot diftinguifh rye from barley, or an oak from a crab-tree ? You are fenfible that I know the full extent of your country-fkill is in fifhing for roaches, or gudgeons at the higheft.

I love to do you good offices with your friends, and therefore defire you will fhow this letter to the Duchefs, to improve her Grace's good opinion of your qualifications, and convince her how ufeful you are like to be in the family. Her Grace fhall have the honour of my correfpondence again when fhe goes to Aimfbury. Hear a piece of Irifh news. I buried the famous General Meredyth's father laft night in my cathedral ; he was ninety-fix years old : fo that Mrs Pope may live feven years longer. You faw Mr Pope in health ; pray is he generally more healthy than when I was amongft you ? I would know how your own health is, and how much wine you drink in a day. My ftint in company is a pint at noon, and half as much at night ; but I often dine at home like a hermit, and then I drink little or none at all. Yet I differ from you ; for I would have fociety, if I could get what I like, people of middle underftanding, and middle rank.

Adieu.

L E T T E R LIX.

Dublin, July 10. 1732.

I Had your letter by Mr Ryves a long time after the date, for I fuppofe he ftaid long in the way. I am glad you determine upon fomething. There is no writing I efteem more than fables, nor any thing fo difficult to fucceed in ; which however you have done excellently well ; and I have often admired your happinefs in fuch a kind of performance, which I have frequently endeavoured at in vain. I remember I acted as you feem to hint. I found a moral firft, and ftudied for a fable ; but could do nothing that

D d 3

pleafed

pleafed me, and fo left off that fcheme for ever.
I remember one, which was, to reprefent what fcoundrels rife in armies by a long war; wherein I fuppofed the lion was engaged, and having loft all his a-
nimals of worth, at laft Serjeant Hog came to be
a brigadier, and Corporal Afs a colonel, &c. I agree
with you likewife about getting fomething by the
ftage; which, when it fucceeds, is the beft crop for
poetry in England. But, pray, take fome new
fcheme, quite different from any thing you have already touched. The prefent humour of the players,
who hardly (as I was told in London) regard any
new play, and your prefent fituation at the court, are
the difficulties to be overcome; but thofe circumftances may have altered (at leaft the former) fince I
left you. My fcheme was, to pafs a month at Aimfbury, and then go to Twickenham, and live a winter between that and Dawley, and fometimes at
Rifkins; without going to London, where I now can
have no occafional ledgings. But I am not yet in any
condition for fuch removals. I would fain have you
get enough againft you grow old, to have two or
three fervants about you, and a convenient houfe. It
is hard to want thofe *fubfidia fenectuti*, when a man
grows hard to pleafe, and few people care whether he
be pleafed or no. I have a large houfe, yet I fhould
hardly prevail to find one vifiter, if I were not able
to hire him with a bottle of wine: fo that, when I
am not abroad on horfeback, I generally dine alone,
and am thankful if a friend will pafs the evening
with me. I am now with the remainder of my pint
before me, and fo here is your health,—and the fecond and chief is to my Tunbridge acquaintance,
my Lady Duchefs.— And I tell you, that I fear my
Lord Bolingbroke and Mr Pope, (a couple of philofophers), would ftarve me; for even of Port wine I
fhould require half a pint a-day, and as much at
night: and you were growing as bad, unlefs your
Duke and Duchefs have mended have. Your colic
is owing to intemperance of the philofophical kind:
                                                    you

you eat without care; and if you drink lefs than I,
you drink too little. But your inattention I cannot
pardon, becaufe I imagined the caufe was removed;
for I thought it lay in your forty millions of fchemes,
by court-hopes and court-fears. Yet Mr Pope has
the fame defect, and it is of all others the moft mortal to converfation; neither is my Lord Bolingbroke
untinged with it: all for want of my rule, *Vive la
bagatelle!* But the Doctor is the king of inattention:
What a vexatious life fhould I lead among you? If
the Duchefs be a *reveufe*, I will never come to Aimfbury; or, if I do, I will run away from you both,
to one of her women; and the fteward and chaplain.

M A D A M,

I mentioned fomething to Mr Gay of a Tunbridge acquaintance, whom we forget of courfe
when we return to town; and yet I am affured that
if they meet again next fummer, they have a better
title to refume their commerce. Thus I look on my
right of correfponding with your Grace, to be better
eftablifhed upon your return to Aimfbury; and I
fhall at this time defcend to forget, or at leaft fufpend
my refentments of your neglect all the time you
were in London. I ftill keep in my heart, that Mr
Gay had no fooner turned his back, than you left the
place in his letter void which he had commanded you
to fill; though your guilt confounded you fo far,
that you wanted prefence of mind to blot out the laft
line, where that command ftared you in the face. But
it is my misfortune to quarrel with all my acquaintance, and always come by the worft: and fortune
is ever againft me; but never fo much as by purfuing
me out of mere partiality to your Grace, for which
you are to anfwer. By your connivance, fhe hath
pleafed, by one ftumble on the ftairs, to give me a
lamenefs that fix months have not been able perfectly to cure: and thus I am prevented from revenging
myfelf by continuing a month at Aimfbury, and
breeding

breeding confufion in your Grace's family. No dif-
appointment through my whole life hath been fo
vexatious by many degrees; and God knows whether I fhall ever live to fee the invifible lady to
whom I was obliged for fo many favours, and whom
I never beheld fince fhe was a brat in hanging-
fleeves. I am, and fhall be ever, with the greateft
refpect and gratitude, Madam, your Grace's moft
obedient and moft humble, &c.

LETTER LX.

Dublin, Aug. 12. 1732.

I Know not what to fay to the account of your
ftewardfhip; and it is monftrous to me, that the
South-fea fhould pay half their debts at one clap.
But I will fend for the money when you put me into
the way; for I fhall want it here, my affairs being in
a bad condition by the miferies of the kingdom, and
my own private fortune being wholly embroiled, and
worfe than ever; fo that I fhail foon petition the
Duchefs, as an object of charity, to lend me three or
four thoufand pounds to keep up my dignity. My
one hundred pound will buy me fix hogfheads of
wine, which will fupport me a year; *provifæ frugis in annum copia.* Horace defired no more; for I
will conftrue *frugis* to be wine. You are young
enough to get fome lucky hint which muft come by
chance, and it fhall be a thing of importance, *quod
et hunc in annum vivat et in plures;* and you fhall not
finifh it in hafte, and it fhall be diverting, and ufe-
fully fatirical, and the Duchefs fhall be your critic;
and, betwixt you and me, I do not find fhe will grow
weary of you till this time feven years. I had lately an offer to change for an Englifh living, which is
juft too fhort by 300 *l.* a-year; and that muft be
made up out of the Duchefs's pin-money, before I
can confent. I want to be minifter of Aimfbury,
Dawley, Twickenham, Rifkins, and Prebendary of
Weftminfter;

Weftminfter; elfe I will nor ftir a ftep, but content
myfelf with making the Duchefs miferable three
months next fummer. But I keep ill company. I
mean the Duchefs and you, who are both out of favour ; and fo I find am I, by a few verfes wherein
Pope and you have your parts. You hear Dr D——y
has got a wife with 1600 *l.* a-year; I, who am his
governour, cannot take one under two thoufand. I
wifh you would inquire of fuch a one in your neighbourhood. See what it is to write godly books! I
profefs, I envy you above all men in England. You
want nothing but three thoufand pounds more, to
keep you in plenty, when your friends grow weary
of you. To prevent which laft evil at Aimfbury,
you muft learn to domineer and be peevifh, to find
fault with their victuals and drink, to chide and direct the fervants, with fome other leffons, which I
fhall teach you, and always practifed myfelf with
fuccefs. I believe I formerly defired to know whe--
ther the vicar of Aimfbury can play at backgammon. Pray afk him the queftion, and give him my
fervice.

To the Ducbefs.

Madam,

I was the moft unwary creature in the world,
when, againft my old maxims, I writ firft to you upon your return to Tunbridge. I beg that this con-
defcenfion of mine may go no farther, and that you
will not pretend to make a precedent of it. I never
knew any man cured of any inattention, although the
pretended caufes were removed. When I was with Mr
Gay laft in London, talking with him on fome poetical
fubjects, he would anfwer, " Well, I am determined
" not to accept the employment of gentleman-ufher :"
and of the fame difpofition were all my poetical
friends; and if you cannot cure him, I utterly defpair.— As to yourfelf, I would fay to you, (though
comparifons

comparisons be odious), what I said to the ——, that
your quality should be never any motive of esteem to
me : my compliment was then lost, but it will not
be so to you. For I know you more by any one of
your letters than I could by six months conversing.
Your pen is always more natural, and sincere, and
unaffected than your tongue : in writing you are too
lazy to give yourself the trouble of acting a part ;
and have indeed acted so indiscreetly, that I have
you at mercy : and although you should arrive
to such a height of immorality as to deny your hand,
yet, whenever I produce it, the world will unite in
swearing this must come from you only.
     I will answer your question. Mr Gay is not dis-
creet enough to live alone, but he is too discreet to
live alone ; and yet (unless you mend him) he will
live alone even in your Grace's company. Your
quarrelling with each other upon the subject of bread
and butter, is the most usual thing in the world.
Parliaments, courts, cities, and kingdoms, quarrel
for no other cause ; from hence, and from hence only, arise all the quarrels between Whig and Tory ;
between those who are in the ministry, and those
who are out ; between all pretenders to employment
in the church, the law, and the army. Even the
common proverb teaches you this, when we say, It
is none of my bread and butter ; meaning it is no
business of mine. Therefore I despair of any re-
concilement between you till the affair of bread and
butter be adjusted, wherein I would gladly be a me-
diator. If Mahomet should come to the mountain,
happy would an excellent lady be, who lives a few
miles from this town ? As I was telling of Mr Gay's
way of living at Aimsbury, she offered fifty guineas
to have you both at her house for one hour over a
bottle of Burgundy, which we were then drinking.
To your question I answer, that your Grace should
pull me by the sleeve till you tore it off ; and when
you said you were weary of me, I would pretend to
be deaf ; and think (according to another proverb)
that.

that you tore my cloaths to keep me from going, I
never will believe one word you fay of my Lord
Duke, unlefs I fee three or four lines in his own hand
at the bottom of yours. I have a concern in the
whole family, and Mr Gay muft give me a particular account of every branch ; for I am not afhamed
of you, though you be Duke and Duchefs, though I
have been of others who are, &c. ; and I do not
doubt but even your own fervants love you, even
down to your poftilions ; and when I come to Aimfbury, before I fee your Grace, I will have an hour's
converfation with the vicar, who will tell me how
familiarly you talk to Goody Dobfon and all the
neighbours, as if you were their equal, and that you
were godmother to her fon Jacky.

I am, and fhall be ever, with the greateft refpect,
your Grace's moft obedient, &c.

L E T T E R   LXI.

Dublin, Oct. 3. 1731.

I Ufually write to friends after a paufe of a few
weeks, that I may not interrupt them in better
company, better thoughts, and better diverfions. I
believe I have told you of a great man, who faid to
me, that he never once in his life received a good
letter from Ireland : for which there are reafons
enough without affronting our underftandings. For
there is not one perfon out of this country, who regards any events that pafs here, unlefs he hath an
eftate or employment.——I cannot tell, that you or I
ever gave the leaft provocation to the prefent miniftry, much lefs to the court; and yet I am ten times
more out of favour than you. For my own part, I
do not fee the politic of opening common letters, directed to perfons generally known ; for a man's underftanding would be very weak to convey fecrets by
the poft ; if he knew any, which I declare I do not :
and, befides, I think the world is already fo well informed

formed by plain events, that I queftion whether the minifters have any fecrets at all. Neither would I be under any apprehenfion if a letter fhould be fent me full of treafon ; becaufe I cannot hinder people from writing what they pleafe, nor fending it to me ; and although it fhould be difcovered to have been opened before it came to my hand, I would on-ly burn it, and think no further. I approve of the fcheme you have to grow fomewhat richer, though, I agree, you will meet with difcouragements ; and it is reafonable you fhould, confidering what kind of pens are at this time only employed and encouraged. For you muft allow that the bad painter was in the right, who, having painted a cock, drove away all the cocks and hens, and even the chickens, for fear thofe who paffed by his fhop might make a compari-fon with his work. And I will fay one thing in fpite of the poft-officers, that fince wit and learning began to be made ufe of in our kingdoms, they were never profeffedly thrown afide, contemned, and punifhed, till within your own memory ; nor dulnefs and igno-rance ever fo openly encouraged and promoted. In anfwer to what you fay of my living among you, if I could do it to my eafe ; perhaps you have heard of a fcheme for an exchange in Berkfhire propofed by two of our friends ; but, befides the difficulty of ad-jufting certain circumflances, it would not anfwer. I am at a time of life that feeks eafe and independence ; you will hear my reafons when you fee thofe friends, and I concluded them with faying, That I would rather be a freeman among flaves, than a flave among freemen. The dignity of my prefent flation damps the pertnefs of inferiour puppies, and 'fquires, which, without plenty and eafe on your fide the channel, would break my heart in a month.

MADAM,

SEE what it is to live where I do. I am utterly ignorant of that fame Strado del Poe ; and yet, if

that

that author be againſt lending or giving money, I
cannot but think him a good courtier; which, I am
ſure, your Grace is not; no not ſo much as to be a
maid of honour. For I am certainly informed, that
you are neither a freethinker, nor can ſell bargains;
that you can neither ſpell, nor talk, nor write, nor
think like a courtier; that you pretend to be reſpect-
ed for qualities which have been out of faſhion ever
ſince you were almoſt in your cradle; that your
contempt for a fine petticoat is an infallible mark of
diſaffection; which is further confirmed by your ill
taſte for wit, in preferring two old-faſhioned poets
before Duck or Cibber. Beſides, you ſpell in ſuch
a manner as no court-lady can read; and write in
ſuch an old-faſhioned ſtyle, as none of them can underſtand.—You need not be in pain about Mr Gay's
ſtock of health. I promiſe you he will ſpend it all
upon lazineſs, and run deep in debt by a winter's
repoſe in town : therefore I entreat your Grace will
order him to move his chops leſs and his legs more
the ſix cold months, elſe he will ſpend all his money in phyſic and coach-hire. I am in much perplexity about your Grace's declaration, of the manner in which you diſpoſe what you call your love
and reſpect; which you ſay are not paid to merit,
but to your own humour. Now, Madam, my miſ-
fortune is, that I have nothing to plead but abundance of merit; and there goes an ugly obſervation,
that the humour of ladies is apt to change. Now,
Madam, if I ſhould go to Aimſbury, with a great
load of merit, and your Grace happen to be out of
humour, and will not purchaſe my merchandiſe at
the price of your reſpect, the goods may be da-
maged, and nobody elſe will take them off my
hands. Beſides, you have declared Mr Gay to hold
the firſt part, and I but the ſecond; which is hard
treatment, ſince I ſhall be the neweſt acquaintance by
ſome years : and I will appeal to all the reſt of your
ſex, whether ſuch an innovation ought to be allowed. I ſhould be ready to ſay in the common forms,

that I was much obliged to the lady who wifhed fhe could give me the beft living, &c. if I did not vehemently fufpeft it was the very fame lady who fpoke many things to me in the fame ftyle; and alfo with regard to the gentleman at your elbow when you writ, whofe dupe he was, as well as of her waiting-woman : but they were both arrant knaves, as I told him and a third friend, though they will not believe it to this day. I defire to prefent my moft humble refpefts to my Lord Duke; and, with my heartieft prayer for the profperity of the whole family, remain your Grace's, &c.

L E T T E R   LXII.

To Mr P o p e.

Dublin, June 12. 1732.

I Doubt, habit hath little power to reconcile ut with ficknefs attended by pain. With me, the lownefs of fpirits hath a moft unhappy effeft : I am grown lefs patient with folitude, and harder to be pleafed with company; which I could formerly better digeft, when I could be eafier without it than at prefent. As to fending you any thing that I have written fince I left you, (either verfe or profe), I can only fay, that I have ordered by my will, that all my papers of any kind fhall be delivered you to difpofe of as you pleafe. I have feveral things that I have had fchemes to finifh, or to attempt; but I very foolifhly put off the trouble, as finners do their repentance : for I grow every day more averfe from writing, which is very natural; and, when I take a pen, fay to myfelf a thoufand times, *Non eft tanti.* As to thofe papers of four or five years paft, that you are pleafed to require foon; they confift of little accidental things writ in the country; family-amufements, never intended further than to divert ourfelves and fome neighbours; or fome effects of anger

on

on public grievances here, which would be infigni-
ficant out of this kingdom. Two or three of us had
a fancy, three years ago, to write a weekly paper,
and called it an *Intelligencer*. But it continued not
long; for the whole volume (it was reprinted in
London, and, I find, you have feen it) was the work
only of two, myfelf and Dr Sheridan. If we could
have got fome ingenious young man to have been
the manager, who fhould have publifhed all that
might be fent to him, it might have continued
longer, for there were hints enough. But the printer
here * could not afford fuch a young man one farthing for his trouble, the fale being fo fmall, and
the price one halfpenny; and fo it dropt. In the
volume you faw, (to anfwer your queftions), the 1ft,
3d, 5th, 7th, were mine. Of the 8th I writ only the
verfes, (very uncorrect, but againft a fellow we all
hated); the 9th mine; the 10th only the verfes, and
of thofe not the four laft flovenly lines. The 15th is
a pamphlet of mine, printed before with Dr Sh——'s
preface, merely for lazinefs not to difappoint the
town; and fo was the 19th, which contains only a
parcel of facts relating purely to the miferies of Ireland, and wholly ufelefs and unentertaining. As to
other things of mine fince I left you; there are, in
profe, a view of the ftate of Ireland; a project for
eating children; and a defence of Lord Carteret:
In verfe, a libel on Dr D—— and Lord Carteret; a
letter to Dr D—— on the libels writ againft him;
the barrack, (a ftolen copy); the lady's journal;
the lady's dreffing-room, (a ftolen copy); the plea
of the damn'd, (a ftolen copy). All thefe have
been printed in London. (I forgot to tell you
that the tale of Sir Ralph was fent from England).
Befides thefe, there are five or fix (perhaps more)
papers of verfes writ in the north, but perfect fa-
mily-things; two or three of which may be tolerable; the reft but indifferent, and the humour
only local; and fome that would give offence to the

* John Harding.

E e 2   times.

times. Such as they are, I will bring them, tolerable or bad, if I recover this lamenefs, and live long enough to fee you either here or there. I forget again to tell you, that the fcheme of paying debts by a tax on vices, is not one fylliable mine, but of a young clergyman whom I countenance. He told me it was built upon a paffage in Gulliver, where a projector hath fomething upon the fame thought. This young man is the moft hopeful we have. A book of his poems was printed in London: Dr D—— is one of his patrons. He is married, and has children, and makes up about 100 *l.* a year; on which he lives decently. The utmoft ftretch of his ambition is, to gather up as much fuperfluous money as will give him a fight of you, and half an hour of your prefence; after which he will return home in full fatisfaction, and in proper time die in peace.

My poetical fountain is drained; and, I profefs, I grow gradually fo dry, that a rhyme with me is almoft as hard to find as a guinea; and even profe fpeculations tire me almoft as much. Yet I have a thing in profe, begun above twenty-eight years ago, and almoft finifhed. It will make a four-fhilling volume; and is fuch a perfection of folly, that you fhall never hear of it till it is printed, and then you fhall be left to guefs *. Nay, I have another † of the fame age, which will require a long time to perfect, and is worfe than the former, in which I will ferve you the fame way. I heard lately from Mr —, who promifes to be lefs lazy in order to mend his fortune. But women who live by their beauty, and men by their wit, are feldom provident enough to confider that both wit and beauty will go off with years; and there is no living upon the credit of what is paft.

I am in great concern to hear of my Lady Boling-

* Polite converfation, in Swift's works, vol. 7.
† Directions to fervants, *ib.*

broke's

broke's ill health returned upon her; and, 1 doubt,
my Lord will find Dawley too solitary without her.
In that, neither he nor you are companions young e-
nough for me; and, 1 believe, the best part of the
reafon why men are faid to grow children when they
are old, is, becaufe they cannot entertain themfelves
with thinking; which is the very cafe of little boys
and girls, who love to be noify among their play-
feHows. I am told Mrs Pope is without pain; and I
have not heard of a more gentle decay, without uneafinefs to herfelf or friends: yet I cannot but pity
you, who are ten times the greater fufferer, by having the perfon you moft love, fo long before you,
and dying daily; and I pray God it may not affect
your mind or your health.

L E T T E R   LXIII.

Mr P O P E to Dr S W I F T. *

Dec. 5, 1732.

IT is not a time to complain that you have not anfwered me two letters (in the laft of which I
was impatient under fome fears). It is not now indeed a time to think of myfelf, when one of the neareft and longeft ties I have ever had, is broken all on
a fudden, by the unexpected death of poor Mr Gay.
An inflammatory fever hurried him out of this life in
three days. He died laft night at nine o'clock, not
deprived of his fenfes entirely at laft, and poffeffing
them perfectly till within five hours. He afked of you
a few hours before, when in acute torment by the inflammation in his bowels and breaft. His effects are
in the Duke of Queenfberry's cuftody. His fifters,
we fuppofe, will be his heirs, who are two widows:

---

* " On my dear friend Mr Gay's death: Received Decem-
" ber 15. but not read till the 20th, by an impulfe, foreboding
" fome misfortune." [This note is indorfed on the original
letter in Dr Swift's hand].

as yet it is not known whether or no he left a will.
— Good God ! how often are we to die before we go
quite off this ſtage ? In every friend we loſe a part of
ourſelves, and the beſt part. God keep thoſe we
have left ! few are worth praying for, and one's ſelf
the leaſt of all.

I ſhall never ſee you now, I believe; one of your
principal calls to England is at an end. Indeed he
was the moſt amiable by far ; his qualities were ſhe
gentleſt : but I love you as well and as firmly. Would
to God the man we have loſt had not been ſo amiable,
nor ſo good ! but that is a wiſh for our own ſakes,
not for his. Sure, if innocence and integrity can deſerve happineſs, it muſt be his. Adieu ; I can add
nothing to what you will feel, and diminiſh nothing
from it. Yet write to me, and ſoon. Believe no
man now living loves you better ; I believe no man
ever did, than

A. Pope.

Dr Arbuthnot, whoſe humanity you know, heartily commends himſelf to you. All poſſible diligence
and affection has been ſhown, and continued attendance, on this melancholy occaſion. Once more a-
dieu, and write to one who is truly diſconſolate.

P. S. By Dr A R B U T H N O T.

Dear SIR,

I am ſorry that the renewal of our correſpondence
ſhould be upon ſuch a melancholy occaſion. Poor
Mr Gay died of an inflammation, and, I believe,
at laſt a mortification of the bowels. It was the moſt
precipitate caſe I ever knew, having cut him off in
three days. He was attended by two phyſicians beſides myſelf. I believed the diſtemper mortal from
the beginning. I have not had the pleaſure of a line
from you theſe two years. I wrote one about your
health, to which I had no anſwer. I wiſh you all
health

health and happinefs; being, with great affection and refpect, Sir,

Your, &c.

LETTER LXIV.

Dublin, 1732-3.

I Received yours with a few lines from the Doctor, and the account of our lofing Mr Gay; upon which event I fhall fay nothing. I am only concerned that long living hath not hardened me: for even in this kingdom, and in a few days paft, two perfons of great merit, whom I loved very well, have died in the prime of their years, but a little above thirty. I would endeavour to comfort myfelf upon the lofs of friends, as I do upon the lofs of money; by turning to my account-book, and feeing whether I have enough left for my fuppert: but in the former cafe I find I have not, any more than in the other; and I know not any man who is in a greater likelihood than myfelf to die poor and friendlefs. You are a much greater lofer than me by his death, as being a more intimate friend, and often his companion; which latter I could never hope to be, except perhaps once more in my life, for a piece of a fummer. I hope he hath left you the care of any writings he may have left; and I wifh, that, with thofe already extant, they could be all publifhed in a fair edition under your infpection. Your poem on the ufe of riches hath been juft printed here; and we have no objection but the obfcurity of feveral paffages by our ignorance in facts and perfons, which makes us lofe abundance of the fatire. Had the printer given me notice, I would have honeftly printed the names at length, where I happened to know them; and writ explanatory notes; which however would have been but few, for my long abfence hath made me ignorant of what paffes out of the fcene where I am. I never had the leaft hint from you about this work, any

more

more than of your former, upon tafte. We are told
here, that you are preparing other pieces of the fame
bulk to be infcribed to other friends, one (for inftance) to my Bolingbroke, another to Lord Oxford,
and fo on.—Dr. Delany prefents you his moft humble
fervice. He behaves himfelf very commendably;
converfes only with his former friends; makes no parade, but entertains them conftantly at an elegant
plentiful table; walks the ftreets as ufual, by day-
light; does many acts of charity and generofity;
cultivates a country-houfe two miles diftant; and is
one of thofe very few within my knowledge, on
whom a great accefs of fortune hath made no manner of change. And particularly he is often without money, as he was before. We have got my Lord
Orrery among us, being forced to continue here on
the ill condition of his eftate by the knavery of an
agent. He is a moft worthy gentleman, whom, I
hope, you will be acquainted with. I am very much
obliged by your favour to Mr P—, which, I defire,
may continue no longer than he fhall deferve by his
modefty; a virtue I never knew him to want, but is
hard for young men to keep, without abundance of
ballaft. If you are acquainted with the Duchefs of
Queenfberry, I defire you will prefent her my moft
humble fervice. I think fhe is a greater lofer by the
death of a friend than either of us. She feems a
lady of excellent fenfe and fpirit. I had often poft-
fcripts from her in our friend's letters to me; and
her part was fometimes longer than his, and they
made up great part of the little happinefs I could
have here. This was the more generous, becaufe I
never faw her fince fhe was a girl of five years old,
nor did I envy poor Mr Gay for any thing fo much
as being a domeftic friend to fuch a lady. I defire
you will never fail to fend me a particular account of
your health. I dare hardly inquire about Mrs Pope,
who, I am told, is but juft among the living, and
confequently a continual grief to you: fhe is fenfible
of your tendernefs, which robs her of the only happiness

pinefs fhe is capable of enjoying. And yet I pity you more than her; you cannot lengthen her days, and I beg fhe may not fhorten yours.

LETTER LXV.

Feb. 16. 1732-3.

IT is indeed impoffible to fpeak on fuch a fubject as the lofs of Mr Gay, to me an irreparable one. But I fend you what I intend for the infcription on his tomb, which the Duke of Queenfberry will fet up at Weftminfter. As to his writings, he left no will, nor fpoke a word of them, or any thing elfe, during his fhort and precipitate illnefs, in which I attended him to his laft breath. The Duke has act-ed more than the part of a brother to him; and it will be ftrange if the fifters do not leave his papers totally to his difpofal, who will do the fame that I would with them. He has managed the comedy (which our poor friend gave to the playhoufe the week before his death) to the utmoft advantage for his relations; and propofes to do the fame with fome fables he left finifhed.

There is nothing of late which I think of more than mortality, and what you mention, of collecting the beft monuments we can of our friends, their own images in their writings: (for thofe are the beft, when their minds are fuch as Mr Gay's was, and as yours is). I am preparing alfo for my own; and have nothing fo much at heart, as to fhew the filly world, that men of wit, or even poets, may be the moft moral of mankind. A few loofe things fome-times fall from them, by which cenforious fools judge as ill of them as poffibly they can, for their own comfort. And indeed, when fuch unguarded and trifling *Jeux d'efprit* have once got abroad, all that prudence or repentance can do, fince they cannot be denied, is, to put them fairly upon that foot; and teach the public (as we have done in the preface to

the

the four volumes of mifcellanies) to diftinguifh betwixt our ftudies and our idlenefles, our works and
our weakneffes. That was the whole end of the laft
volume of mifcellanies, without which our former
declaration in that preface, " That thefe volumes,
contained all that we have ever offended in that way,"
would have been difcredited. It went indeed to my
heart, to omit what you called the libel on Dr D—,
and the beft panegyric on myfelf, that either my
own times or any other could have afforded, or will
ever afford to me. The book, as you obferve,
was printed in great hafte; the caufe whereof was,
that the bookfellers here were doing the fame, in collecting your pieces, the corn with the chaff : I do not
mean that any thing of yours is chaff ; but with
other wit of Ireland, which was fo, and the whole in
your name. I meant principally to oblige them to
feparate what you writ ferioufly from what you writ
carelefsly ; and thought my own weeds might pafs
for a fort of wild flowers, when bundled up with
them.

It was I that fent you thofe books into Ireland,
and fo I did my epiftle to Lord Bathurft, even before
it was publifhed ; and another thing of mine, which
is a parody from Horace *, writ in two mornings. I
never took more care in my life of any thing than
of the former of thefe, nor lefs than of the latter :
yet every friend has forced me to print it ; though,
in truth, my own fingle motive was about twenty lines
toward the latter end, which you will find out.

I have declined opening to you by letters the
whole fcheme of my prefent work, expecting ftill
to do it in a better manner in perfon. But you will
fee pretty foon, that the letter to Lord Barhurft is a
part it of it ; and you will find a plain connection
between them, if you read them in the order juft
contrary to that they were publifhed in. I imitate
thofe cunning tradefmen, who fhow their beft filks

* Sat. 1. lib. 2. vol. 1. of Pope's works.

laft ;

laft ; or, (to give you a truer idea, though it founds
too proudly), my works will in one refpeȼt be like
the works of nature, much more to be liked and
underftood when confidered in the relation they bear
with each other, than when ignorantly looked upon
one by one ; and often thofe parts which attraȼt
moft at firft fight, will appear to be not the moft, but
the leaft confiderable *.

I am pleafed and flattered by your expreffion of
Orna me. The chief pleafure this work can give me
is, that I can in it, with propriety, decency, and
juftice, infert the name and charaȼter of every friend
I have ; and every man that deferves to be loved or
adorned. But I fmile at your applying that phrafe to
my vifiting you in Ireland ; a place where I might
have fome apprehenfion (from their extraordinary
paffion for poetry, and their boundlefs hofpitality)
of being *adorned* to death, and buried under the
weight of garlands, like one I have read of fomewhere or other. My mother lives (which is an anfwer to that point), and, I thank God, though her
memory be in a manner gone, is yet awake and fenfible to me, though fcarce to any thing elfe ; which
doubles the reafon of my attendance, and at the
fame time fweetens it. I wifh, (beyond any other
wifh), you could pafs a fummer here ; I might (too
probably) return with you, unlefs you preferred to
fee France firft, to which country, I think, you
would have a ftrong invitation. Lord Peterborow has
narrowly efcaped death, and yet keeps his chamber.
He is perpetually fpeaking in the moft affeȼtionate
manner of you. He has written you two letters,
which you never received ; and by that has been difcouraged from writing more. I can well believe the
poft-office may do this, when fome letters of his to
me have met the fame fate, and two of mine to
him. Yet let not this difcourage you from writing
to me, or to him, inclofed in the common way, as I

* See note on the epiftle to Lord Cobham, *Of the Knowledge
and Charaȼters of men,* vol. 2. of Pope's works.

do

do to you. Innocent men need fear no detection of their thoughts; and, for my part, I would give them free leave to fend all I write to Curl, if molt of what I write was not too filly.

I defire my fincere fervices to Dr Delany, who, I agree with you, is a man every way efteemable. My Lord Orrery is a molt virtuous and good-natured nobleman, whom I fhould be happy to know. Lord B. received your letter through my hands. It is not to be told you how much he wifhes for you. The whole lift of perfons to whom you fent your fervices, return you theirs, with proper fenfe of the diftinc-tion.——Your Lady friend is *femper eadem*; and I have written an epiftle to her on that qualification, in a female character; which is thought by my chief critic, in your abfence, to be my *chef d'oeuvre:* but it cannot be printed perfectly, in an age fo fore of fa-tire, and fo willing to mifapply characters.

As to my own health, it is as good as ufual. I have lain ill feven days of a flight fever, (the com-plaint here), but recovered by gentle fweats, and the care of Dr Arbuthnot. The play Mr Gay left fucceeds very well; it is another original in its kind. Adieu. God preferve your life, your health, your limbs, your fpirits, and your friendfhips!

LETTER LXVI.

April 2. 1733.

YOU fay truly, that death is only terrible to us, as it feparates us from thofe we love; but I really think thofe have the worft of it who are left by us, if we are true friends. I have felt more (I fancy) in the lofs of Mr Gay, than I fhall fuffer in the thought of going away myfelf into a ftate that can feel none of this fort of loffes. I wifhed vehe-mently to have feen him in a condition of living in-dependent, and to have lived in perfect indolence the reft of our days together, the two moft idle,

moft

most innocent, undesigning poets of our age. I now
as vehemently wish you and I might walk into the
grave together, by as flow steps as you pleafe, but
contentedly and cheerfully. Whether that ever can
be, or in what country, I know no more, than into
what country we shall walk out of the grave. But it
fuffices me to know, it will be exactly what region or
state our maker appoints; and that whatever *is*, is
right. Our poor friend's papers are partly in my
hands; and for as much as is fo, I will take care to
fupprefs things unworthy of him. As to the epitaph,
I am forry you gave a copy; for it will certainly by
that means come into print; and I would correct
it more, unlefs you will do it for me, (and that I
shall like as well). Upon the whole, I earnestly
wish your coming over hither; for this reafon,
among many others, that your influence may be
joined with mine, to fupprefs whatever we may judge
proper of his papers. To be plunged in my neighbour's and my papers, will be your inevitable fate as
foon as you come. That I am an author whofe characters are thought of fome weight, appears from the
great noife and brittle that the court and town make
about any I give: and I will not render them lefs
important, or lefs interesting, by fparing vice and
folly, or by betraying the caufe of truth and virtue.
I will take care they shall be fuch as no man can be
angry at, but the perfons I would have angry. You
are fenfible, with what decency and juffice I paid
homage to the Royal family, at the fame time that I
fatirifed falfe courtiers, and fpies, &c. about them.
I have not the courage, however, to be fuch a fatirift as
you, but I would be as much, or more, a philofopher.
You call your fatires, *libels*; I would rather call my fatires, *epiftles*. They will confift more of morality than
of wit, and grow graver, which you will call duller.
I shall leave it to my antagonifts to be witty, (if they
can), and content myfelf to be ufeful, and in the
right. Tell me your opinion as to Lady ———'s or
Lord * *'s performance? They are certainly the

top-wits of the court, and you may judge by that
fingle piece what can be done againſt me ; for it was
laboured, correcked, præ-commended, and poſt-diſ-
approved, ſo far as to be diſowned by themſelves, after
each had highly cried it up, for the others *. I have
met with ſome complaints, and heard at a diſtance
of ſome threats, occaſioned by my verſes. I ſent fair
meſſages to acquaint them where I was to be found
in town, and to offer to call at their houſes to ſatisfy
them, and ſo it dropped. It is very poor in any
one to rail and threaten at a diſtance, and have nothing to ſay to you when they ſee you.— I am glad
you perſiſt and abide by ſo good a thing as that
poem †, in which I am immortal for my morality.
I never took any praiſe ſo kindly ; and yet, I think,
I deſerve that praiſe better than I do any other.
When does your collection come out, and what will
it conſiſt of ? I have but laſt week finiſhed another
of my epiſtles, in the order of the ſyſtem ; and this
week (exercitandi gratia) I have tranſlated (or rather parodied) another of Horace's, in which I introduce you adviſing me about my expenſes, houſe-
keeping, &c. But theſe things ſhall lie by, till you
come to carp at them, and alter rhymes, and grammar, and triplets, and cacophonies of all kinds.
Our parliament will ſit till midſummer ; which, I
hope, may be a motive to bring you rather in ſummer than ſo late as autumn. You uſed to love what I
hate, a hurry of politics, &c. Courts I ſee not, courtiers
I know not, kings I adore not, queens I compliment
not ; ſo I am never like to be in faſhion, nor in dependence. I heartily join with you in pitying our
poor Lady for her unhappineſs ; and ſhould only pity
her more, if ſhe had more of what they at court call
happineſs. Come then, and perhaps we may go all
together into France, at the end of the ſeaſon, and
compare the liberties of both kingdoms. Adieu.

---

* See Pope's epiſtle written on this occaſion, above.
† The ironical libel on Dr Delany.

Believe

Believe me, dear Sir, (with a thoufand warm wifhes, mixed with fhort fighs), ever yours.

LETTER LXVII.

To Mr POPE.

Dublin, May 1. 1733.

I Anfwer your letter the fooner, becaufe I have a particular reafon for doing fo. Some weeks ago came over a poem called, *The life and charaƈter of Dr S. written by himfelf.* It was reprinted here, and is dedicated to you. It is grounded upon a maxim in Rochefoucault; and the dedication, after a formal ftory, fays, that my manner of writing is to be found in every line. I believe I have told you, that I writ a year or two ago near five hundred lines upon the fame maxim in Rochefoucault, and was a long time about it, as that impoftor fays in his dedication; with many circumftances, all pure invention. I defire you to believe, and to tell my friends, that in this fpurious piece there is not a fingle line, or bit of a line, or thought, any way refembling the genuine copy, any more than it does Virgil's Æneis; for I never gave a copy of mine, nor lent it out of my fight. And although I fhewed it to all common acquaintance indifferently, and fome of them (efpecially one or two females) had got many lines by heart here and there, and repeated them often; yet it happens, that not one fingle line, or thought, is contained in this impofture; although it appears, that they who counterfeited me, had heard of the true one. But even this trick fhall not provoke me to print the true one; which indeed is not proper to be feen, till I can be feen no more. I therefore defire you will undeceive my friends; and I will order an advertifement to be printed here, and tranfmit it to England, that every body may know the delufion, and acquit me; as, I am fure,

F f 2

you

you muſt have done yourſelf, if you have read
any part of it; which is mean, and trivial, and full
of that cant that I moſt deſpiſe.   I would ſink
to be a vicar in. Norfolk, rather than be charged
with ſuch a performance.   Now I come to your
letter.

When I was of your age, I thought every day of
death, but now every minute; and a continual giddy
diſorder, more or leſs, is a greater addition than that
of my years.   I cannot affirm, that I pity our friend
Gay; but I pity his friends, I pity you, and would
at leaſt equally pity myſelf, if I lived amongſt you;
becauſe I ſhould have ſeen him oftener than you did,
who are a kind of hermit,   how great a noiſe ſoever
you make by your ill nature, in not letting the honeſt villains of the times enjoy themſelves in this
world, which is their only happineſs, and terrifying
them with another. I ſhould have added in my libel, that, of all men living, you are the moſt happy
in your enemies and your friends.   And I will ſwear
you have fifty times more charity for mankind
than I could ever pretend to.   Whether the pro-
duction you mention came from the Lady or the
Lord, I did not imagine that they were at leaſt ſo
bad verſifiers.   Therefore *facit indignatio verſus*,
is only to be applied when the indignation is againſt
general villany, and never operates when ſome ſort
of people write to defend themſelves.   I love to hear
them reproach you for dulneſs; only I would be ſa-
tisfied, ſince you are ſo dull, why are they ſo angry?
Give me a ſhilling, and I will enſure you, that
poſterity ſhall never know you had one ſingle enemy, excepting thoſe whoſe memory you have preſerved.

I am ſorry for the ſituation of Mr Gay's papers.
You do not exert yourſelf as much as I could wiſh in
this affair. I had rather the two ſiſters were hanged,
than ſee his works ſwelled by any loſs of credit to
his memory.   I would be glad to ſee the moſt valuable printed by themſelves; thoſe which ought
not

not to be feen, burned immediately; and the others
that have gone abroad, printed feparately. like *opuf-
cula*, or rather be ftifled and forgotten. I thought
your epitaph was immediately to be engraved, and
therefore I made lefs fcruple to give a copy to Lord
Orrery, who earneftly defired it, but to nobody
elfe; and he tells me, he gave only two, which he
will recall. I have a fhort epigram of his upon it;
wherein I would correct a line or two at moft, and
then I will fend it you (with his permiffion). I have
nothing againft yours, but the laft line, *Striking
their aching*; the two participles, as they are fo
near, feem to found too like. I fhall write to the
Duchefs, who hath lately honoured me with a very
friendly letter, and I will tell her my opinion freely
about our friend's papers. I want health, and my
affairs are enlarged: but I will break through the
latter, if the other mends. I can ufe a courfe of
medicines, lame and giddy. My chief defign, next
to feeing you, is to be a fevere critic on you and
your neighbour; but firft kill his father, that he
may be able to maintain me in my own way of living, and particularly my horfes. It coft me near
600 *l*. for a wall to keep mine; and I never ride
without two fervants for fear of accidents. *Hic vivi-
mus ambitiofa paupertate.* You are both too poor
for my acquaintance, but he much the poorer.
With you I will find grafs, and wine, and fervants;
but with him not.—The collection you fpeak of is
this. A printer came to me, to defire he might print
my works (as he called them) in four volumes, by
fubfcription. I faid I would give no leave, and
fhould be forry to fee them printed here. He faid
they could not be printed in London. I anfwered,
they could, if the partners agreed. He faid, he
" would be glad of my permiffion; but as he could
" print them without it, and was advifed that it
" could do me no harm, and having been affured
" of numerous fubfcriptions, he hoped I would not
" be angry at his purfuing his own intereft, &c."

Much

Much of this difcourfe paffed ; and he goes on with
the matter ; wherein I determine not to intermeddle,
though it be much to my difcontent: and I wifh it
could be done in England, rather than here, although
I am grown pretty indifferent in every thing of that
kind. This is the truth of the ftory.

My vanity turns at prefent on being perfonated in
your *Quæ virtus*, &c. You will obferve in this letter many marks of an ill head and a low fpirit, but
a heart wholly turned to love you with the greateft
earneftnefs and truth.

LETTER LXVIII.

May 28. 1733.

I Have begun two or three letters to you by
fnatches, and been prevented from finifhing
them by a thoufand avocations and diffipations. I
muft firft acknowledge the honour done me by Lord
Orrery, whofe praifes are that precious ointment Solomon fpeaks of, which can be given only by men
of virtue. All other praife, whether from poets or
peers, is contemptible alike : and I am old enough
and experienced enough to know, that the only
praifes worth having, are thofe beftowed *by* virtue
for virtue. My poetry I abandon to the critics, my
morals I commit to the teftimony of thofe who know
me ; and therefore I was more pleafed with your
libel, than with any verfes I ever received. I wifh
fuch a collection of your writings could be printed
here, as you mention going on in Ireland. I was
furprifed to receive from the printer that fpurious
piece, called *The life and character of Dr Swift,*
with a letter, telling me, the perfon " who publifhed
" it, had affured him, the dedication to me was what
" I would not take ill, or elfe he would not have
" printed it." I cannot tell who the man is, who
took fo far upon him as to anfwer for my way of
thinking ; though, had the thing been genuine, I
should

should have been greatly difpleafed at the publifher's part, in doing it without your knowledge.

I am as earneft as you can be, in doing my beft to prevent the publifhing of any thing unworthy of Mr Gay ; but I fear his friends partiality. I wifh you would come over. All the myfteries of my philofophical work fhall then be cleared to you, and you will not think that I am not merry enough, nor angry enough. It will not want for fatire ; but as for anger, I know it not; or at leaft only that fort of which the apoftle fpeaks, " Be ye angry, and " fin not."

My neighbour's * writings have been metaphyfi- cal, and will next be hiftorical. It is certainly from him only that a valuable hiftory of Europe in thefe latter times can be expected. Come, and quicken him ; for age, indolence, and contempt of the world, grow upon men apace, and may often make the wifeft indifferent whether pofterity be any wifer than we. To a man in years, health and quiet become fuch rarities, and confequently fo valuable, that he is apt to think of nothing more than of enjoying them whenever he can, for the remainder of life : and this, I doubt not, has caufed fo many great men to die without leaving a fcrap to pofterity.

I am fincerely troubled for the bad account you give me of your own health. I wifh every day to hear a better, as much as I do to enjoy my own, I faithfully affure you.

L E T T E R LXIX.

From Dr S w i f t.

Dublin, July 8. 1733.

I Muft condole with you for the lofs of Mrs Pope, of whofe death † the papers have been full. But I

* Lord Bolingbroke.,
† Mrs Pope died June 7. 1733, aged 93.

would

would rather rejoice with you ; becaufe, if any circumftances can make the death of a dear parent and
friend a fubject for joy, you have them all. She
died in an extreme old age, without pain, under the
care of the moft dutiful fon that I have ever known
or heard of; which is a felicity not happening to one
in a million. The worft effect of her death falls upon me ; and fo much the worfe, becaufe I expected
aliquis damno ufus in illo, that it would be followed
by making me and this kingdom happy with your
prefence. But I am told, to my great misfortune,
that a very convenient offer happening, you waved
the invitation preffed on you, alleging the fear you
had of being killed here with eating and drinking.
By which I find, that you have given fome credit to a
notion, of our great plenty and hofpitality. It is
true, our meat. and wine is cheaper here, as it is
always in the pooreft countries, becaufe there is no
money to pay for them. I believe there are not in
this whole city three gentlemen out of employment,
who are able to give entertainments once a-month.
Thofe who are in employments of church or ftate,
are three parts in four from England, and amount to
little more than a dozen. Thofe indeed may once
or twice invite their friends, or any perfon of diftinction that makes a voyage hither. All my acquaintance tell me, they know not above three families where they can occafionally dine in a whole
year. Dr Delany is the only gentleman I know,
who keeps one certain day in the week to entertain
feven or eight friends at dinner ; and to pafs the
evening, where there is nothing of excefs, either in
eating or drinking. Our old friend Southern (who
hath juft left us) was invited to dinner once or twice
by a judge, a bifhop, or a commiffioner of the revenues ; but moft frequented a few particular friends,
and chiefly the Doctor, who is eafy in his fortune,
and very hofpitable. The conveniencies of taking
the air, winter or fummer, do far exceed thofe in
London. For the two large ftrands, juft at two ends
of

of the town, are as firm and dry in winter as in fummer. There are at leaft fix or eight gentlemen of
fenfe, learning, good humour, and tafte, able and
defirous to pleafe you; and orderly females, fome
of the better fort, to take care of you. Thefe were
the motives that I have frequently made ufe of to
entice you hither. And there would be no failure
among the beft people here, of any honours that
could be done you. As to myfelf, I declare, my
health is fo uncertain that I dare not venture amongft
you at prefent. I hate the thoughts of London;
where I am not rich enough to live otherwife than
by fhifting, which is now too late. Neither can I
have conveniencies in the country for three horfes
and two fervants, and many others, which I have
here at hand. I am one of the governours of all the
hackney-coaches, carts, and carriages round this
town; who dare not infult me, like your rafcally
waggoners or coachmen, but give me the way: nor
is there one Lord or Squire for a hundred of yours,
to turn me cut of the road, or run over me with
their coaches and fix. Thus I make fome advantage of the public poverty; and give you the reafons
for what I once writ, why I chufe to be a freeman
among flaves, rather than a flave among freemen,
Then, I walk the ftreets in peace without being
juftled, nor ever without a thoufand bleffings from
my friends the vulgar. I am Lord Mayor of 120
houfes; I am abfolute Lord of the greateft cathedral
in the kingdom; am at peace with the neighbouring
princes, the Lord Mayor of the city, and the Archbifhop of Dublin; only the latter, like the K. of
France, fometimes attempts incroachments on my
dominions, as old Lewis did upon Lorrain. In the
midft of this raillery, I can tell you, with ferioufnefs,
that thefe advantages contribute to my eafe, and
therefore I value them. And in one part of your
letter, relating to my Lord B——— and yourfelf,
you agree with me entirely, about the indifference,
the love of quiet, the care of health, &c. that grow
upon

upon men in years. And if you difcover thofe inclinations in my Lord and yourfelf, what can you
expect from me, whofe health is fo precarious? and
yet, at your or his time of life, I could have leaped
over the moon.

LETTER LXX.

Sept. 1. 1733.

I Have every day wifhed to write to you, to fay a
thoufand things; and yet, I think, I fhould not
have writ to you now, if I was not fick of writing
any thing, fick of myfelf, and (what is worfe) fick
of my friends too. The world is become too bufy
for me; every body is fo concerned for the public;
that all private enjoyments are loft or difrelifhed. I
write more to fhow you I am tired of this life, than
to tell you any thing relating to it. I live as I did, I
think as I did, I love you as I did: but all thefe are
to no purpofe; the world will not live, think, or
love, as I do. I am troubled for, and vexed at all
my friends by turns. Here are fome whom you love,
and who love you; yet they receive no proofs of that
affection from you, and they give none of it to you.
There is a great gulf between. In earneft, I would
go a thoufand miles by land to fee you, but the fea I
dread. My ailments are fuch, that I really believe
a fea-ficknefs (confidering the oppreffion of colical
pains, and the great weaknefs of my breaft) would
kill me: and if I did not die of that, I muft of the
exceffive eating and drinking of your hofpitable
town, and the exceffive flattery of your moft poetical country. I hate to be crammed, either way;
Let your hungry poets and your rhyming poets digeft it, I cannot. I like much better to be abufed
and half-ftarved, than to be fo over-praifed and over-
fed. Drown Ireland! for having caught you, and
for having kept you. I only referve a little charity
for her, for knowing your value, and efteeming you
                                                      You.

You are the only patriot I know, who is not hated for ſerving his country. The man who drew your character and printed it here, was not much in the wrong in many things he ſaid of you : yet he was a very impertinent fellow, for ſaying them in words, quite different from thoſe you had yourſelf employed before on the ſame ſubject : for ſurely to alter your words is to prejudice them, and I have been told, that a man himſelf can hardly ſay the ſame thing twice over with equal happineſs; nature is ſo much a better thing than artifice.

I have written nothing this year. It is no affectation to tell you, my mother's loſs has turned my frame of thinking. The habit of a whole life is a ſtronger thing than all the reaſon in the world. I know I ought to be eaſy, and to be free; but I am dejected, I am confined : my whole amuſement is in reviewing my paſt life, not in laying plans for my future. I wiſh you cared as little for popular applauſe as I; as little for any nation, in contradiſtinction to others, as I : and then I fancy, you that are not afraid of the ſea, you that are a ſtronger man at ſixty than ever I was at twenty, would come and ſee ſeveral people, who are (at laſt), like the primitive Chriſtians, of one ſoul and of one mind. The day is come, which I have often wiſhed, but never thought to ſee; when *every mortal that I eſteem, is of the ſame ſentiment in politics and in religion.*

Adieu. All you love, are yours; but all are buſy, except (dear Sir) your ſincere friend.

LETTER LXXI.

Jan. 6. 1734.

I Never think of you, and can never write to you, now, without drawing many of thoſe ſhort ſighs of which we have formerly talked. The reflection both of the friends we have been deprived of by death, and of thoſe from whom we are ſeparated almoſt

-moſt as eternally by abſence, checks me to that degree that it takes away, in a manner, the pleaſure
(which yet I feel very ſenſibly too) of thinking I am
now converſing with you. You have been ſilent to
me as to your works; whether thoſe printed here àre,
or are not genuine. But one, I am ſure, is yours;
and your method of concealing yourſelf, puts me in
mind of the Indian bird I have read of, who hides
his head in a hole, while all his feathers and tail ſtick
out. You will have immediately, by ſeveral franks,
(even before it is here publiſhed), my epiſtle to Lord
Cobham, part of my *opus magnum*, and the laſt Eſſay on Man; both which, I conclude, will be grateful
to your bookſeller, on whom you pleaſe to beſtow
them ſo early. There is a woman's war declared a-
gainſt me by a certain Lord; his weapons are the
ſame which women and children uſe, a pin to ſcratch,
and a ſquirt to beſpatter. I writ a ſort of anſwer;
but was aſhamed to enter the liſts with him, and after ſhewing it to ſome people, ſuppreſſed it: otherwiſe it was ſuch as was worthy of him and worthy of
me. I was three weeks this autumn with Lord Peterborow, who rejoices in your doings, and always
ſpeaks with the greateſt affection of you. I need not
tell you who elſe do the ſame; you may be ſure almoſt all thoſe whom I ever ſee, or deſire to ſee. I
wonder not that B— paid you no ſort of civility while
he was in Ireland: he is too much a half-wit to love
a true wit; and too much half-honeſt, to eſteem any
entire merit. I hope and think he hates me too, and
I will do my beſt to make him: he is ſo inſupporta-
bly inſolent in his civility to me, when he meets me
at one third place, that I muſt affront him to be rid
of it. That ſtrict neutrality as to public parties,
which I have conſtantly obſerved in all my writings,
I think gives me the more title to attack ſuch men
as ſlander and belie my character in private, to thoſe
who know me not. Yet even this is a liberty I will
never take, unleſs at the ſame time they are peſts of
private ſociety, or miſchievous members of the public;

blic; that is to fay, unlefs they are enemies to all men, as well as to me.———Pray write to me when you can. If ever I can come to you, I will: if not, may Providence be our friend and our guard through this fimple world, where nothing is valuable but fenfe and friendfhip. Adieu, dear Sir; may health attend your years, and then may many years be added to you.

P. S. I am juft now told, a very curious lady intends to write to you to pump you about fome poems faid to be yours. Pray tell her, that you have not anfwered me on the fame queftions, and that I fhall take it as a thing never to be forgiven from you, if you tell another what you have concealed from me.

LETTER LXXII.

Sept. 15. 1734.

I Have ever thought you as fenfible as any man I knew, of all the delicacies of friendfhip; and yet I fear (from what Lord B. tells me you faid in your laft letter) that you did not quite underftand the reafon of my late filence. I affure you it proceeded wholly from the tender kindnefs I bear you. When the heart is full, it is angry at all words that cannot come up to it; and you are now the man in all the world I am moft troubled to write to, for you are the friend I have left whom I am moft grieved about. Death has not done worfe to me in feparating poor Gay, or any other, than difeafe and abfence in dividing us. I am afraid to know how you do; fince moft accounts I have, give me pain for you, and I am unwilling to tell you the condition of my own health. If it were good, I would fee you; and yet if I found you in that very condition of deafnefs, which made you fly from us while we were together, what comfort could we derive from it? In writing

often I should find great relief, could we write freely; and yet, when I have done fo, you feem, by not
anfwering in a very long time, to feel either the fame
uneafinefs as I do, or to abftain, from fome prudential reafon. Yet I am fure, nothing that you and I
would fay to each other, (though our whole fouls were
to be laid open to the clerks of the poft-office), could
hurt either of us fo much, in the opinion of any honeft man or good fubject, as the intervening, offi-
cious impertinence of thofe goers between us, who
in England.pretend to intimacies with you, and in
Ireland to intimacies with me. I cannot but receive
any that call upon me in your name; and in truth
they take it in vain too often. I take all opportunities of juftifying you againft thefe friends, efpecially
thofe who know all you think and write, and repeat
your flighter verfes. It is generally on fuch little
fcraps that witlings feed; and it is hard the world
fhould judge of our houfekeeping, from what we fling
to our dogs; yet this is often the confequence. But
they treat you ftill worfe, mix their own with yours,
print them to get money, and lay them at your door.
This I am fatisfied was the cafe in the epiftle to a lady. It was juft the fame hand (if I have any judgment in ftyle) which printed your life and character
before, which you fo ftrongly difavowed in your letters to Lord Carteret, myfelf, and others. I was very well informed of another fact, which convinced
me yet more. The fame perfon who gave this to be
printed, offered to a bookfeller a piece in profe as
yours, and as commiffioned by you, which has fince
appeared, and been owned to be his own. I think
(I fay once more) that I know your hand, though you
did not mine in the Effay on Man. I beg your pardon for not telling you, as I fhould, had you been in
England: but no fecret can crofs your Irifh fea, and
every clerk in the poft-office had known it. I fancy,
though you loft fight of me in the firft of thofe effays,
you faw me in the fecond. The defign of concealing myfelf was good, and had its full effect. I was
                                                    thought

thought a divine, a philofopher, and what not; and my doctrine had a fanction I could not have given to it. Whether I can proceed in the fame grave march like Lucretius, or muft defcend to the gaieties of Horace, I know not, or whether I can do either: but be the future as it will, I fhall collect all the paft in one fair quarto this winter, and fend it you, where you will find frequent mention of yourfelf. I was glad you fuffered your writings to be collected more completely than hitherto, in the volumes I daily expect from Ireland; I wifhed it had been in more pomp, but that will be done by others: yours are beauties, that can never be too finely dreffed, for they will ever be young. I have only one piece of mercy to beg of you: do not laugh at my gravity, but permit me to wear the beard of a philofopher, till I pull it off, and make a jeft of it myfelf. It is juft what my Lord B. is doing with metaphyfics. I hope you will live to fee, and ftare at the learned figure he will make, on the fame fhelf with Locke and Malbranche.

You fee how I talk to you, (for this is not writing). If you like I fhould do fo, why not tell me fo? if it be the leaft pleafure to you, I will write once a-week moft gladly: but can you abftract the letters from the perfon who writes them, fo far, as not to feel more vexation in the thought of our feparation, and thofe misfortunes which occafion it, than fatisfaction in the nothings he can exprefs? If you can, really and from my heart, I cannot. I return again to melancholy. Pray, however, tell me, is it a fatisfaction? that will make it one to me; and we will think alike, as friends ought, and you fhall hear from me punctually juft when you will.

P. S. Our friend, who is juft returned from a progrefs of three months, and is fetting out in three days with me for the Bath, where he will ftay till towards the middle of October, left this letter with me yefterday, and I cannot feal and difpatch it till I have

fcribbled

fcribbled the remainder of this page full.. He talks
very pompoufly of my metaphyfics, and places them
in a very honourable ftation. It is true, I have
writ-fix letters and an half to him on fubjects of that
kind, and I propofe a letter and an half more, which
would fwell.the whole up to a confiderable volume.
But he thinks me fonder of the name of an author
than I am. When he and you, and one or two other
friends, have feen them, *fatis magnum theatrum mihi
eftis*, I fhall not have the itch of making them more
public *. I know how little regard you pay to writings of this kind. But I imagine, that if you can
like any fuch, it muft be thofe that ftrip metaphyfics
of all their bombaft, keep within the fight of every
well-conftituted eye, and never bewilder themfelves
whilft they pretend to guide the reafon of others. I
writ to you a long letter fome time ago, and fent it
by the poft. Did it come to your hands? or did the
infpectors of private correfpondence ftop it, to revenge themfelves of the ill faid of them in it? *Vale,
et me ama.*

LETTER LXXIII.

From Dr SWIFT.

Nov. 1. 1734.

I Have yours with my Lord B———'s poftfcript
of September 15. It was long on its way; and
for fome weeks after the date, I was very ill with my
two inveterate diforders, giddinefs and deafnefs.
The latter is pretty well off; but the other makes
me totter towards evenings, and much difpirits me.
But I continue to ride and walk; both of which, although they be no cures, are at leaft amufements.
I did never imagine you to be either inconftant, or to
want right notions of friendfhip: but I apprehend
your want of health; and it hath been a frequent

* As Lord B. (let. 49.) tells us, they fhew that *all our meta-*
phyfical theology is ridiculous and abominable.

wonder

wonder to me how you have, been able to entertain
the world so long, so frequently, so happily, under so
many bodily diforders. My Lord B. fays you have
been three months rambling, which is the beft thing
you can poffibly do in a fummer-feafon; and when
the winter recalls you, we will, for our own interefts,
leave you to your fpeculations. God be thanked I
have done with every thing, and of every kind, that
requires writing, except now and then a letter; or,
like a true old man, fcribbling trifles only fit for children, or fchoolboys of the loweft clafs at beft, which
three or four of us read and laugh at to-day, and
burn to-morrow. Yet, what is fingular, I never am
without fome great work in view, enough to take
up forty years of the moft vigorous healthy man;
although I am convinced, that I fhall never be able to
finifh three treatifes, that have lain by me feveral
years, and want nothing but correction. My Lord
B. faid in his poftfcript, that you would go to Bath
in three days. We fince heard, that you were dan-
geroufly ill there, and that the news-mongers gave
you over. But a gentleman of this kingdom, on his
return from Bath, affured me he left you well; and
fo did fome others, whom I have forgot. I am forry
at my heart that you are peftered with people who
come in my name; and I profefs to you, it is without my knowledge. I am confident I fhall hardly
ever have occafion again to recommend; for my
friends here are very few, and fixed to the freehold,
from whence nothing but death will remove them.
Surely I never doubted about your Effay on Man;
and I would lay any odds, that I would never fail
to difcover you in fix lines, unlefs you had a mind
to write below, or befide yourfelf, on purpofe. I confefs I did never imagine you were fo deep in morals,
or that fo many new and excellent rules could be
produced fo advantageoufly and agreeably in that
fcience, from any one head. I confefs in fome few
places I was forced to read twice. I believe I told
you before what the Duke of D——faid to me on

that

that occafion, how a judge here, who knows you,
told him, that, on the firſt reading thoſe eſſays, he
was much pleaſed, but found ſome lines a little dark :
on the ſecond moſt of them cleared up, and his
pleaſure increaſed : on the third he had no doubt
remained ; and then he admired the whole. My
Lord B——'s attempt of reducing metaphyſics to
intelligible ſenſe and uſefulneſs, will be a glorious
undertaking ; and as I never knew him fail in any
thing he attempted, if he had the ſole management,
ſo I am confident he will ſucceed in this. I defire
you will allow that I write to you both at preſent,
and ſo I ſhall while I live. It ſaves your money and
my time ; and he being your genius, no matter to
which it is addreſſed. I am happy that what you
write is printed in large letters ; otherwiſe, between
the weakneſs of my eyes, and the thickneſs of my
hearing, I ſhould loſe the greateſt pleaſure that is
left me. Pray command my Lord B—— to follow
that example, if I live to read his metaphyſics. Pray
God bleſs you both. I had a melancholy account
from the Doctor of his health. I will anſwer his
letter as ſoon as I can. I am ever entirely yours.

LETTER LXXIV.

Twickenham, Dec. 19. 1734.

I AM truly ſorry for any complaint you have ; and
it is in regard to the weakneſs of your eyes, that
I write (as well as print) in folio. You will think,
(I know you will, for you have all the candour of a
good underſtanding), that the thing which men of
our age feel the moſt, is the friendſhip of our equals ;
and that therefore whatever affects thoſe who are ſlept
a few years before us, cannot but ſenſibly affect us
who are to follow. It troubles me to hear you complain of your memory ; and, if I am in any part of
my conſtititution younger than you, it will be in my
remembering every thing that has pleaſed me in you,

longer

longer than perhaps you will. The two fummers we
paffed together dwell always on my mind, like a vifion which gave me a glimpfe of a better life and
better company, than this world otherwife afforded.
I am now an individual, upon whom no other depends ; and may go where I will, if the wretched
carcafe I am annexed to, did not hinder me. I
rambled by very eafy journeys this year to Lord Bathurft and Lord Peterborow, who, upon every occafion, commemorate, love, and wifh for you. I now
pafs my days between Dawley, London, and this
place; not ftudious, nor idle, rather polifhing old
works than hewing out new. I redeem now and
then a paper that hath been abandoned feveral years ;
and of this fort you will foon fee one which I infcribe to our old friend Arbuthnot.

Thus far I had written ; and thinking to finifh my
letter the fame evening, was prevented by company ;
and the next morning found myfelf in a fever, highly difordered, and fo continued in bed for five days ;
and in my chamber till now ; but fo well recovered,
as to hope to go abroad to-morrow, even by the advice of Dr Arbuthnot. He himfelf, poor man, is
much broke, though not worfe than for thefe two
laft months he has been. He took extremely kind
your letter. I wifh to God, we could once meet a-
gain, before that feparation, which yet, I would be
glad to believe, fhall re-unite us. But he who made
us, not for ours, but his purpofes, knows only whether it be for the better or the worfe, that the affections of this life fhould, or fhould not continue into
the other : and doubtlefs it is as it fhould be. Yet
I am fure, that while I am here, and the thing that I
am, I fhall be imperfect without the communication
of fuch friends as you. You are to me like a limb
loft, and buried in another country. Though we feem
quite divided, every accident makes me feel you
were once a part of me. I always confider you fo
much as a friend, that I forget you are an author,
perhaps too much ; but it is as much as I would defire

fire you would do to me.: However, if I could in-:
fpirit you to beftow correction upon thofe three treatifes, which you fay are fo near completed ; I fhould
think it a better work than any I can pretend to of
my own. I am almoft at the end of my morals, as
I have been long ago of my wit. My fyftem is a
fhort one, and my circle narrow. Imagination has
no limits, and that is a fphere in which you may
move on to eternity : but where one is confined to
truth, (or, to fpeak more like a human creature, to
the appearances of truth), we foon find the fhortnefs
of our tether. Indeed, by the help of a metaphy- ·
fical chain of ideas, one may extend the circulation,
go round and round for ever, without making any
progrefs beyond the point to which Providence has
pinned us. But this does not fatisfy me ; who would
rather fay a little to no purpofe, than a great deal.
Lord B. is voluminous, but he is voluminous only
to deftroy volumes. I fhall not live, I fear, to fee
that work printed. He is fo taken up ftill (in fpite
of the monitory hint given in the firft line of my
effay) with particular men, that he neglects mankind, and is ftill a creature of this world, not of the
univerfe ; this world, which is a name we give to
Europe, to England, to Ireland, to London, to
Dublin, to the court, to the caftle, and fo diminifh-
ing, till it comes to our own affairs, and to our own
perſons. When you write either to him or to me,
(for we accept it all as one), rebuke him for it ; as
a divine, if you like it ; or as a badineur, if you think
that more effectual.

What I write will fhew that my head is yet weak.
I had written to you by that gentleman from the
Bath, but I did not know him ; and every body that
comes from Ireland, pretends to be a friend of the
Dean's. I am always glad to fee any that are truly
fo ; and therefore do nor miftake any thing I faid,
fo as to difcourage you ſ......ding any fuch to me.
Adieu. ·

LET-

LETTER LXXV.

From Dr SWIFT.

May 12. 1735.

YOur letter was sent me yesterday by Mr Stopford, who landed the same day, but I have
not yet seen him. As to my silence, God knows it
is my great misfortune. My little domestic affairs
are in great confusion, by the villany of agents,
and the miseries of this kingdom, where there is
no money to be had. Nor am I unconcerned, to
see all things tending towards absolute power in
both nations.*, (it is here in perfection already), although I shall not live to see it established. This
condition of things, both public, and personal to myself, hath given me such a kind of despondency, that
I am almost unqualified for any company, diversion,
or amusement. The death of Mr Gay and the
Doctor †, hath been terrible wounds near my heart.
Their living would have been a great comfort to me,
although I should never have seen them ; like a sum
of money in a bank, from which I should receive at
least annual interest, as I do from you, and have
done from my Lord Bolingbroke. To shew in how
much ignorance I live, it is hardly a fortnight since I
heard of the death of my Lady Masham, my constant
friend in all changes of times. God forbid that I
should expect you to make a voyage that would in
the least affect your health. But in the mean time
how unhappy am I, that my best friend should have
perhaps the only kind of disorder for which a sea-
voyage is not in some degree a remedy? The old
Duke of Ormond said, he would not change his
dead son (Ossory) for the best living son in Europe.

* The Dean was frequently troubled, he tells us, with a
giddiness in his head.
† Arbuthnot. He died Feb. 27. 1734 5.

Neither.

Neither would I change you, my abfent friend, for the beft prefent friend round the globe.

I have lately read a book imputed to Lord B; called, *A differtation upon parties.* I think it very mafterly written.

Pray God reward you for your kind prayers. I believe your prayers will do me more good than thofe of all the prelates in both kingdoms, or any prelates in Europe, except the bifhop of Marfeilles *. And God preferve you for contributing more to mend the world, than the whole pack of (modern) parfons in a lump.

I am ever entirely yours.

L E T T E R LXXVI.

From Dr S w i f t.

Sept. 3. 1735.

This letter will be delivered to you by Faulkner the printer, who goes over on his private affairs. This is an anfwer to yours of two months ago, which complains of that profligate fellow Curl. I heartily wifh you were what they call difaffected, as I am. I may fay as David did, *I have finned greatly, but what have thefe fheep done?* You have given no offence to the miniftry, nor to the lords, nor commons, nor queen, nor the next in power. For you are a man of virtue, and therefore muft abhor vice and all corruption, although your difcretion holds the reins. " You need not fear any con-" fequence in the commerce that hath fo long paff-" ed between us, although I never deftroyed one " of your letters. But my executors are men of ho-" nour and virtue, who have ftrict orders in my " will to burn every letter left behind me." Nei-

---

* Who continued there with his flock all the time a dreadful pefilence defolated that city, in 1720. He fold all his plate, &c. for the relief of the poor.

ther.

ther did our letters contain any turns of wit, or fancy, or politics, or fatire, but mere innocent friendfhip. Yet I am loath that any letters from you, and
a very few other friends, fhould die before me. I
believe we neither of us ever leaned our head upon
our left hand, to ftudy what we fhould write next;
yet we have held a conftant intercourfe from your
youth and my middle age, and from your middle
age it muft be continued till my death, which my
bad ftate of health makes me expect every month.
I have the ambition, and it is very earneft as well as
in hafte, to have one epiftle infcribed to me while I
am alive, and you juft in the time when wit and wifdom are in the height. I muft once more repeat
Cicero's defire to a friend, *Orna me.* A month ago
were fent me over by a friend of mine, the works of
John Hughes, Efq; They are in verfe and profe.
I never heard of the man in my life; yet I find your
name as a fubfcriber too. He is too grave a poet for
me; and, I think, among the *mediocribus* in profe
as well as verfe. I have the honour to know Dr
Rundle *. He is indeed worth all the reft you ever
fent us; but that is faying nothing, for he anfwers
your character. I have dined thrice in his company.
He brought over a worthy clergyman of this kingdom as his chaplain, which was a very wife and popular action. His only fault is, that he drinks no
wine, and I drink nothing elfe.

This kingdom is now abfolutely ftarving, by the
means of every oppreffion than can be inflicted on
mankind. — *Shall I not vifit for thefe things? faith
the Lord.* You advife me right, not to trouble myfelf about the world. But oppreffion tortures me,
and I cannot live without meat and drink, nor get
either without money; and money is not to be had,
except they will make me a bifhop, or a judge, or a
colonel, or a commiffioner of the revenues.

Adieu.

* Bifhop of Derry.

L E T-

LETTER LXXVII.

TO anfwer your queftion as to Mr Hughes, what he wanted as to genius, he made up as an honeft man : but he was of the clafs you think him.

I am glad you think of Dr Rundle as I do. He will be an honour to the bifhops, and a difgrace to one bifhop ; two things you will like : but what you will like more particularly, he will be a friend and benefactor even to your unfriended, unbenefited nation ; he will be a friend to human race, where-ever he goes. Pray tell him my beft wifhes for his health and long life. I wifh you and he came over together, or that I were with you. I never faw a man fo feldom whom I liked fo much as Dr Rundle.

Lord Peterborow I went to take a laft leave of, at his fetting fail for Lifbon. No body can be more wafted, no foul can be more alive. Immediately af-ter the fevereft operation, of being cut into the blad-der, for a fuppreffion of urine, he took coach, and got from Briftol to Southampton. This is a man that will neither live nor die like any other mortal.

Poor Lord Peterborow! there is another ftring loft, that would have helped to draw you hither! He ordered, on his deathbed, his watch to be given me, (that which had accompanied him in all his tra-vels), with this reafon, " That I might have fome-" thing to put me every day in mind of him." It was a prefent to him from the King of Sicily, whofe arms and *infignia* are graved on the inner cafe. On the outer, I have put this infcription. *Victor Ama-deus, Rex Siciliæ, Dux Sabaudiæ, &c. &c. Carolo Mordaunt, Comiti de Peterborow, D. D. Car. Mor. Com. de Pet. Alexandro Pope moriens legavit,* 1735.)

Pray write to me a little oftener : and if there be a thing left in the world that pleafes you, tell it one who will partake of it. I hear with approbation and pleafure, that your prefent care is to relieve the

moft

most helpless of this world, those objects * which
most want our compassion, though generally made
the scorn of their fellow-creatures, such as are less
innocent than they. You always think generously ;
and of all charities, this is the most disinterested, and
least vain-glorious, done to such as never will thank
you, or can praise you for it.

God bless you with ease, if not with pleasure ;
with a tolerable state of health, if not with its full
enjoyment; with a refigned temper of mind, if not
a very cheerful one. It is upon these terms I live
myself, though younger than you ; and I repine not
at my lot, could but the presence of a few that I
love be added to these.

Adieu;

LETTER LXXVIII.

From Dr SWIFT.

Oct. 21. 1735.

I Answered your letter relating to Curl, &c. I believe my letters have escaped being published,
because I writ nothing but nature and friendship, and
particular incidents which could make no figure in
writing. I have observed, that not only Voiture, but
likewise Tully and Pliny, writ their letters for the
public view, more than for the fake of their corre-
spondents ; and I am glad of it, on account of the
entertainment they have given me. Balfac did the
fame thing ; but with more stiffness, and confequently lefs diverting : now I must tell you, that you are
to look upon me as one going very fast out of the
world ; but my flesh and bones are to be carried to
Holyhead, for I will not lie in a country of flaves.
It pleafeth me to find that you begin to dislike things,
in spite of your philofophy. Your Muse cannot forbear her hints to that purpose. I cannot travel to

* Idiots.

fee you ; otherwife I folemnly proteft I would do it.
I have an intention to pafs this winter in the country, with a friend forty miles off, and to ride only
ten miles a-day ; yet is my health fo uncertain, that
I fear it will not be in my power. I often ride a dozen miles, but I come to my own bed at night. My
beft way would be to marry ; for in that cafe any bed
would be better than my own. I found you a very
young man, and I left you a middle-aged one ; you
knew me a middle-aged man, and now I am an old
one. Where is my Lord ——— ? methinks, I am inquiring after a tulip of laft year. — " You need
" not apprehend any Curls meddling with your let-
" ters to me. I will not deftroy them, but have or-
" dered my executors to do that office." I have a
thoufand things more to fay ; *longævitas eft garrula* ;
but I muft remember I have other letters to write, if
I have time, which I fpend to tell you fo. I am e-
ver, deareft Sir,

Your, &c.

LETTER LXXIX.

From Dr SWIFT.

Feb. 9. 1735-6.

I Cannot properly call you my beft friend, becaufe
I have not another left who deferves the name ;
fuch a havock have time, death, exile, and oblivion
made. Perhaps you would have fewer complaints of
my ill health and lownefs of fpirits, if they were not
fome excufe for my delay of writing even to you. It
is perfectly right what you fay of the indifference in
common friends, whether we are fick or well, happy or miferable. The very maid-fervants in a family have the fame notion : I have heard them often
fay, Oh, I am very fick, if any body cared for it !
I am vexed when my vifitors come with the compliment ufual here, Mr Dean, I hope you are very
well. My popularity that you mention, is wholly
confined

confined to the common people, who are more conftant than thofe we mifcall their betters. I walk
the ftreets, and fo do my lower friends ; from whom,
and from whom alone, I have a thoufand hats and
bleffings upon old fcores, which thofe we call the
gentry have forgot. But I have not the love, or
hardly the civility, of any one man in power or ftation ; and I can boaft, that I neither vifit nor am acquainted with any lord temporal or fpiritual in the
whole kingdom; nor am able to do the leaft good
office to the moft deferving man, except what I can
difpofe of in my own cathedral upon a vacancy.
What hath funk my fpirits more than even years and
ficknefs, is reflecting on the moft execrable corruptions that run through every branch of public management.

I heartily thank you for thofe lines tranflated,
Singula de nobis anni, &c. You have put them in a
ftrong and admirable light : but, however, I am fo
partial, as to be more delighted with thofe which
are to do me the greateft honour I fhall ever receive
from pofterity, and will outweigh the malignity of
ten thoufand enemies. I never faw them before ; by
which it is plain, that the letter you fent me mifcar-
ried. — I do not doubt that you have choice of new
acquaintance, and fome of them may be deferving :
for youth is the feafon of virtue ; corruptions grow
with years, and I believe the oldeft rogue in England
is the greateft. You have years enough before you,
to watch whether thefe new acquaintance will keep
their virtue, when they leave you, and go into the
world ; how long will their fpirit of independency,
laft againft the temptations of future minifters and
future kings. — As to the new Lord Lieutenant *, I
never knew any of the family ; fo that I fhall not be
able to get any job done by him, for any deferving
friend.

* The Duke of Devonfhire.

L E T T E R LXXX.

From Dr SWIFT.

Feb. 7. 1735 6.

IT is fome time fince I dined at the Bifhop of Derry's, where Mr Secretary Cary told me with great concern, that you were taken very ill. I have heard nothing fince ; only I have continued in great pain of mind : yet for my own fake and the world's more than for yours ; becaufe I well know how little you value life both as a philofopher and a Chriftian, particularly the latter, wherein hardly one in a million of us heretics can equal you. If you are well recovered, you ought to be reproached for not putting me efpecially out of pain, who could not bear the lofs of you ; although we muft be for ever diftant as much as if I were in the grave, for which my years and continual indifpofition are preparing me every feafon. I have ftaid too long from preffing you to give me fome eafe by an account of your health ; pray do not ufe me fo ill any more. I look upon you as an eftate from which I receive my beft annual rents, although I am never to fee it. Mr Tickell was at the fame meeting under the fame real concern ; and fo were a hundred others of this town who had never feen you.

I read to the bifhop of Derry the paragraph in your letter which concerned him, and his Lordfhip expreffed his thankfulnefs in a manner that became him. He is efteemed here as a perfon of learning, and converfation, and humanity ; but he is beloved by all people.

I have nobody now left but you. Pray, be fo kind to outlive me ; and then die as foon as you pleafe, but without pain ; and let us meet in a better place, if my religion will permit, but rather my virtue, although much unequal to yours. Pray, let my Lord Bathurft know how much I love him ; I ftill infift

on

on his remembering me, although he is too much in
the world to honour an abfent friend with his letters.
My ftate of health is not to boaft of; my giddinefs
is more or lefs too conftant; I fleep ill, and have a
poor appetite. I can as eafily write a poem in the
Chinefe language as my own. I am as fit for matrimony as invention; and yet I have daily fchemes for
innumerable effays in profe, and proceed fometimes
to no lefs than half a dozen lines, which the next
morning become wafte paper. What vexes me moft
is, that my female friends, who could bear me very
well a dozen years ago, have now forfaken me; although I am not fo old in proportion to them, as I
formerly was: which I can prove by arithmetic; for
then I was double their age, which now I am not.
Pray, put me out of fear as foon as you can, about
that ugly report of your illnefs; and let me know
who this Chefelden is, that hath fo lately fprung
up in your favour. Give me alfo fome account of
your neighbour * who writ to me from Bath. I hear
he refolves to be ftrenuous for taking off the teft;
which grieves me extremely, from all the unprejudiced
reafons I ever was able to form, and againft the
maxims of all wife Chriftian governments †, which
always had fome eftablifhed religion, leaving at beft
a toleration to others.

Farewell, my deareft friend! ever and upon every
account that can create friendfhip and efteem.

LETTER LXXXI.

March 25, 1736.

IF ever I write more epiftles in verfe, one of them
fhall be addreffed to you. I have long concerted
it, and begun it: but I would make what bears your
name as finifhed as my laft work ought to be, that is

* Lord Bolingbroke.
† The author of the *Differtation on parties* appears to be of
the fame opinion.

H h 3   to

to fay, more finifhed than any of the reft. The
fubject is large, and will divide into four epiftles,
which naturally follow the Eſſay on Man, *viz.*
1. Of the extent and limits of human reaſon and
ſcience. 2. A view of the uſeful and therefore at-
tainable, and of the unuſeful and therefore unattain-
able arts. 3. Of the nature, ends, application,
and uſe of different capacities. 4. Of the uſe of
learning, of the *ſcience* of the *world*, and of *wit*. It
will conclude with a ſatire againſt the miſapplication
of all theſe, exemplified by pictures, characters,
and examples.

But alas! the taſk is great, and *non ſum qualis
eram !* My underſtanding indeed, ſuch as it is, is
extended rather than diminiſhed. I ſee things more
in the whole, more confiſtent, and more clearly de-
duced from, and related to each other. But what
I gain on the ſide of philoſophy, I loſe on the ſide of
poetry : the flowers are gone, when the fruits begin
to ripen, and the fruits perhaps will never ripen
perfectly. The climate (under our heaven of a court)
is but cold and uncertain ; the winds riſe, and the
winter comes on. I find myſelf but little diſpoſed
to build a new houſe ; I have nothing left but to gather up the relics of a wreck, and look about me to
ſee how few friends I have left. Pray, whoſe eſteem
or admiration ſhould I deſire now to procure by my
writings ? whoſe friendſhip or converſation to obtain
by them ? I am a man of deſperate fortunes, that is,
a man whoſe friends are dead : for I never aimed at
any other fortune than in friends. As ſoon as I
had ſent my laſt letter, I received a moſt kind one
from you, expreſſing great pain for my late illneſs at
Mr Cheſelden's. I conclude you was eaſed of that
friendly apprehenſion in a few days after you had
diſpatched yours, for mine muſt have reached you
then. I wondered a little at your quære, who
Cheſelden was ? It ſhews that the trueſt merit does
not travel ſo far any way as on the wings of poetry ;
he is the moſt noted, and moſt deſerving man, in the
whole

whole profeffion of chirurgery; and has faved the lives of thoufands by his manner of cutting for the ftone.—I am now well, or what I muft call fo.

I have lately feen fome writings of Lord B's, fince he went to France. Nothing can deprefs his genius: whatever befals him, he will ftill be the greateft man in the world, either in his own time, or with pofterity.

Every man you know or care for here, inquires of you, and pays you the only devoir he can, that of drinking your health. I wifh you had any motive to fee this kingdom. I could keep you; for I am rich, that is, I have more than I want. I can afford room for yourfelf and two fervants. I have indeed room enough, nothing but myfelf at home; the kind and hearty houfewife is dead! the agreeable and inftrudive neighbour is gone! yet my houfe is enlarged, and the gardens extend and flourifh, as knowing nothing of the guefts they have loft. I have more fruit-trees and kitchen-garden than you have any thought of; nay, I have good melons and pine-apples of my own growth. I am as much a better gardener, as I am a worfe poet, than when you faw me. But gardening is near akin to philofophy; for Tully fays, *Agricultura proxima fapientiæ*. For God's fake, why fhould not you (that are a ftep higher than a philofopher, a divine, yet have too much grace and wit than to be a bifhop) e'en give all you have to the poor of Ireland, (for whom you have already done every thing elfe), fo quit the place, and live and die with me? And let *tales animæ concordes* be our motto and our epitaph.

LETTER LXXXII.

From Dr SWIFT.

Dublin, April 22. 1736.

MY common illnefs is of that kind which utterly difqualifies me for all converfation; I mean
my

my deafnefs : and indeed it is that only which dif-
courageth me from all thoughts of coming to England : becaufe I am never fure that it may not return
in a week. If it were a good honeft gout, I could
catch an interval, to take a voyage ; and in a warm
lodging get an eafy chair, and be able to hear and
roar among my friends. " As to what you fay of
" your letters, fince you have many years of life
" more-than I, my refolution is to direct my execu-
" tors to fend you all your letters, well fealed and
" packeted, along with fome legacies mentioned
" in my will, and leave them entirely to your dif-
" pofal. Thofe things are all tied up, indorfed, and
" locked in a cabinet ; and I have not one fervant
" who can properly be faid to write or read. No
" mortal fhall copy them ; but you fhall furely have
" them when I am no more." I have a little re-
pined at my being hitherto flipped by you in your
epiftles, not from any other ambition than the title
of a friend ; and in that fenfe I expect you fhall perform your promife, if your health, and leifure, and
inclination will permit. I deny your lofing on the
fide of poetry : I could reafon againft you a little
from experience : you are, and will be fome years to
come, at the age when Invention ftill keeps its
ground, and Judgment is at full maturity. But
your fubjects are much more difficult when confined
to verfe. I am amazed to fee you exhauft the whole
fcience of morality in fo mafterly a manner. Sir W.
Temple faid, that the lofs of friends was a tax upon
long life. It need not be very long, fince you have
had fo great a fhare ; but I have not above one left ;
and in this country I have only a few general companions of good nature and middling underftandings.
How fhould I know Chefelden ? On your fide, men
of fame ftart up and die, before we here (at leaft I)
know any thing of the matter. I am a little comforted with what you fay of Lord B's genius ftill
keeping up, and preparing to appear by effects worthy of the author, and ufeful to the world.—Com-
men

mon reports have made me very uneafy about your
neighbour Mr P. It is affirmed that he hath been
very near death. I love him for being a patriot in
moſt corrupted times, and highly eſteem his excellent underſtanding. Nothing but the perverfe nature of my diſorders, as I have above deſcribed
them, and which are abſolute diſqualifications for
converfe, could hinder me from waiting on you at
Twickenham, and nurſing you to Paris. In ſhort,
my ailments amount to a prohibition ; although I
am, as you deſcribe yourſelf, what *I muſt call well,*
yet I have not ſpirits left to ride out, which (excepting walking) was my only diverſion. And I muſt
expe*ct* to decline every month, like one who lives
upon his principal fum, which muſt leſſen every
day ; and indeed I am likewife literally almoſt in the
fame cafe, while every body owes me, and nobody
pays me. Inſtead of a young race of patriots on
your ſide, which gives me fome glimpfe of joy ;
here we have the direct contrary, a race of young
dunces and atheiſts, or old villains and monſters,
whereof four fifths are more wicked and ſtupid than
Chartres. Your wants are fo few, that you need not
be rich to fupply them ; and my wants are fo many,
that a King's ſeven millions of guineas would not
fupport me.

LETTER LXXXIII.

Aug. 17. 1736.

I Find, though I have lefs experience than you,
the truth of what you told me fome time ago,
that increafe of years makes men more talkative, but
lefs writative ; to that degree, that I now write no
letters but of plain bufinefs, or plain how d'ye's to
thofe few I am forced to correfpond with, either out
of neceſſity, or love. And I grow Laconic even beyond Laconicifm ; for fometimes I return only Yes,
or No, to queſtionary or petitionary epiſtles of half

a

a.yard long. You and Lord Bolingbroke are the only men to whom I write, and always in folio.. You are indeed almoſt the only men I know, who either can write in this age, or whoſe writings will reach the next: others are mere mortals. Whatever failings ſuch men may have, a reſpeƈt is due to them, as luminaries whoſe exaltation renders their motion a little irregular, or rather cauſes it to ſeem ſo to others. I am afraid to cenſure any thing I hear of Dean Swift, becauſe I hear it only from mortals, blind and dull. And.you ſhould be cautious of cenſuring any aƈtion or motion of Lord B. becauſe you hear it only from ſhallow, envious, or malicious reporters. What you writ to me about him, I find to my great ſcandal repeated in one of yours to ———. Whatever you might hint to me, was this for the profane ? The thing, if true, ſhould be concealed :- but it is, I aſſure you, abſolutely untrue, in every circumſtance. He has fixed in a very agreeable retirement near Fontainbleau, and makes it his whole buſineſs *vacare literis*. But tell me the truth, were you not angry at his omitting to write to you ſo long ? I may, for I hear from him. ſeldomer than from you, that is, twice or thrice a year at moſt. Can you poſſibly think he can negleƈt you, or diſregard you ? If you catch yourſelf at thinking ſuch nonſenſe, your parts are decayed. For, believe me, great geniuſes muſt and do eſteem one another, and I queſtion if any others can eſteem or comprehend uncommon merit. Others only gueſs at that merit or ſee glimmerings of their minds. A genius has the intuitive faculty. Therefore, imagine what you will, you cannot be ſo ſure of any man's eſteem as of his. If I can think that neither he nor you deſpiſe me, it is a greater honour to me by far, and will be thought ſo by poſterity, than if all the houſe of Lords writ commendatory verſes upon me, the Commons ordered me to print my works, the univerſities gave me public thanks, and the King, Queen, and Prince, crowned me with laurel. You are

are a very ignorant man : you do not know the figure
his name and yours will make hereafter : I do, and
will preferve all the memorials I can, that I was of
your intimacy; *longo, fed proximus, intervallo.* I
will not quarrel with the prefent age; it has done
enough for me, in making and keeping you two my
friends. Do not you be too angry at it; and let
not him be too angry at it : it has done and can do
neither of you any manner of harm, as long as it has
not; and cannot burn your works: while thofe
fubfift, you will both appear the greateft men of
the time, in fpite of princes and minifters; and the
wifeft, in fpite of all the little errours you may pleafe
to commit.

Adieu. May better health attend you, than, I
fear, you poffefs : may but as good health attend
you always as mine is at prefent; tolerable, when an
eafy mind is joined with it.

LETTER LXXXIV.

From Dr SWIFT.

Dec. 2. 1736.

I Think you owe me a letter; but whether you do
or not, I have not been in a condition to write.
Years and infirmities have quite broke me; I mean
that odious continual diforder in my head. I neither
read, nor write, nor remember, nor converfe. All
I have left is to walk and ride : the firft I can do tolerably; but the latter, for want of good weather at
this feafon, is feldom in my power; and having not
an ounce of flefh about me, my fkin comes off in ten
miles riding, becaufe my fkin and bone cannot agree
together. But I am angry, becaufe you will not fuppofe me as fick as I am, and write to me out of perfect charity, although I fhould not be able to anfwer.
I have too many vexations, by my ftation and the impertinence of people, to be able to bear the mortification

cation of not hearing from a very few diftant friends that are left; and, confidering how time and fortune have ordered matters, I have hardly one friend left but yourfelf. What Horace fays, *Singula de nobis anni prædantur,* I feel ever month at fartheft; and by this computation, if I hold out two years, I fhall think it a miracle. My comfort is, you begun to diftinguifh fo confounded early, that your acquaintance with diftinguifhed men of all kinds was almoft as ancient as mine. I mean Wycherley, Rowe, Prior, Congreve, Addifon, Parnell, &c. and in fpite of your heart, you have owned me a contemporary. Not to mention Lords Oxford, Bolingbroke, Harcourt, Peterborow. In fhort, I was t'other day recollecting twenty-feven great minifters, or men of wit and learning, who are all dead, and all of my acquaintance, within twenty years paft; neither have I the grace to be forry, that the prefent times are drawn to the dregs as well as my own life.—May my friends be happy in this and a better life; but I value not what becomes of pofterity when I confider from what monfters they are to fpring.—My Lord Orrery writes to you to-morrow, and you fee I fend this under his cover, or at leaft franked by him. He has 3000 *l.* a-year about Cork, and the neighbourhood, and has more than three years rent unpaid. This is our condition, in thefe bleffed times. I writ to your neighbour about a month ago, and fubfcribed my name. I fear he hath not received my letter, and wifh you would afk him: but perhaps he is ftill a-rambling; for we hear of him at Newmarket, and that Boerhaave hath reftored his health.—How my fervices are leffened of late with the number of my friends on your fide! yet my Lord Bathurft, and Lord Mafham, and Mr Lewis remain; and being your acquaintance, I defire, when you fee them, to deliver my compliments; but chiefly to Mrs P. B. and let me know whether fhe be as young and agreeable as when I faw her laft. Have you got a fupply of new friends to make up for thofe who are gone? and are

they

they equal to the firſt? I am afraid it is with friends
as with times; and that the *laudator temporis aſti ſe
puero*, is equally applicable to both. I am leſs grieved
for living here, becauſe it is a perfeſt retirement, and
conſequently fitteſt for thoſe who are grown good for
nothing: for this town and kingdom are as much
out of the world as North Wales.—My head is ſo ill
that I cannot write a paper full as I uſed to do; and
yet I will not forgive a blank of half an inch from
you.—I had reaſon to expeſt from ſome of your letters, that we were to hope for more epiſtles of morality; and, I aſſure you, my acquaintance reſent that
they have not ſeen my name at the head of one. The
ſubjeſts of ſuch epiſtles are more uſeful to the public,
by your manner of handling them, than any of all
your writings; and although, in ſo profligate a world
as ours, they may poſſibly not much mend our manners, yet poſterity will enjoy the benefit, whenever
a court happens to have the leaſt reliſh for virtue and
religion.

LETTER LXXXV.

To Dr SWIFT.

Dec. 30. 1736.

YOur very kind letter has made me more melancholy, than almoſt any thing in this world now
can do. For I can bear every thing in it, bad as it
is, better than the complaints of my friends. Though
others tell me you are in pretty good health, and in
good ſpirits, I find the contrary when you open your
mind to me. And indeed it is but a prudent part, to
ſeem not ſo concerned about others, nor ſo crazy ourſelves as we really are: for we ſhall neither be beloved nor eſteemed the more, by our common acquaintance, for any affliſtion or any infirmity. But to our
true friend we may, we muſt complain, of what (it
is a thouſand to one) he complains with us: for if

we have known him long, he is old; and if he has
known the world long, he is out of humour at it.
If you have but as much more health than others at
your age, as you have more wit and good temper,
you ſhall not have much of my pity: but if you
ever live to have leſs, you ſhall not have leſs of my
affection. A whole people will rejoice at every year
that ſhall be added to you, of which you have had a
late inſtance in the public rejoicings on your birthday.
I can aſſure you, ſomething better and greater than
high birth and quality muſt go toward acquiring
thoſe demonſtrations of public eſteem and love. I
have ſeen a royal birthday uncelebrated, but by one
vile ode, and one hired bonfire. Whatever years
may take away from you, they will not take away
the general eſteem for your ſenſe, virtue, and charity.

The moſt melancholy effect of years is that you
mention, the catalogue of thoſe we loved and have
loſt, perpetually increaſing. How much that reflection ſtruck me, you will ſee from the motto I have
prefixed to my book of letters, which ſo much a-
gainſt my inclination has been drawn from me. It
is from Catullus:

Quo deſiderio veteres revocamus amores,
Atque olim amiſſas flemus amicitias!

I detain this letter till I can find ſome ſafe conveyance; innocent as it is, and as all letters of mine
muſt be, of any thing to offend my ſuperiours, except the reverence I bear to true merit and virtue.
" But I have much reaſon to fear, thoſe which you
" have too partially kept in your hands, will get
" out in ſome very diſagreeable ſhape, in caſe of
" our mortality: and the more reaſon to fear it,
" ſince this laſt month Curl has obtained from Ire-
" land two letters; (one of Lord Bolingbroke, and
" one of mine, to you, which we wrote in the year
" 1723), and he has printed them, to the beſt of
" my memory, rightly, except one paſſage concern-
" ing

" ing Dawley, which muſt have been ſince inſerted,
" ſince my Lord had not that place at that time.
" Your anſwer to that letter he has not got ; it has
" never been out of my cuſtody ; for whatever is
" lent is loſt (wit as well as money) to theſe needy
" poetical readers."

The world will certainly be the better for his
change of life. He ſeems, in the whole turn of his
letters, to be a ſettled and principled philoſopher,
thanking fortune for the tranquillity he has been led
into by her averſion, like a man driven by a violent
wind, from the ſea into a calm harbour. You aſk
me, if I have got any ſupply of new friends to make
up for thoſe that are gone ? I think that impoſſible ;
for not our friends only, but ſo much of ourſelves is
gone, by the mere flux and courſe of years, that, were
the ſame friends to be reſtored to us, we could not be
reſtored to ourſelves, to enjoy them. But as when
the continual waſhing of a river takes away our
flowers and plants, it throws weeds and ſedges in
their room * ; ſo the courſe of time brings us ſomething, as it deprives us of a great deal ; and inſtead
of leaving us what we cultivated, and expected to
flouriſh, and adorn us, gives us only what is of ſome
little uſe, by accident. Thus I have acquired, without my ſeeking, a few chance-acquaintance, of young
men, who look rather to the paſt age than the preſent, and therefore the future may have ſome hopes
of them. If I love them, it is becauſe they honour
ſome of thoſe whom I, and the world, have loſt, or
are loſing. Two or three of them have diſtinguiſhed
themſelves in parliament ; and you will own, in a very uncommon manner, when I tell you, it is by their
aſſerting of independency, and contempt of corruption. One or two are linked to me, by their love of

* There are ſome ſtrokes in this letter, which can be accounted for no otherwiſe than by the author's extreme compaſ-
ſion and tenderneſs of heart, too much affected by the complaints
of a peeviſh old man, (labouring and impatient under his infirmities), and too intent in the friendly office of mollifying them.

the fame studies and the fame authors: but I will own to you, my moral capacity has got fo much the better of my poetical, that I have few acquaintance on the latter fcore, and none without a cafting weight on the former. But I find my heart hardened, and blunt to new impreffions; it will fcarce receive or retain affections of yefterday; and thofe friends who have been dead thefe twenty years, are more prefent to me now, than thofe I fee daily. You, dear Sir, are one of the former fort to me in all refpects, but that we can yet correfpond together. I do not know whether it is not more vexatious, to know we are both in one world, without any further intercourfe. Adieu. I can fay no more, I feel fo much. Let me drop into common things.—Lord Mafham has juft married his fon. Mr Lewis has juft buried his wife. Lord Oxford wept over your letter in pure kindnefs. Mrs B. fighs more for you, than for the lofs of youth. She fays, fhe will be agreeable many years hence, for fhe has learned that fecret from fome receipts of your writing.—Adieu.

LETTER LXXXVI.

March 23. 1736-7.

THough you were never to write to me, yet what you defired in your laft, that I would write often to you, would be a very eafy tafk: for every day I talk with you, and of you, in my heart; and I need only fet down what that is thinking of. The nearer I find myfelf verging to that period of life which is to be labour and forrow, the more I prop myfelf upon thofe few fupports that are left me. People in this ftate are like props indeed; they cannot ftand alone, but two or more of them can ftand, leaning and bearing upon one another. I wifh you and I might pafs this part of life together. My only neceffary care is at an end. I am now my own mafter master too much; my house is too large; my gardens furnish too much wood and provision for my use. My servants are sensible and tender of me. They have intermarried, and are become rather low friends than servants; and to all those that I see here with pleasure, they take a pleasure in being useful. I conclude this is your case too in your domestic life; and I sometimes think of your old housekeeper as my nurse; though I tremble at the sea, which only divides us. As your fears are not so great as mine, and, I firmly hope, your strength still much greater, is it utterly impossible, it might once more be some pleasure to you to see England? My sole motive in proposing France to meet in, was the narrowness of the passage by sea from hence; the physicians having told me, the weakness of my breast, &c. is such, as a sea-sickness might endanger my life. Though one or two of our friends are gone, since you saw your native country *, there remain a few more who will last so till death, and who, I cannot but hope, have an attractive power, to draw you back to a country, which cannot quite be sunk or enslaved, while such spirits remain. And let me tell you, there are a few more of the same spirit, who would awaken all your old ideas, and revive your hopes of her future recovery and virtue. These look up to you with reverence, and would be animated by the sight of him, at whose soul they have taken fire, in his writings, and derived from thence as much love of their species as is consistent with a contempt for the knaves of it.

I could never be weary, except at the eyes, of writing to you; but my real reason (and a strong one it is) for doing it so seldom, is fear; fear of a very great and experienced evil, that of my letters being kept by the partiality of friends, and passing into the hands and malice of enemies; who publish

---

* The Dean was born in Ireland. This I mention, because the sentence may be understood in a double sense. *Dub. edit.*

them

them with all their imperfections on their head; so that I write not on the common terms of honest men.

Would to God you would come over with Lord Orrery, whose care of you in the voyage I could so certainly depend on; and bring with you your old housekeeper, and two or three servants. I have room for all, a heart for all, and (think what you will) a fortune for all. We could, were we together, contrive to make our last days easy, and leave some sort of monument, what friends two wits could be, in spite of all the fools in the world.

Adieu.

L E T T E R   LXXXVII.

From Dr S w i f t.

Dublin, May 31. 1737.

IT is true, I owe you some letters; but it has pleased God, that I have not been in a condition to pay you. When you shall be at my age, perhaps you may lie under the same disability to your present or future friends. But my age is not my disability; for I can walk six or seven miles, and ride a dozen. But I am deaf for two months together. This deafness unqualifies me for all company, except a few friends with counter-tenor voices, whom I can call names, if they do not speak loud enough for my ears. It is this evil that hath hindered me from venturing to the Bath, and to Twickenham: for deafness being not a frequent disorder, hath no allowance given it; and the scurvy figure a man affected that way makes in company, is utterly insupportable.

It was I began with the petition to you of *Orna mie*, and now you come like an unfair merchant, to charge me with being in your debt; which by your way of reckoning I must always be, for yours are always guineas, and mine farthings; and yet I have a pretence to quarrel with you, because I am not at

the

the head of any one of your epiftles. I am often
wondering, how you come to excel all mortals on the
fubject of morality, even in the poetical way; and
fhould have wondered more, if nature and education
had not made you a profeffor of it from your infancy. " All the letters I can find of yours, I have
" faftened in a folio cover, and the reft in bundles
" indorfed: but, by reading their dates, I find a
" chafm of fix years, of which I can find no copies;
" and yet I keep them with all poffible care. But
" I have been forced, on three or four occafions, to
" fend all my papers to fome friends; yet thofe pa-
" pers were all fent fealed in bundles, to fome faith-
" ful friends; however, what I have are not much
" above fixty." I found nothing in any one of
them to be left out. None of them have any thing to
do with party, of which you are the cleareft of all
men by your religion, and the whole tenour of your
life; while I am raging every moment againft the
corruption of both kingdoms, efpecially of this;
fuch is my weaknefs.

I have read your epiftle of Horace to Auguftus.
It was fent me in the Englifh edition, as foon as it
could come. They are printing it in a fmall octavo.
The curious are looking out, fome for flattery, fome
for ironies in it. The four folks think they have
found out fome: but your admirers here, I mean e-
very man of tafte, affect to be certain, that the profeffion of friendfhip to me in the fame poem, will
not fuffer you to be thought a flatterer. My happinefs is, that you are too far engaged; and in fpite of
you the ages to come will celebrate me, and know
you were a friend who loved and efteemed me, although I died the object of court and party hatred.

Pray, who is that Mr Glover who writ the epic
poem called *Leonidas,* which is reprinting here, and
hath great vogue? We have frequently good poems
of late from London. I have juft read one upon
converfation, and two or three others. But the croud
do not incumber you, who, like the orator or preacher,

er, ſtand aloft, and are ſeen above the reſt, more
than the whole aſſembly below.

I am able to write no more ; and this is my third
endeavour, which is too weak to finiſh the paper. I
am, my deareſt friend, yours entirely, as long as I
can write, or ſpeak, or think.

J. Swift.

LETTER LXXXVIII.

From Dr Swift.

Dublin, July 23. 1737.

I Sent a letter to you ſome weeks ago, which my
Lord Orrery incloſed in one of his, to which I
received as yet no anſwer; but it will be time enough
when his Lordſhip goes over, which will be, as he
hopes, in about ten days; and then he will take with
him " all the letters I preſerved of yours, which
" are not above twenty-five. I find there is a great
" chaſm of ſome years, but the dates are more ear-
" ly than my two laſt journeys to England ; which
" makes me imagine, that in one of thoſe journeys
" I carried over another cargo." But I cannot truſt
my memory half an hour ; and my diſorders of deafneſs and giddineſs increaſe daily. So that I am declining as faſt as it is eaſily poſſible for me, if I were
a dozen years older.

We have had your volume of letters, which, I am
told, are to be printed here. Some of thoſe who
highly eſteem you, and a few who know you perſo-
nally, are grieved to find you make no diſtinction
between the Engliſh gentry of this kingdom, and
the ſavage old Iriſh, (who are only the vulgar, and
ſome gentlemen who live in the Iriſh parts of the
kingdom) ; but the Engliſh colonies, who are three
parts in four, are much more civilized than many
counties in England, and ſpeak better Engliſh, and
are much better bred. And they think it very hard,
that

that an American, who is of the fifth generation
from England, fhould be allowed to preferve that
title, only becaufe we have been told by fome of
them, that their names are entered in fome parifh in
London. I have three or four coufins here, who were
born in Portugal, whofe parents took the fame care,
and they are all of them Londoners. Dr Delany,
who, as I take it, is of an Irifh family, came to vifit me three days ago, on purpofe to complain of
thofe paffages in your letters. He will not allow fuch
a difference between the two climates; but will affert that North Wales, Northumberland, Yorkfhire,
and the other northern fhires, have a more cloudy
ungenial air than any part of Ireland. In fhort, I
am afraid your friends and admirers here will force
you to make a palinody.

As for the other parts of your volume of letters,
my opinion is, that there might be collected from
them the beft fyftem that ever was wrote for the conduct of human life, at leaft to fhame all reafonable
men out of their follies and vices. It is fome recommendation of this kingdom, and of the tafte of
the people, that you are at leaft as highly celebrated
here, as you are at home. If you will blame us for
flavery, corruption, Atheifm, and fuch trifles, do it
freely; but include England, only with an addition
of every other vice.—I wifh you would give orders
againft the corruption of Englifh by thofe fcribblers,
who fend us over their trafh in profe and verfe, with
abominable curtailings and quaint modernifms:—
I am now daily expecting an end of life. I have loft
all fpirit, and every fcrap of health. I fometimes recover a little of my hearing, but my head is ever
out of order. While I have any ability to hold a
commerce with you, I will never be filent; and this
chancing to be a day that I can hold a pen, I will
drag it as long as I am able. Pray, let my Lord
Orrery fee you often: next to yourfelf, I love no
man fo well; and tell him what I fay, if he vifits
you. I have now done; for it is evening, and my
head

head grows worfe. May God always protect you, and preferve you long, for a pattern of piety and virtue.

Farewell, my deareft and almoft only conftant friend. I am ever, at leaft in my efteem, honour, and affection to you, what I hope you expect me to be,

Yours, &c.

L E.T T E R LXXXIX.

From Dr S w i f-t.

My dear friend,   *Dublin, Aug.* 8. 1738.

I Have yours of July 25.-and firft I defire you will look upon me as a man worn with years, and funk by public as well as perfonal vexations. I have entirely loft my memory, incapable of converfation, by a cruel deafnefs, which has lafted almoft a year, and I defpair of any cure. I fay not this to increafe your compaffion, (of which you have already too great a part), but as an excufe for my not being regular in my letters to you, and fome few other friends. I have an ill name in the poft-office of both kingdoms; which makes the letters addreffed to me not feldom mifcarry, or be opened and read, and then fealed in a bungling manner, before they come to my hands. Our friend Mrs B. is very often in my thoughts, and high in my efteem. I defire you will be the meffenger of my humble thanks and fervice to her. That fuperiour univerfal genius you defcribe, whofe hand-writing I know towards the end of your letter, hath made me both proud and happy; but by what he writes, I fear, he will be too foon gone to his foreft abroad. He began in the Queen's time to be my patron, and then defcended to be my friend.

It is a great favour of heaven, that your health grows better by the addition of years. I have abfolutely

folutely done with poetry for feveral years paft; and
even at my beft times I could produce nothing but.
trifles. I therefore. reject your compliments on that
fcore: and it is no compliment in me; for I take
your fecond dialogue that you lately fent me, to,
equal almoft any thing you ever writ; although I
live fo much out of the world, that I am ignorant of
the facts and perfons, which, I prefume, are- very
well known from Temple bar to St James's; (I
mean the court exclufive).

" I can faithfully affure you, that every letter you
" have favoured me with; thefe twenty years and
" more, are fealed up in bundles, and delivered to
" Mrs W———, a very worthy, rational, and ju-
" dicious coufin of mine, and the only relation
" whofe vifits I can fuffer. All thefe letters fhe is
". directed to fend fafely to you, upon my deceafe."

My Lord Orrery is gone with his lady to a part.
of her eftate in the north. She is a perfon of very.
good underftanding, as any I know of her fex. Give
me leave to write here a fhort anfwer to my Lord B's
letter, in the laft page of yours.

My dear Lord,
    I am infinitely obliged to your Lordfhip for the
honour of your letter, and kind remembrance of me.
I do here confefs, that I have more obligations to
your Lordfhip than to all the world befides. You
never deceived me, even when you were a great minifter of ftate: and yet I love you ftill more, for
your condefcending to write to me, when you had
the honour to be an exile. I can hardly hope
to live till you publifh your hiftory, and am vain
enough to wifh that my name could be fqueezed in
among the few fubalterns, *quorum pars parva fui.*
If not, I will be revenged, and contrive fome way
to be known to futurity, that I had the honour to
have your Lordfhip for my beft patron; and I will
live and die, with the higheft veneration and gratitude, your moft obedient, &c.

                                              P. S. I

P. S. I will here, in a poſtſcript, correct (if it be poſſible) the blunders I have made in my letter. I ſhewed my couſin the above letter; and ſhe aſſures me, that a great collection of
* your   me,
      letters to   are put up and ſealed,
 my   you,
and in ſome very ſafe hand †. I am, my moſt dear and honoured friend, entirely yours,

J. Swift.

It is now Aug. 24.
1 7 3 8.

* It is written juſt thus in the original. The book that is now printed, ſeems to be part of the collection here ſpoken of; as it contains not only the letters of Mr Pope, but of Dr Swift, both to him and to Mr Gay, which were returned him after Mr Gay's death: though any mention made by Mr P. of the return or exchange of letters, has been induſtriouſly ſuppreſſed in the publication, and only appears by ſome of the anſwers.

† The Earl of Orrery to Mr Pope.

S I R,

I am more and more convinced that your letters are neither loſt nor burnt; but who the Dean means by a ſafe hand in Ireland, is beyond my power of gueſſing; though I am particularly acquainted with moſt, if not all, of his friends. As I knew you had the recovery of thoſe letters at heart, I took more than ordinary pains to find out where they were; but my inquiries were to no purpoſe; and, I fear, whoever has them, is too tenacious of them to diſcover where they lie. " *Mrs W—— did aſſure me, ſhe had not one of them;* " *and ſeemed to be under great uneaſineſs, that you* " *ſhould imagine they were left with her. She like-* " *wiſe told me ſhe had ſtopped the Dean's letter which* " *gave you that information; but believed he would* " *write ſuch another; and therefore deſired me to* " *aſſure you from her, that ſhe was totally ignorant* " *where they were.*" *You may make what uſe you pleaſe, either to the Dean, or any other perſon, of what I have told you.*

I

I am reedy to teſtify it ; and I think-it ought to be known, " That the Dean ſays they are deli·vered into "a ſafe hand, and Mrs W—— declares ſhe has "them not. The conſequence of their being hereafter "publiſhed, may give uneaſineſs to ſome of your friends, "and of courſe to you : ſo I would do all in my power "to make you entirely eaſy in that point."*

This is the firſt time I have put pen to paper ſince my late misfortune ; and I ſhould ſay, (as an excuſe for this letter), that it has coſt me ſome pain, did it not allow me an opportunity to aſſure you, that I am,

> *Dear Sir,*
>
> *With the trueſt eſteem,*
>
> *Your very faithful and obedient ſervant,*

Marſton, Oct. 4. 1738.   ORRERY.

* This lady ſince gave Mr Pope the ſtrongeſt aſſurances that ſhe had uſed her utmoſt endeavours to prevent the publication ; nay, went ſo far, as to ſecrete the book, till it was commanded from her, and delivered to the Dublin printer. Whereupon her ſon-in-law, D. Swift, Eſq; inſiſted upon writing a preface to juſtify Mr P. from having any knowledge of it, and to lay it upon the corrupt practices of the printers in London ; but this he would not agree to, as not knowing the truth of the fact.

LETTERS to RALPH ALLEN, Efq;

LETTER XC.

Mr POPE *to Mr* ALLEN.

Twitnam, April 30. 1736.

I Saw Mr M. yefterday, who has readily allowed Mr V. to copy the picture. I have inquired for the beft originals of thofe two fubjects, which, I found, were favourite ones with you, and well deferve to be fo ; the difcovery of Jofeph to his brethren, and the refignation of the captive by Scipio. Of the latter, my Lord Burlington has a fine one done by Ricci ; and I am promifed the other in a good print, from one of the chief Italian painters. That of Scipio is of the exact fize ; one would wifh for a baffo relievo, in which manner, in my opinion, you would beft ornament your hall, done in chiaro ofcuro.

A man not only fhews his tafte, but his virtue, in the choice of fuch ornaments. And whatever example moft ftrikes us, we may reafonably imagine, may have an influence upon others. So that the hiftory itfelf, if well chofen, upon a rich man's walls, is very often a better leffon than any he could teach by his converfation. In this fenfe, the ftones may be faid to fpeak, when men cannot, or will not. I cannot help thinking, (and I know you will join with me, you who have been making an altar-piece), that the zeal of the firft reformers was ill placed, in removing *pictures* (that is to fay, examples) out of churches ; and yet fuffering *epitaphs* (that is to fay, flatteries, and falfe hiftory) to be the burthen of church-walls, and the fhame, as as well derifion, of all honeft men.

I

·I have heard little yet of the fubfcription *. I
intend to make a vifit for a fortnight from home to
Lady Peterborow at Southampton, about the middle
of May. After my return I will inquire what has
been done; and, I really believe, what I told you
will prove true; and I fhall be honourably acquitted
of a tafk I am not fond of †. I have run out my
leaf, and will only add my fincere wifhes for your
happinefs of all kinds.

I am, &c.

LETTER XCI.

Mr POPE *to Mr* ALLEN.

Southampton, June 5. 1736.

I Need not fay I thank you for a letter, which
proves fo much friendfhip for me. I have much
more to fay upon it than I can till we meet. But in
a word, I think your notion of the value of thofe
things ‡ is greatly too high, as to any fervice they
can do to the public: and, as to any advantage they
may do to my own character, I ought to be content
with what they have done already. I affure you, I
do not think it the leaft of thofe advantages that
they have occafioned me the good-will (in fo great a
degree) of fo worthy a man ‖. I fear (as I muft rather retrench than add to their number, unlefs I
would publifh my own commendations) that the
common run of fubfcribers would think themfelves
injured by not having every thing, which difcretion

* For his own edition of the 1ft volume of his letters; un-
dertaken at Mr Allen's requeft.
† The printing his letters by fubfcription.
‡ His letters.
‖ Mr Allen's friendfhip with the author was contracted on the
reading his volume of letters, which gave the former the higheft opinion of the other's general benevolence and goodnefs of
heart.

K k 2. muft

muſt ſupprefs; and this they (without any other
confideration than as buyers of a book) would call
giving them an imperfect collection: whereas the
only uſe to my own character, as an author, of ſuch
a publication, would be the ſuppreſſion of many
things. And as to my character as a man, it would
be but juſt where it is; unlefs I could be ſo vain,
for it could not be virtuous, to add more and more
honeſt fentiments; which, when done *to be printed,*
would ſurely be wrong and weak alſo.

I do grant it would be ſome pleafure to me to ex-
punge ſeveral idle paſſages, which will otherwiſe, if
not go down to the next age, pafs, at leaſt, in this,
for mine; although many of them were not; and,
God knows, none of them are my prefent ſentiments, but, on the contrary, wholly difapproved by
me.

And I do not flatter you when I ſay, that pleafure
would be increaſed to me, in knowing I ſhould do
what would pleaſe *you*. But I cannot perfuade myfelf to let the whole burden, even though it were a
public good, lie upon you, much lefs to ſerve my
private fame entirely at another's expenſe *.

But underſtand me rightly. Did I believe half ſo
well of them as you do, I would not ſcruple your
aſſiſtance; becaufe I am fure, that to occaſion you to
contribute to a real good, would be the greateſt benefit I could oblige you in. And I hereby promiſe you,
if ever I am ſo happy as to find any juſt occaſion
where your generoſity and goodnefs may unite for
ſuch a worthy end, I will not ſcruple to draw upon
you for any ſum to effect it.

As to the prefent affair: that you may be convinced what weight your opinion and your deſires
have with me, I will do what I have not yet done.
I will tell my friends I am as willing to publiſh this
book as to let it alone. And, rather than ſuffer you

* Mr Allen offered to print the letters at his own expenſe.

to be taxed at your own rate, will publiſh, in the news, next winter, the propoſals, &c.

I tell you all theſe particulars to ſhew you how willing I am to follow your advice, nay, to accept your aſſiſtance in any moderate degree. But I think you ſhould reſerve ſo great a proof of your benevolence to a better occaſion.

Since I wrote laſt, I have found, on further inquiry, that there is another fine picture on the ſubject of Scipio and the captive, by Pietro da Cortona, which Sir Paul Methuen has a ſketch of: and, I believe, is more expreſſive than that of Ricci, as Pietro is famous for expreſſion. I have alſo met with a fine print of the diſcovery of Joſeph to his brethren ; a deſign, which I fancy, is of La Sueur, and will do perfectly well.

I am, &c.

L E T T E R   XCII.

Mr P o p e *to Mr* A l l e n.

Nov. 6. 1736.

I Do not write too often to you for many reaſons ; but one, which I think a good one, is, that friends ſhould be left to think of one another for certain intervals without too frequent memorandums : it is an exerciſe of their friendſhip, and a trial of their memory. And moreover, to be perpetually repeating aſſurances, is both a needleſs and ſuſpicious kind of treatment with ſuch as are ſincere. Not to add the tautology one muſt be guilty of, who can make out ſo many idle words as to fill pages with ſaying one thing. For all is ſaid in this word, *I am truly yours.*

I am now as buſy in planting for myſelf as I was lately in planting for another. And I thank God for every wet day and for every fog, that gives me the headach, but proſpers my works. They will indeed

outlive me, (if they do not die in their travels from
place to place; for my garden, like my life, feems,
to me, every day to want correction ; I hope, at leaft,
for the better) ; but I am pleafed to think my trees
will afford fhade and fruit to others, when I fhall
want them no more. And it is no fort of grief to
me, that thofe others will not be things of my own
poor body : but it is enough, they are creatures of
the fame fpecies, and made by the fame hand that
made me. I wifh (if a wifh would tranfport me) to
fee you in the fame employment. And it is no partiality even to you, to fay it would be as pleafing
to the full to me, if I could improve your works as
my own.

Talking of works, mine in profe are above three
quarters printed ; and will be a book of fifty and
more fheets in quarto. As I find, what I imagined,
the flownefs of fubfcribers, I will do all I can to difappoint *you* in particular ; and intend to publifh in
January, when the town fills, an advertifement, that
the book will be delivered by Lady-day, to oblige
all that will fubfcribe, to do it. In the mean time,
I have printed receipts, which put an end to any perfons delaying upon pretence of *doubt*, by determi-
ning that time. I fend you a few that you may fee I
am in earneft, endeavouring all I can to fave your
money ; at the fame time, that nothing can leffen the
obligation to me.

I thank God for your health, and for my own,
which is better than ufual.

I am, &c.

LETTER XCIII.

Mr POPE *to Mr* ALLEN.

June 8. 1737.

I Was very forry to hear how much concern your
humanity and friendfhip betrayed you into upon
the

the falfe report which occafioned your grief. I am
now fo well, that I ought not to conceal it from you,
as the juft reward of your goodnefs which made you
fuffer for me. Perhaps when a friend is really dead,
(if he knows our concern for him), he knows us to
be as much miftaken in our forrow as you now were :
fo that what we think a real-evil, is, to fuch fpirits
as fee things truly, no more of moment than a mere
imaginary one. It is equally as God pleafes ; let
us think or call it good or evil.

I wifh the world would let me give myfelf more to
fuch people in it as I like, and difcharge me of half
the honours which perfons of higher rank beftow on
me ; and for which one generally pays a little too
much of what they cannot beftow, time and life.
Were I arrived to that happier circumftance, you
would fee me at Widcombe, and not at Bath.
But whether it will be as much in my power as in
my wifh, God knows. I can only fay, I think of
it with the pleafure and fincerity becoming one who
is, &c.

L E T T E R   XCIV.

M̃r P O P E *to M̃r* A L L E N.

Nov. 24. 1737.

THE event * of this week or fortnight has filled
every body's mind and mine fo much, that I
could not get done what you defired as to Dr P.
but as foon as I can get home, where my books lie,
I will fend them to Mr K. The death of great perfons is fuch a fort of furprife to *all*, as every one's
death is to himfelf, though both fhould equally be
expected and prepared for. We begin to efteem and
commend our fuperiours, at the time that we pity
them ; becaufe then they feem not above ourfelves.
The Queen fhewed, by the confeffion of all about
her, the utmoft firmnefs and temper to her laft mo-

* The Queen's death.

ments,

ments, and through the courfe of great torments.
What chara&er hiftorians will allow her, I do not
know; but all her domeftic fervants, and thofe
neareft her, give her the beft teftimony, that of fincere tears. But the public is always hard; rigid at
beft, even when juft, in its opinion of any one. The
only pleafure which any one, either of high or low
rank, muft depend upon receiving, is in the candour
or partiality - of friends, and that fmall circle we
are converfant in : and it is therefore the greateft
fatisfaction to fuch as wifh us well, to know we
enjoy that. I therefore thank you particularly for
telling me of the continuance, or rather increafe of
thofe bleffings which make your domeftic life happy. I have nothing fo good to add, as to affure you :
I pray for it, and am always faithfully and affectionately, &c.

L E T T E R   XCV.

Mr P O P E *to Mr* A L L E N.

Twickenham, April 28. 1738.

IT is a pain to me to hear your old complaint fo
troublefome to you ; and the fhare I have borne,
and ftill bear too often, in the fame complaint, gives
me a very feeling fenfe of it. I hope we agree in
every other fenfation befides this : for your *heart* is
always right, whatever your body may be. I will
venture to fay, my body is the worft part of me, or
God have mercy on my foul. I cannot help telling
you the rapture you accidentally gave the poor woman ; (for whom you left a guinea, on what I told
you of my finding her at the end of my garden) : I
had no notion of her want being fo great, as I then
told you, when I gave her half a one. But I find I
have a pleafure to come, for I will allow her fomething yearly; and that may be but one year; for,
I think, by her looks fhe is not lefs than eighty. I

am

am determined to take this charity out of your hands, which, I know, you will think hard upon you. But fo it fhall be.

Pray tell me if you have any objection to my putting your name into a poem of mine (incidentally, not at all going out of the way for it), provided I fay fomething of you, which moft people would take ill, for example, that you are no man of high birth or quality? You muft be perfectly free with me on this, as on any, nay, on every other occafion.

I have nothing to add but my wifhes for your health : every other enjoyment you will provide for yourfelf, which becomes a reafonable man. Adieu, I am, &c.

LETTER XCVI.

Mr POPE to Mr ALLEN.

Jan. 20.

I Ought fooner to have acknowledged yours ; but I have been feverely handled by my afthma, and, at the fame time, hurried by bufinefs that gave an increafe to it by catching cold. I am truly forry to find that neither yours nor Mrs A's diforder is totally removed: but God forbid your pain fhould continue to return every day, which is worfe by much than I expected to hear. I hope your next will give me a better account. Poor Mr Bethel too is very ill in Yorkfhire. And, I do affure you, there are no two men I wifh better to. I have known and efteemed him for every moral virtue thefe twenty years and more. He has all the charity, without any of the weaknefs of ——; and, I firmly believe, never faid a thing he did not think, nor did a thing he could not tell. I am concerned he is in fo cold and remote a place, as in the Wolds of Yorkfhire, at a hunting-feat. If he lives till fpring, he talks of returning to London ; and, if I poffibly can, I would
get

get him to lie out of it at Twickenham ; though we went backward and forward every day in a warm coach ; which would be the propereft exercife for both of us, fince he is become fo weak as to be deprived of riding a horfe.

L. Bolingbroke ftays a month yet, and I hope Mr Warburton will come to town before he goes. They will both be pleafed to meet each other ; and nothing, in all my life, has been fo great a pleafure to my nature, as to bring deferving and knowing men together. It is the greateft favour that can be done, either to great geniufes or ufeful men. I wifh too, he were a while in town, if it were only to lie a little in the way of fome proud and powerful perfons, to fee if they have any of the beft fort of pride left, namely, to ferve learning and merit, and by that means diftinguifh themfelves from their pedeceffors.

I am, &c.

L E T T E R   XCVII.

Mr P o p e to Mr A l l e n.

March 6.

I Thank you very kindly for yours. I am fure we fhall meet with the fame hearts we ever met ; and I could wifh it were at Twickenham, though only to fee you and Mrs Allen twice there inftead of once. But, as matters have turned out, a decent obedience to the government has fince obliged me to refide here, ten miles out of the capital ; and therefore I muft fee you here or no where. Let that be an additional reafon for your coming and ftaying what time you can.

The utmoft I can do, I will venture to tell you in your ear. I may flide along the Surrey fide (where no Middlefex juftice can pretend any cognifance) to Batterfea, and thence crofs the water for an hour or
two,

two, in a clofe chair, to dine with you, or fo. But
to be in town, I fear, will be imprudent, and thought
infolent.   At leaft, hitherto, all comply with the
proclamation *.

I write thus early, that you may let me know if
your day continues, and I will have every room in
my houfe as warm for you as the owner always would
be. It may poffibly be, that I fhall be taking the
fecret flight I fpeak of to Batterfea, before you come,
with Mr Warburton, whom I have promifed to make ⁻
known to the only great man in Europe, who knows
as much as he.   And from thence we may return
the 16th, or any day, hither, and meet you, without fail, if you fix your day.⁻

I would not make ill health come into the fcale,
as to keeping me here (though, in truth, it now bears
very hard upon me again, and the leaft accident of
cold, or motion almoft, throws me into a very dangerous and fuffering condition.) God fend you long
life, and an eafier enjoyment of your breath than I
now can expect, I fear, &c.

* On the invafion, at that time threatened from France and
the pretender.

LETTERS of Mr POPE to Mr WARBURTON.

LETTER XCVIII.

April 11. 1739.

I Have juſt received from Mr R. two more of your *letters* *.. It is in the greateſt hurry imaginable that I write this, but I cannot help thanking you in particular for your third *letter*, which is ſo extremely clear, ſhort, and full, that I think Mr Crouzaz † ought never to have another anſwer, and deſerved not ſo good an one. I can only ſay, you do him too much honour, and me too much right, ſo odd as the expreſſion ſeems; for you have made my ſyſtem as clear as I ought to have done, and could not. It is indeed the ſame ſyſtem as mine, but illuſtrated with a ray of your own, as they ſay our natural body is the ſame ſtill when it is glorified. I am ſure I like it better than I did before, and ſo will every man elſe. I know I meant juſt what you explain, but I did not explain my own meaning ſo well as you. You underſtand me as well as I do myſelf, but you expreſs me better than I could expreſs myſelf. Pray accept the ſincereſt acknowledgments. I cannot but wiſh theſe letters were put together in one book, and intend (with your leave) to procure a tranſlation of part, at leaſt, or of all of them into French ‡; but I ſhall not proceed a ſtep without your conſent and opinion, &c.

* Commentaries on the *Eſſay on Man*.
† A German profeſſor, who wrote remarks upon the philoſophy of that *Eſſay*.
‡ They were all tranſlated into that language by a French gentleman of condition, who is now in an eminent ſtation in his own country,

LET-

LETTER XCIX.

May 26. 1739.

THE diffipation in which I am obliged to live through many degrees of civil obligation, which ought not to rob a man of himfelf who paffes for an independent one, and yet make me every body's fervant more than my own; this, Sir, is the occafion of my filence to you, to whom I really have more obligation than to almoft any man. By writing, indeed, I propofed no more than to tell you my fenfe of it: as to any corrections of your *letters*, I could make none, but what refulted from inverting the order of them, and thofe expreffions relating to myfelf which I thought exaggerated. I could not find a word to alter in the laft letter, which I returned immediately to the bookfeller. I muft particularly thank you for the mention you have made of me in your poftfcript * to the laft edition of the *Legation of Mofes*. I am much more pleafed with a compliment that links me to a virtuous man, and by the beft fimilitude, that of a good mind, (even a better and ftronger tie than the fimilitude of ftudies), than I could be proud of any other whatfoever. May that independency, charity, and competency attend you, which fets a good prieft above a bifhop, and truly makes his fortune; that is, his happinefs in this life as well as in the other.

* He means, a *vindication of the author of the Divine legation*, againft fome papers in the Weekly Mifcellany: in which Mr Warburton applied to himfelf thofe lines in the epiftle to Dr Arbuthnot,

Me let the tender office long engage, &c.

LETTER C.

Twitenham, Sept. 20. 1739.

I Received with great pleasure the paper you sent me; and yet with greater, the prospect you give me of a nearer acquaintance with you when you come to town. I shall hope what part of your time you can afford me, amongst the number of those who esteem you, will be passed rather in this place than in London; since it is here only I live as I ought, *mihi et amicis.* I therefore depend on your promise; and so much as my constitution suffers by the winter, I yet assure you, such an acquisition will make the spring much the more welcome to me, when it is to bring you hither, *cum zephyris et hirundine prima.*

As soon as Mr R. can transmit to me an entire copy of your *letters*, I wish he had your leave so to do; that I may put the book into the hands of a French gentleman to translate, who, I hope, will not subject your work to as much ill-grounded criticism, as my French translator * has subjected mine. In earnest, I am extremely obliged to you, for thus espousing the cause of a stranger whom you judged to be injured; but my part, in this sentiment, is the least. The generosity of your conduct deserves esteem, your zeal for truth deserves affection from every candid man: and as such, were I wholly out of the case, I should esteem and love you for it. I will not therefore use you so ill as to write in the general style of compliment; it is below the dignity of the occasion: and I can only say (which I say with sincerity and warmth) that you have made me, &c.

* *Refnel,* on whose very faulty and absurd translation Crouzaz founded his only plausible objections.

LETTER CI.

Jan. 4. 1739.

IT is a real truth that I ſhould have written to you
oftener, if I had not a great reſpect for you, and
owed not a great debt to you. But it may be no un-
neceſſary thing to let you know, that moſt of my
friends alſo pay you their thanks; and ſome of the
moſt knowing, as well as moſt candid judges, think
me as much beholden to you as I think myſelf. Your
letters * meet from ſuch with the approbation they
merit; and I have been able to find but two or three
very ſlight inaccuracies in the whole book, which I
have, upon their obſervation, altered in an exemplar
which I keep againſt a ſecond edition. My very uncertain ſtate of health, which is ſhaken more and
more every winter, drove me to Bath and Briſtol two
months ſince; and I ſhall not return towards London
till February. But I have received nine or ten letters,
from thence on the ſucceſs of your book †, which
they are earneſt to have tranſlated. One of them is
begun in France. A French gentleman, about
Monſieur Cambis the ambaſſador, hath done the
greateſt part of it here. But I will retard the impreſ-
ſion till I have your directions, or till I can have a
pleaſure I earneſtly wiſh for, to meet you in town;
where you gave me ſome hopes you ſometimes paſſed
a part of the ſpring, for the beſt reaſon, I know, of
ever viſiting it, the converſation of a few friends.
Pray, ſuffer me to be what you have made me, one
of them, and let my houſe have its ſhare of you: or,
if I can any way be inſtrumental in accommodating
you in town during your ſtay, I have lodgings and a
library or two in my diſpoſal; which, I believe, I
need not offer to a man to whom all libraries ought
to be open, or to one who wants them ſo little; but

---

* On the *Eſſay on Man.*
† The commentary on the Eſſay on Man.

that

that it is poffible you may be as much a ftranger to
this town, as I wifh with all my heart I was. I fee
by certain fquibs in the *Mifcellanies* *, that you have
as much of the uncharitable fpirit poured out upon
you as the author you defended from Crouzaz. I
only wifh you gave them no other anfwer than that
of the fun to the frogs, fhining out, in your fecond
book, and the completion of your argument. No
man is, as he ought to be, more, or fo much a
friend to your merit and character, as, Sir,

Your, &c.

L E T T E R CII.

Jan. 17. 1739-40.

THough I writ to you two pofts ago, I ought to
acknowledge now a new and unexpected favour of the remarks on the fourth epiftle †; which
(though I find by yours attending them, they were
fent laft month) I received but this morning. This
was occafioned by no fault of Mr R. but the neglect,
I believe, of the perfon to whofe care he configned
them. I have been full three months about Bath and
Briftol, endeavouring to amend a complaint which
more or lefs has troubled me all my life. I hope the
regimen this has obliged me to, will make the remainder of it more philofophical, and improve my
refignation to part with it at laft. I am preparing
to return home, and fhall then revife what my French
gentleman has done, and add *this* to it. He is the
fame perfon who tranflated the *effay* into profe, which
Mr Crouzaz fhould have profited by, who, I am
really afraid, when I lay the circumftances all together, was moved to his proceeding in fo very unrea-
fonable a way, by fome malice either of his own, or
fome others; though I was very willing, at firft, to

* The Weekly Mifcellany, by Dr Webfter, Dr Waterland,
Dr Sebbing, Mr Venn, and others.
† Of the *Effay on Man*.

impute

impute it to ignorance or prejudice. I fee nothing to
be added to your work; only fome commendatory
deviations from the argument itfelf, in my favour, I
ought to think might be omitted.

I muft repeat my urgent defire to be previoufly acquainted with the precife time of your vifit to London; that I may have the pleafure to meet a man in
the manner I would, whom I muft efteem one of the
greateft of my benefactors. I am, with the moft
grateful and affectionate regard, &c.

LETTER CIII.

April 16. 1740.

YOU could not give me more pleafure than by
your fhort letter, which acquaints me that I
may hope to fee you fo foon. Let us meet like men
who have been many years acquainted with each
other, and whofe friendfhip is not to begin, but continue. All forms fhould be paffed, when people know
each other's mind fo well. I flatter myfelf you are a
man after my own heart, who feeks content only from
within, and fays to greatnefs, *Tuas habeto tibi res,
egomet habebo meas.* But as it is but juft your other
friends fhould have fome part of you, I infift on my
making you the firft vifit in London; and thence after a few days, to carry you to Twitenham, for as
many as you can afford me. If the prefs be to take
up any part of your time, the fheets may be brought
you hourly thither by my waterman: and you will
have more leifure to attend to any thing of that fort
than in town. I believe alfo I have moft of the books
you can want, or can eafily borrow them. I earneftly defire a line may be left at Mr. R.'s, where and
when I fhall call upon you; which I will daily inquire for, whether I chance to be here or in the
country. Believe me, Sir, with the trueft regard,
and the fincereft wifh to deferve,

Yours, &c.

L l 3 LET-

LETTER CIV.

Twitenham, June 24. 1740.

IT is true that I am a very unpunctual correspondent, though no unpunctual agent or friend; and
that, in the commerce of words, I am both poor and
lazy. Civility and compliment generally are the
goods that letter-writers exchange; which, with honest men, seems a kind of illicit trade, by having
been, for the most part, carried on, and carried fur-
thest by designing men. I am therefore reduced to
plain inquiries, how my friend does, and what he
does? and to repetitions, which I am afraid to tire
him with, *how much I love him.* Your two kind
letters gave me real satisfaction, in hearing you were
safe and well; and in shewing me you took kindly
my unaffected endeavours to prove my esteem for
you, and delight in your conversation. Indeed my
languid state of health, and frequent deficiency of
spirits, together with a number of dissipations, et
aliena negotia centum, all conspire to throw a faint-
ness and cool appearance over my conduct to those I
best love; which I perpetually feel, and grieve at.
But, in earnest, no man is more deeply touched with
merit in general, or with particular merit towards
me, in any one. You ought therefore in both views
to hold yourself what you are to me in my opinion
and affection; so high in each, that I may perhaps
seldom attempt to tell it you. The greatest justice,
and favour too that you can do me, is to take it for
granted.
Do not therefore commend my talents, but in-
struct me by your own. I am not really learned
enough to be a judge in works of the nature and
depth of yours. But I travel through your book
as through an amazing scene of ancient Egypt or
Greece; struck with veneration and wonder; but at
every step wanting an instructor to tell me all I wish
to

to know. Such you prove to me in the walks of
antiquity ; and fuch you will prove to all mankind :
but with this additional character, more than any
other fearcher into antiquities, that of a genius equal
to your pains, and of a tafte equal to your learning.

I am obliged greatly to you for what you have
projected at Cambridge, in relation to my Effay * ;
but more for the motive which did originally, and
does confequentially in a manner, animate all your
goodnefs to me, the opinion you entertain of my honeft intention in that piece, and your zeal to demonftrate me no irreligious man. I was very fincere
with you in what I told you of my own opinion of
my own character as a poet, and I think I may
confcientioufly fay, I fhall die in it. I have nothing
to add, but that I hope fometimes to hear you are
well, as you fhall certainly now and then hear the
beft I can tell you of myfelf.

L E T T E R   CV.

Oct. 27. 1740.

I AM grown fo bad a correfpondent, partly through
the weaknefs of my eyes, which has much increafed of late, and partly through other difagreeable accidents (almoft peculiar to me), that my oldeft, as well as beft friends, are reafonable enough to
excufe me. I know you are of the number who deferve all the teftimonies of any fort, which I can give
you of efteem and friendfhip ; and I confide in you,
as a man of candour enough, to know it cannot be
otherwife, if I am an honeft one. So I will fay no
more on this head, but proceed to thank you for your
conftant memory of whatever may be ferviceable or
reputable to me. The tranflation you † are a much
better judge of than I, not only becaufe you under-

* Mr Pope defired Mr Warburton to procure a good tranflation of the *Effay on Man* into Latin profe.
† Of his *Effay on Man* into Latin profe.

ftand

ftand my work better than I do myfelf, but as your
continued familiarity with the learned languages,
makes you infinitely more a mafter of them. I
would only recommend that the tranflator's attention
to Tully's Latinity may not preclude his ufage of
fome *terms* which may be more *precife* in modern philofophy than fuch as he could ferve himfelf of, efpecially in matters metaphyfical. I think this fpecimen
clofe enough, and clear alfo, as far as the claffical
phrafes allow; from which yet I would rather he
fometimes deviated, than fuffered the fenfe to be either dubious, or clouded too much. You know my
mind perfectly as to the intent of fuch a verfion; and
I would have it accompanied with your own remarks
tranflated, fuch only I mean as are general, or explanatory of thofe paffages, which are concife to any
degree of obfcurity, or which demand perhaps too
minute an attention in the reader.

I have been unable to make the journey I defigned to Oxford, and Lord Bathurft's, where I hoped
to have made you of the party. I am going to Bath
for near two months. Yet pray let nothing hinder
me fometimes from hearing you are well. I have had
that contentment from time to time from Mr G.

Scriblerus * will or will not be publifhed, according to the event of fome other papers coming, or
not coming out; which it will be my utmoft endeavour to hinder †. I will not give you the pain of
acquainting you what they are. Your fimile of B.
and his nephew, would make an excellent epigram.
But all fatire is become fo ineffectual, (when the laft
ftep that Virtue can ftand upon, *fhame*, is taken
away), that Epigram muft expect to do nothing even
in its own little province, and upon its own little
fubjects. Adieu. Believe I wifh you nearer us; the
only power I wifh, is that of attaching, and at the
fame time fupporting, fuch congenial bodies, as you
are to, dear Sir,

Your, &c.

* The *Memoirs of Scriblerus.*
† The letters publifhed by Dr Swift.

L E T-

LETTER CVI.

Bath, Feb. 4. 1740-1.

IF I had not been made by many accidents fo fick of letter-writing, as to be almoft afraid of the fhadow of my own pen, you would be the perfon I, fhould ofteneft pour myfelf out to : indeed for a good reafon ; for you have given me the ftrongeft proofs of underftanding, and accepting my meaning in the beft manner ; and of the candour of your heart, as well as the clearnefs of your head. My vexations I would not trouble you with, but I muft juft mention the two greateft I now have. They have printed, in Ireland, my letters to Dr Swift, and (which is the ftrangeft circumftance) by his own confent and direction, without acquainting me till it was done: The other is one that will continue with me till fome profperous event to your fervice fhall bring us nearer to each other. I am not content with thofe glimpfes of you, which a fhort fpring-vifit affords ; and from which you carry nothing away with you, but my fighs and wifhes, without any real benefit.

I am heartily glad of the advancement of your *fecond volume* * ; and particularly of the *digreffions*, for they are *fo much more of you* ; and I can truft your judgment enough to depend upon their being pertinent. You, will, I queftion not, verify the good proverb, That the furtheft about way is the neareft way home : and much better than plunging through thick and thin, *more theologorum* ; and per- fifting in the fame old track, where fo many have either broken their necks, or come off very lamely. This leads me to thank you for that very enter- taining, and, I think, inftructive ftory of Dr W***, who was, in this, the image of ***, who never admit of any remedy from a hand they diflike. But

---

* *Of the Divine Legation.*

I

I am forry he had fo much of the modern Chriftian
rancour, as, I believe, he may be convinced by
this time, that the kingdom of heaven is not for
fuch.

I am juft returning to London, and fhall the
more impatiently expect your book's appearance,
as I hope you will follow it ; and that I may have
as happy a month through your means as I had the
laft fpring.

I am, &c.

L E T T E R CVII.

April 14. 1741.

YOU are every way kind to me, in your partiality to what is tolerable in me; and in your
freedom where you find me in an errour. Such, I
own, is the inftance given of ——. You owe me much
friendfhip of this latter fort, having been too pro-
fufe of the former.

I think every day a week till you come to town,
which, Mr G. tells me, will be in the beginning of
the next month. When, 1 expect, you will contrive
to be as beneficial to me as you can, by paffing with
me as much time as you can : every day of which,
it will be my fault, if I do not make of fome ufe to
me, as well as pleafure. This is all I have to tell
you ; and, be affured, my fincereft efteem and affection are yours.

L E T T E R CVIII.

Twitenham, Aug. 12. 1741,

THE general indifpofition I have to writing,
unlefs upon a belief of the neceffity or ufe of
it, muft plead my excufe in not doing it to you. I
know it is not (I feel it is not) needful to repeat affurances of the true and conftant friendfhip and

efteem

efteem I bear you. Honeft and ingenuous friends are
fure of each other's; the tie is mutual and folid.
The ufe of writing letters refolves wholly into the gratification given and received in the knowledge of
each other's welfare. Unlefs I ever fhould be fo fortunate, (and a rare fortune it would be), to be able
to procure, and acquaint you of, fome real benefit
done you by my means. But Fortune feldom fuffers
one difinterefted man to ferve another. It is too
much an infult upon her to let two of thofe who moft
defpife her favours, be happy in them at the fame
time, and in the fame inftance. I wifh for nothing
fo much at her hands, as that fhe would permit fome
great perfon or other to remove you nearer the banks
of the Thames; though very lately a nobleman,
whom you efteem much more than you know, had
deftined, &c.

I thank you heartily for your hints; and am afraid
if I had more of them, not on this only, but on
other fubjects, I fhould break my refolution, and become an author anew : nay a new author, and a better than I yet have been ; or God forbid I fhould go
on jingling only the fame bells!

I have received fome chagrin at the delay of your
degree at Oxon. As for mine, I will die before I
receive one, in an art I am ignorant of, at a place
where there remains any fcruple of beftowing one on
you, in a fcience of which you are fo great a mafter.
In fhort, I will be doctored with you, or not at all. I
am fure, where-ever honour is not conferred on the
deferving, there can be none given to the undeferving,
no more from the hands of priefts, than of princes.
Adieu. God give you all *true bleffings.*

L E T T E R CIX.

Sept. 20. 1741.

IT is not my friendſhip, but the diſcernment of
that nobleman * 1 mentioned, which you are to
thank for his intention to ſerve you. And his judgment is ſo uncontroverted, that it would really be a
pleaſure to you to owe him any thing ; inſtead of a
ſhame, which often is the caſe in the favours of men
of that rank. I am ſorry I can only wiſh you well,
and not do myſelf honour in doing you any good.
But I comfort myſelf when I reflect, few men could
make you happier, none more deſerving than you
have made yourſelf.

I do not know how I have been betrayed into a
paragraph of this kind. I aſk your pardon, though
it be truth, for ſaying ſo much.——

If I can prevail on myſelf to complete the Dunciad, it will be publiſhed at the ſame time with a general edition of all my verſes, (for poems I will not
call them), and, I hope, your friendſhip to me will
be then as well known, as my being an author ; and
go down together to poſterity. I mean to as much of
poſterity as poor moderns can reach to ; where the
commentator (as uſual) will lend a crutch to the
weak poet to help him to limp a little further,
than he could on his own feet. We ſhall take our
degree together in fame, whatever we do at the uni-
verſity. And I tell you once more, I will not have
it there without you.——

L E T T E R CX.

Bath, Nov. 12. 1741.

I AM always naturally ſparing of my letters to my
friends ; for a reaſon 1 think a great one ; that it

* Lord Cheſterfield.

is

is needlefs after experience, to repeat affurances of friendfhip; and no lefs irkfome to be fearching for words, to exprefs it over and over. But I have more calls than one for this letter. Firft, to exprefs a fatisfaction at your refolution not to keep up the ball of difpute with Dr M. though, I am fatisfied, you could have done it; and to tell you that Mr L. is pleafed at it too, who writes me word upon this occafion, that he muft infinitely efteem a divine, and an author who loves peace, better than victory. Secondly, I am to recommend to you as an author, a bookfeller in the room of the honeft one you have loft, Mr G.; and I know none who is fo worthy, and has fo good a title in that character to fucceed him as Mr Knapton. But my third motive of now troubling you is my own proper intereft and pleafure. I am here in more leifure than I can poffibly enjoy even in my own houfe, *vacare literis*. It is at this place, that your exhortations may be moft effectual, to make me refume the ftudies I have almoft laid afide, by perpetual avocations and diffipations. If it were practicable for you to pafs a month or fix weeks from home, it is here I could wifh to be with you. And if you would attend to the continuation of your own noble work, or unbend to the idle amufement of commenting upon a poet, who has no other merit, than that of aiming by his moral ftrokes to merit fome regard from fuch men as advance truth and virtue in a more effectual way; in either cafe, this place and this houfe would be an inviolable afylum to you, from all you would defire to avoid, in fo public a fcene as Bath. The worthy man, who is the mafter of it, invites you in the ftrongeft terms; and is one who would treat you with love and veneration, rather than what the world calls civility and regard. He is fincerer and plainer than almoft any man now in this world, *antiquis moribus.* If the waters of the Bath may be ferviceable to your complaints, (as I believe from what you have told me of them), no opportunity can ever be better. It is juft

the beſt feaſon. We are told the Biſhop of Saliſbury
is expected here daily, who, I know, is your friend :
at leaſt, though a biſhop, is too much a man of
learning to be your enemy. You ſee I omit nothing
to add to the weight in the balance ; in which, however, I will not think myſelf light, ſince I have
known your partiality, You will want no ſervant
here. Your room will be next to mine, and one man
will ſerve us. Here is a library, and a gallery nine-
ty feet long to walk in, and a coach whenever you
would take the air with me. Mr ALLEN tells me,
you might on horſeback be here in three days ; it is
leſs than 100 miles from Newark, the road through
Leiceſter, Stow in the Wolde in Glouceſterſhire, and
Cirenceſter by Lord Bathurſt's. I could engage to
carry you to London from hence, and I would accommodate my time and journey to your conveniency.

Is all this a dream ? or can you make it a reality ?
can you give ear to me ?

Audiſtin' ? an me ludit amabilis
Inſania ?

Dear Sir, adieu ; and give me a line to Mr Allen's
at Bath. God preſerve you ever.

LETTER CXI.

Nov. 22. 1741.

YOurs is very full and very kind, it is a friendly and ſatisfactory anſwer, and all I can deſire.
Do but inſtantly fulfil it. — Only I hope this will
find you before you ſet out. For I think (on all con-
ſiderations) your beſt way will be to take London in
your way. It will ſecure you from accidents of weather to travel in the coach, both thither, and from
thence hither. But in particular, I think you ſhould
take ſome care as to Mr G's executors. And I am of
opinion, no man will be more ſerviceable in ſettling
any

any fuch accounts than Mr Knapton, who fo well knows the trade, and is of fo acknowledged a credit in it. If you can ftay but a few days there, I fhould be glad; though I would not have you omit any necef-fary thing to yourfelf. I wifh too you would juft fee * * *, though when you have paffed a month here, it will be time enough, for all we have to do in town; and they will be lefs bufy, probably, than juft before the feffion opens, to think of men of letters.

When you are in London, I beg a line from you, in which pray tell us what day you fhall arrive at Bath by the coach, that we may fend to meet you, and bring you hither.

You will owe me a real obligation by being made acquainted with the mafter of this houfe; and by fharing with me, what I think one of the chief fa-tisfactions of my life, his friendfhip. But whether I fhall owe you any in contributing to make me a fcribbler again, I know not.

L E T T E R   CXII.

April 23. 1742.

MY letters are fo fhort, partly becaufe I could by no length of *writings* (not even by fuch as lawyers write) *convey* to you more than you have already of my heart and efteem; and partly becaufe I want time and eyes. I cannot fufficiently tell you both my pleafure and my gratefulnefs, in and for your two laft letters, which fhew your zeal fo ftrong for that piece of my idlenefs, which was literally written only to keep *me* from fleeping in a dull win-ter; and perhaps to make others fleep unlefs awa-kened by my commentator: no uncommon cafe a-mong the learned. I am every day in expectation of Lord Bolingbroke's arrival; with whom I fhall feize all the hours I can; for his ftay (I fear by what he writes) will be very fhort. —— I do not

think

think it impoffible but he may go to Bath for a few
weeks, to fee (if he be then alive, as yet he is) his
old fervant.——In that cafe I think to go with him ;
and if it fhould be at a feafon when the waters are
beneficial, (which agree particularly with him too),
would it be an impoffibility to meet you at Mr Allen's ; whofe houfe, you know, and heart, are yours ?
Though this is a mere chance, I fhould not be forry
you faw fo great a genius, though he and you were
never to meet again.—Adieu. The world is not
what I wifh it ; but I will not repent being in it while
two or three live.

I am, &c.

LETTER CXIII.

Bath, Nov. 27. 1742.

THis will fhew you I am ftill with our friend ;
but it is the laft day ; and I would rather you
heard of me pleafed, as I yet am, than chagrined as
I fhall be in a few hours. We are both pretty well.
I wifh you had been more explicit if your leg be
quite well. You fay no more than that you got
home well. I expect a more particular account of
you when you have repofed yourfelf a while at your
own fire-fide. I fhall inquire as foon as I am in
London, which of my friends have feen you. There
are two or three who knew how to value you. I
wifh I was as fure they would ftudy to ferve you.—
A project has arifen in my head to make you, in
fome meafure, the editor of this new edition of the
Dunciad *, if you have no fcruple of owning fome
of the graver notes, which are now added to thofe of
Dr Arbuthnot. I mean it as a kind of prelude, or
advertifement to the public, of your commentaries,
on the Effays on man, and on criticifm, which I propofe to print next in another volume proportioned to

* That is, of the four books complete.

this.

this. I only doubt whether an avowal of thefe notes
to fo ludicrous a poem, be fuitable to a character fo
eftablifhed as yours for more ferious ftudies. It was
a fudden thought fince we parted ; and I would have
you treat it as no more ; and tell me if it is not better to be fuppreffed; freely and friendlily. I have
a particular reafon to make you intereft yourfelf in
me and my writings. It will caufe both them and
me to make the better figure to pofterity. A very
mediocre poet, one Drayton, is yet taken fome
notice of becaufe Selden writ a few notes on one of
his poems.——

Adieu. May every domeftic happinefs make you
unwilling to remove from home ; and may every
friend you do that kindnefs for, treat you fo as to
make you forget you are not at home.

I am, &c.

LETTER CXIV.

Dec. 28. 1742.

I Have always fo many things to take kindly of
you, that I do not know which to begin to
thank you for. I was willing to conclude our whole
account of the Dunciad, at leaft, and therefore ftaid
till it was finifhed. The encouragement you gave
me to add the fourth book, firft determined me to do
fo ; and the approbation you feemed to give it, was
what fingly determined me to print it. Since that,
your notes and your difcourfe in the name of Ariftar-
chus have given its laft finifhings and ornaments.——
I am glad you will refrefh the *memory* of fuch readers
as have no other faculty to be readers ; efpecially of
fuch works as the *Divine Legation*. But I hope you
will not take too much notice of another and duller
fort ; thofe who become writers through malice, and
muft die whenever you pleafe to fhine out in the completion of the work : which I wifh were now your
only anfwer to any of them : except you will make

ufe

ufe of that fhort and excellent one you gave me in the ftory of the *reading-glafs*.

The world here grows very bufy. About what time is it you think of being amongft us? My health, I fear, will confine me, whether in town or here, fo that I may expect more of your company as one good refulting out of evil.

I write, you know, very laconically. I have but one formula which fays every thing to a friend, " I am yours, and beg you to continue mine." Let me not be ignorant (you can prevent my being fo of *any thing*, but firft and principally) of your health and well-being; and depend on my fenfe of all the *kindnefs* over and above all the *juftice* you fhall ever do me.

I never read a thing with more pleafure than an additional fheet to * Jervas's preface to Don Quixote. Before I got over two paragraphs, I cried out, *Aut Erafmus aut diabolus!* I knew you as certainly as the ancients did the gods by the firft pace and the very gait. I have not a moment to exprefs myfelf in; but could not omit this, which delighted me fo greatly.

My law-fuit with L. is at an end. — Adieu! Believe no man can be more yours. Call me by any title you will but a *Doctor of Oxford: Sit tibi cura mei, fit tibi cura tui.*

LETTER CXV.

Jan. 18. 1742.

I AM forced to grow every day more laconic in my letters, for my eyefight grows every day fhorter and dimmer. Forgive me then that I anfwer you fummarily. I can even lefs bear an equal part in a correfpondence than in a converfation with you. But be affured once for all, the more I read of you, as the more I hear from you, the better I am inftructed and

* On the origin of the books of chivalry.

pleafed.

pleafed. And this misfortune of my own dulnefs, and my own abfence, only quickens my ardent wifh that fome good fortune would draw you nearer, and enable me to enjoy both, for a greater part of our lives in this neighbourhood; and in fuch a fituation, as might make more beneficial friends than I efteem and enjoy you equally. — I have again heard from Lord * * and another hand, that the Lord † I writ to you of, declares an intention to ferve you. My anfwer (which they related to him) was, that he would be fure of your acquaintance for life, if once he ferved or obliged you; but that I was certain you would never trouble him with your expectation, though he would never get rid of your gratitude.— Dear Sir, adieu; and let me be fometimes certified of your health. My own is as ufual; and my affection the fame, always yours.

L E T T E R   CXVI.

Twitenham, March 24. 1743.

I Write to you amongft the very few I now defire to have my friends merely, *Si valeas, valeo.* It is in effect all I fay: but it is very literally true, for I place all that makes my life defirable in their welfare. I may truly affirm, that vanity or intereft have not the leaft fhare in any friendfhip I have; or caufe me now to cultivate that of any one man by any one letter. But if any motive fhould draw me to flatter a great man, it would be to fave the friend I would have him ferve from doing it. Rather than lay a deferving perfon under the neceffity of it, I would hazard my own character, and keep his in dignity. Though, in truth, I live in a time when no meafures of conduct influence the fuccefs of one's applications, and the beft thing to truft to is chance and opportunity.

† Granville.

I

I only mean to tell you, I am wholly yours, how few words foever I make of it.—A greater pleafure to me is, that I chanced to make Mr Allen fo, who is not only worth more than — intrinfically ; but, I forefee, will be effectually more a comfort and glory to you every year you live. My confidence in any man lefs truly great than an honeſt one is but fmall.————

I have lived much by myfelf of late, partly through ill health, and partly to amufe myfelf with little improvements in my garden and houfe, to which poſſibly I fhall (if I live) be foon more confined. When the Dunciad may be publifhed, I know not. I am more defirous of carrying on the beſt, that is, your edition of the reſt of the *Epiſtles* and *Eſſ'y on Criticiſm*, &c. I know it is there I fhall be feen moſt to advantage. But I inſiſt on one condition, that you never think of this when you can employ yourfelf in finifhing that noble work of the *Divine Legation*, (which is what, above all, *iterum iterumque monebo*), or any other ufeful fcheme of your own. It would be a fatisfaction to me at prefent only to hear that you have fupported your health among thefe epidemical diforders, which, though not mortal to any of my friends, have afflicted almoſt every one.

L E T T E R   CXVII.

June 5.

I Wifh that, inſtead of writing to you once in two months, I could do you fome fervice as often ; for I am arrived to an age when I am as fparing of words as moſt old men are of money, though I daily find lefs occafion for any. But I live in a time when benefits are not in the power of an honeſt man to beſtow ; nor indeed of an honeſt man to receive ; confidering on what terms they are generally to be had. It is certain you have a full right to any I could do you, who not only monthly, but weekly of late, have
loaded

loaded me with favours of that kind, which are moſt acceptable to veteran authors ; thoſe garlands which a commentator weaves to hang about his poet, and which are flowers both of his own gathering and painting too ; not bloſſoms ſpringing from the dry author.

It is very unreaſonable after this, to give you a ſecond trouble in reviſing the *Eſſay on Homer*. But I look upon you as one ſworn to ſuffer no errours in me : and though the common way with a commentator be to erect them into beauties, the beſt office of a critic is to correct and amend them. There being a new edition coming out of *Homer*, I would willingly render it a little leſs defective, and the bookſeller will not allow me time to do ſo myſelf.

Lord B. returns to France very ſpeedily, and it is poſſible I may go for three weeks or a month to Mr Allen's in the ſummer ; of which I will not fail to advertiſe you, if it ſuits your conveniency to be there, and drink the waters more beneficially.

Forgive my ſcribbling ſo haſtily and ſo ill. My eyes are at leaſt as bad as my head ; and it is with my heart only that I can pretend to be, to any real purpoſe,

Your, &c.

LETTER CXVIII.

July 18.

YOU may well expect letters from me of thanks : but the kind attention you ſhew to every thing that concerns me is ſo manifeſt, and ſo repeated, that you cannot but tell yourſelf how neceſſarily I muſt pay them in my heart, which makes it almoſt impertinent to ſay ſo. Your alterations to the preface and eſſay * are juſt ; and none more obliging to me than where you prove your concern, that my notions in

* Prefixed to his Homer's Iliad.

my

my firft writings fhould not be repugnant to thofe in
my laft. And you will have the charity to think,
when I was then in an errour, it was not fo much
that I thought wrong or perverfely, as that I had not
thought fufficiently. What I could correct in the
diffipated life I am forced to lead here, I have : and
fome there are which ftill want your help to be made
as they fhould be.—Mr Allen depends on you at the
end of the next month or in September, and I will
join him as foon as I can return from the other party, I believe not till September at fooneft. — You
will pardon me (dear Sir) for writing to you but juft
like an attorney or agent. I am more concerned for
your finances * than your fame ; becaufe the firft, I
fear, you will never be concerned about yourfelf ;
the fecond is fecure to you already, and (whether
you will or not) will follow you.

I have never faid one word to you of the public.
I have known the greater world too long to be very
fanguine. But accidents and occafions may do what
virtue would not, and God fend they may ! Adieu.
Whatever becomes of public virtue, let us preferve
our own poor fhare of the private. Be affured, if I
have any, I am, with a true fenfe of your merit and
friendfhip, &c.

LETTER CXIX.

Oct. 7.

I Heartily thank you for yours, from which I learned your fafe arrival. And that you found all
yours in health, was a kind addition to the account ;
as I truly am interefted in whatever is, and deferves
to be dear to you, and to make a part of your happinefs. I have many reafons and experiences to
convince me, how much you wifh health to me, as
well as long life to my writings. Could you make

* His debt from the executor of Mr G.

as.

as much a better man of me as you can make a better author, I were fecure of immortality both here and hereafter by your means. The Dunciad I have ordered to be advertifed in quarto. Pray order as many of them as you will; and know that whatever is mine is yours.

LETTER CXX.

Jan. 12. 1743.

AN unwillingnefs to write nothing to you, whom I refpect; and worfe than nothing (which would afflict you) to one who wifhes me fo well, has hitherto kept me filent. Of the public I can tell you nothing worthy the reflection of a reafonable man; and of myfelf only an account that would give you pain; for my afthma has increafed every week fince you laft heard from me, to the degree of confining me totally to the fire-fide; fo that I have hardly feen any of my friends but two, who happen to be divided from the world as much as myfelf, and are conftantly retired at Batterfea. There I have paffed moft of my time, and often wifhed you of the company, as the beft I know to make me not regret the lofs of all others, and to prepare me for a nobler fcene than any mortal greatnefs can open to us. I fear by the account you gave me of the time you defign to come this way, one of them (whom I much wifh you had a glimpfe of) will be gone again, unlefs you pafs fome weeks in London before Mr Allen arrives there in March. My prefent indifpofition takes up almoft all my hours, to render a very few of them fupportable: yet I go on foftly to prepare the great edition of my things with your notes; and as faft as I receive any from you, I add others in order.——

I am told the laureat is going to publifh a very abufive pamphlet. That is all I can defire; it is enough, if it be abufive, and if it be his. He threat-

ens

ens you ; but, I think, you will not fear or love him
fo much as to anfwer him, though you have anfwered one or two as dull. He will be more to me than
a dofe of hartfhorn : and as a ftink revives one who
has been oppreffed with perfumes, his railing will
cure me of a courfe of flatteries.

I am much more concerned to hear that fome of
your clergy are offended at a verfe or two of mine *,
becaufe I have a refpect for *your* clergy, (though the
verfes are harder upon *ours*). But if they do not
blame *you* for defending thofe verfes, I will wrap
myfelf up in the layman's cloak, and fleep under
your fhield.

I am forry to find by a letter two pofts fince from
Mr Allen, that he is not quite recovered yet of all
remains of his indifpofition, nor Mrs Allen quite well.
Do not be difcouraged from telling me how you are :
for no man is more yours than, &c.

LETTER CXXI.

IF I was not afhamed to be fo behindhand with
you, that I can never pretend to fetch it up,
(any more than I could, in my prefent ftate, to overtake you in a race) ; I would particularife which of
your letters I fhould have anfwered firft. It muft
fuffice to fay I have received them all : and whatever
very little refpites I have had, from the daily care
of my malady, have been employed in revifing the
papers *on the ufe of riches*, which I would have ready
for your laft revife, againft you come to town, that
they may be begun with while you are here. — I
own, the late incroachments upon my conftitution
make me willing to fee the end of all further care
about me or my works. I would reft for the one,
in a full refignation of my being to be difpofed of by
the Father of all mercy ; and for the other (though
indeed a trifle, yet a trifle may be fome example), I

* Ver. 355. — 358. of the 2d book of the Dunciad.

would

would commit them to the candour of a fenfible and.
reflecting judge, rather than to the malice of every
fhort-fighted and malevolent critic, or inadvertent
and cenforious reader. And no hand can fet them
in fo good a light, or fo well turn their beft fide to
the day as your own. This obliges me to confefs I
have for fome months thought myfelf going, and
that not flowly, down the hill. The rather as every
attempt of the phyficians, and ftill the laft medicines
more forcible in their nature, have utterly failed to
ferve me. I was at laft, about feven days ago, taken
with fo violent a fit at Batterfea, that my friends
Lord M. and Lord B. fent for prefent help to the
furgeon ; whofe bleeding me, I am perfuaded, faved
my life, by the inftantaneous effect it had ; and
which has continued fo much to amend me, that I
have paffed five days without oppreffion, and recovered, what I have three months wanted, fome
degree of expectoration, and fome hours together of
fleep. I am now got to Twitenham, to try if the
air will not take fome part in reviving me, if I can
avoid colds ; and between that place and Batterfea
with my Lord B. I will pafs what I have of life, while
he ftays, (which I can tell you, to my great fatif-
faction, will be this fortnight or three weeks yet).
What if you came before Mr Allen, and ftaid till
then, inftead of poftponing your journey longer ?
Pray, if you write, juft tell him how ill I have been,
or I had wrote again to him : but that I will do, the
firft day I find myfelf alone with pen, ink, and paper, which I can hardly be even here, or in any fpirits yet to hold a pen. You fee I fay nothing, and
yet this writing is labour to me.

I am, &c.

L E T T E R   CXXII.

April   1744.

I Am forry to meet you with fo bad an account of myfelf, who fhould otherwife with joy have flown to the interview. I am too ill to be in town; and within this week fo much worfe, as to make my journey thither, at prefent, impracticable, even if there was no proclamation in my way. I left the town in a decent compliance to that; but this additional prohibition from the higheft of all powers I muft bow to without murmuring. I wifh to fee you here. Mr Allen comes not till the 16th, and you will probably chufe to be in town chiefly while he is there. I received yours juft now, and I writ to hinder — from printing the comment on the *ufe of riches* too haftily, fince what you write me, intending to have forwarded it otherwife, that you might revife it during your ftay. Indeed my prefent weaknefs will make me lefs and lefs capable of any thing. I hope at leaft, now at firft, to fee you for a day or two here at Twitenham, and concert meafures how to enjoy for the future what I can of your friendfhip *.

I am, &c.

* He died May 30. following.

The

The LAST WILL and TESTA-MENT of ALEXANDER POPE of *Twickenham*, Efq;

IN THE NAME OF GOD, AMEN. I Alexander Pope, of Twickenham, in the county of Middlefex, make this my laft will and teftament. I refign my foul to its Creator in all humble hope of its future happinefs, as in the difpofal of a Being infinitely good. As to my body, my will is, that it be buried near the monument of my dear parents at Twickenham, with the addition, after the words *filius fecit*— of thefe only, *et fibi : Qui obiit anno* 17 — *ætatis* — ; and that it be carried to the grave by fix of the pooreft men of the parifh, to each of whom I order a fuit of grey coarfe cloth, as mourning. If I happen to die at any inconvenient diftance, let the fame be done in any other parifh, and the infcription be added on the monument at Twickenham. I hereby make and appoint my particular friends, Allen Lord Bathurft, Hugh Earl of Marchmont, the Honourable William Murray, his Majefty's Solicitor-General, and George Arbuthnot, of the court of exchequer, Efq; the furvivors or furvivor of them, executors of this my laft will and teftament.

But all the manufcript and unprinted papers which I fhall leave at my deceafe, I defire may be delivered to my Noble Friend, Henry St John, Lord Bolingbroke, to whofe fole care and judgment I commit them, either to be preferved or deftroyed ; or, in cafe he fhall not furvive me, to the above-faid Earl of Marchmont. Thefe, who in the courfe of my life have done me all other good offices, will not refufe me this laft after my death : I leave them therefore this trouble, as a mark of my truft and friendfhip ; only defiring them each to accept of fome fmall memorial of me : That my Lord Bolingbroke

N n 2   will

will add to his library all the volumes of my works
and tranflations of Homer, bound in red morocco,
and the eleven volumes of thofe of Erafmus: That
my Lord Marchmont will take the large paper edition
of Thuanus, by Buckley, and that portrait of Lord
Bolingbroke, by Richardfon, which he fhall prefer:
That my Lord Bathurft will find a place for the three
ftatues of the Hercules of Farnefe, the Venus of Medicis, and the Apollo in chiaro ofcuro, done by
Kneller: That Mr Murray will accept of the marble
head of Homer, by Bernini; and of Sir Ifaac New-
ton, by Guelfi: and that Mr Arbuthnot will take
the watch I commonly wore, which the King of
Sardinia gave to the late Earl of Peterborow, and
he to me on his deathbed; together with one of the
pictures of Lord Bolingbroke.

Item, I defire Mr Lyttelton to accept of the bufts
of Spenfer, Shakefpear, Milton, and Dryden, in
marble, which his Royal mafter the Prince was pleafed to give me. I give and devife my library of
printed books to Ralph Allen of Widcombe, Efq;
and to the Reverend Mr William Warburton, or to
the furvivor of them, (when thofe belonging to Lord
Bolingbroke are taken out, and when Mrs Martha
Blount has chofen threefcore out of the number.) I
alfo give and bequeath to the faid Mr Warburton the
property of all fuch of my works already printed, as
he hath written, or fhall write commentaries or notes
upon, and which I have not otherwife difpofed of
or alienated; and all the profits which fhall arife after my death, from fuch editions as he fhall publifh
without future alterations.

Item, In cafe Ralph Allen, Efq; above faid, fhall
furvive me, I order my executors to pay him the
fum of one hundred and fifty pounds, being, to the
beft of my calculation, the amount of what I have
received from him; partly for my own, and partly
for charitable ufes. If he refufe to take this himfelf, I defire him to employ it in a way, I am perfuaded, he will not diflike, to the benefit of the Bath
hofpital.

I give and devise to my fifter-in-law, Mrs Magdalen Racket, the fum of three hundred pounds; and to her fons, Henry and Robert Racket, one hundred pounds each. I alfo releafe, and give to her all my right and intereft in and upon a bond of five hundred pounds due to me from her fon Michael. I alfo give her the family-pictures of my father, mother, and aunts, and the diamond ring my mother wore, and her golden watch. I give to Erafmus Lewis, Gilbert Weft, Sir Clement Cotterell, William Rollinfon, Nathaniel Hook, Efqs, and to Mrs Anne Arbuthnot, to each the fum of five pounds, to be laid out in a ring, or any memorial of me; and to my fervant, John Searl, who has faithfully and ably ferved me many years, I give and devife the fum of one hundred pounds over and above a year's wages to himfelf, and his wife; and to the poor of the parifh of Twickenham, twenty pounds, to be divided among them by the faid John Searl: and it is my will, if the faid John Searl die before me, that the faid fum of one hundred pounds go to his wife or children.

Item, I give and devife to Mrs Martha Blount, younger daughter of Mrs Martha Blount, late of Welbeck-Street, Cavendifh-Square, the fum of one thoufand pounds immediately on my deceafe: and all the furniture of my grotto, urns in my garden, houfehold goods, chattels, plate, or whatever is not otherwife difpofed of in this my will, I give and devife to the faid Mrs Martha Blount, out of a fincere regard and long friendfhip for her. And it is my will, that my above-faid executors, the furvivors or furvivor of them, fhall take an account of all my eftate, money, or bonds, &c. and, after paying my debts and legacies, fhall place out all the refidue upon government or other fecurities, according to their beft judgment; and pay the produce thereof, half-yearly, to the faid Mrs Martha Blount, during her natural life: and after her deceafe, I give the fum of one thoufand pounds to Mrs Magdalen Racket,

ket, and her fons Robert, Henry, and John, to be
divided equally among them, or to the furvivors or
furvivor of them ; and after the deceafe of the faid
Mrs Martha Blount, I give the fum of two hundred
pounds to the above-faid Gilbert Weft ; two hundred
to Mr George Arbuthnot ; two hundred to his fifter,
Mrs Anne Arbuthnot ; and one hundred to my fervant, John Searl, to which foever of thefe fhall be
then living : and all the refidue and remainder to
be confidered as undifpofed of, and go to my next
of kin.

This is my laft will and teftament, written with
my own hand, and fealed with my feal, this twelfth
day of December, in the year of our Lord, one
thoufand feven hundred and forty-three.

ALEX. POPE.

Signed, fealed, and declared
by the teftator, as his laft
will and teftament, in prefence of us,

RADNOR.
STEPHEN HALES, Minifter of Teddington.
JOSEPH SPENCE, Profeffor of Hiftory in the univer-
fity of Oxford.

FINIS.